C PROGRAMMING

TEST YOUR SKILLS

Ashok N. Kamthane
Department of Electronics and Telecommunication Engineering
Shri Guru Gobind Singhji Institute of Engineering and Technology
Nanded, Maharashtra

Pearson

ISBN 978-81-317-3209-0

First Impression

Published by Pearson India Education Services Pvt. Ltd, CIN: U72200TN2005PTC057128.

Head Office: 15th Floor, Tower-B, World Trade Tower, Plot No. 1, Block-C, Sector 16, Noida 201 301, Uttar Pradesh, India.
Registered Office: 7th Floor, SDB2, ODC 7, 8 & 9, Survey No. 01 ELCOT IT/ ITES-SEZ, Sholinganallur,
Chennai – 600 119, Tamilnadu, India.
Phone: 044-66540100
Website: in.pearson.com, Email: companysecretary.india@pearson.com

Printed in India at Repro India Limited

CONTENTS

C PROGRAMMING

TEST YOUR SKILLS

1

Computer Fundamentals and Brief Information on C

CHAPTER OUTLINE

PREFACE

This book is handy for students of various disciplines such as engineering, science, diploma and computer training institutes. It is also useful for those who prepare and appear for the interviews, recruitment test and technical tests conducted by various software companies. It may not be useful for the practicing professionals such as software engineers working in the area of software developments but it will definitely enhance their C skills once they go through it.

It contains self-test questions, multiple choice questions, fill in the blanks and true or false type questions that will make the text more student friendly. It contains numerous programming examples and exercises make the book most interesting. This book can be used as a reference for the course on C, a guide for self C learning and practical material for conducting training courses in C.

To a certain extent, an attempt has been made to cover the C syllabi of different branches of various universities. In this view, the book can be adopted in one semester of engineering as well as in degree and other courses. Tests in C have been written for beginners, those who do not have knowledge of C or other programming languages and also for those who want to learn or expand their knowledge of C.

In order to bridge the gap between theory and practical, each concept is explained in short in an easy-to-understand manner, supported with numerous worked-out examples and programs. The book contains solved illustrative problems and exercises. The programmer can run the solved programs and check the output.

The programs in Chapters 1 to 14 are fully tested and executed with mostly available C compilers. The programmer may also use Turbo C or ANSI C compilers.

ORGANIZATION OF THE BOOK

Chapter 1 describes the basic concepts of computer, components of a computer, sequence, selection iteration and flowcharts. An overview of compilers and interpreters, structure of a C program and programming rules are presented. How to execute C program is also demonstrated using sample programs.

After becoming familiar with the basics of a computer and C Language in the first chapter, the reader can now follow the other basics of C in Chapter 2. It covers C keywords, character set, delimiters, types of tokens, identifiers, constants variables, rules for defining variables, data types, initializing variables, dynamic initialization, type modifiers, type conversion, wrapping around and volatile variable.

Chapter 3 explains various details of the language which are useful to write a program. This chapter covers various C operators including arithmetic operators, relational operators, logical operators, increment operators, decrement operators (unary operators) and assignment operators. Other operators such as comma, conditional operator and bitwise operators are also presented here with programming examples.

Chapter 4 is essential for knowing the decision making statements in a programming language. This chapter demonstrates how to transfer the control from one to other part of the program. The programmer can make the program powerful by using control statements, such as `if`, `if-else`, nested `if-else` statements and `switch`.

Chapter 5 describes program loop in which statements are executed several times until a condition is satisfied. In this chapter, reader follows the program loop which is also known as iterative structure or repetitive structure. Three types of loop control statements are shown in this chapter as `for`, `while` and `do-while`. Syntaxes of these control statements are briefed together with programming examples. The other statements, such as the `break`, `continue` and `goto` statements, are also narrated.

Chapter 6 deals with the array in which the reader can follow the similar types and ordered data elements. Here one can follow array declaration, initialization and accessing array elements. After learning arrays and pointers, the reader can develop programs on one-, two- and multi-dimensional arrays.

Chapter 7 explains importance of string. It covers definition of a string, declaration and initialization of a string and string functions.

Chapter 8 deals with pointers and they are used to allocate memory dynamically. How memory is handled efficiently with pointers is also explained in this chapter.

Chapter 9 is one more important chapter on functions. How a large size program is divided into smaller ones and how a modular program has to be developed is learnt in this chapter. Here, we learn definition and declaration of a function. Also, the `return` statements, types of functions, functions with operators, functions and loop statements, function and arrays, pointers, etc. are discussed here.

Chapter 10 covers local and global variables. Also, explanation on `auto`, `external`, `static` and `register` variables is presented in this chapter.

Chapter 11 narrates how to make use of preprocessor directives. How various macros are to be used is discussed in this chapter. It covers `#define` directive, undefining a macro, token pasting and stringizing operators, include file and pre-defined macros in ANSI and Turbo C.

Chapter 12 covers structures and unions. This is another powerful feature of C language. One can get derived data type using structures and unions. User can decide the data types to be included in the body of a structure. By using structures, we can make a group of variables, arrays, pointers, etc. Declaration and initialization of structure and union are learnt in this chapter. Other concepts, such as arrays of structures, pointer to structure, structure and functions, `typedef`, enumerating data type and calling BIOS, also are explained in this chapter.

Chapter 13 is on files. How to read a file, append in it, and reading operations of a file. Lot many file handling commands are explained and discussed in this chapter. Text and binary files are also explained in this chapter.

Chapter 14 is on graphics. How to draw various figures/images using C is explained in this chapter. Initialization of graphics and graphic functions are also presented here.

Every chapter contains multiple choice questions and a brief theoretical discussion on the various aspects of C.

ACKNOWLEDGEMENTS

I express my deep sense of gratitude to the former Minister for Higher and Technical Education of Maharashtra, honourable Dilip Walse-Patil, who complimented me for writing books while he was in Nanded for the distribution of gold medals to the outstanding students and teachers of SGGS College of Engineering and Technology in 2002.

I would also like to thank all those who have encouraged me to write this book, especially Prof B. M. Naik, former Principal of SGGS College of Engineering and Technology, Nanded, who is a source of inspiration.

Special thanks are due to members of Board of Governors of the college who motivated me for writing this book: Shri Baba Kalyani, Chairman and Managing Director of Bharat Forge Ltd, Pune, Prof K. G. Narayankhedkar, Vijay Ghate, Kamlesh Pande, Dr V. P. Dimri, Chandra Iyangar and Dr S. R. Kajale Director of our institute. I am also thankful to the director for extending his help to write this book.

My sincere thanks to Prof S. D. Mahajan, who is holding the position of the director of Technical Education, Maharashtra State, and ex-board of governors of this college, Dr M. B. Kinhalkar, Former

Home Minister, Dr J. G. Wadekar, Dr V. A. Hambire and the ex-principal, Dr T. R. Sontakke for inspiring me to write this book.

I am grateful to all my colleagues, friends and students who extended moral support and helped me in preparing this book. My sincere thanks to Prof Dr S. G. Kahalekar, Dr P. D. Jadhav, Dr P. Pramanik, Dr B. M. Dabde, Dr U. V. Kulkarni, Dr V. M. Nandedkar, Dr M. L. Waikar, Dr R. S. Holambe, Dr B. M. Patre, R. K. Chavan, Dr J. V. L. Venkatesh, Dr Y. V. Joshi , S. S. Kandhare, P. S. Nalawade, S. S. Hatkar, Dr R. C. Thool, Narayan Patil, Dr A. V. Nandedkar, A. B. Gonde, Dr S. V. Bonde, Dr P. B. Londhe, Dr S. S. Gajre, Dr M. B. Kokre, Dr R. R. Manthalkar, N. G. Megde, Dr A. S. Sontakke, Deepak Bacchewar, Dr L. M. Waghmare and A. I. Tamboli for moral support. I am also thankful to my friends S. L. Kotgire, Balaji Bacchewar, M. M. Jahagirdar, R. M. Medabalmewar, L. M. Buddhewar, K. M. Buddhewar, D. V. Deshpande, S. R. Kokne, M. G. Damkondawar, R. D. Yeramwar, S. R. Tumma and S. R. Mana for their help.

I am also thankful to Thomas Mathew Rajesh, Sachin Saxena, Ruchi Sachdev and the editorial team of Pearson Education for specific invaluable inputs and bringing this book out in a record time. Ruchi Sachdev has extended her help in bringing out this book in this present form. I am thankful for her help.

Last but not the least, my thanks are due to my wife Surekha for her patience and support while writing this book. My sons Amol and Amit, daughter Sangita and daughter-in-law Swaroopa were also of great help and extended support to me all the times.

Ashok N. Kamthane

ABOUT THE AUTHOR

Ashok N. Kamthane is Assistant Professor in the Department of Electronics and Telecommunication Engineering, SGGS Institute of Engineering and Technology, Nanded, Maharashtra. He has over 25 years of teaching experience, and was associated with the development of hardware and software using 8051 on acoustic transceiver system for submarines.

Professor Kamthane is also the author of bestselling books, *Programming with ANSI and Turbo C* and *Object Oriented Programming with ANSI and Turbo C++* published by Pearson. His other books are *Computer Programming for Anna University* and *C and Data Structures for JNTU.*

1.1 COMPONENTS OF A COMPUTER

A computer is a programmable electronic machine that accepts instructions and data through input devices, manipulates data according to instructions and provides the final result through the output device. Figure 1.1, a conventional block diagram, shows the components of a conventional computer.

Figure 1.2 shows a computer. In brief, the various blocks/components of a computer are summarized below.

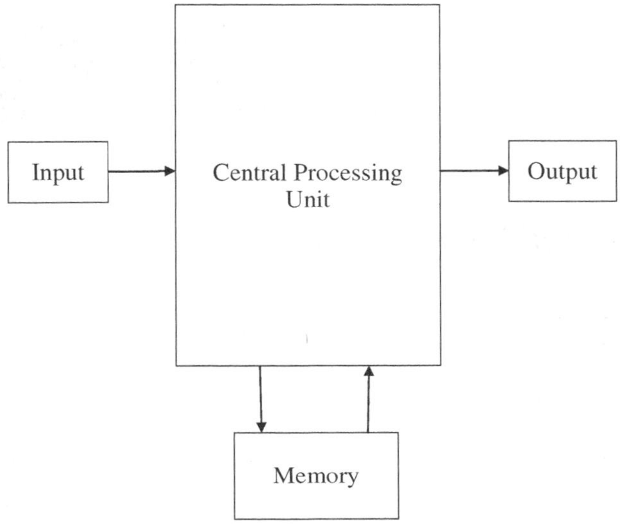

FIGURE 1.1 **Block diagram of a conventional computer**

Input devices: An input device feeds instructions and data, which are stored in the computer's memory. Consequently, computer reads data from the memory and manipulates it according to instructions. The various input devices to the central processor are keyboard, mouse, analog to digital converters, light pen, track ball, optical character reader, scanner, etc. Figure 1.3 shows the input devices of a computer. For example, a floppy and a compact disc can be used either as input or output device.

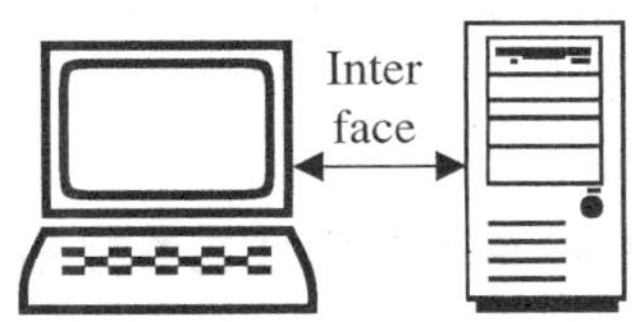

FIGURE 1.2 **Computer as a single unit**

Output devices: The processed data will be sent to the output device by the computer. The output device can be a monitor, printer, LED, seven-segment display, digital-to-analog converter, plotter, etc. Figure 1.4 shows the different output devices of a computer.

Memory: Volatile semiconductor memory is used for storing instructions and data in the form of ones and zeros. The memory can be called as user's memory or read-write memory. The processor first reads the instructions and data then executes the instructions.

One more memory device is used in the computer which is called as 'read only memory' (non-volatile memory), in which a program is installed permanently/fixed for providing certain operations.

Central processing unit: The heart of the computer system is a central processing unit. It comprises arithmetic and logical unit, registers and control unit. The arithmetic and logical unit performs operations

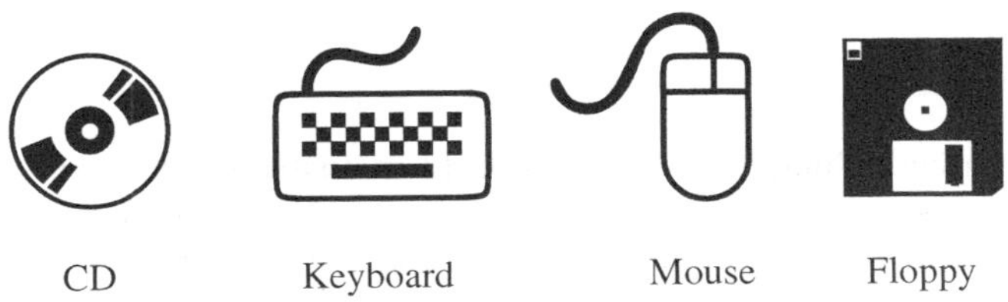

FIGURE 1.3 **Input devices of a computer**

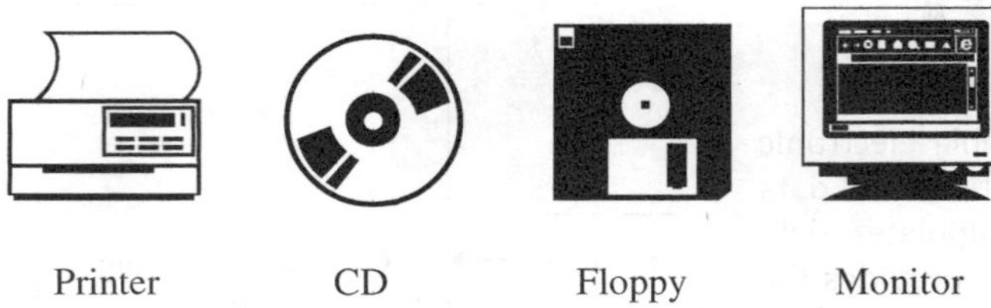

FIGURE 1.4 Output devices of a computer

based on instructions. The control unit generates the timing and control signals for carrying out the operations within the processor. The registers are used for storing the results temporarily.

1.2 LATEST COMPUTERS

Today's portable computers are just like notebooks, or even require less space than a notebook. They are handy, light weighted and portable, hence users now carry laptops while travelling for their day-to-day work.

1.3 ALGORITHM

The algorithm is defined as 'the finite set of the steps, which provide a chain of actions for solving a definite nature of problem'. Each step in the algorithm should be well defined. Every step is known as an instruction.

1.4 SEQUENCE, SELECTION AND ITERATION

The steps/instructions of an algorithm/program can be either in sequence or out of sequence based on true or false condition or repeatedly the same set of steps/instructions are executed over a number of times. The three types of control structures are narrated as follows.

Sequence: The steps described in algorithm are performed one by one successively without skipping any step. Each instruction of such algorithm is executed, because no selection procedure or conditional branching exists in sequence algorithm.

Selection: An algorithm written in a sequence is not powerful. There must be a procedure to handle control structures such as 'if' or 'if else' in the algorithm/program.

Iteration: It is very necessary to perform the same step for a number of times. If the same statement is written repetitively, it will increase the program code. To avoid this problem, iteration mechanism is applied. The statement written in iteration block is executed for a given number of times, based on certain conditions.

1.5 FLOWCHARTS

A flowchart is an alternative technique for solving a problem. Instead of descriptive steps of algorithm, we use pictorial representation for every step. It shows a sequence of operations. A flowchart is a set of symbols, which indicates various operations in the program. For every process, there is a corresponding symbol in flowchart.

We have given below some commonly used symbols in flowcharts.

Start and stop: The start and stop symbols indicate both the beginning and the end of a flowchart. This symbol could be flat, oval or egg shaped. Figure 1.5 shows the symbol of start/stop. Usually, this symbol is used twice in a flowchart, that is at the beginning and end.

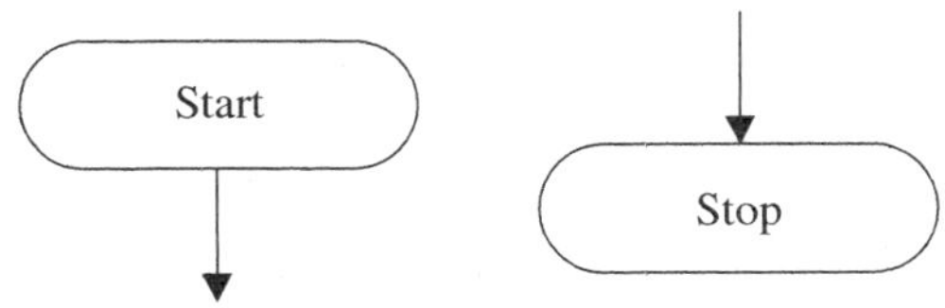

FIGURE 1.5 **Start/stop symbol**

Decision or test symbol: The decision symbol is diamond shaped. This symbol is used to take one of the decisions. Depending on the condition, the decision block selects one of the alternatives. In case the condition is satisfied, a set of statements will be executed, otherwise for 'false' the control transfers to exit.

Single alternative decision: Here, more than one flow line can be used depending upon the conduction. It is usually in the form of 'Yes' or 'No' question, with branching flow lines depending upon the answer. With single alternative, the flow diagram will be as shown in Figure 1.6.

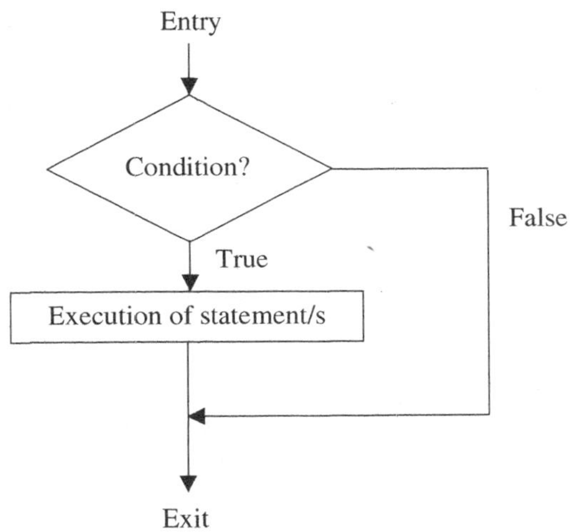

FIGURE 1.6 **Single alternative decision**

Two alternative decisions: In Figure 1.7, two alternative paths have been shown. On satisfying the condition, statement/s pertaining to 'action 1' will be executed otherwise the other statement/s for 'action 2' will be executed.

Multiple alternative decisions: In Figure 1.8, multiple decision blocks are shown. Every decision block has two branches. In case the condition is satisfied,

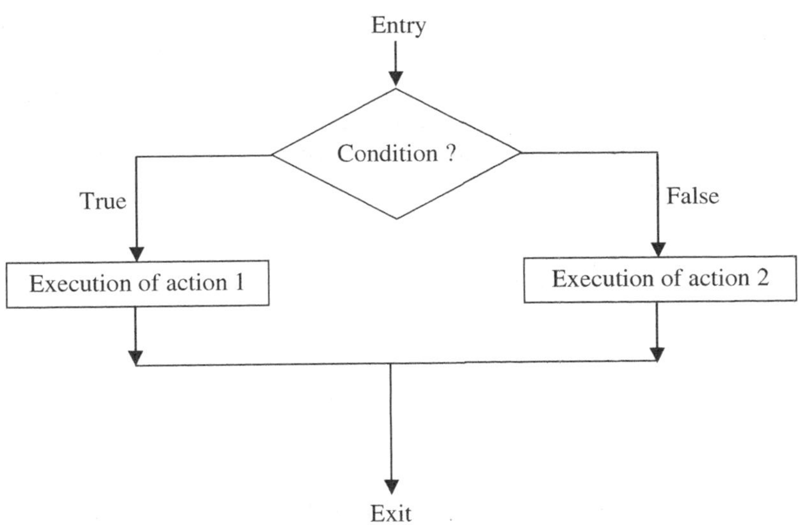

FIGURE 1.7 **Two alternative decisions**

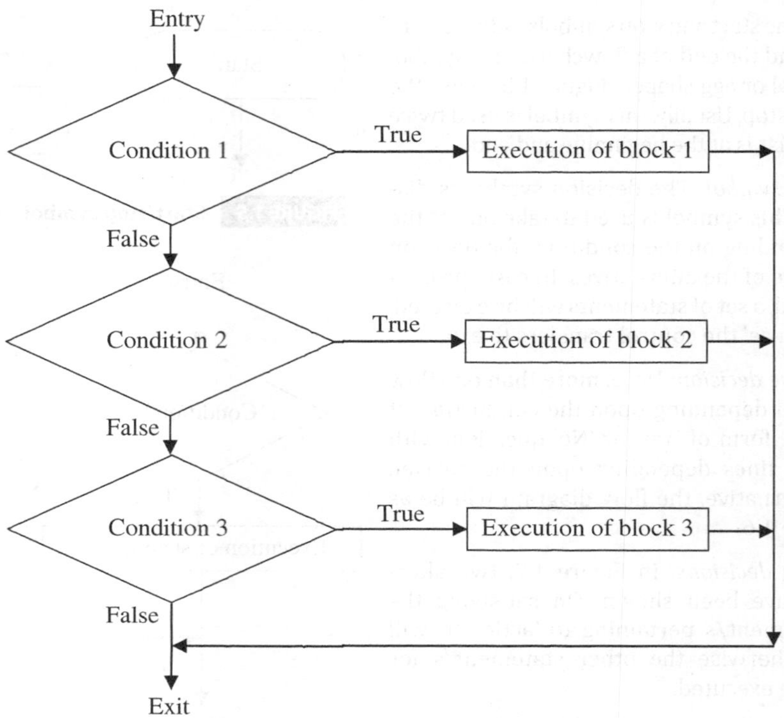

FIGURE 1.8 Multiple alternative decisions

execution of statements of appropriate blocks takes place, otherwise next condition will be verified. If condition 1 is satisfied, then block 1 statements are executed. In the same way, other decision blocks are executed.

Connector symbol: Connector symbol has to be shown in the form of a circle. It is used to establish the connection whenever it is impossible to directly join two parts in a flowchart. Quite often, the two parts of a flowchart may be on two separate pages. In such a case, connector can be used for joining the two parts. Figure 1.9 shows the connector symbol.

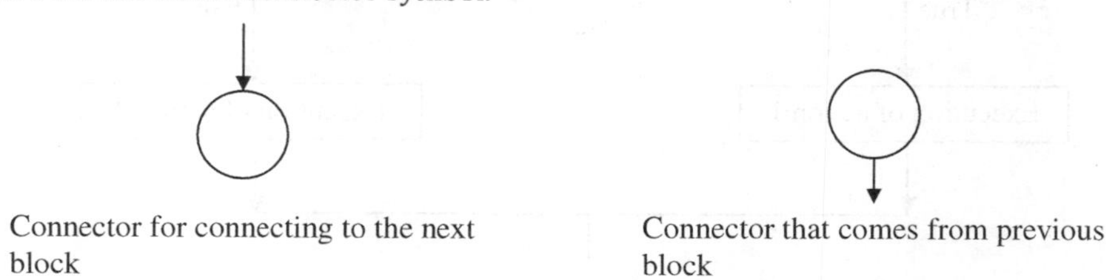

FIGURE 1.9 Connector symbol

Process symbol: A rectangle shape should show the symbol of process block. It is usually used for data handling, and values are assigned to the variables in this symbol. Figure 1.10 shows the process symbol. The operations mentioned within the rectangular block will be executed when this kind of block appears in the flowchart. There are two flow lines connected with the process symbol, one is incoming and another line is outgoing.

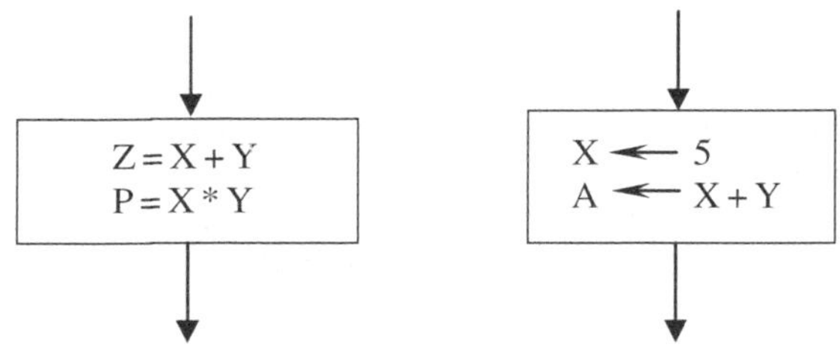

FIGURE 1.10 **Process symbol**

Loop symbol: This symbol looks like a hexagonal. It is used for the implementation of 'for' loops only. Four flow lines are associated with this symbol. Two lines are used to indicate the sequence of the program and the remaining two lines are used to show the looping area, i.e. from the beginning till the end.

For the sake of understanding, Figure 1.11 illustrates the working of 'for' loop. The variable j is initialized to 0 and it is to be incremented by step 2 until it reaches the final value 10. For every increased value of j, body of the loop is executed. This process will continue until the value of j reaches 10. Here, the next block is shown for the repetitive operation.

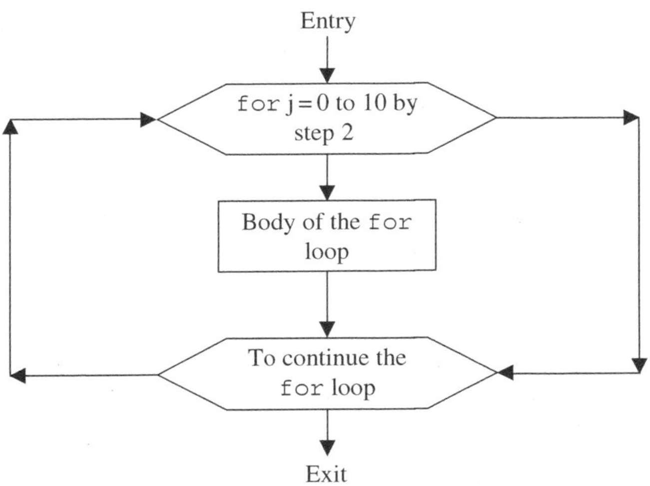

FIGURE 1.11 **For loop**

Input–output symbol: Input–output symbol looks like a parallelogram as shown in Figure 1.12. The input–output symbol is used to input and output the data. While the data is provided to the program for processing, then this symbol is used. There are two flow lines connected with the input–output symbol. One line comes to this symbol and another line goes from this symbol.

As shown in Figure 1.12, compiler reads the values of X and Y, and, as in the second figure, the result is either displayed on the monitor or printed using the printer.

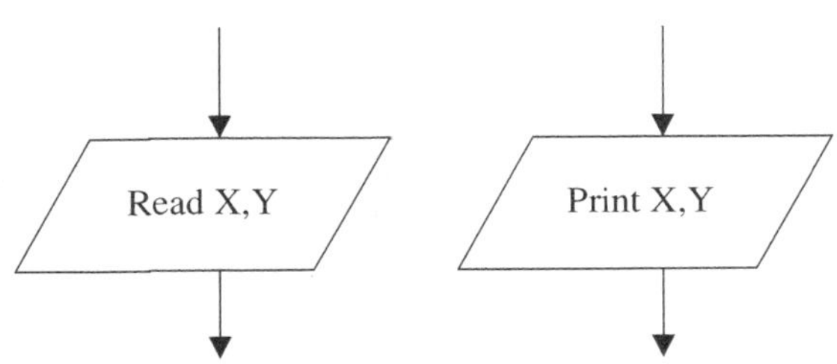

FIGURE 1.12 **Input–output symbol**

Delay symbol: Symbol of delay is just like 'AND' gate. It is used for adding delay to the process. It is associated with two lines. One is incoming and the another is outgoing as shown in Figure 1.13.

Manual input symbol: This is used for assigning the variable values through the keyboard, where, as in data symbol, the values are assigned directly without manual intervention. Figure 1.14 represents the symbol of manual input.

In addition, following symbols (Figure 1.15) can be used in the flowchart, and they are parts of flowcharts.

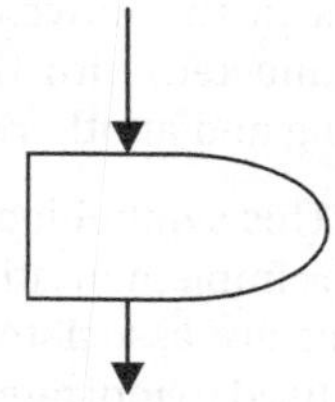

FIGURE 1.13 **Delay symbol**

1.6 AN OVERVIEW OF COMPILERS AND INTERPRETERS

A program is a set of instructions for performing a particular task. A program can be written in an assembly language as well as in a high-level language. This written program is called as source program. The source program is to be transformed into the machine language which is called as object program. Either an interpreter or a compiler will do this activity. Figure 1.16 shows the process of conversion of a source program into machine program.

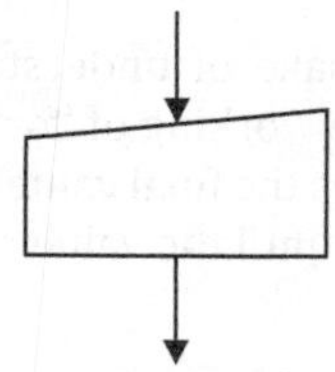

FIGURE 1.14 **Manual input symbol**

Interpreters: An interpreter reads only one line of a source program at a time, and converts it into object code. In case of errors, the same will be indicated

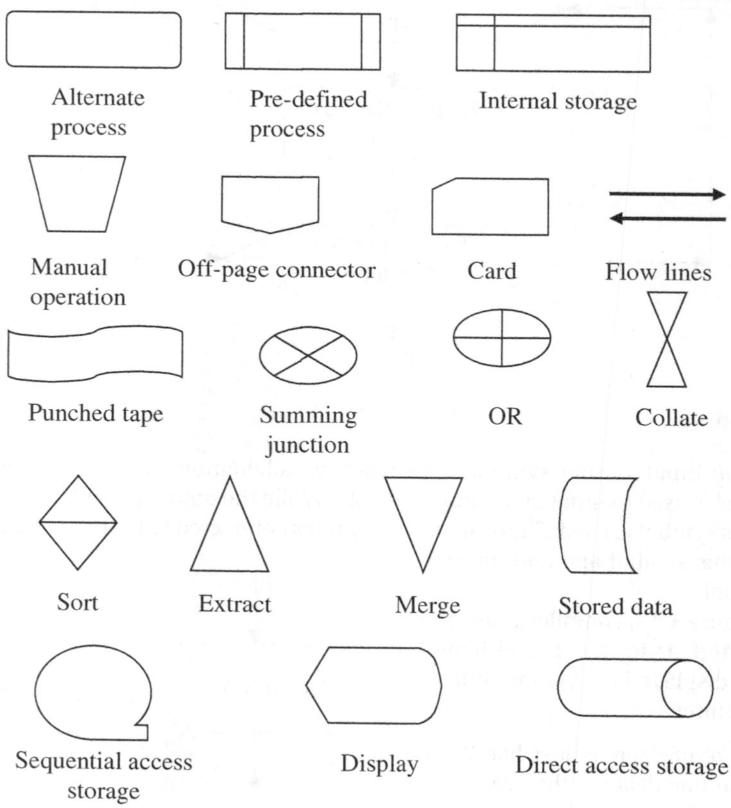

FIGURE 1.15 **Some other symbols used in the flowcharts**

FIGURE 1.16 **Translation of a source program into a machine code**

instantly. The program written with an interpreter can easily be read and understood by other users as well. So security is not provided. Any one can modify the source code. Hence, it is easier than compilers. But the disadvantage is that it consumes more time for converting a source program into an object program.

Compilers: Compiler reads the entire program and converts it into object code in one stroke. Figure 1.17 shows translation of a C program into machine codes. Hence, compilers are faster than interpreters. It needs more amount of memory than interpreters do. It provides errors of not just one line, but errors of the entire program. It shows syntax and other errors in case the program is wrong. Only error free programs are executed.

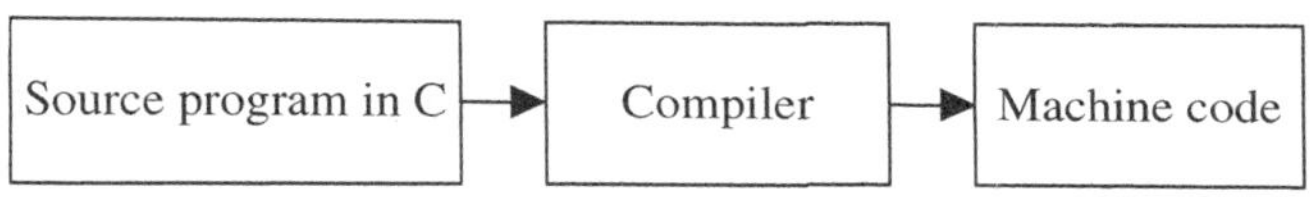

FIGURE 1.17 **Translation of a C source program to machine code**

The compiler creates a file that contains executable codes, and then the execution process starts. With this process of a compiler, the execution of a program will be performed with machine code.

When the program length for any application is large, compilers are preferred.

1.7 STRUCTURE OF A C PROGRAM

A C program comprises different sections which are shown in Figure 1.18.

(i) *Include header file section*: C program depends upon some header files for function definition that are used in a program. Each header file by default is extended with `.h`. The file should be included using `#include` directive as given below.

Example:
`#include <stdio.h>` or `#include "stdio.h."`

In this example, `<stdio.h>` file is included, i.e. all the definitions and prototypes of function defined in this file are available in the current program. This file is also compiled with original program.

(ii) *Global declaration*: This section declares some variables that are to be used in more than one function. These variables are known as global variables. This section must be declared outside of all the functions.

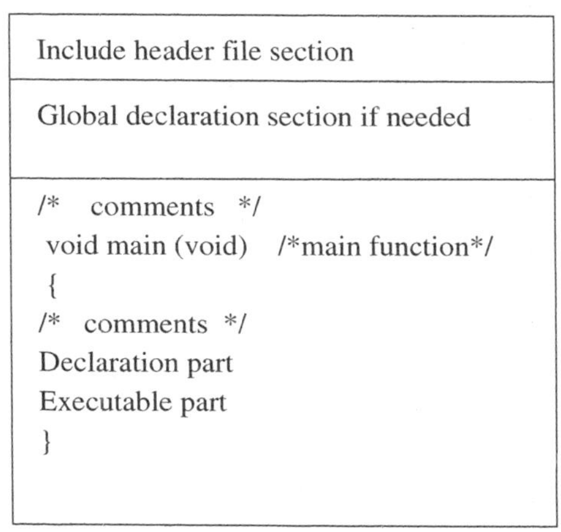

FIGURE 1.18 **Various sections of a C program**

(iii) *Function* `main(void)`: Program written in C language contains a `void main(void)` function. Arguments, if needed, are specified within the parentheses following the function name `main`. Here in this program `void` enclosed within a bracket indicates that no arguments are passed to the main function. The keyword `void` before `main` returns nothing. If keyword `int` before `main` is observed, it indicates that function `main` returns integer. The function `main()` is a starting point of every C program. The execution of the program always begins with the function `main()`. Except the `main()` function, other sections may not be necessary. The program execution starts from the opening brace '{' and ends with the closing brace '}'. Between these two braces, the programmer should declare declaration and executable parts.

(iv) *Declaration part*: The declaration part declares the entire variables that are used in executable part. The initialization of variables is also done in this section. The initialization means providing initial value to the variables.

(v) *Executable part*: This part contains the statements following the declaration of the variables. It also contains a set of statements or a single statement.

(vi) *User-defined function*: The functions defined by the user are called user-defined functions. These functions are generally defined after the `main()` function. They can also be defined before `main()` function. This portion is not compulsory. Programmer can follow this concept in the chapter on Functions.

(vii) *Comments*: Comments are not necessary in the program. However, to understand the flow of programs, programmers can include comments in the program. They are to be inserted by the programmer, and it is useful for documentation. The clarity of the program can be followed if it is properly documented.

Comments should be placed between the delimiters /* and */. The compiler does not execute comments. Thus, we can say that comments are not the part of executable programs.

The user can frequently use any number of comments that can be placed anywhere in the program. Please note that the comment statements can be nested. The user can use the C compiler and should select the Option Menu of the editor and select the Compiler-Source-Nested Comments ON/OFF. The comments can be inserted with single statement or in nested statements in the program. Examples are as follows.

***Example*:**

```
/* This is single comment */
/* This is an example of /* nested comments */*/
/* This is an example of
   of comments with
   multiple lines */ /* It can be nested */
```

1.8 C PROGRAMMING RULES

(i) Statements should be written in lower case letters. Upper case letters are only used for symbolic constants.

(ii) Blank spaces may be inserted between the words. This improves the readability of the statements. However, it is not used while declaring a variable, keyword, constant and functions.

(iii) It is not necessary to fix the position of statement in the program, i.e. the programmer can write the statement anywhere between the two braces following the declaration part. The user can also write one or more statements in one line separating them with semicolon (;). Hence, it is often called a free-form language. The following statements are valid.

a=b+c;
d=b*c;
or
a=b+c; d=b*c;

(iv) The opening and closing braces should be balanced, i.e. if opening braces are four, then closing braces should also be four.

1.9 EXECUTING THE PROGRAM

The following steps are essential to execute a program in C.

Creation of program: The program should be written in C editor. The file name does not necessarily include extension '.C'. The default extension is '.C'. The user can also specify his/her own extension.

Compilation and linking a program: With `alt-c` keys, the source program statements should be translated into object program, which is suitable for execution by the computer. The translation is done after correcting each statement as per C syntax. If there is no error, compilation proceeds and translated program is stored in another file with the same file name, but with an extension '.obj'. If at all errors are there, the programmer should correct them. The linking is also an essential process. It puts all other program files and functions together that are required by the program. For example, if the programmer is using `pow()` function, then the object code of this function should be brought from `math.h` library of the system and linked to the `main()`program.

Executing the program: After the compilation, the executable object code will be loaded in the computers main memory and the program is executed. This is done with keys `alt-r`.

All the above steps can be performed using menu options of the editor.

1.10 AN EXAMPLE OF A C PROGRAM

Following is a sample program when executed with C compiler, the output of the program would be as follows.

"Hello! Welcome you in the C world"

```
void main()
{
/* First sample Program */
printf("Hello! Welcome you in the C world");
}
```

Look at the program. Execution of every C program always starts from `main()`. The `main()` is a special function designed for starting the C program.

Following the main, a pair of empty parentheses are seen. Nothing is enclosed between a pair of parentheses which indicates that no arguments to the main function.

Following the `main()`, program is written between opening and closing braces. Opening brace is '{' and closing brace is '}'. Opening brace indicates that immediately following this brace the program statement should be started, and immediately after closing brace program statement ends. A function body contains all the statements within the two braces for performing a specific task. Here, in this example, our task is to print a message "Hello! Welcome you in the C world". Two statements are written within the braces in the above program. First line is a comment line and the second line is printf()function. Within the quotation mark in the printf()function, whatever is written gets printed at the output device. Here, within the quotation mark message is "Hello! Welcome you in the C world", and hence the same is displayed on the screen.

EXERCISES

1.A Fill in the blanks

1. Computer is a ______ electronic machine.
   (a) programmable
   (b) non-programmable
   (c) none of the above
2. Scanner is an ______ device.
   (a) output
   (b) input
   (c) input and output
3. Floppy is an ______ device.
   (a) output
   (b) input
   (c) input and output
4. Hard disc is a ______ device.
   (a) semiconductor
   (b) magnetic
   (c) conductor
5. Program execution takes place in ______ memory.
   (a) CD
   (b) tape
   (c) RAM
6. In ______ structure, the steps described in algorithm are executed one by one without skipping any step.
   (a) iterative
   (b) selection
   (c) sequential
7. Program looping is done with ______ structure.
   (a) iterative
   (b) selection
   (c) sequential
8. Header files appear in the C program at the ______.
   (a) beginning
   (b) middle
   (c) end
9. Comments in C are written within ______.
   (a) /* */
   (b) { }
   (c) ( )
10. ______ language is CPU dependent.
    (a) compiler
    (b) assembler
    (c) interpreter
11. C is a ______ language.
    (a) portable
    (b) non-portable
    (c) none of the above
12. Opening and closing braces in C should be ______.
    (a) unbalanced
    (b) balanced
    (c) uncontrolled
13. ______ are pre-defined in the compiler.
    (a) ASCII
    (b) keywords
    (c) none of the above
14. ______ processes instructions and data.
    (a) keys
    (b) CPU
    (c) hard disc

1.B True or false

1. Human's intellectual capability is superior than computer's capability.
2. Computers are slaves to the humans.
3. Computer is a non-programmable system.
4. The control unit of a CPU generates the timing and control signals.
5. Palmtop is a programmable gadget.
6. Algorithms are used for solving problems with a step by step procedure.
7. Flowchart is a visual representation of the sequence of steps for solving a problem.
8. Iteration mechanism is normally implemented in the program for avoiding repetition of similar statements in a program.
9. Embedded systems are the same as that of computers.
10. Compilers are slower than interpreters.
11. Interpreters need more memory than the compilers.
12. Embedded systems are reprogrammable systems.
13. User-defined functions can be defined after and before the `main()`function.
14. The opening and closing braces should not be balanced in C program.
15. The program execution in C starts from the opening brace and ends with the closing brace.

1.C Match the following correct pairs given in Group A with Group B

I

Group A		Group B	
Serial No.	**Hardware**	**Serial No.**	**Meaning**
1.	Monitor	A	Both input and output
2.	Floppy	B	Output
3.	RAM	C	Magnetic
4.	Hard disc	D	Semiconductor

II

Group A		Group B	
Serial No.	**Device**	**Serial No.**	**Meaning**
1.	RAM	A	Non-volatile
2.	ROM	B	Volatile
3.	Hard disc	C	Optical disc
4.	CD	D	Magnetic

III

Group A		Group B	
Serial No.	**Software**	**Serial No.**	**Meaning**
1.	Assembler	A	Complete source code execution at a time
2.	Linker	B	One line execution at a time
3.	Compiler	C	Assembly language to machine language
4.	Interpreter	D	Linking different modules

IV

Group A		Group B	
Serial No.	**Items**	**Serial No.**	**Meaning**
1.	Notepad	A	Software package
2.	Database management system	B	Single program
3.	Microsoft office suit	C	System utility
4.	Disc cleanup	D	Set of programs

V

Group A		Group B	
Serial No.	**Items**	**Serial No.**	**Meaning**
1.	Loader	A	System functions
2.	Firewall	B	Part of OS
3.	Virus	C	System utility
4.	Disc management	D	Small program

1.D Select the appropriate option from the multiple choices given below

1. Hard disc is an
   (a) input device
   (b) output device
   (c) input as well as output
   (d) none of the above

2. Mouse is an
   (a) input device
   (b) output device
   (c) input as well as output
   (d) none of the above

3. Brain of the computer system is
   (a) mouse
   (b) printer
   (c) keyboard
   (d) central processing unit

4. Monitor of computer system is an
   (a) input
   (b) output
   (c) input as well as output

5. Random access memory is
   (a) non-volatile
   (b) volatile
   (c) both of the above

6. ALU is a part of
   (a) input
   (b) output
   (c) CPU

7. Laptop device is
   (a) non-portable
   (b) portable
   (c) desktop

8. Which control structure is used based on condition
   (a) sequence
   (b) selection
   (c) iterative

9. Iterative structure means that the instructions are executed
   (a) once
   (b) repetitively for finite times
   (c) infinitely

10. Compiler executes at a time
    (a) one single line
    (b) complete source code
    (c) two lines

11. Interpreter is a
    (a) hardware
    (b) software
    (c) none of the above

12. C source program is in
    (a) upper case
    (b) lower case
    (c) none of the above

13. Keys used for compiling the source program in C
    (a) alt-c
    (b) alt-r
    (c) alt-f

14. Keys used for running the source program in C
    (a) alt-c
    (b) alt-r
    (c) alt-f

15. Keys used for closing the C editor
    (a) alt-c
    (b) alt-x
    (c) alt-f

16. Interpreter converts source code into
    (a) machine code
    (b) ASCII code
    (c) BCD code

1.E Answer the following questions

1. What is the impact of computers in our life?
2. List the specifications of personal computer system consisting Pentium based CPU.
3. Which technology has brought important revolution in computer networking? Explain its features.
4. What are the functions of an interpreter and a compiler?
5. What is the difference between an interpreter and a compiler?
6. Compare and contrast between assembler and compiler.

7. Describe the functions of peripheral devices of a central processing unit.
8. What is meant by compilation? Explain in detail. How a compiler executes the subprograms of a program?
9. Write the rules for writing a C program.
10. Elaborate different sections of C program.
11. Explain the functions of a linker.
12. What is the role of curly braces ({ }) in C program?
13. What are the user-defined functions?
14. What is the role of a flowchart? Explain various symbols used in flowcharts.
15. What are the benefits of algorithms? Describe the characteristics of a good algorithm.
16. List the features and specifications of a laptop.

ANSWERS

1.A Fill in the blanks

1. (a) programmable
2. (b) input
3. (c) input and output
4. (b) magnetic
5. (c) RAM
6. (c) sequential
7. (a) iterative
8. (a) beginning
9. (a) /* */
10. (b) assembler
11. (a) portable
12. (b) balanced
13. (b) keywords
14. (b) CPU

1.B True or false

1. T 2. T 3. F 4. T 5. T 6. T 7. T 8. T 9. F
10. F 11. F 12. F 13. T 14. F 15. T

1.C Match the following correct pairs given in Group A with Group B

I 1. B, 2. A, 3. D, 4. C
II 1. B, 2. A, 3. D, 4. C
III 1. C, 2. D, 3. A, 4. B
IV 1. B, 2. A, 3. D, 4. C
V 1. B, 2. C, 3. D, 4. A

1.D Select the appropriate option from the multiple choices given below

1. (c) input as well as output
2. (a) input device
3. (d) central processing unit
4. (b) output
5. (b) volatile
6. (c) CPU
7. (b) portable
8. (b) selection
9. (b) repetitively for finite times
10. (b) complete source code
11. (b) software
12. (b) lower case
13. (a) alt-c
14. (b) alt-r
15. (b) alt-x
16. (a) machine code

2

The C Declarations

CHAPTER OUTLINE

2.1 Introduction
2.2 The C Character Set
2.3 Delimiters
2.4 Types of Tokens
2.5 The C Keywords
2.6 Identifiers
2.7 Constants
2.8 Variables
2.9 Rules for Defining Variables
2.10 C Data Types
2.11 Initializing Variables
2.12 Dynamic Initilization
2.13 Type Modifiers
2.14 Type Conversion
2.15 Wrapping Around
2.16 Constant and Volatile Variables

2.1 INTRODUCTION

In this chapter, various elements of C are described, which include character set, the type of variables, data types, types of tokens, delimiters, variable initialization, dynamic initialization, etc.

2.2 THE C CHARACTER SET

A character is indicated by any alphabets in lowercase or uppercase, digits or special symbol/characters. These characters are used to write any kind of C program.

Figure 2.1 presents valid categories of C character set.

(i) Alphabets (A, B, C, ..., Z and a, b, c, ..., z)

(ii) Digits (numbers 0 to 9)

(iii) White spaces (blank space, tabs, etc.)

(iv) Special characters: list of special characters are given in Table 2.1

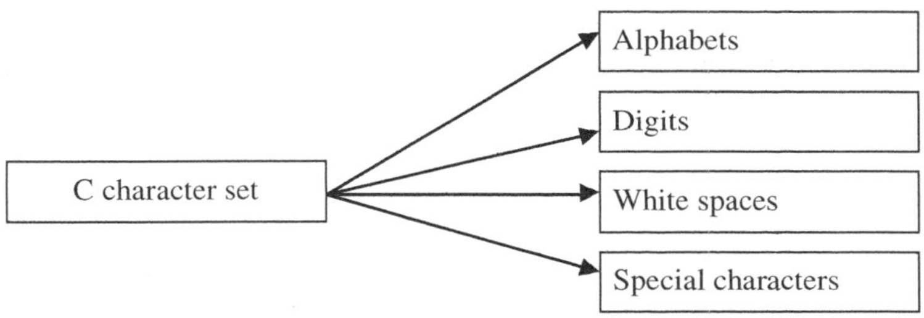

FIGURE 2.1 C character set

The complete character set is listed in the Tables 2.1 and 2.2.

TABLE 2.1 List of special characters

<table>
<tr><th>Symbol</th><th>Name</th><th>Symbol</th><th>Name</th></tr>
<tr><td>,</td><td>Comma</td><td>&</td><td>Ampersand</td></tr>
<tr><td>.</td><td>Period or dot</td><td>∧</td><td>Caret</td></tr>
<tr><td>;</td><td>Semicolon</td><td>*</td><td>Asterisk</td></tr>
<tr><td>:</td><td>Colon</td><td>−</td><td>Minus</td></tr>
<tr><td>‘</td><td>Apostrophe</td><td>+</td><td>Plus</td></tr>
<tr><td>“</td><td>Quotation mark</td><td><</td><td>Less than</td></tr>
<tr><td>!</td><td>Exclamation mark</td><td>></td><td>Greater than</td></tr>
<tr><td>|</td><td>Vertical bar</td><td>()</td><td>Parenthesis left/right</td></tr>
<tr><td>/</td><td>Slash</td><td>[]</td><td>Bracket left/right</td></tr>
<tr><td>\</td><td>Back slash</td><td>{}</td><td>Braces left/right</td></tr>
<tr><td>~</td><td>Tilde</td><td>%</td><td>Percent sign</td></tr>
<tr><td>$</td><td>Dollar</td><td>=</td><td>Equal to</td></tr>
<tr><td>?</td><td>Question mark</td><td>@</td><td>At the rate</td></tr>
</table>

TABLE 2.2 Character set

Letters	*Digits*	*White Spaces*
Capital letters A to Z Small case letters a to z	All decimal digits 0 to 9	Blank space Horizontal tab Vertical tab New line Form feed

2.3 DELIMITERS

Language pattern of C uses special kind of symbols which are called as delimiters. They are given in Table 2.3.

TABLE 2.3 Delimiters

Symbol	*Delimiters*	*Use*
:	Colon	Useful for label
;	Semicolon	Terminate statements
()	Parentheses	Used in expression and function
[]	Square bracket	Used for array declaration
{}	Curly brace	Scope of statement
#	Hash	Pre-processor directive
,	Comma	Variable separator

2.4 TYPES OF TOKENS

A compiler designer prescribes rules for constructing a program using statements. The smallest unit of a program/statement is called as token. The compiler identifies them as token. Tokens are classified as follows. Figure 2.2 shows types of tokens supported by C.

The tokens are as follows.

(i) Keywords – Reserved by the compiler and there are 32 keywords (ANSI standard).

(ii) Variables – User-defined. Any number of variables can be defined.

(iii) Constants – Constants are assigned to variables.

(iv) Operators – Operators are of different types and are used in expressions.

(v) Special characters – These characters are used in different declarations in C.

(vi) Strings – Sequence of characters enclosed in double quotation marks.

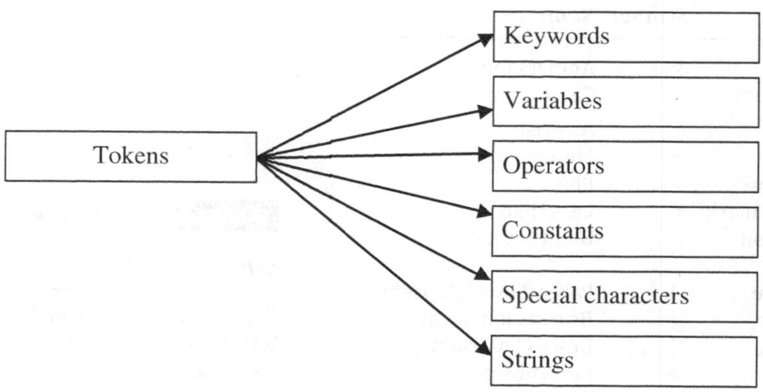

FIGURE 2.2 Types of tokens

2.5 THE C KEYWORDS

The C keywords are reserved words by the compiler, and they have been assigned fixed meaning. The keywords cannot be used as variable names because they have been assigned fixed meanings.

The 32 C keywords provided in ANSI C are listed in Table 2.4. Besides, additional keywords provided in Borland C are shown at the end of this table.

TABLE 2.4 C keywords

auto		double		int		struct
break		else		long		switch
case		enum		register		typedef
char		extern		return		union
const		float		short		unsigned
continue		for		signed		void
default		goto		sizeof		volatile
do		if		static		while
		Additional keywords for Borland C				
asm	cdecl	far	huge	interrupt	near	pascal

2.6 IDENTIFIERS

A symbolic name is used to refer to a variable. This process is done with identifiers. In other words, identifiers are names of variables, functions and arrays. They refer to variety of entities such as structures, unions, enumeration, constants, `typedef` names, functions and objects (see Figure 2.3). An identifier always starts with an alphabet, and it is a plain sequence of alphabets and/or digits. C identifier does not allow blank spaces, punctuations, signs, etc.

Identifiers are user-defined names. They are generally defined in lowercase letters. However, the uppercase letters are also permitted. The under score (_) symbol can be used as an identifier. In general, a programmer uses underscore as link between two words for long identifiers.

Valid identifiers are as follows.

`length, area, volume, SUM, Average,` etc.

Invalid identifiers are as follows.

`length of line, S+um, year's,` etc.

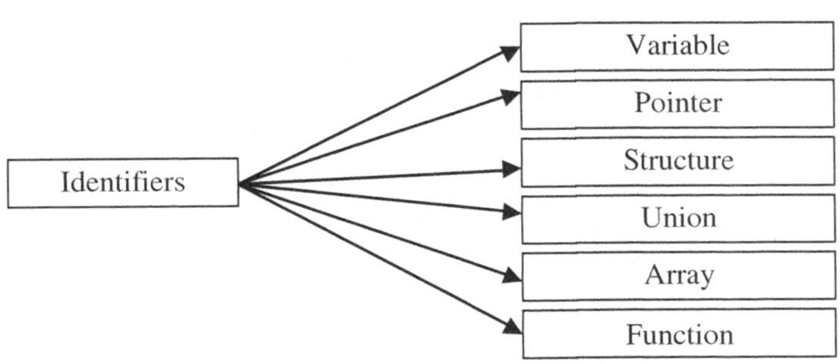

FIGURE 2.3 Identifiers

Examples:

User-defined identifiers are as follows.

(i) `#define N 10`

(ii) `#define a 15`

Here, 'N' and 'a' are user-defined identifiers.

2.7 CONSTANTS

Constant values are assigned to the variables which do not change during execution of a program. They are classified into following groups as given in Figure 2.4.

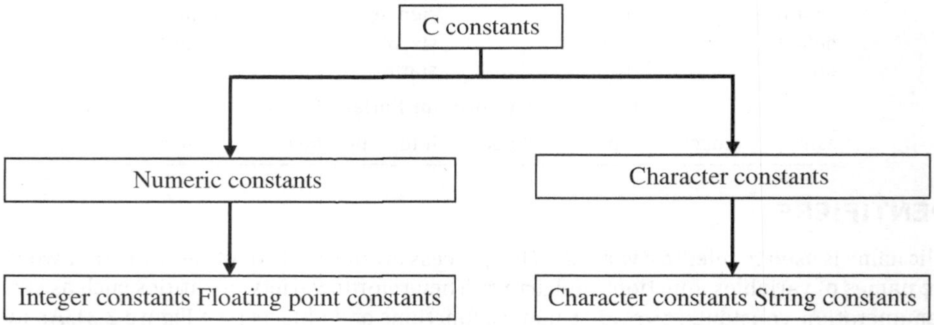

FIGURE 2.4 **C constants**

2.7.1 Numeric Constants

(i) *Integer constants*: these constants are represented with whole numbers. It requires minimum two bytes and maximum four bytes of memory.

Valid examples: 10, 20, +30, −15
Invalid integer constants: 2.3, .235, $76, 3*^6

Besides representing the integers in decimal, they can also be represented in octal or hexadecimal, based on the requirement.

An octal has base 8 and hexadecimal 16. The octal numbers are 0, 1, 2, 3, 4, 5, 6, 7 and hexadecimal numbers are 0, 1, 2, 3, 4, 5, 6, 7, 8, 9, A, B, C, D, E, F.

The representation of octal numbers in C would be done with leading digit 0 and for hexadecimal representation with leading 0X or 0x.

Following are few examples of octal and hexadecimal numbers:

Octal numbers: 027, 037, 072, etc.
Hexadecimal numbers: 0X9, 0Xab, 0X4, etc.

(ii) *Floating point constants*: floating point constants are often known as real constants. Real constants can be represented in exponential or fractional form. Integer constants are unfit to represent many quantities such as length, breadth, height, etc.

Examples of real numbers are as follows.

Examples:
2.5, 5.521, 3.14

In an exponential notation, the value 2456.123 can be written as 2.4561 × e+3. The part that precedes e is called as mantissa and followed by it is an exponent. In this case, 2.4561 is mantissa and +3 is an exponent.

Valid examples: 5.2e2, −2, 5.0e−5 , 0.5e−3

In double type also the real numbers can be expressed with mantissa and exponent parts.

2.7.2 Character Constants

(i) *Single character constants*: A character constant in C is represented with a single character, and it is enclosed within single quotes. Each character constant has a particular integer value associated with it.

Each character has one ASCII value. A character can also be represented with single digit or a single special symbol or white space enclosed within a pair of single quotes.

Examples:
'a', '8', '&'

Character constants have integer values known as ASCII values. For example, the statement `printf("%c %d", 65, 'B');` will display character 'A' and 66.

(ii) *String constant*: String constants are sequence of characters or zeros enclosed within double quotes. The string may be a combination of all kinds of symbols.

Valid examples of string constants are : "Hello", "India", "444", "a".

2.8 VARIABLES

Variables are the basic objects manipulated in the program. Declaration gives an introduction of a variable to compiler and its properties like scope, range of values and memory required for storage. A variable is used to store values, and it must be declared before it is used in the program. It has memory location. The variable can store single value at a time.

Example:
Height, average, sum, avg12, etc.

2.9 RULES FOR DEFINING VARIABLES

(i) A variable must begin with a letter without spaces, but an underscore is permitted. The underscore is treated as one type of character.

(ii) The variable should not be a C keyword.

(iii) The variable names may be combination of uppercase and lowercase letters. For example, suM and sum are not the same. The traditional practice is to use lowercase letters for variable names and uppercase letters for symbolic constants.

(iv) The variable name should not start with a digit.

(v) Blanks and commas are not permitted within a variable name.

2.10 C DATA TYPES

The basic data types are `char`, `int` , `float` and `double`.

The C supports a number of qualifiers that can be applied to these basic data type. The qualifiers `short` and `long` provide different length to `int`. The `short` is always 16 bits and `long` 32 bits, i.e. `int` is either 16 or 32 bits. The compiler is free to choose suitable size depending upon the hardware. However, the restriction is that `short` or `int` is at least of 2 bytes and `long` at least of 4 bytes. The `short` should not be longer than `int`, and `int` which is no longer than `long`.

The qualifier `unsigned` and `signed` can be applied to `char`, `int` and `long`. The `unsigned` data types always hold values only zero or positive. This data type follows the law of arithmetic modulo 2^n, where n is the number of bits in the type. For example, `char` are 8 bits with a combination of negative and positive values (−128 to 127). The `unsigned char` supports values 0 to 255. The characters are `signed` or `unsigned`, the printable `char` are always positive.

C data type can be classified as follows.

(i) Basic data type: Basic data types are:

(a) Integer (`int`), (b) Character (`char`), (c) Floating point (`float`) and (d) Double floating point (`double`).

(ii) Derived data type: Derived data types are pointers , functions and arrays. Explanation on these data types is given in the respective chapters.

(iii) User-defined data type: `struct`, `union`, `enum` and `typedef` are user-defined data types. Explanation on these data types is given in chapter 12.

(iv) Void data type: It is an empty data set.The chapter on Functions can be referred for void data type.

2.10.1 Basic Data Type

(i) *Integer Data Type*

(a) *Short and long integer*: all C compilers offer different integer data types. They are `short` and `long`. Short integer requires half the space in memory than the long. The short integer requires 2 bytes and the long integer 4 bytes.

Brief description on them is given in the Table 2.5

TABLE 2.5 Difference between short and long integers

Short Integer	*Long Integer*
Occupies 2 bytes in memory	Occupies 4 bytes in memory
Range: −32768 to 32767	Range: −2147483648 to 2147483647
Program runs faster	Program runs slower
Format string is `%d` or `%i`	Format String is `%ld`
Example:	Example:
`int a=2;`	`long b;`
`short int b=2;`	`long int c;`

When variable is declared without short or long keyword, the default is short-signed `int`.

(b) *Signed and unsigned integers*: both signed and unsigned integers occupy 2 bytes in memory. But the range varies differently in singed integers and unsigned integers. In signed integers, the range is −32768 to 32767, whereas unsigned in integers the range is 0 to 65535.

The difference between the signed and unsigned integers is provided in Table 2.6

TABLE 2.6 Difference between signed and unsigned integers

Signed Integer	*Unsigned Integer*
Occupies 2 bytes in memory	Occupies 2 bytes in memory
Range: −32768 to 32767	Range: 0 to 65535
Format string is `%d` or `%i`	Format string is `%u`
By default signed `int` is short-signed `int`	By default unsigned `int` is short unsigned `int`
There are also long signed `int` having range from -2147483648 to 2147483647	There are also long unsigned `int` with range from 0 to 4294967295
Example:	Example:
`int a=2;`	`unsigned long b;`
`long int b=2;`	`unsigned short int c;`

When a variable is declared as unsigned, the negative range of the data type is transferred to positive, i.e. doubles the largest size of the possible value. This is due to declaring unsigned `int`; the 16th bit is free and not used to store the sign of the number.

(ii) `char`, *Signed and Unsigned*

Brief description on these data types are illustrated in Table 2.7

TABLE 2.7 Difference between signed and unsigned characters

Signed Character	*Unsigned Character*
Occupies 2 bytes in memory	Occupies 2 bytes in memory
Range: −128 to 127	Range: 0 to 255
Format string: `%c`	Format string: `%c`
When printed using `%d` control string, corresponding ASCII number is printed	When printed using `%d` control string, corresponding ASCII number is printed

(iii) *Floats and Doubles*

Table 2.8 shows the description of floats and doubles.

TABLE 2.8 Difference between float and double

Float	*Doubles*
Occupies 4 bytes in memory	Occupies 8 bytes in memory
Range: $3.4e^{-38}$ to $+3.4e^{+38}$	Range: $1.7\ e^{-308}$ to $+1.7e^{+308}$
Format string: `%f`	Format string: `%lf`
Example:	Example:
`float a;`	`double y;`
	There also exists `long double` which occupies 10 bytes in memory
	Example: `long double k;`

(iv) *Entire Basic Data Types in C*

The entire data types supported by the C, as illustrated above, are given in Table 2.9 for the convenience of the reader's understanding.

TABLE 2.9 Data types and their control strings

Data Type	*Size (bytes)*	*Range*	*Format String*
`char`	1	−128 to 127	`%c`
`unsigned char`	1	0 to 255	`%c`
`short or int`	2	−32768 to 32767	`%i` or `%d`
`unsigned int`	2	0 to 65535	`%u`
`long`	4	−2147483648 to 2147483647	`%ld`
`unsigned long`	4	0 to 4294967295	`%lu`
`float`	4	$3.4e^{-38}$ to $3.4e^{+38}$	`%f` or `%g`
`double`	8	$1.7e^{-308}$ to $1.7e^{+308}$	`%lf`
`long double`	10	$3.4e^{-4932}$ to $1.1e^{+4932}$	`%lf`
`enum`	2	-32768 to 32767	`%d`

2.10.2 The Void Data Type

The void type is added in ANSI C and it is also known as empty data type. It can be used in two ways.

(i) When specified as a function return type, void means that the function does not return a value.

```
void message(char *name)
{
  printf("Hello, %s.", name);
}
```

Here, message () is a void function. The keyword void is preceded by the function name. This function, when executed, displays only message and does not return any value to the calling function.

(ii) The void keyword is also used as argument for function. When found in a function heading, void means the function does not take any arguments.

```
int fun(void)
{
  return 1;
}
```

Here, the function `fun()` does not require any argument. It returns an integer value.

(iii) When specified as a function return type and in function heading, the function neither returns a value nor requires any argument.

```
void fun(void);
```

The above function neither returns a value nor requires any argument.

2.11 INITIALIZING VARIABLES

Variables declared can be assigned or initialized using assignment operator '='. The declaration and initialization can also be done in the same line.

***Syntax*:**
variable_name = constant
or
data_type variable_name = constant

***Example*:**
`x=2`; where `x` is an integer variable.
```
int y=2;
int x,y,z; x=y=z=1;
```

2.12 DYNAMIC INITIALIZATION

The initialization of variable at run-time is called dynamic initialization. Dynamic refers to process during execution. In C, initialization can be done at any place in the program, however, the declaration should be done at the declaration part only.

2.13 TYPE MODIFIERS

The keywords `signed`, `unsigned`, `short` and `long` are type modifiers. A type modifier changes the meaning of basic data type and produces a new data type. Each of these type modifiers is applicable to the basic data type `int`. The modifiers `signed` and `unsigned` are also applicable to the type `char`. The `long` type modifier can be applicable to `double` type.

***Examples*:**
```
long l;  //int data type is applied
int s; //signed is default
unsigned long int;     //int keyword is optional
```

2.14 TYPE CONVERSION

Some times the programmer needs the result in certain data type, for example, division of 5 with 2 should return float value. Practically, the compiler always returns integer values because both arguments are of integer data type. This can be followed by execution of the following program.

2.1 Write a program to change data type of results obtained by division operations.

```
void main()
{
clrscr();
printf("\n Division operation                    Result" );
printf("\n Two Integers (5 & 2)                : %d",5/2);
printf("\n One int & one float (5.5 & 2)       : %g",5.5/2);
printf("\n Two Integers (5 & 2)                : %g",(float)5/2);
}
```

Output

```
Division operation                     Result
Two Integers (5 & 2)                 : 2
One int & one float (5.5 & 2)        : 2.75
Two Integers (5 & 2)                 : 2.5
```

2.15 WRAPPING AROUND

When the value of a variable goes beyond its limit, the compiler would not flag any error message. It just wraps around the value of a variable. For example, the range of unsigned integer is 0 to 65535. In this type, negative values and values greater than 65535 are compatible.

```
unsigned int x=65536;
```

The value assigned is greater by one than the range. Here, the compiler starts again from the beginning after reaching the end of the range.

Consider the following example.

2.2 Write a program to demonstrate wrapping around.

```
#include <stdio.h>
#include <stdio.h>
void main()
{
   unsigned u=65537;
   clrscr();
   printf("\n u=%u",u);
}
```

Output

```
u=1
```

2.16 CONSTANT AND VOLATILE VARIABLES

2.16.1 Constant Variable

If we want the value of a certain variable remain the same or unchanged during the program execution, it can be done by declaring the variable as a constant. The keyword `const` is then prefixed before the declaration. It tells the compiler that the variable is a constant. Thus, variables declared as constant are protected from modification.

***Example*:**

```
const int m=10;
```

where `const` is a keyword, 'm' is the variable name and 10 is a constant.

The compiler protects the value of 'm' from modification. The user cannot assign any value to 'm', but using pointer the value can be changed. When user attempts to modify the value of a constant variable, the message 'cannot modify the constant object in function main' will be displayed.

2.3 Write a program to assign a constant value to `const` and make an attempt to change its value.

```
void main()
{
 const int num=12;
```

```
++num;
 printf("%d",num);
getche();
}
```

The above program code will not be executed and end with error message. Here, an attempt is made to modify a constant's value.

2.16.2 Volatile Variable

The volatile variables are those variables that can be changed at any time by other external program or the same program. The syntax is as follows.

```
volatile int d;
```

If the value of a variable in the current program is to be maintained constant and desired to be changed by other external operation, then the declaration of variable will be as follows:

```
volatile const d=10;
```

2.4 Write a program to use volatile variable and make an attempt to change its value.

```
void main()
{
 volatile num=12;
 num=num-1;
 printf("%d",num);
 getche();
}
```

Output

```
11
```

EXERCISES

2.A Fill in the blanks

1.

Serial No.	*Escape Sequence*	*Use*
(i)	\n	------
(ii)	--------	Backspace
(iii)	\v	--------

Serial No.	*Escape Sequence*	*Use*
(iv)	-----------	Alert bell
(v)	\t	-------
(vi)	-------	Null

2. The `short` integer data type occupies ______ bytes.

   (a) 2 (b) 3 (c) 4 (d) 1

3. `Long` integer occupies ______ bytes.

   (a) 2 (b) 4 (c) 8 (d) 1

4. `Unsigned int` range is from ______ to ______.

   (a) 0 to 65535 (b) 0 to 65536
   (c) −32768 to 32767 (d) 0 to 255

5. The `char` data type occupies ______ bytes.

   (a) 2 (b) 3 (c) 4 (d) 1

6. The `char` range is from ______ to ______.

   (a) −128 to 127
   (b) 128 to −127
   (c) 0 to 255

7. The format string for `char` data type is ______.

   (a) `%c` (b) `%d` (c) `%u` (d) `%f`

8. The format string for `int` is ______.

   (a) `%c` (b) `%d` (c) `%u` (d) `%f`

9. The format string for `long double` is ______.

   (a) `%c` (b) `%d` (c) `%u` (d) `%lf`

10. The format string for data type ______.

    (a) `%f` (b) `%d` (c) `%u` (d) `%lf`

11.

Serial No.	*Data Type*	*Range*	*Bytes*
(i)	`char`	----------	1
(ii)	---------	0 to 255	1
(iii)	`short` or `int`	−32768 to 32767	----------
(iv)	`unsigned int`	0 to 65535	----------
(v)	`long`	-------------	4
(vi)	-------------	0 to 4294967295	4
(vii)	`float`	-------------	-------
(viii)	------------	$1.7e^{-308}$ to $1.7e^{+308}$	8
(ix)	`long double`	-----------------------	10

12. In C, quantity that varies during program execution is called ______. Variables are names given to ______ in the memory of a computer.

    (a) identifiers
    (b) variables
    (c) memory locations
    (d) values

13. C program is ______ of ______. ______ is the beginning point of execution.

    (a) combination
    (b) collection
    (c) functions
    (d) sub-routines
    (e) `main()`
    (f) `#include`

2.B True or false

1. Data means combination of letters, digits, symbols, etc.
2. In C, A to Z and a to z are treated as same.
3. The `signed` is a C keyword.
4. The `new` is a C keyword.
5. 10.120 is an integer constant.
6. Identifiers are names of variables, arrays, functions, etc.
7. The constant in C applicable to values which do not change during program execution.
8. 'A' is a character constant.
9. 'India' is a string constant.
10. A variable is data name used for storing data values.
11. The value of a variable can be changed during program execution.

12. A variable name can start with a digit.

13. The C keyword can act as variable name

14. In C, the variable names sum and Sum are the same.

15. `short int` and `int` are different from each other.

16. `int`, `short int` and `long int` belong to one category with different size and range of values.

17. `int` occupies 4 bytes in the memory.

18. `const int a=10;` value of 'a' cannot be changed during program execution.

19. a, b, c are valid variable names.

2.C Match the following correct pairs given in Group A with Group B

I

Group A		Group B	
Serial No.	**Data Type**	**Serial No.**	**Size (bytes)**
1.	char	A	2
2.	short or int	B	1
3.	float	C	8
4.	double	D	4
5.	long double	E	10

II

Group A		Group B	
Serial No.	**Data Type**	**Serial No.**	**Range**
1.	char	A	0 to 255
2.	unsigned char	B	−128 to 127
3.	short or int	C	0 to 65535
4.	unsigned int	D	−32768 to 32767

III

Group A		Group B	
Serial No.	**Data Type**	**Serial No.**	**Control string**
1.	unsigned char	A	%lu
2.	unsigned int	B	%ld
3.	long	C	%u
4.	unsigned long	D	%c

IV

Group A		Group B	
Serial No.	**Data Types**	**Serial No.**	**Keyword**
1.	signed char	A	unsigned long int
2.	signed int	B	signed long int
3.	signed long int	C	signed int
4.	unsigned long integer	D	signed char

V

Group A		Group B	
Serial No.	**Delimiters**	**Serial No.**	**Use**
1.	: Colon	A	Used for array declaration
2.	; Semicolon	B	Used in expression and function
3.	() Parenthesis	C	Terminate statements
4.	[] Square bracket	D	Useful for label

VI

Group A		Group B	
Serial No.	**Delimiters**	**Serial No.**	**Use**
1.	{} Curly brace	A	Variable separator
2.	# Hash	B	Pre-processor directive
3.	, Comma	C	Scope of statement

2.D Select the appropriate option from the multiple choices given below

1. A character variable occupies

   (a) one memory location
   (b) two memory locations
   (c) three memory locations
   (d) none of the above

2. A long integer variable occupies

   (a) 4 byes (b) 2 bytes
   (c) 1 byte (d) none of the above

3. Which one of the following is reserved word in C ?

   (a) Keywords (b) Variables
   (c) Header files (d) List

4. Each header files extension in C program is done with

   (a) .h (b) .p
   (c) .c (d) none of the above

5. In C, variables are initialized in

   (a) executable section
   (b) header section
   (c) function section
   (d) declaration section

6. The word 'default' is a

   (a) keyword (b) password
   (c) header file (d) none of the above

7. The identifiers are defined by

   (a) compiler (b) user
   (c) function (d) none of the above

8. An unsigned integer value ranges from

   (a) 0 to 65535
   (b) 0 to 35354
   (c) −32235 to 32236
   (d) none of the above

9. The word 'volatile' in C is pre-defined by

   (a) compiler
   (b) assembler
   (c) debugger
   (d) none of the above

10. Identifiers are

    (a) user-defined names
    (b) reserved keywords
    (c) C statements
    (d) none of the above

11. In C, every variable has

    (a) a type
    (b) a name
    (c) a value
    (d) a size
    (e) all of the above

12. The range of character data type is

    (a) −128 to 127
    (b) 0 to 255
    (c) −32768 to 32767
    (d) none of the above

13. Variables must begin with character without spaces, but it permits

    (a) underscore symbol (_)
    (b) asterisk symbol (*)
    (c) ampersand symbol (&)
    (d) none of the above

14. The C program should be written only in

    (a) lowercase letters
    (b) uppercase letters
    (c) title case
    (d) sentence case

15. Declaration part declares

    (a) variables
    (b) only characters
    (c) only integers
    (d) none of the above

16. In C, a variable cannot start with

    (a) a number
    (b) an alphabet
    (c) a character
    (d) none of the above

17. An `unsigned integer` variable occupies memory

    (a) 2 byes (b) 4 bytes
    (c) 1 bytes (d) 8 bytes

18. In C, double variable needs memory size of

(a) 8 bytes (b) 2 bytes
(c) 10 bytes (d) all of the above

19. In C, `main()` is a

(a) function where program starts
(b) user created function
(c) string function
(d) number of variables

20. The word 'continue' is a

(a) keyword
(b) password
(c) header file
(d) none of the above

21. An `unsigned integer` variable contains values

(a) greater or equal to zero
(b) less than zero
(c) only zeros
(d) (a) and (b) both

22. The volatile variables are those variables that remain/can be

(a) constant
(b) changed at any time
(c) both of the above
(d) none of the above

23. In C, the statements following `main()` are enclosed within

(a) { } (b) ( )
(c) < > (d) none of the above

24. In C, the maximum value of unsigned character is

(a) 255
(b) 127
(c) 65535
(d) none of the above

25. The range of long signed integer is

(a) −2147483648 to 2147483647
(b) 0 to 255
(c) 0 to 4294967295
(d) none of the above

26. In C, '`sizeof`' is a/an

(a) variable
(b) operator
(c) keyword
(d) none of the above

27. Which is the incorrect variable name

(a) else (b) name
(c) age (d) cha_r

28. How many keywords are there in ANSI C?

(a) 32 (b) 33 (c) 42 (d) 15

29. Integer constants in C can be

(a) positive
(b) negative
(c) positive or negative
(d) none of the above

30. Which of the following statement is wrong

(a) 5+5=a; (b) ss=12.25;
(c) st='m' * 'b'; (d) is ='A'+10;

31. The ANSI standard recognizes the maximum length of a variable up to

(a) 31characters
(b) 8 characters
(c) 25 characters
(d) unlimited characters

32. In C, the first character of the variable should be

(a) integer
(b) an alphabet
(c) floating number
(d) none of the above

33. The error message 'Cannot modify a constant object' is displayed when user

(a) attempts to modify the constant variable
(b) attempts to use the variable in expressions
(c) attempts to assign value of constant variable to another variable

34. The following program will display the warning message

```
int x=2,y=2;
printf("x=%d",x);
```

(a) 'y' is assigned a value which is never used in function main()
(b) expression syntax in main
(c) possible use of'y'before definition in function main

35. The following program will display the warning message

```
int x,y;
printf("x=%d",x);
```

(a) 'y' is assigned a value which is never used in function main()
(b) expression syntax in main
(c) possible use of 'x' before definition in function main

2.E What will be the output/s of the following program/s?

Character constants

1. Program to print a character

```
void main()
{
char c=65;
clrscr();
printf("%c",c);
}
```

2. Program to print characters

```
void main()
{
clrscr();
printf("%c %c",74+32,
    80+32);
}
```

Character constants with ASCII values

3.

```
void main()
{
unsigned char c=65;
clrscr();
printf("%d %c %d ",c,c,c);
}
```

4.

```
void main()
{
signed char c=80;
c+=10;
c-=26;
c=++c;
clrscr();
printf("%d %c %d ",c,c,c);
}
```

5.

```
void main()
{
int a=12,b=78;
char c=a+b;
clrscr();
printf("\n c=%c c=%d",c,c);
}
```

Integers, float, long integers, etc.

6.

```
void main()
{
unsigned u=65536;
clrscr();
printf("%u",u);
}
```

7.

```
void main()
{
int x=5;
clrscr();
printf("%g",x/2.);
}
```

8.

```
void main()
{
int x=2.5;
float f=2.800000;
char c='s';
clrscr();
printf("x=%d f=%g c=%c",x,f,c-32);
}
```

9.

```
void main()
{
char c=78.5;
float f='C';
int k=2.5;
clrscr();
printf("%c %g %d" ,c,f,k);
}
```

10.

```
void main()
{
char r=127,q=130;
int x=r+q;
clrscr();
printf("\n x=%d",x);
}
```

11.

```
void main()
{
int sum, Keyword,a=21,b=29;
clrscr();
sum=a+b;
Keyword=a-b;
printf("\n %d %d ",Keyword,sum);
}
```

12.

```
void main()
{
int r=33000,q=-2000;
int x=r+q;
clrscr();
printf("\n x=%d",x);
}
```

13.

```
void main()
{
unsigned u=2147483647;
long     l=2147483647;
clrscr();
printf("\n u=%u l=%ld",u,l);
}
```

Integers with exponentiation

14.

```
void main()
{
  int x,a=3e1,b=2e2;
  clrscr();
  x=a+b;
  printf("x=%d",x);
}
```

15.

```
void main()
{
  int x,a=1e1, b=0;
  clrscr();
  b+=1e1;
  printf("a= %d b=%d",a,b);
}
```

16.

```
void main()
{
  float a=3e2,b=2e4;
  clrscr();
  printf("a=%g b=%g",a,b);
}
```

Float numbers

17.

```
void main()
{
 float a=3e-1,b=2e-2;
 clrscr();
 printf("a=%g b=%g",a,b);
}
```

18.

```
void main()
  {
    float a=1e3, b=2e4,c;
    clrscr();
    c=(a*b)/(a+b);
    printf("\n %f ",c);
    getche();
  }
```

String display and operation on it

19.

```
void main()
{
char arry[10]="PEARSON";
int i=0;
clrscr();
arry[i]=arry[i++];
printf("%s",arry);
}
```

20.

```
void main()
{
clrscr();
printf("HELLO!");
printf("\r\rC Programming");
}
```

21.
```
void main()
{
  clrscr();
  printf("\t\a1b\bt/t2");
  printf("\\\\\\");
}
```

22.
```
void main()
{
 char
 name[]={'I','N','D','I','A','\0'};
 char
 name1[]={'I','N','D','I','A','\0'};
 clrscr();
 printf(name); "\t";
 printf(name1);
}
```

Dynamic initilization

23.
```
void main()
{
 int r=2;
 float perimeter=2*3.14*r;
 float area=3.14*r*r;
 clrscr();
 printf(" Perimeter=%g \nArea=%g ",
 perimeter,area);
 getche();
 }
```

Type conversion

24.
```
void main()
{
clrscr();
printf("\n%d",10/3);
printf("\n%g",10.8/2);
printf("\n%g",(float)11/2);
getche();
}
```

25.
```
void main()
 {
   int a=50,b=2,c;
  clrscr();
  c=(a*b)/(a+b);
  printf("\n %d ",c);
  getche();
  }
```

Constant and volatile variables

26.
```
void main()
{
 const int a=11;
 volatile num=12;
 clrscr();
 num=num-1;
 printf("%d %d",num,a);
 getche();
 }
```

2.F Find the bug/s in the following program/s

Characters, integers, long, unsigned, etc.

1.
```
void main()
{
unsigned int d=65535;
unsigned char p=65;
clrscr();
printf("%c %c",d,p);
getche();
}
```

2.
```
void main()
{
char x=-127;
unsigned char p=-127;
clrscr();
printf("\n%d %d"x,p);
getche();
}
```

3.
```
void main()
{
int x=2,
printf("%d",x);
}
```

4.
```
void main()
{
```

```
int 2x=2;
printf("%d",2x);
}
```

5.

```
void main()
{
int abcdefghijklmnopqrstuvwxyz=10
   0;
printf("%d",++abcdefghijklmnopqrstu
vwxyz);
}
```

6.

```
void main()
{
 int case=8;
 printf ("%d",case);
 }
```

7.

```
void main()
{
int x,y;
x=8;
y=9;
z=x+y;
printf("%d",z);
}
```

8.

```
void main()
{
int x=-32769;
unsigned int p=-65534;
clrscr();
printf("\n%d %d", x p);
getche();
}
```

9.

```
void main()
{
int x=-32768;
unsigned int p=65535;
clrscr();
printf("\n%d %d", x p);
getche();
}
```

10.

```
void main()
{
int x=5,y=2;
printf("%f",x/y);
}
```

11.

```
void main()
{
unsigned x=-5;
clrscr();
printf("%u",x);
}
```

12.

```
void main()
{
clrscr();
int x=5;
x++;
printf("%d",x);
}
```

13.

```
void main()
{
LONG x=500000;
x++;
clrscr();
printf
("%ld",x);
}
```

14.

```
void main()
{
int x,y=5;
x+=y;
clrscr();
printf("%d",x);
}
```

Integers with micros

15.

```
#define N=90
void main()
{
int x=10,p;
clrscr();
p=x*N;
printf("\n%d ", p);
getche();
}
```

16.

```
#define N >90
#define M >100
void main()
{
```

```
int x=10,p;
clrscr();
p=x*N;
p=p+M;
printf("\n%d ", p);
getche();
}
```

17.

```
#define N 2
#define M 3
void main()
{
int x=10,p;
clrscr();
p=x*n;
p=p*m;
printf("\n%d ", p);
getche();
}
```

Float and double floats

18.

```
void main()
{
float f=2.5;
clrscr();
printf("%d %f",f);
}
```

19.

```
void main()
{
 float f=5/2;
 clrscr();
 printf("\n %f",f);
 }
```

20.

```
void main()
{
float d=65535.43;
double p=65789.987654;
clrscr();
printf("%d %d",d,p);
getche();
}
```

21.

```
void main()
{
float d=1234567.43;
double p=987654321.1234567;
clrscr();
printf("\n%f %lf",d,p);
printf("\n%d %d",size of(d),size
of(p));
getche();
}
```

Typecasting

22.

```
void main()
{
clrscr();
printf("\n %d", 7/2);
printf("\n%g",7.0/2);
printf("\n%g", float7/2);
getche();
}
```

Volatile and constants

23.

```
void main()
{
volatile d=15;
const p=25;
clrscr();
printf("%d %d"d+10,p+1);
getche();
}
```

24.

```
void main()
{
const x=5;
clrscr();
x++;
printf("%d",x);
}
```

2.G Attempt the following programming exercises

1. Write a program to display A 65 a.
2. Write a program to display X Y Z and corresponding ASCII values.
3. Write a program to display AAA 656565 aaa.
4. Write a program to display Z z X x.
5. Write a program to display the size of float and long double number.
6. Write a program to use volatile keyword and explain how can it be used to change the

variable's value? (Hint: Refer to solved program of this type)

7. Write a program to display float and unsigned numbers. (Hint: Refer to solved programs)

Answers

2.A Fill in the blanks

1. (i) New line, (ii) \b, (iii) Vertical tab, (iv) \a, (v) Horizontal tab, (vi) \0
2. (a) 2
3. (b) 4
4. (a) 0 to 65535
5. (d) 1
6. (a) −128 to 127
7. (a) %c
8. (b) %d
9. (d) %lf
10. (a) %f
11. (i) −128 to 127, (ii) unsigned char, (iii) 2, (iv) 2, (v) −2147483648 to 2147483647, (vi) unsigned long, (vii) $3.4e^{-38}$ to $3.4\ e^{+38}$ & 4, (viii) double, (ix) $3.4e^{-4932}$ to $1.1\ e^{+4932}$.
12. (b) variable, (c) memory locations
13. (a) combination, (c) functions, (e) `main()`

2.B True or false

1. T 2. F 3. T 4. F 5. F 6. T 7. T 8. T
9. T 10. T 11. T 12. F 13. F 14. F 15. F 16. T
17. F 18. T 19. T

2.C Match the following correct pairs given in Group A with Group B

I 1. B, 2. A, 3. D, 4. C, 5. E
II 1. B, 2. A, 3. D, 4. C
III 1. D, 2. C, 3. B, 4. A
IV 1. D, 2. C, 3. B, 4. A
V 1. D, 2. C, 3. B, 4. A
VI 1. C, 2. B, 3. A

2.D Select the appropriate option from the multiple choices given below

1. (a) one memory location
2. (a) 4 byes
3. (a) keywords
4. (a) .h
5. (d) declaration section
6. (a) keyword
7. (b) user
8. (a) 0 to 65535
9. (a) compiler
10. (a) user-defined names
11. (a) a type
12. (a) −128 to 127
13. (a) underscore symbol (_)
14. (a) lowercase letters
15. (a) Variables
16. (a) a number
17. (a) 2 byes
18. (a) 8 bytes
19. (a) function where program starts
20. (a) keyword
21. (a) greater or equal to zero
22. (b) changed at any time
23. (a) { }
24. (a) 255
25. (a) −2147483648 to 2147483647
26. (c) keyword
27. (a) else
28. (a) 32
29. (c) positive or negative
30. (a) 5+5=a;
31. (a) 31characters.
32. (b) an alphabet
33. (a) attempts to modify the constant variable
34. (a) 'y' is assigned a value which is never used in function main()
35. (c) Possible use of 'x' before definition in function main

2.E What will be the output/s of the following program/s?

1. A (ASCII equivalent of 65 is A)
2. j p (ASCII equivalent of 106 and 112 are j and p, respectively)
3. 65 A 65 (Decimal equivalent of A, ASCII equivalent of 65 and decimal equivalent of A)
4. 65 A 65 (With the arithmetic operations 'c' becomes 65, hence the values displayed are decimal 65 and its equivalent ASCII)
5. c=Z c=90 (Refer character set and data type. Addition of two integers is 90 and its ASCII is Z)

6. 0 (Refer range of unsigned number. Last number of unsigned is 65535. After this next number is 0. Compiler restarts from the beginning after reaching the final value)
7. 2.5 (Division of two numbers 5 and 2 with `%g` format string results real number 2.5)
8. x=2 f=2.8 c=S (As per `printf()` statement `%d %g %c`, the output should be integer, float and character that too uppercase letter S because of s-32. Refer to ASCII table)
9. N 67 2 (Refer to the `printf()` statement and format strings specified in it. Accordingly, a letter and numbers are displayed)
10. x=1 (Data type is initially `char` and then operation is in `int`, because of `char` range)
11. −8 50 (Subtraction and addition of two numbers)
12. 31000 (Subtraction of 33000 and 2000)
13. u=65535 l=2147483647 (Last values of unsigned integer 65535 and long integer 2147483647)
14. x=230 (Simple operation 3*10+2*100)
15. a=10 b=10 (The value of 'a' is assigned to 'b' and value of 'a' is not changed)
16. a=300 b=20000 (Simple operations 3*e2 and 2*e4 which are equal to 2*100 and 2*10000)
17. a=0.3 b=0.02 (Float values are assigned to 'a' and 'b' and operation 3^*e^{-1}=.3 and 2^*e^{-2}=.02)
18. 952.380981 (Multiplication and division operation 1000*20000/(1000+20000)=952.380981
19. PEARSON (With format string `%s` PEARSON is displayed)
20. C Programming (Due to \r (carriage return) next line C Programming is displayed)
21. 1t 2\\\(\a provides audible sound and horizontal tab)
22. INDIAINDIA (Two arrays are displayed one after the other)
23. Perimeter=12.56

    Area=12.56 (Perimeter and area are calculated with simple formulae)
24. (Refer to type conversion section)

    3

    5.4

    5.5
25. 1 (100 divided by 52 provides 1 in this program)
26. 11 11(Refer to constant and volatile section. Volatile means value can be changed. Values assigned to num and a are displayed)

2.F Find the bug/s in the following program/s

1. First `%c` is to be replaced by `%u` and then answer will be 65535 A.
2. Missing , (comma) in `printf()`. Answer would be −127 129.
3. Statement terminated by comma. Answer after correction will be 2.
4. 2x is a invalid variable. Declaration error.
5. No Bug. Answer will be 101.
6. `case` is a keyword. Keyword is not permitted. Answer with permitted variable name would be 8.
7. Variable 'z' is not declared in the program following `main()`.
8. Missing , (comma) in the `printf()` statement. Unsigned must be +ve.

   Answer after correction 32767 2.
9. Mistakes in `printf()`. Second `%d` replace with `%u` and put , (comma) in between 'x' and 'p'.

   −32768 65535
10. Format string `%f` is not suitable. Replace `%f` by `%d`. Answer will be 2.
11. `unsigned integer` should not contain negative values.
12. `clrscr()` is not allowed in declaration part.
13. Capital letters may not allowed.
14. Variable 'x' should be analysed. Assign value to x.
15. Syntax error in first line `#define`. Remove =. Answer will be 900.
16. Expression syntax in first two lines. Answer after removing > from them will be 1000.
17. Undefined symbols 'n' and 'm'. Replace them with N and M. Answer will be 60.
18. `%f` is unnecessarily written.
19. No bug. But to get the desired output as 2.5, either 5 or 2 should be float or explicit type casting is required.
20. No bug. But to get the desired results one must use the control strings `%f` and `%lf`. Answer would be

    65535.429688 65789.98754

21. Space between size and of should be removed. The answer will be

    1234567.375000 987654321.1234574 8

22. `float` must be enclosed within bracket, then answer will be
    3
    3.5
    3.5

23. Missing , (comma) in the `printf()`. Answer after correction 25 26.

24. Constant variable cannot be modified.

3

Operators and Expressions

CHAPTER OUTLINE

3.1 OPERATORS

Operators perform operations on operands. An operand is a data item on which the operation is to be performed. C supports numerous operators, which fall into different categories.

C provides the following four basic classes of operators:

(i) Arithmetic, (ii) Relational, (iii) Logical and (iv) Bitwise.

Besides these four basic operators, C also supports additional operators such as increment, decrement, conditional and assignment. Basic operators and others along with their symbolic representation are shown in the Table 3.1.

TABLE 3.1 Types of operators

Type of Operator	*Symbolic Representation*
Arithmetic operators	+, − , *, / and %
Relational operators	>, <, = =, >=, <= and !=
Logical operators	&&, || and !
Increment and decrement operator	+ + and − −
Assignment operator	=
Bitwise operators	&, |, ^, >>, << and ~
Comma operator	,
Conditional operator	?, :

3.2 ARITHMETIC OPERATORS

The various arithmetic operators such as + (addition), − (subtraction), * (multiplication), / (division), % (modulus) are used in C. They are shown in the Tables 3.2a and 3.2b with examples.These are binary operators as operation is performed on two operands.

Suppose ' x ' and ' y ' are the integer variables whose values are 10 and −5. On evaluating arithmetic expressions as cited in the table using the variables, result can be obtained as follows.

In another way, the results of various arithmetic operations can be as per Table 3.2b.

TABLE 3.2a Arithmetic expressions with results

Arithmetic Operator	*Expression*	*Result*
+	x+y	5
−	x−y	15
*	x*y	−50
/	x/y	−2
%	x%y	0

TABLE 3.2b Arithmetic operators

Arithmetic Operator	*Operator Explanation*	*Example*
+	Addition	2+2=4
−	Subtraction	5−3=2
*	Multiplication	2*5=10
/	Division	10/2=5
%	Modular division	11%3=2 (Remainder 2)

Please note that the variables can be float numbers or characters too. In case of the division of two integers is concerned, the result is truncated to integer only. The % operator provides remainder only when the operation is carried on integers.

3.3 RELATIONAL OPERATORS

These operators provide relationship between two quantities. If the relation is true, then it returns a value 1 otherwise 0 for false. The relational operators together with their descriptions, examples and return values are described in Table 3.3.

TABLE 3.3 Relational operators

Operator	*Description or Action*	*Example*	*Return Value*
>	Greater than	5>4	1
<	Less than	10<9	0
<=	Less than or equal to	10<=10	1
>=	Greater than equal to	11>=5	1
= =	Equal to	2= =3	0
!=	Not equal to	3!=3	0

3.4 LOGICAL OPERATORS

The logical relationship between the two quantities is checked with logical operators. Using these operators, two expressions can be joined and conditions can be checked. Such an expression provides result either logically true (1) or false (0). The operands could be constants, variables and expressions. Table 3.4 illustrates the three logical operators together with examples and their return values.

TABLE 3.4 Logical operators: examples on logical operators

Operator	*Description or Action*	*Example*	*Return Value*
&&	Logical AND	5>3 && 5<10	1
||	Logical OR	8>5 || 8<2	1
!	Logical NOT	8!=8	0

From the above table following rules can be followed for logical operators:

(i) The logical AND (&&) operator provides 1 result when both expressions are true, otherwise 0.

(ii) The logical OR (||) operator provides 1 result when one of the expressions is true, otherwise 0.

(iii) The logical NOT operator (!) returns 0 if the condition is false otherwise 1.

3.5 INCREMENT AND DECREMENT OPERATORS (UNARY OPERATORS)

The operator that needs one operand is called unary operator. Unary operators are increment operator (++), decrement operator (−−), minus (−) and plus (+). These operators and their descriptions are given in the Table 3.5.

TABLE 3.5 Unary arithmetic operators

Operator	*Description or Action*
−	Minus
+	Plus
++	Increment
−−	Decrement
&	Address operator
`sizeof()`	Gives the size of operator

(i) *Minus* (−) *and plus* (+): This unary minus operator is used for indicating or changing the algebraic sign of a value.

For example `int x=-50;`

```
int y=-x;
```

This assigns the value of −50 to '`x`' and the value of 50 to '`y`' through '`x`'. The − sign used in this way is called the unary operator because it takes just one operand. There is no unary plus (+) used in C. A value assigned with plus sign is also valid. For example, `int x=+50;` here, + is valid but in practice this sign should not be used.

(ii) *Increment* (++) *and decrement* (−−) *operators*: These are also unary operators. The operator ++ adds one to its operand, whereas the operator −− subtracts one from its operand. For justification, `x=x+1;` can be written as `x++;` and `x=x-1;` can be written as `x--;`. Both of these operators may either follow or precede the operand, i.e. `x=x+1;` can be represented as `x++;` or `++x;`.

If '++' or '−−' are used as a suffix to the variable name, then post-increment/decrement operation take place. Consider an example for understanding '++' operator as a suffix to the variable:

```
x=20;
y=10;
z=x*y++;
```

In the above equation, the current value of ' y ' is used for the product. The result is 200, which is assigned to ' z '. After multiplication, the value of ' y ' is incremented by one.

If '++' or '−−' are used as a prefix to the variable name, then pre increment/decrement operation take place. Consider an example for understanding '++' operator as a prefix to the variable.

```
x=20;
y=10;
z=x*++y;
```

In the above equation, the value of ' y ' is incremented and then multiplication is carried. The result is 220, which is assigned to ' z '. Programmer can run the programs as illustrated in this chapter for verification of increment and decrement operations.

(iii) `sizeof()` *and '&' Operator*: The `sizeof()` operator is a unary operator and it provides the number of bytes occupied by a variable, i.e. the size in terms of bytes required in memory to store the value. The number of bytes occupied varies from variable to variable depending upon its data types. The '&' operator prints address of the variable in the memory. Examples on this issue are illustrated in this chapter.

3.6 ASSIGNMENT OPERATORS AND EXPRESSIONS

Assigning a value to a variable is very simple. For example, `int x=5;` here, 5 is assigned to ' x ' and this is carried out by the operator =. As and when compiler encounters equal to (=) sign, the value on the right side of the equal to (=) operator is assigned to the variable on the left side. List of assignment operators are shown in Table 3.6.

TABLE 3.6 Assignment operators

=	*=	/=	%=
+=	−=	<<=	>>=
&=	^=	!=	

Consider the following example `K=K+3;` in this expression, the variable of the left side of = is repeated on the right. The same can be written follows.

```
K+=3;
```

The operators = and += are called assignment operator. The binary operators which need two operands to their either side are sure to have a corresponding assignment operator operand = to the left side.

Example:

```
j*=x+1;
```

or

```
j=j*(x+1);
```

3.7 COMMA AND CONDITIONAL OPERATOR

(i) *Comma operator (,)*: The comma operator is used to separate two or more expressions. The comma operator has the lowest priority among all the operators. It is not essential to enclose the expressions with comma operators within the parenthesis. For example, the statements given below are valid.

Example:

```
a=2,b=4,c=a+b;
(a=2,b=4,c=a+b;)
```

(ii) *Conditional operator (?)*: The conditional operator contains condition followed by two statements or values. The conditional operator is also called as ternary operator. If the condition is true, the first statement is executed otherwise the second statement.

The conditional operators (?) and (:) are sometimes called ternary operators because they take three arguments. The syntax of conditional operator is as given below.

Syntax:

```
Condition ? (expression1) : (expression2);
```

Two expressions are separated by colon. If the condition is true expression1 gets evaluated, otherwise expression2. The condition is always written before ? (question mark). Question mark is followed condition statement.

3.8 BITWISE OPERATORS

C supports a set of bitwise operators, as listed in the Table 3.7, for bit manipulation. C supports six bit operators. These operators can operate only on integer operands such as `int`, `char`, `short`, `long`, etc.

TABLE 3.7 Bitwise operators: examples on bitwise operators

Operator	*Meaning*
>>	Right shift
<<	Left shift
^	Bitwise XOR (exclusive OR)
~	One's complement
&	Bitwise AND
|	Bitwise OR

EXERCISES

3.A Fill in the blanks

Arithmetic operators

1. There are five arithmetic operators. They are +, −, _____, * and %.
   (a) /
   (b) ++
   (c) \

2. The expression x++ is equivalent with ________ expressions.
   (a) x=x+1
   (b) x ++1
   (c) x+=2

3. The expression x+=2 is not equivalent with ________.
   (a) x=x+2
   (b) x++=2

Relational operator

4. Relational operator results are either ________ or ________.
   (a) 1, 0
   (b) 0, 0
   (c) 1, 1

Logical operator

5. Logical AND is performed with ________ operator.
   (a) $$
   (b) &&
   (c) ||
   (d) @@

6. Logical OR is performed by ________ operator.
   (a) ||
   (b) &&
   (c) ^^
   (d) $$

7. The logical OR (||) operator provides ________ result when one of the expressions is true, otherwise 0.
   (a) 1
   (b) 0
   (c) none of the above

8. The _____ operator provides _____ result when both expressions are true otherwise ___.
   (a) logical AND (&&)
   (b) logical OR
   (c) logical NOT (!)
   (d) 1
   (e) 0

9. The ______ operator negates the input value.
   (a) logical AND (&&)
   (b) logical OR (||)
   (c) logical NOT (!)

10. The ________ operator provides true result when one of the expressions is true otherwise 0.
   (a) logical AND (&&)
   (b) logical OR (||)
   (c) logical NOT (!)

Increment and decrement operator

11. The x++ is a ________ increment.
   (a) postfix
   (b) prefix
   (c) none of the above

12. Unary increment operator is ________.
   (a) ++
   (b) +
   (c) none of the above

13. Unary decrement operator is ________.
   (a) –
   (b) – –
   (c) none of the above

14. If x=2, then expression −x++ gives _______.
   (a) 3
   (b) −3
   (c) −2
   (d) 2

Comma and `sizeof()` operator

15. The __________ has the ________ among all the operators. It is not essential to enclose the expressions with comma operators within the _________.
   (a) lowest priority
   (b) comma operator
   (c) parentheses
   (d) brackets

16. The ______ gives the _____ occupied by a variable. The number of bytes occupied varies from variable to variable depending upon its ______.
   (a) `fsize()` function
   (b) `sizeof()` operator
   (c) bits
   (d) bytes
   (e) data types

Bitwise operator

17. In C, the lvalue stands for _______.
   (a) long value
   (b) left value
   (c) last value

18. The rvalue stands for _____.
   (a) right value
   (b) remainder value
   (c) none of the above

19. Fill the columns

Serial No.	*Type of Operator*	*Operators*
(i)	Arithmetic operators	----------
(ii)	--------	<, >, =, >=, !=
(iii)	Logical operators	-------
(iv)	--------	++, &, --
(v)	Bitwise operator	-------

20. Fill the columns

Serial No.	*Operator*	*Description*	*Example*	*Result*
(i)	>	Greater than	5>4	-----
(ii)	<	Less than	10<9	----
(iii)	<=	Less than or equal to	10<=10	----
(iv)	>=	Greater than or equal to	11>=5	----
(v)	==	Equal to	2==3	----
(vi)	!=	Not equal to	3!=3	----

21. Fill the columns

Serial No.	*Operator*	*Description*	*Example*	*Return Value*
(i)	&&	Logical AND	5>3 && 5<10	----
(ii)	||	Logical OR	8>5 || 8<2	----
(iii)	!	Logical Not	8!=8	----

22. Fill in the columns

Consider j=4 and k=3.

Serial No.	*Expressions*	*Value of j*
(i)	j+=k	------
(ii)	j-=k	------
(iii)	j*=k	------
(iv)	j/=k	------
(v)	j%=k	------
(vi)	j<<=k	------
(vii)	j>>=k	------
(viii)	j&=k	------
(ix)	j | =k	------
(x)	j^=k	------

3.B True or false

Arithmetic operator

1. + is a symbolic representation of increment operator.
2. −− is a symbolic representation of decrement operator.

Relational operator

3. >> is the relational operator.
4. >= is the binary operator.
5. != is the relational operator.

Logical operator

6. The logical AND (&&) operator provides true result when both expressions are true.
7. The logical NOT operator (!) provides 0 if the input value is true, otherwise 1.
8. The logical OR (||) operator provides false result when one of the expressions is true.

Increment and decrement operator

9. In C, x=x−1 can be written as x−−.
10. In C, a=9 then ++a and a++ are having the same values.

Comma and conditional operator

11. Comma operator has the highest priority among all the operators.
12. Conditional operator performs the same function as `if-else` statement.

`sizeof()` *and & operators*

13. Number of bytes needed to store a variable is indicated by `sizeof()` operator.
14. The '&' operator prints address of the variable.

Bitwise operator

15. Bitwise EX-OR operation is performed by operator &.
16. One's complement is performed by operator ~.
17. Bitwise OR is performed by operator | .

3.C Match the following correct pairs given in Group A with Group B

Arithmetic Operators

I Group A / Group B

Serial No.	Arithmetic Operators	Serial No.	Operator Explanation
1.	−	A	Addition
2.	+	B	Subtraction
3.	/	C	Multiplication
4.	*	D	Division

Relational Operators

II Group A / Group B

Serial No.	Operator	Serial No	Description or Action
1.	<	A	Greater than
2.	>	B	Less than
3.	>=	C	Less than or equal to
4.	<=	D	Greater than equal to

III

Group A		Group B	
Serial No.	Operator	Serial No.	Description or Action
1.	= =	A	Equal to
2.	!=	B	Not equal to

Relational and logical operators

IV

Group A		Group B	
Serial No.	Example	Serial No.	Return Value
1.	5>3 && 5<10	A	0
2.	8>5 || 8<2	B	1
3.	8!=8	C	1

Logical operators

V

Group A		Group B	
Serial No.	Operator	Serial No.	Description or Action
1.	||	A	Logical AND
2.	&&	B	Logical OR
3.	!	C	Logical NOT

VI

Group A		Group B	
Serial No.	Type	Serial No.	Operators
1.	Arithmetic operators	A	>, <, = =, >=, <= and !
2.	Relational operators	B	+, −, *, / and %
3.	Logical operators	C	&&, || and !

VII

Group A		Group B	
Serial No.	Type of Operator	Serial No.	Operators
1.	Increment and decrement operator	A	?:
2.	Assignment operator	B	,
3.	Bit wise operators	C	&, |, ^, >>, << and ~
4.	Comma operator	D	=
5.	Conditional operator	E	+ + and − −

3.D Select the appropriate option from the multiple choices given below

Examples on arithmetic operators

1. Addition of two numbers is performed using
   (a) arithmetic operator
   (b) logical operator
   (c) unary operator
   (d) comma operator

2. What is the result of 5% 10?
   (a) 5
   (b) 2
   (c) 1
   (d) 0

3. What is the result of the expression ((10/3)*3+5)%10?
   (a) 4
   (b) 10
   (c) 8
   (d) none of the above

4. What is the result of expression (10/3) * (`int`) 5. 5?
   (a) 15
   (b) 1
   (c) 3
   (d) none of the above

5. The expressions y=5+2%−9 evaluates to
   (a) 8
   (b) 7
   (c) −7
   (d) 0

6. What is the result of 4/2?
   (a) 1
   (b) 6
   (c) 2
   (d) 0

7. Which of the following is suitable in C arithmetic instructions?

   (a) [ ]
   (b) { }
   (c) ( )
   (d) none of the above

8. Multiplication (*) and division (/) operators have _____ priority than addition (+) operator.

   (a) lower
   (b) higher
   (c) similar

9. The following one operator has 2nd priority range

   (a) *
   (b) /
   (c) <<
   (d) |

10. If m = −12 and c = −5, what is the result of m%c

   (a) −2
   (b) −1
   (c) −3
   (d) −4

Examples on logical operators

11. What is the result of 10&&2?

   (a) 0
   (b) 1
   (c) 2
   (d) 5

12. The && operator is used to

   (a) compare two numeric value
   (b) compare two float values
   (c) compare two boolean values
   (d) none of the above

Examples on unary, increment and decrement operator

13. The associativity of unary minus, increment and decrement operators is from

   (a) right to left
   (b) left to right
   (c) both (a) and (b)
   (d) none of the above

Examples on bitwise operators

14. What is the result of 2<<2?

   (a) 8
   (b) 16
   (c) 2
   (d) 0

15. The associativity of bitwise operators is from

   (a) right to left
   (b) left to right
   (c) both (a) and (b)
   (d) none of the above

16. What is the result of the following program?

```
void main()
{
int a,x=10,y=20;
clrscr();
a=--x*y++;
printf("\n %d",a);
}
```

   (a) 180
   (b) 200
   (c) 380
   (d) 210

17. What is the result of the following program?

```
void main()
{
int m,a=12,b=10;
clrscr();
m =(++a*b++)/a;
printf("\n %d",m);
}
```

   (a) 10
   (b) 12
   (c) 11
   (d) 14

18. What is the result of the following program?

```
void main()
{
unsigned int m,a=65515,b=10;
clrscr();
m=(a+b)/b;
printf("\n %d",m);
}
```

   (a) 6552
   (b) 6552.5
   (c) 6551
   (d) 6553

19. What will be the output of the following program?

```
void main()
{
    int ans=2;
    int m=10;
    int k;
    k=!((ans<2)&&(m>2));
    printf("\n %d",k);
}
```

(a) 1
(b) 0
(c) −1
(d) 2

20. What will be the output of the following program?

```
void main()
{
    int m,j=3,k;
    m=2*j/2;
    k=2*(j/2);
      clrscr()
    ;printf ("\n m=%d k=%d",m,k);
}
```

(a) m=3 k=2
(b) m=3 k=3
(c) m=2 k=3
(d) m=2 k=2

21. What will be the value of x, y and z after the execution of the following program?

```
void main()
{
    int x,y,z;
    y=2;
    x=2;
    x=2*(y++);
    z=2*(++y);
    printf("\n x=%d y=%d
    z=%d",x,y,z);
}
```

(a) x=4 y=4 z=8
(b) x=6 y=4 z=8
(c) x=2 y=4 z=8
(d) x=4 y=4 z=4

22. What will be the value of 'x' after the execution of the following program?

```
void main()
{
    int x=!0*10;
}
```

(a) 10
(b) 1
(c) 0
(d) None of the above

23. What will be the value of 'k' after the execution of the following program?

```
void main()
{
int k=8;
(k++-k++);
}
```

(a) k=10
(b) k=0
(c) k=8
(d) k=9

24. What will be the value of 'b' after the execution of the following program?

```
void main()
{
int b,k=8;
b=(k++-k++-k++,k++);
}
```

(a) b=11
(b) b=12
(c) b=7
(d) b=9

25. What will be the value of 'k' after the execution?

```
void main()
{
    int a=3,m=10,k;
    k= !( (a<5) != (m>3) );
}
```

(a) 1
(b) 0
(c) −1
(d) 2

26. What will be the value of 'm' and 'k'?

```
void main()
{
    int m,s,k;
    s=5;
    m=2*s/3;
    k=2*(s/3);
    clrscr();
    printf("%d %d",m,k);
}
```

(a) m=3 k=2
(b) m=2 k=3
(c) m=2 k=2
(d) m=3 k=3

27. What will be the output of the following program?

```
void main()
{
    int i=1,j=2,k=3;
    clrscr();
    printf("%d",!((j+k)>(i+5)));
}
```

(a) 0
(b) 1
(c) −1
(d) 2

28. What will be the value of 'j' after the execution?

```
void main()
{
    float j=8,k=5;
    j*=k*+3.145;
    clrscr();
    printf("j=%g",j);
}
```

(a) j=125.8
(b) 124.9
(c) 124.8
(d) 0

29. What will be the value of 'y'?

a)
```
void main()
{
float y;
y=22/8*(3.145+2)*8/5;
clrscr();
printf("y=%g",y);
}
```

a) y=16.464
(b) 16.064
(c) 16
(d) 0

3.E What will be the output/s of the following program/s?

Questions on arithmetic operators

1. Program on some arithmetic operators.

```
void main()
{
int y;
clrscr();
y=5+4*6-8;
printf("%d\n",y);
y=(5+4)*10/2-8;
printf("%d\n",y);
y=5+4/2-5;
printf("%d\n",y);
y=5+4*6+90/10-8;
printf("%d\n",y);
getche();
}
```

2. Assign the basic salary of an employee as Rs 20000 to some variable and compute the output of the following program.

```
void main()
{
float bas=20000,tot;
clrscr();
tot=bas+0.30*bas+0.18*bas;
printf("Total salary = %10.2f\
   n",tot);
getche();
}
```

3. Program on some arithmetic operators.

```
void main()
{
int a=32763, b=5,c;
unsigned int p=65535,q=1,r;
clrscr();
c=a+b,
r=p+q;
printf("\n c= %d",c);
printf("\n r= %u",r);
getche();
}
```

4. Program on some arithmetic operators.

```
void main()
{
unsigned long p=4294967295,q=1,r;
```

```
long a=2147483646,b=1,c;
clrscr();
r=p+q;
c=a+b;
printf("\n r= %lu",r);
printf("\n c= %ld",c);
getche();
}
```

5. Program on some arithmetic operators.

```
void main()
{
float p=355/10*10,a;
clrscr();
printf("\n %f ",p);
a=10.0/2+5.0/2+1.0/2;
printf("\n %f",a);
getche();
}
```

6. Assign the principal amount, year and rate of interest as 2000, 2 and 5, respectively to the variables.

```
void main()
{
int prin=2000,year=2;
float rate=5,simple;
clrscr();
simple=prin*rate*year/100;
printf("\n %5.2f \n",simple);
getche();
}
```

7. Assign the radius as 3.5 and compute the area of the circle.

```
void main()
{
float area,radius=3.5;
const float pi=3.1413;
clrscr();
area=pi*radius*radius;
printf("\nArea of a circle
    =%2.2f",area);
getche();
}
```

8. Program to find reminder and quotient.

```
void main()
{
int y=125,x=10, z,p;
clrscr();
z=y%x;
p=y/x;
printf("Remainder after division
    operation=%d\n",z);
printf("Quotient of the division
    operation=%d\n",p);
getche();
}
```

9. Program on arithmetic operators.

```
void main()
{
int y=!0*100;
clrscr();
printf("%d",y);
getche();
}
```

10. Program to convert decimal 10 into binary.

```
void main()
{
    int n=10,i,x=7,y=3;
    clrscr();
    printf("Binary equivalent of
    decimal numer 10 is");
    while(n!=0)
    {
    i=n%2;
    n=n/2;
    gotoxy(x,y);
    printf("%d",i);
    x--;
    }
    getch();
    }
```

11. Program on arithmetic operators.

```
void main()
{
    clrscr();
    printf("%d",1000%5);
    printf("%d",1010%10);
    printf("%d",11010%15);
    printf("%d",0101110%20);
    getche();
}
```

Examples on relational and bitwise operators

12. Program on relational operators.

```
void main()
{
int x=40,y=80;
clrscr();
x<<=1,y>>=2;
printf ("%d %d ",x,y);
getche();
}
```

13. Program on simple problem.
```
void main()
{
clrscr();
printf("\n %d",15==15);
printf(" %d",11>=15);
printf(" %d",7<8);
printf(" %d", 'C'=='c');
getche();
}
```

14. Program on simple problem.
```
void main()
{
clrscr();
printf("%d %d ",2>3,5+8>15-2);
printf("%d %d",
    8*5>4/2*5,(100*2)==100/2*4);
getche();
}
```

15. Program on simple problem.
```
void main()
{
clrscr();
printf("\nCondition : Return
    Values\n" );
printf("\n10!=10 : %5d",10!=10);
printf("\n10==10 : %5d",10==10);
printf("\n10>=10 : %5d",10>=10);
printf("\n10<=100 : %5d",10<=100);
printf("\n10!=9 : %5d",10!=9);
}
```

Examples on logical operators

16. Program on simple logical problem.
```
void main()
{
int a=4,b=2,m,n,o;
clrscr();
m=a&&b;
n=a||b;
o=a==b;
printf("\n%d",m);
printf("\n%d",n);
printf("\n%d",o);
getche();
}
```

Examples on relational and logical operators

17. Program on simple logical problem.
```
void main()
{
int x=2,y=0,z=8,p;
clrscr();
z=x>y&&y;
p=x||z;
printf("\n%d\n%d",z,p);
getch();
}
```

18. Program on logical problem.
```
void main()
{
int x=2000,y=1000,z=20,p;
clrscr();
p=(x>z && y<z);
printf("\n%d",p);
getch();
}
```

19. Program on logical problem.
```
void main()
{
clrscr();
printf ("\nCondition : Return
    Values\n" );
printf("\n5>3 && 5<10 : %5d",5>3 &&
    5<10);
printf("\n 8>5 || 8<2 : %5d",8>5 || 8<2);
printf("\n !(8==8) : %5d",!(8==8));
}
```

20. Program on logical problem.
```
void main()
{
clrscr();
printf("\n %d",1>2 && 2<1);
printf(" %d",11!=15 || 51>100);
printf(" %d", 'C'!='c');
getche();
}
```

Examples are given on (+) unary operator

21. Program on unary operator.
```
void main()
{
float a=+15.4,c=-4.6;
clrscr();
c+=a;
printf("%10.2f",c);
getche();
}
```

22. Program on unary operator.
```
void main()
{
```

```
int x=40,y=50,z=10;
clrscr();
x+=y;
z+=x;
printf("%d\n%d ",x,z);
getch();
}
```

23. Program on unary operator.

```
void main()
{
int x=2,y=2;
clrscr();
x*=x+3;
y+=x+2;
printf("\n%d\n%d",x,y);
getch();
}
```

Examples are given on (–) unary operator

24. Program on unary operator.

```
void main()
{
    int a=45,b=60,c=75;
    clrscr();
    c-=a;
    a-=b;
    printf("a=%d",a);
    printf("\nb=%d",b);
    printf("\nc=%d",c);
    getch();
}
```

Examples on ++ and -- operators

25. Some tricky problem.

```
void main()
{
int a,z,x=10,y=20;
clrscr();
z=x*y++;
a=x*y;
printf("\n%d \n%d",z,a);
}
```

26. Some tricky problem.

```
void main()
{
int x=36,y=31,z,p,k;
clrscr ();
z=(++x)%(--y);
printf("%d ", z);
p=x/y++;
printf("%d ", p);
k=z+p+y;
printf("%d ",k);
getch();
}
```

27. Some tricky problem.

```
void main()
{
int y=10,x=12,z;
clrscr();
z=y+x;
printf("%d\n",z);
z=++y+x;
printf("%d\n",z);
y++;
++x;
z=y+x;
printf("%d\n",z);
getche();
}
```

28. Some tricky problem.

```
void main()
{
int x=27,y=15,z;
clrscr();
x=3*(x++);
printf("%d ",x);
z=x+(++y);
printf("%d",z);
getche();
}
```

29. Some tricky problem.

```
void main()
{
int p,q,r;
clrscr();
p=6;
q=7;
r=2*(p++);
p=2*(++q);
printf("\n r=%d p=%d q=%d",r,p,q);
getche();
}
```

30. Some tricky problem.

```
void main()
{
int k=10,y;
clrscr();
y=(++k + k++);
```

```
printf("%d",y);
getche();
}
```

31. Some tricky problem.

```
void main()
{
int a=2,b=4,c=4,d;
clrscr();
a=d=b++ + ++c;
printf("a=%d d=%d",a,d);
getche();
}
```

32. Some tricky problem.

```
void main()
{
int x=2,y;
-x++;
y=-x++;
clrscr();
printf("%d\n%d",x,y);
getche();
}
```

33. Some tricky problem.

```
void main()
{
 int x=25,y=12,z;z=x++/--y;
 clrscr();
 printf("\n x = %d y = %d z = %d",x,y,z);
 getche();
}
```

Examples on `sizeof ()` and & operators

34. Find size of bytes for integer, character and long integers.

```
void main()
{
clrscr();
printf("\n size of int
   =%d",sizeof(int));
printf("\n size of char
   =%d",sizeof(char));
printf("\n size of long
   =%d",sizeof(long));
getche();
}
```

35. Same as above.

```
void main()
{
char x='a';
int y=2;
long int z=23456;
float p=2.345;
double q=12e10;
clrscr();
printf("\n size of a character(x)=%d
   byte",sizeof(x));
printf("\n size of an integer(y)=%d
   bytes",sizeof(y));
printf("\n size of long
   integer(z)=%d bytes",sizeof(z));
printf("\n size of float(p)=%d
   bytes",sizeof(p));
printf("\n size of double float
   (q)=%d bytes",sizeof(q));
printf("\n Address of x=%u y=%u
   z=%u p=%u q=%u",&x,&y,
   &z,&p,&q);
getche();
}
```

36. Some tricky problem.

```
void main()
{
int x=5;
float y=6;
char z='a';
double p=1234567;
long double q=987654321;
clrscr();
printf("\n sizeof(x)=%d
   bytes",sizeof(x));
printf("\n sizeof(y)=%d
   bytes",sizeof(y));
printf("\n sizeof(z)=%d
   bytes",sizeof(z));
printf("\n sizeof(p)=%d
   bytes",sizeof(p));
printf("\n sizeof(q)=%d
   bytes",sizeof(q));
printf("\n Address of x=%u
   , y=%u,z=%u,p=%u,q=%u
   ",&x,&y,&z,&p,&q);
getche();
}
```

37. Some tricky problem.

```
void main()
{
   clrscr();
   printf("%d",sizeof(4e2));
getche();
}
```

38. Some tricky problem.

```
void main()
{
   float y=6;
int x=5;
char z='h';
long double q=987654321;
clrscr();
printf("\n sizeof(y)=%d
   bytes",sizeof(y));
printf("\n sizeof(x)=%d
   bytes",sizeof(x));
printf("\n sizeof(z)=%d
   bytes",sizeof(z));
printf("\n sizeof(q)=%d
   bytes",sizeof(q));
getche();
}
```

39. Some tricky problem.

```
void main()
{
clrscr();
printf("%c",sizeof("printf"));
getche();
}
```

Following programs are provided on relational and assignment operators together with conditional operators.

Examples on assignment operators

40. Number and its ASCII.

```
void main()
{
char X=65;
unsigned char a=97;
clrscr();
printf("\n X=%d X=%c a=%c",X,X,a);
getche();
}
```

41. Display assigned values to the variables.

```
void main()
{
int x=8.00000,q=4.0000;
clrscr();
printf("\n %d %d",x,q);
getche();
}
```

42. Display assigned value to the variable and some additional operation.

```
void main()
{
int x=8.00000;
clrscr();
printf("\n %d %.2f",x,4.00/2);
getche();
}
```

43. Number and its ASCII.

```
void main()
{
int x=65;
char y='B';
clrscr();
printf("\n %d %c",x,x);
printf("\n %d %c\n", y,y);
getche();
}
```

44. Number formatting.

```
void main()
{
float x=34.455;
int y=3512;
long z=234567;
clrscr();
printf("%d\n",y);
printf("%8d\n",y);
printf("%08d\n",y);
printf("%8.4f\n",x);
printf("%ld\n",z);
printf("%10ld\n",z);
printf("%010ld\n",z);
getche();
}
```

45. Formatting.

```
void main()
{
clrscr();
printf(1+"Hello");
printf("\n2 3 4");
getche();
}
```

46. Hexadecimal and octal numbers.

```
void main()
{
int z=0x40;
int y=0x50;
int x=050;
clrscr();
printf(" %d\n",z);
printf(" %d\n",y);
printf(" %d\n",x);
getche();
}
```

Examples on comma (,) operators

47. Some addition and subtraction with comma operator.

```
void main()
{
clrscr();
printf("Addition = %d\nSubtraction
    = %d",2+3,5-4);
}
```

Examples on conditional operator

48. Conditional operator.

```
void main()
{
clrscr();
3>2 ? printf("True.") :
    printf("False.");
}
```

49. Conditional operator

```
void main()
{
clrscr();
printf("Result = %d",2==3 ? 4 : 5 );
}
```

50. Conditional operator.

```
void main()
{
int a=5,b=10;
clrscr();
printf("Result of the following
    conditional operation=" );
printf("%d",a==b ? 10 :15 );
getche();
}
```

51. Conditional operator.

```
void main()
{
clrscr();
5!=8 ? printf("True") :
    printf("False");
}
```

52. Conditional operator.

```
void main()
{
    int x=100,k,z;
    clrscr();
    for (z=0;z<5;z++)
{
printf("%d",k=(x%2==z ? 1:0));
}
}
```

53. Conditional operator.

```
void main()
{
int a=5,b=15;
clrscr();
printf("Result on execution =" );
printf("%d",!((a*b)>30) ? a:b );
getche();
}
```

54. Conditional operator.

```
void main()
{
int x=17,y=15;
clrscr();
printf("Result on execution =" );
printf("%d",!((x*y)>(x+y+100)) ?
    x+y:x-y );
getche();
}
```

55. Conditional operator.

```
void main()
{
int x=12,y=15,z;
clrscr();
z=!((x++>++y))?x:y;
printf("%d ",z);
getche();
}
```

Examples on bitwise operators

56. Left and right shift.

```
void main()
{
int x=2,y=16,z;
clrscr();
x<<=2,y>>=1;
x&=y;
z=y|x;
printf("%d %d ",x,z);
getche();
}
```

57. Complement and Bitwise OR operation.

```
void main()
{
int p=2,x=8,y=5,z;
clrscr();
x=~x;
z=y|p;
printf("%d %d",x,z);
```

```
getche();
}
```

58. EX-OR and OR.

```
void main()
{
int p=10,x=12,y,z;
clrscr();
y=p^x;
z=p|y;
printf("%d %d ",y,z);
getche();
}
```

59. AND operation.

```
void main()
{
int y=12,x=8, z;
clrscr();
z=y&x;
printf("%d\n",z);
getche();
}
```

60. Binary operations.

```
void main()
{
int y=1,x=2, z,p,k;
clrscr();
z=x&y;
printf("%d\n",z);
p=z|x;
printf("%d\n",p);
k=p^y;
printf("%d\n",k);
getche();
}
```

61. Binary operations.

```
void main()
{
int a=4,b=16,m,n,o;
clrscr();
m=a<<2;
n=b>>3;
o=~0;
printf("\n%d",m);
printf("\n%d",n);
printf("\n%d",o);
getche();
}
```

62. Binary operations.

```
void main()
{
int x=2,y;
clrscr();
x<<=3;
y=x;
printf("\n y=%d",y);
getche();
}
```

63. Binary operations.

```
void main()
{
int a=8,b=4,c;
c=a & b;
clrscr();
printf("\n c=%d",c);
getche();
}
```

64. Binary operations.

```
void main()
{
int a=4,b=2,m,n,o;
clrscr();
m=a^b;
n=a|b;
o=a&b;
printf("\nExclusive OR operation in
    m=%d",m);
printf("\nOR operation in n=
    %d",n);
printf("\nAND operation in o=
    %d",o);
getche();
}
```

65. Binary operations.

```
void main()
{
int k=-2,j=2,s,q;
s=~k;
q=~j;
clrscr();
printf("s=%d q=%d",s,q);
getche();
}
```

66. Binary operations.

```
void main()
{
int k=0,s;
s=~k>>2;
clrscr();
printf("s=%d",s);
getche();
}
```

3.F Find the bug/s in the following program/s

Arithmetic operators

1.

```
void main()
{
int x=2,y=2,z=4;
clrscr();
z=((x+y)*z/2);
printf("%f",z);
}
```

2.

```
void main()
{
int x=10,y=20,z=30;
clrscr();
z=((x+y)*z/2);
z=z%4;
print("%d",z);
}
```

3.

```
void main()
{
int x=2,y=3,z;
x+y=z;
printf("z=%d",z);
}
```

4.

```
void main()
{
clrscr();
printf("%d %d",+2,2+);
}
```

Relational operators

5.

```
void main()
{
clrsr();
printf("\n %d",20==15);
printf(" %d",10>=15);
printf(" %d",9<8);
printf(" %d", 'A'=='a');
}
```

6.

```
void main()
{
char a=4,b=16,m,n,o;
clrscr();
m=a<2;
n=b>3;
o=a!=b;
printf("\n%c",m);
printf("\n%c",n);
printf("\n%c",o);
getche();
}
```

7.

```
void main()
{
int x=2,z;
clrscr();
z=x=>2;
printf("%d",z);
}
```

Logical operators and conditional operators

8.

```
void main()
{
char p=90;
int a;
clrscr();
a=(p>=65 && p<=90 ? 1 : 0);
printf("Y :%c",a);
getche();
}
```

9.

```
void main()
{
int a,b,c;
clrscr();
a=4;
b=2;
c=(a<<b && b>>1 );
printf("\n c=%c",c);
getche();
}
```

10.

```
void main()
{
int x=150 ,z;
clrscr();
z=(x==1 || x==100 ? 1 : 0);
printf("Z=%lf", z);
getche();
}
```

Conditional operators

11.
```
void main()
{
3>2 ? printf("True") ;
   printf("False");
}
```

12.
```
void main()
{
int a=5,b;
clrscr();
b=(a==5 ? 3 : 4);
printf("b= %c\n ",b);
getche();
}
```

13.
```
void main()
{
int x=2,y=5,z;
z=x!>y;
clrscr();
printf("%d",z);
}
```

Increment and decrement operators

14.
```
void main()
{
int x=2,y=2,z=4;
clrscr();
z=x+-y+++z;
printf("%d",z);
}
```

15.
```
void main()
{
int a,z,x==5,y==6;
clrscr();
z=x++*y++;
a=x*y;
printf("\n%d %d",z,a);
}
```

16.
```
void main()
{
int x=2; ++ x ++;}
```

17.
```
void main()
{
printf("%d",++8);
}
```

18.
```
void main()
{
   int x=2;
   ++++x;
   clrscr();
   printf("%d",x);
}
```

Assignment operators

19.
```
void main()
{
float a=12345678;
clrscr();
printf("\n %.2d",a);
getche();
}
```

20.
```
void main()
{
double a=987654321;
clrscr();
printf("\n %.2c",a);
getche();
}
```

Bitwise operators

21.
```
void main()
{
int a=2,b=4,c;
clrscr();
printf("\nBitwise operation");
c=a || b;
printf("\nThe Oring operation
   between a & b in c = %d",c);
getche();
}
```

22.
```
void main()
{
char a=2,b=16,m,n,o;
clrscr();
m=a^^b;
n=b||a;
```

```
o=~b;
printf("\n%d",m);
printf("\n%d",n);
printf("\n%d",o);
getche();
}
```

23.

```
void main()
{
int x;
clrscr();
x=>>2;
printf("%d",x);
}
```

`sizeof()` *operator*

24.

```
void main()
{
longint x;
clrscr();
 printf("%d",sizeof(x));
}
```

3.G Attempt the following programming exercises

1. Write a program to shift the entered number by 4 bits right and display the result. (Hint: Right shift operator)

2. Write a program to shift the entered number by 6 bits left and display the result. (Hint: Left shift operator)

3. Assume `x`, `y` and `z` are the integer variables whose values are to be assigned as 20,10 and 5. Compute the value of each of the following expressions:

   (a) `x+y-z`, (b) `x+y/z`, (c) `x*y*z`

4. Write a program to mask the least significant digit of the entered number. Use AND operator.

5. Write a program to enter three numbers and find the smallest and the largest out of them. (Hint: Relational operator)

6. Write a program to enter numbers 1 to 10, and carry out modular division operations on them with 2, 3 and 4 and display the remainders.

7. Write a program to enter a hexadecimal number and convert it into decimal and binary. (Hint: mod operator)

8. Write a program to find the average rainfall of 10 rainy days.

9. Write a program to enter two unsigned numbers. Compare them with conditional operator. If the first number is greater than the second, perform factorial of the larger number otherwise perform addition of them.

10. Write a program to calculate the total cost of the four wheeler vehicle by adding basic cost with (a) excise duty (8%), (b) sales tax (10%), (c) Octroi (2%), (d) road tax (1%) and (e) insurance (1%). Input the basic cost.

11. Write a program to display ASCII equivalents of

    (a) `"Z"`, `"A"`, `"Y"` and `"a"`, `"b"`, `"c"`

    (b) `"A"-"C"`, `"B"-"A"` and `"c" - "B"`

    (c) `"c"+"a"`, `"b"*"a"` and `"c"+12`

12. Write a program to count total even and odd numbers out of 10 entered numbers. (Hint: mod operator)

13. Write a program to enter a six-digit number. Display the digits of the number in the reverse order using modular division and division operation.

14. Write a program to display numbers from 0 to 9. Use ASCII range 48 to 59 and control string `%c`.

15. Write a program to evaluate the following expressions and display their results.

    (a) $x^2 + x^3 * (2*x)$

    (b) $x^1 + y^2 + z^3$

    where `x`, `y` and `z` are integers.

16. Write a program to print whether the number entered is even or odd, use conditional operator. (Hint: mod operator)

17. Assume `x`, `y` and `z` are the floating variables whose values are to be assigned as 20.20, 10.10 and 5.5. Compute the value of each of the following expressions:

    (a) `x+y+z`, (b) `(x+y)/z`, (c) `(x*y*z)/(x-y)` (Use arithmetic operators)

18. Assume x1, x2 and x3 are the character type variables whose values are to be assigned as A, B and C. Find the numerical value of each of the following expressions using ASCII characters.

    (a) `x1+x2`, (b) `x1-x3`, (c) `x1%x2` (Use ASCII table)

ANSWERS

3.A Fill in the blanks

1. (a) /
2. (a) x=x+1
3. (b) x++=2
4. (a) 1,0
5. (b) &&
6. (a) ||
7. (a) 1
8. (a) logical AND (&&), (d) 1, (e) 0
9. (c) logical NOT (!)
10. (b) logical OR
11. (a) postfix
12. (a)++
13. (b)−−
14. (c) −2
15. (b) comma operator, (a) lowest priority, (c) parentheses
16. (b) `sizeof ()`operator, (d) bytes, (e) data types
17. (b) left value
18. (a) right value
19. (i) +, −, *, / and %, (ii) Relational operators, (iii) &&, || and !, (iv) increment, decrement, (v) &, |, ^, >>, << and ~
20. (i) 1, (ii) 0, (iii) 1, (iv) 1, (v) 0, (vi) 0
21. (i) 1, (ii) 1, (iii) 0
22. (i) 7, (ii) 1, (iii) 12, (iv) 1, (v) 1, (vi) 32, (vii) 0, (viii) 0, (ix) 7, (x) 7

3.B True or false

1. F 2. T 3. F 4. F 5. T 6. T 7. T 8. F 9. T 10. T 11. F 12. T 13. T 14. T 15. F 16. T 17. T

3.C Match the following correct pairs given in Group A with Group B

I. 1. B, 2. A, 3. D, 4. C
II. 1. B, 2. A, 3. D, 4. C
III. 1. A, 2. B
IV. 1. B, 2. C, 3. A
V. 1. B, 2. A, 3. C
VI. 1. B, 2. A, 3. C
VII. 1. E, 2. D, 3. C, 4. B, 5. A

3.D Select the appropriate option from the multiple choices given below

1. (a) arithmetic operator
2. (a) 5
3. (a) 4
4. (a) 15
5. (b) 7
6. (c) 2
7. (c) ()

8. (b) higher
9. (a) *
10. (a) −2
11. (b) −1
12. (c) compare two boolean values
13. (a) right to left
14. (a) 8
15. (b) left to right
16. (a) 180
17. (a) 10
18. (a) 6552
19. (a) 1
20. (a) m=3 k=2
21. (a) x=4 y=4 z=8
22. (a) 10
23. (a) k=10
24. (a) b=11
25. (a) 1
26. (a) m=3 k=2
27. (b) 1
28. (a) j = 125.8
29. (a) y = 16.464

3.E What will be the output/s of the following program/s?

1. 21

   37

   2

   30

   (Multiplication and division have higher priorities than + and −, hence the answers are as above)

2. Total salary = 29600.00

   (Multiplication and division have higher priorities than + and −, hence the answer is as cited above)

3. c = −32768
   r = 0
   (Refer ranges of singed integers and unsigned integers. Any attempt to increase the numbers beyond the limits cause wrapping)

4. r = 0
   c = 2147483647
   (Refer the ranges of unsigned and long integer numbers)

5. 350.000000
   8.000000
   (Evaluation of 355/10 is 35.0, and multiplication to it by 10 provides result 350.0. The value operation computed is as per division, i.e.5+2.5+.5=8.0)

6. 200.00
   (Simple interest calculation, i.e. (2000*5*2)/100=200.00)

7. Area of a circle = 38.48
   (Area of a circle is calculated for the given data and the value of pi is constant)

8. Remainder after division operation=5
   Quotient of the division operation=12
   (125%10 provides 5 as remainder and quotient of 125/10 is 12)

9. 100

10. Binary equivalent of 10 is
    1 0 1 0
    (Repetitive division of 10 by 2 provides the remainders and the remainders are displayed from some coordinates with 'x' and 'y'. 'y' coordinate is fixed and 'x' coordininate is changed with x −−)

11. 00010
    (Remainders are displayed in one line)

12. 80 20
    (Binary left and right shift operation on data 40 by one shift and on 80 by two shifts provide the result 80 and 20, respectively)

13. 1010
    (Relational operators' results)

14. 0 0 1 1
    (Relational operators' results)

15. Condition : Return values
    10!=10 : 0
    10==10 : 1

10>=10 : 1
10<=100 : 1
10!=9 : 1

16. 1
1
0
(Logical operations provide results either 1 or 0. Refer to logical operations section)

17. 0
1
(Logical operations provide results either 1 or 0. Refer to logical operations section)

18. 0
(Logical operations provide results either 1 or 0. Refer to logical operations section)

19. Condition : Return values
5>3 && 5<10 : 1
8>5 || 8<2 : 1
!(8==8) : 0
(Conditional operations provide results either 1 or 0. Refer to logical operations section)

20. 0 1 1
(Logical operations provide results either 1 or 0. Refer logical operations section)

21. 10.80

22. 90
100

23. 10
14

24. a=−15
b=60
c=30

25. 200
210
(It is based on unary post-increment operation)

26. 7 1 39
(Pre-increment and post-increment operations)

27. 22
23
25
(Pre-increment and post-increment operations)

28. 82 98

29. r=12 p=16 q=8

30. 22

31. a=9 d=9

32. 4
−3

33. x = 26 y = 11 z = 2

34. size of `int` =2
size of `char` =1
size of `long` =4

35. size of a character(x)=1 byte
size of an integer(y)=2 bytes
size of long integer(z)=4 bytes
size of float(p)=4 bytes
size of double float (q)=8 bytes
Address of x=65481 y=65482 z=65484 p=65488 q=65492

36. sizeof(x)=2 bytes
sizeof(y)=4 bytes
sizeof(z)=1 bytes
sizeof(p)=8 bytes
sizeof(q)=10 bytes
Address of x=65470, y=65472, z=65477, p=65478, q=65486

37. 8

38. sizeof(y)=4 bytes
sizeof(x)=2 bytes
sizeof(z)=1 bytes
sizeof(q)=10 bytes

39. 7
(`printf` string needs 7 characters, hence total length of string is 7) Replace %c by %d in printf() and verify answer

40. X=65 X=A a=a
(Refer to assignment operators and ASCII table)

41. 8 4
(Refer to assignment operators)

42. 8 2.00
(Simple example on assignment operator)

43. 65 A
66 B
(Refer to assignment operators and ASCII table)

44. 3512
    3512
00003512

34.4550
234567
   234567
0000234567
(Formatting example)

45. ello
2 3 4
(H is skipped and displayed 2, 3 and 4)

46. 64
80
40
(Refer to hexadecimal and octal numbers)

47. Addition = 5
Subtraction = 1
(Simple example on comma operator)

48. 'True.'
(Simple conditional operation provides result true)

49. Result = 5

50. Result of the following conditional operation=15

51. True

52. 10000

53. Result on execution =15

54. Result on execution =2

55. 13

56. 8 8

57. −9 7

58. 6 14

59. 8

60. 0
2
3

61. 16
2
−1

62. y=16

63. C=0

64. Exclusive OR operation in m= 6
OR operation in n= 6
AND operation in o= 0

65. s=1 q=−3

66. s=−1

3.F Find the bug/s in the following program/s

1. `%f` is not expected in `printf()`. With `%d` the answer would be 8.
2. `printf()` is needed instead of `print`.
   Answer with correction would be 4.
3. variable must be at left side.
4. 2+ is not allowed.
5. Replace `clrsr` with `clrscr()`, and the answer of all conditional statements would be 0.
6. Replace `c` by `d` in all `printf()` statements. The answer will be
   0
   1
   1
7. => operator is invalid.
8. Replace `%c` with `%d` in `printf()` and the answer would be Y :1.
9. Replace `%c` with `%d` in `printf()` and the answer would be c=1.
10. Replace `%d` in place of `%lf` in `printf()` and the answer would be Z=0.
11. Semicolon is not allowed in between two `printf()`. Put the : and see the result. It should be "True".
12. Answer: b= 3 provided `%d` in place of `%c`.
13. Operator !> is invalid.
14. No bug.
15. Declaration syntax error in declaration `int` statement. The result after removing one of the '=' from it would be 30 42.
16. At a time both postfix and prefix operations are not allowed.
17. Operator ++ cannot be applicable to constant.
18. Lvalue required in function `main()`.

19. Replace `%d` with `%f` and the answer would be 12345678.00.

20. Replace `%lf` with `%c` in `printf()` statement. The answer would be 987654321.00.

21. Following answer would be obtained by removing one | symbol from c=a||b.

    Bitwise operation

    The Oring operation between a & b in c = 6

22. Syntax error in statement `m` . Single ^ is needed. With this the answer would be
    18
    1
    −17

23. x=>>2;

24. `longint` is not permitted.

4

Decision Control

CHAPTER OUTLINE

4.1 CONTROL STRUCTURES

Decision making statements in a programming language facilitate the programmer to transfer the control from one part to other part of the program. The programmer can make the program powerful by using control statements. Thus, using control statements the flow of program/execution of the statements is not in sequence. On the basis of real-time applications, it is essential

- ⇨ to alter the flow of a program
- ⇨ to test the logical conditions
- ⇨ to control the flow of execution as per the selection

C supports three kinds of controls structures in the program, such as

(i) sequential
(ii) selective
(iii) iterative

In sequential structure, the statements are executed one after the other in the sequence in which they appear. In selection control structures, choice of the path is decided based on the conditional statement. In iterative control structure, the program statements are repeatedly executed for numerous times even though they appear only once in the program.

C language supports the control statem ents as listed below.

(i) `if` statement
(ii) `if-else` statement
(iii) `if-else if` ladder statement
(iv) `switch()` statement
(v) `goto` unconditional jump
(vi) `for` loop statement
(vii) `while` loop
(viii) `do-while` loop

Besides the above mentioned statements, C also supports the other control statements such as `continue`, `break`, etc. In this chapter, we describe the operation of selective control structures.

4.2 `if` STATEMENT

C uses the keyword `if` to execute a set of command lines or one command line when the logical condition is true. It has only one option. The sets of command lines are executed only when the logical condition is true. Syntax of `if` statement is given in Figure 4.1.

```
/*Syntax for the simplest if
statement :-*/

if(condition) /* no semi-colon */
    statement;
```

FIGURE 4.1 **Syntax of `if` statement**

4.3 `if-else` STATEMENT

The `if-else` statement takes care of true as well as false conditions. It has two blocks. One block is for `if` and it is executed when the condition is true. The other block is of `else` and it is executed when the condition is false. The `else` statement cannot be used without `if`. The operation `if-else` can be understood from Figures 4.2 and 4.3.

Flow chart for `if-else` statement:

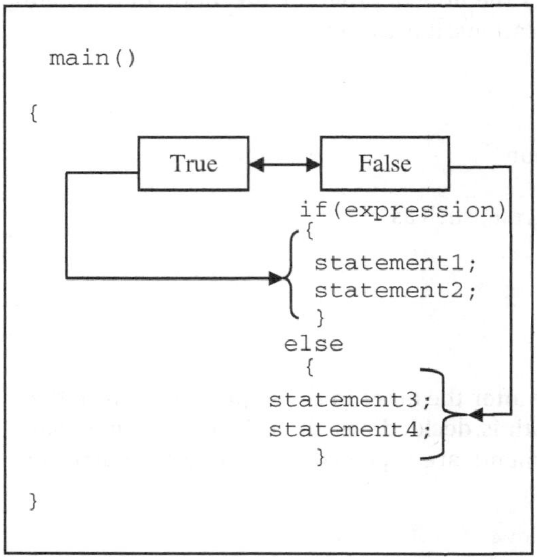

FIGURE 4.2 `if-else` statement

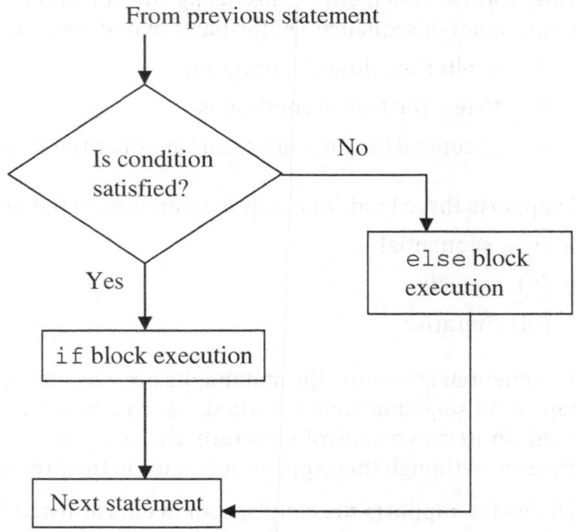

FIGURE 4.3 Flowchart with `if-else`

4.4 NESTED `if-else` STATEMENT

In this kind of statements, number of logical conditions are checked for executing various statements. Figure 4.4 describes the nested `if-else-if` blocks.
The syntax of the `if-else-if` ladder is shown in Figure 4.5.

4.5 `switch` STATEMENT

The `switch` statement is a multi-way branch statement. In the program, if there is a possibility to make a choice from a number of options, then structured selection is useful. It requires only one argument of any data type, which is checked with number of `case` options. The statement evaluates expression and then looks for its value among the case constants. If the value matches with the `case` constant, this particular `case` statement is executed. If not, `default` is executed. Here `switch`, `case` and `default` are reserved keywords. Every `case` statement terminates with ':'. The `break` statement is used to exit from current `case` structure. The `switch()` statement is useful for writing menu driven program.

The syntax of the `switch() case` statement is provided in Figure 4.6.

4.5.1 `switch` Execution

When one of the cases satisfies, the statements following it are executed. In case there is no match, the `default` case is executed. The `default` can be put anywhere in the `switch()` expression. The `switch()` statement can also be written without `default` statement. The `break` statement used in `switch()` passed control outside the `switch()` block. By mistake, if no `break` statements are given, all the cases following to it are executed (see Figure 4.7).

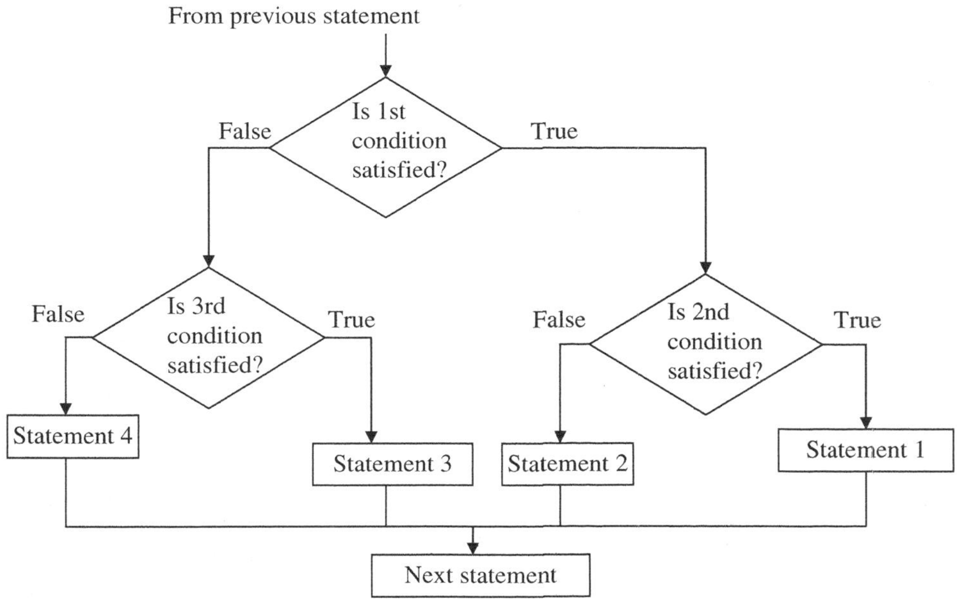

FIGURE 4.4 **`if-else-if` ladder statement**

```
/* Syntax of if-else-if statement is as
follows.*/

if(condition 1)
   {
   statement 1;  /* →  if block  */
   statement 2;
   }

else if(condition 2)
   {
   statement 3;  /* →  else if block */
   statement 4;
   }

else
   {
   statement 5;  /* →  else if block */
   statement 6;
   }
```

FIGURE 4.5 **The syntax of the `if-else-if`**

```
switch(variable   or
expression)
{
case  constant A:
statement;
break;

case constant B:
statement;
break;

default:
statement;
}
```

FIGURE 4.6 **The syntax of the `switch` `case` statement**

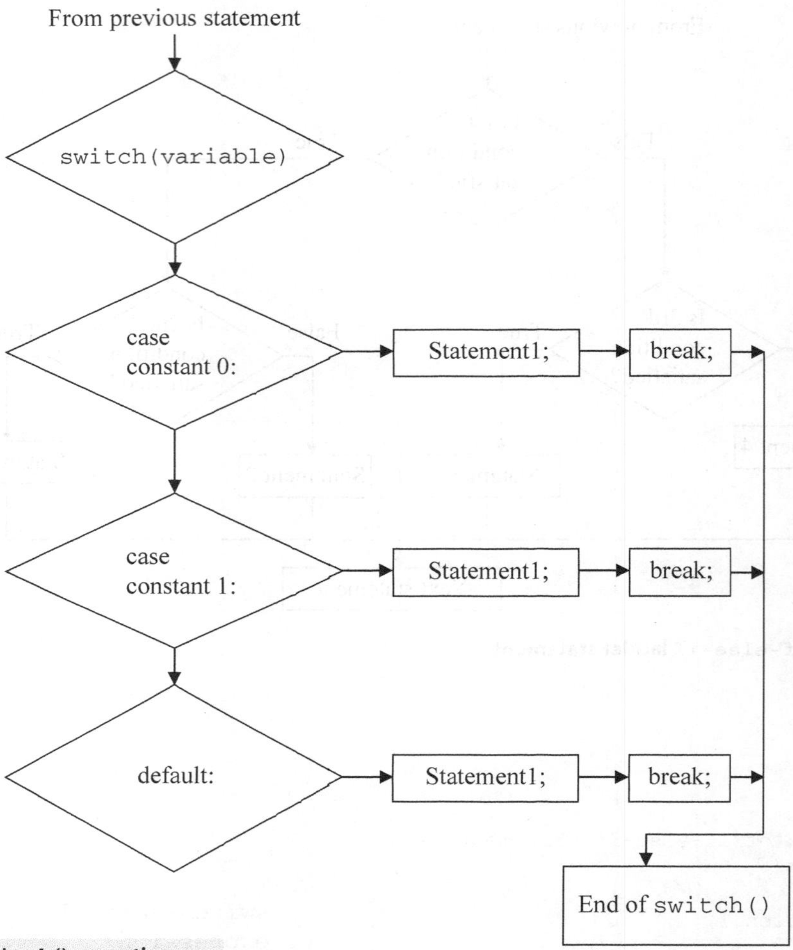

FIGURE 4.7 `switch()` **execution**

Following examples are provided for testing the programmer's skills.

EXERCISES

4.A Fill in the blanks

1. The `if` statement can evaluate logical and ______ operations.

   (a) relational
   (b) modular
   (c) addition

2. The `if-else` statement takes care of ______ as well as ______ conditions.

   (a) true, false
   (b) floats, integers
   (c) double, unsigned
   (d) none of the above

3. Same conditions may be repeated for a number of times in _______ structure.

   (a) `if-else`
   (b) `switch` case
   (c) none of the above

4. The `switch` can only test for _______ .

   (a) equality
   (b) non-equality
   (c) none of the above

5. Only _______ values are applicable in `switch` structure.

   (a) constants
   (b) variables
   (c) objects

6. No two `case` statements have _______ in the same switch.

   (a) identical constants
   (b) different constants
   (c) variables

7. In `switch`, character constants are automatically converted to _______.

   (a) `floats`
   (b) `integers`
   (c) `bool` values

8. If `switch` block is defined like `switch(x) { }` _______.

   (a) program will run
   (b) program will not run
   (c) compile error

9. The `switch` expression should neither be terminated with _______ and nor with any other symbol.

   (a) semicolon
   (b) colon
   (c) comma

10. The entire `case` structure following `switch()` should be enclosed with _______.

    (a) ()
    (b) {}
    (c) []

11. The keyword _______ is preceded by a constant.

    (a) `switch`
    (b) `case`
    (c) `break`

12. Every constant terminates with a _______. Each `case` statement must contain different constant values.

    (a) semicolon
    (b) colon
    (c) comma

13. The `break` statement separates the two _______ statements.

    (a) `case` statements
    (b) `else` statements
    (c) default

14. After matching constant of the `case` found, `break` takes the control to _______.

    (a) next case
    (b) out of `switch()` block
    (c) default

15. The statement _______ also can be used in `switch()` in place of break.

    (a) `continue`
    (b) `exit(0)`
    (c) `goto`

16. The `case` can be used in_______ .

    (a) `if-else`
    (b) `switch()`
    (c) select case

4.B True or false

1. The statement `if(1)` executes `if` block.
2. The `if()` statement can evaluate relational and logical expressions.
3. The `if()` statement works with expressions as well as constants.
4. The `else` block is executed when the condition is false.
5. The `else` is associated with `if` .
6. The `if` statement can have multiple `else` statements.

7. Like `if-else` the `switch` statement can be nested.
8. One `switch` statement can have multiple `case` statements but only one default statement.
9. The default statement can be written anywhere in the `switch` block.
10. The `switch` statement accepts only constant as an argument.
11. The default statement is compulsory for `switch` statement.
12. The `switch` statement testes for equality only.
13. The `default` case in `switch` gets executed when none of the `case` value matches.
14. The default statement can be placed at the beginning of `switch`, without any statement in its block.
15. The `switch` block can be terminated by a semicolon.
16. The `break` statement is used to separate two `case` statements.
17. The `case` statement is always terminated by semicolon.
18. The `break` statement is terminated by colon.
19. The `break` and `exit()` are similar.
20. The `break` statement terminates the particular `case`.

4.C Match the following correct pairs given in Group A with Group B

I

Group A		Group B	
Condition		**Meaning**	
1.	`if`	A	`switch`
2.	`break`	B	`label`
3.	`continue`	C	`default case`
4.	`goto`	D	`else`
5.	`default`	E	`for loop`

II

Group A		Group B	
Condition		**Meaning**	
1.	`if(0)`	A	Always true
2.	`if(1)`	B	Always false
3.	`else if(1)`	C	Nested else

III

Group A		Group B	
Characters		**ASCII Value**	
1.	A–Z	A	97–122
2.	a–z	B	65–90
3.	0–9	C	48–57

IV

Group A		Group B	
Function		**Meaning**	
1.	`isalnum()`	A	Provides True if input is a letter
2.	`isalpha()`	B	True if input is in lower case
3.	`islower`	C	True if input is in upper case
4.	`isupper()`	D	Provides True if input is either a letter or a digit

V

Group A		Group B	
Keywords		**Meaning**	
1.	`break;`	A	Control goes to the top of the loop
2.	`continue;`	B	Program termination
3.	`exit();`	C	Exit from the loop

4.D Select the appropriate option from the multiple choices given below

if

1. The statement `if(0)` means
   - (a) the expression is always false
   - (b) the expressions is always true
   - (c) the invalid expressions
2. The statement `if(−1)` means
   - (a) the expression is always false
   - (b) the expression is always true
   - (c) the invalid expressions
3. The condition given in `if(condition)` is true then
   - (a) `if` block executed
   - (b) `else` block executed
   - (c) both blocks are executed

4. The scope of `if()` can be defined with

   (a) `{}`
   (b) `[]`
   (c) `()`

5. The keyword `else` can be used with

   (a) `if` statement
   (b) `switch()` statement
   (c) `do-while()` statement
   (d) none of the above

6. Which warning message will be flagged by the compiler for the following program?
   `main() { if(0)printf("1"s));}`

   (a) unreachable code in function `main`
   (b) constant expression required
   (c) statement missing

switch()

7. The `if-else` and `switch` statements belong to

   (a) repetitive structure
   (b) sequential structure
   (c) selective structure
   (d) none of the above

8. The `default` is a

   (a) keyword in C
   (b) function
   (c) pointer
   (d) none of the above

9. The keyword `switch` is followed by

   (a) `switch` variable
   (b) `constant`
   (c) `float` variable
   (d) `goto`

10. The `default` statement can appear

    (a) anywhere within the switch
    (b) at the end of each `case`
    (c) default must be at the end of `switch case`

11. By mistake if no `break` statements are given in each `case`

    (a) all the `cases` following it are executed
    (b) statements following one `case` executes
    (c) none of the above

12. What will be the output of the program?

```
void main()
{
if(1)
printf("1"),
printf("0");
else
printf("2"));
}
```

    (a) 10
    (b) 2
    (c) No output

13. What will be the output of the following program?

```
void main()
{
  char y='p';
  clrscr();

  switch(y)
    {
    if(y=='p')
    {
    case 'p': printf("%s"," Pleasant");
    case 'B': printf("%s","mood");
    }

    else
    case 'G': printf("%s","moo");
    default : printf("%s", " ");
    }
}
```

    (a) pleasantmood
    (b) moo
    (c) mood
    (d) none of the above

14. What will be the output of the following program?

```
void main()
{
  char x='H';
  clrscr();
  switch(x)
  {
  case 'H': printf("%c",'H');
  case 'E': printf("%c",'a');
  case 'L': printf("%c",'i');
  case 'l': printf("%c",'!');break;
  case 'O': printf("%c",'O');
  }
}
```

    (a) Hai!
    (b) Hao
    (c) oHai
    (d) none of the above

15. What will be the output of the following program?

```
void main()
{
  int x='2';
  clrscr();

    switch(x)
    {
    case 1:
    printf( "0 1 001");
    break;
    case 2:
    printf("1 2 3");
    break;
    default:
    printf("I II III");
    }
}
```

(a) 1 2 3
(b) 0 1 001
(c) I II III
(d) none of the above

16. What will be the output of the following program?

```
void main()
{
char x=0;
clrscr();
switch(x)
{
  case 0 : printf("%c",'C');
      break;
  case 0 : printf("%c",'d');
      break;
  default :;
}
}
```

(a) cd
(b) program error
(c) C

4.E. What will be the output/s of the following program/s?

`if` statements

1. Program to compute salary of an employee.

```
void main()
{
int bas=1000,hra,years=7,nets=0;
clrscr();
  if(years >5)
  {
  hra=700;
  nets=bas+hra;
  printf("\n Salary of an employee =
     Rs %d",nets);
  }
getche();
}
```

2. Program to calculate profit and incentive.

```
void main()
{
float sales=100000,cost=50000,profit;
float incen;
clrscr();
profit=sales-cost;
printf("Profit= Rs ");
printf("%.2f",profit);
if(profit>20000)
{
incen=(float)profit*24/100;
printf("\nIncentive = Rs %.2f",
   incen);
}
getche();
}
```

3. Some tricky Program.

```
void main()
{
int k=10,y=0,z;
clrscr();
for(z=0;z<10;z++)
{
  y++;
  k--;
  printf("%d ",k+y);
  if(y==k)
  break;
}
}
```

Multiple `if` statements

4. Program to compare two numbers.

```
void main()
{
  int n=5,b=7;
  clrscr();
   if(n>b)
```

```
    printf("%d is Greater than %d",n,b);
    if(n<b)
    printf("%d is smaller than %d",n,b);
    if(n==b)
    printf("%d is equal to %d\n",n,b);
    getche();
}
```

5. Program to find energy bill using conditions.

```
void main()
{
    int startr=1000,endr=1345,differ;
    float amount;
    clrscr();
    differ=endr-startr;
    if(differ==100)
      {
      amount=1.30*differ;
      printf("Total bill will be Rs
         %.2f",amount);
      }
      if(differ>101 && differ<300)
      {
      amount=3.50*differ;
      printf("Total bill will be Rs
         %.2f",amount);
      }
      if(differ>=300)
      {
      amount=4.50*differ;
      printf("Total bill will be Rs
         %.2f",amount);
      }
      getche();

}
```

6. Program to display result use exit() statement.

```
void main()
{
    float percen=80;
    clrscr();
    if(percen<0||percen>100)
    {
        printf("Invalid percentage\n");
        exit();
        }
    if(percen<50)
        printf("Fail");
    if(percen>=50&&percen<60)
        printf("Pass\n");
    if(percen>=61&&percen<70)
        printf("First class\n");
    if(percen>=70)
        printf("Distinction class\n");
    getche();
}
```

7. Program to print the strings.

```
void main()
{
    clrscr();
    if('A'<'B')
    printf("Hello ");
    printf(" How R U ");

    if('A'<'a')
    printf(" Sir ?");
}
```

`if-else` statement

8. Program to detect the given number as to whether it is even or odd.

```
void main()
{
    int number=7;
    clrscr();
    if(number %2==0)
    printf("\n The entered number %d
       is even",number);
    else
    printf("\n The Entered number %d
       is odd",number);
    getche();
}
```

9. Program to find energy bill.

```
void main()
{
int initial=1000,final=1300,
   consumed;
float total;
clrscr();
consumed = final-initial;
if(consumed>=200)
total=consumed * 2.50;
else
total=consumed * 1.50;
printf("Total bill for %d units is
   Rs %.2f",consumed,total);
getche();
}
```

10. Program on tricky operation.

```
void main()
{
```

```
int j=5,k=8,l=-9;
clrscr();
if(j< k && l>k)
{
  j+=2;
  l-=1;
}
else
j--;
printf("\n %d %d %d",j,k,l);
}
```

11. Program to compare two numbers using **if** statement.

```
void main()
{
  int j=8;
  int k=8;
  clrscr();
  if(j>k)
  printf("Numbers are not equal");
  else
  if(k==j/2*2)
  printf("Numbers are equal");
}
```

12. Program to print the string 'Wel- Come' or 'Good Bye'.

```
void main()
{
  int j,k,l;
  j=k=l=12;
  j++; k++; l++;
  clrscr();
  if(j==k==l)
  printf("Wel -Come");
  else
  printf("Good Bye");
}
```

13. Program to print the string.

```
void main()
{
  int j,k,l;
  j=k=12;
  l=12;
  j++; k++; l++;
  clrscr();
  if(j==k && k==l && j==l)
  printf("Welcome");
  else
  printf ("Good Bye");
}
```

14. Program to print values of three variables.

```
void main()
{
  int a=1,b=3,c=8;
  if (a>b)
  b=a;
  if (a>c)
  a=c;
  else
  a=b;
  clrscr();
  printf ("\na =%d b=%d c=%d",a,b,c);
}
```

15. Program to check whether the entered year is leap year or not. Use `goto` and `exit()` statements.

```
void main()
{
int year=2005;
clrscr();
if(year%4==0 && year%100!=0 ||
   year%400==0)
goto leap;
else goto noleap;
leap:printf("\%d is a leap year
   ",year);
exit();
noleap:printf("\%d is a not a leap
   year",year);
getche();
}
```

16. Program to print value of a variable.

```
void main()
{
  int x=10;
  if(x==x++)
  x-=!3;
  else
  x-=2;
  clrscr();
  printf("\nx=%d",x);
}
```

Nested `if-else` statements

17. Program on comparison of three numbers.

```
void main()
{
int x=6,y=5,z=10;
clrscr();
printf("\nAnswer is :");
if(x>y)
```

```
{
if(x>z)
printf("%d\n",x);
else
printf("%d\n",z);
}
else
{
if(z>y)
printf("%d\n",z);
else
printf("%d\n",y);
}
getche();
}
```

18. Program to detect person has made profit or loss.

```
void main()
{
  int sprize=200,cprize=300,profit,
      loss;
  clrscr();
  if(sprize>cprize)
  {
    profit=sprize-cprize;
    printf("\n Person has made the
       profit of Rs %d",profit);
  }
  else
  {
        if(sprize<cprize)
        loss=cprize-sprize;
        printf("\n Person has
          incurred the loss of
          Rs %d",loss);
  }
  getche();
}
```

19. Program to print smallest number from the three given numbers.

```
void main()
{
int a=2,b=4,c=1,temp;
clrscr();
if(a<b)
{
if(a<c)
temp=a;
else
temp=c;
}
else
{
if(b<c)
temp =b;
else
temp =c;
}
printf("Answer out of three
    numbers (%d %d %d)is %d \n",
    a,b,c, temp);
getche();
}
```

20. Program to print largest number amongst three entered numbers.

```
void main()
{
  int x=1,y=9,z=7;
  clrscr();
   if(x>y)
   {
   if(x>z)
   printf("x=%d\n",x);
   else
   printf("z=%d\n",z);
   }
  else
   {
   if(z>y)
   printf("z=%d\n",z);
   else
   printf("y=%d\n",y);

   }
   getche();
}
```

21. Program on mathematical operation on a variable.

```
void main()
{
  unsigned b=0;
  short hand=42;
  clrscr();
  if(hand<50 & !b)
  hand++;
  if(hand<50);
  else if(hand > 40)
 {
  hand+=7;
  hand++;
 }
  else
  --hand;
  printf("\n %d",hand);
}
```

22. Program on mathematical operation on variables.

```
void main()
{
  int x=0,b1=0,b2=0;
  clrscr();
  if(!b1)
{
  if(!b2)
{
   b1=1;
   x++;
  if(5>6)
{
  x++;
  }
  if(!b1)x=x+10;
  else if(b2==1)x=x+100;
  else if(b1 | b2)x=x+1000;
  }
  }
  printf(" %d ",x);
  getche();
  }
```

23. Program to detect the entered variable is a letter, symbol or digit.

```
void main()
{
    int p=10;
    clrscr();
    fflush(stdin);
    if(isalnum(p)!=0)
    {
    printf("\n It is neither a
      letter nor a character");
    exit();
    }
  if(isalpha(p))
  printf("\n It is a character");
  else
  printf("\n It is a digit");
  getche();
}
```

24. Program to detect whether entered character is alphabet, upper case or lower case.

```
void main()
{
       char p='H';
       clrscr();
           if(!isalpha(p))
           {
           printf("\n It is not an
             alphabet");
           exit();
           }
     if(isupper(p))
     printf("\n It is a upper case
        character");
     else
     printf("\n It is a lower case
        character");
     getche();
}
```

25. Program to convert & print entered lower case character into upper case character.

```
void main()
{
        char p='h',z;
        clrscr();
        if(!isalpha(p))
        {
        printf("\n It is not an
            alphabet");
        exit();
        }
     if(isupper(p))
     z=tolower(p);
     else
     z=toupper(p);
     printf("\n%c",z);
       getche();
}
```

else-if ladder

26. Some tricky program.

```
void main()
{
int nc=250;
clrscr();
if(nc<100)
goto free;
else if(nc>99 && nc<200)
goto charge1;
else if(nc>199 && nc<300)
goto charge2;
else
goto charge3;
free :
printf("\n No charges.");
return;
charge1:
printf("\n Total Charges in Rs :
    %d .",nc*1);
getche();
exit();
charge2:
```

```
printf("\n Total Charges in Rs:
   %d .",nc*2);
getche();
exit();
charge3:
printf("\n Total Charges in Rs :
   %d .",nc*3);
}
```

switch() case statement

27. Program to print entered number is even or odd.

```
void main()
{
int x=6,y;
clrscr();
switch(x)
{
case 0 :
printf("\n Number is Even.");
break;
case1:
printf("\number is odd ");
default :
y=x%2;
switch(y)
{
case 0:
printf("\n x is even");
break;
default :
printf("\n x is Odd.");
}
}
getche();
}
```

28. Program to print the characters and make a string.

```
void main()
{
int ch;
clrscr();
for(ch=1;ch<=5;ch++)
switch(ch)
{
case 1 :
printf(" L");
break;
case 2 :
printf(" O");
break;
case 3 :
printf(" V");
break;
case 4 :
printf(" E");
break;
case 5 :
printf("\n ");
break;
default :
printf("\n Invalid Choice");
}
getch();
}
```

29. Program to calculate addition, subtraction, multiplication and division of two numbers.

```
void main()
{
int ch,a=20,b=10;
clrscr();
for(ch=1;ch<=4;ch++)
switch(ch)
{
case 1 :
printf("%3d",a+b);
break;
case 2 :
printf("%3d",a-b);
break;
case 3 :
printf("%4d",a*b);
break;
case 4 :
printf("%4d",a/b);
break;
default :
printf("\n Invalid Choice");
}
getch();
}
```

30. Program to find addition and multiplication of numbers. Use `continue` statement.

```
void main()
{
  int x=9,y=9,z,m;
  clrscr();
  for(m=1;m<=2;m++)
  {
  switch(m)
  { case 1:
  z=x+y;
  printf("\n %d",z);
  continue;
  case 2:
  z=x*y;
```

```
    printf("\n %d",z);
    break;
    default:
    printf("Invalid number");
    }
    }
    getche();
}
```

31. Program to find area and perimeter of square and rectangle using `switch()` `case` statement.

```
void main()
{
    int s=5,b=4,w=6,
        as,ar,ps,pr,choice;
    clrscr();
    for(choice=1;choice<=4;choice++)
    switch(choice)
    {
    case 1:
    as=s*s;
    printf("\n Area of the square
        =%d",as);
    break;
    case 2:
    ar=b*w;
    printf("\n Area of the
        Rectangle=%d",ar);
    break;

    case 3:
    ps=4*s;
    printf("\n Perimeter of the square
        =%d",ps);
    break;

    case 4:
    pr=2*(b+w);
    printf("\n Perimeter of the
        Rectangle =%d",pr);
    break;

    default:
    printf("Invalid case");
    break;
    }
    getche();
    }
```

32. Program to calculate area, circumference and diameter of a circle.

```
void main()
{
    int r=3,ch;
    float a,c,d,pi=3.14;
    clrscr();
    for(ch=1;ch<=3;ch++)
    switch(ch)
    {
    case 1:
    a=(float)pi*r*r;
    printf("\n Area of a circle:-
        %.2f",a);
    break;

    case 2:
    c=(float)2*pi*r;
    printf("\circumference of a
        circle:- %.2f",c);
    break;

    case 3:
    d=2*r;
    printf("\n Diameter of a circle:-
        %.2f",d);
    break;
    default:
    printf("Invalid choice");
      }
      getch();
}
```

33. Program to calculate volume of a cylinder, sphere, cone and area of a trapezium.

```
void main()
{
    int r=3,h=8,tra,s=5,p=6,ch,d;
    float a,pi=3.14,v,c;
    clrscr();
    for(ch=1;ch<=4;ch++)
    switch(ch)
    {
    case 1:
    a=pi*r*r*h;
    printf("\n Volume of a Cylinder:-
        %.2f",a);
    break;

    case 2:
    v=(float)4/3*pi*r*r*r;
    printf("\n volume of a sphere:-
        %.2f",v);
    break;

    case 3:
    c=(float)1/3*pi*r*r*h;
    printf("\n Volume of cone:- %.2f",c);
    break;

    case 4:
    tra=(s+p)*h/2;
```

```
    printf("\n Area of trapezium:-
        %d",tra);
    break;

    default:
    printf("Invalid choice");
        }
        getch();
}
```

34. Program to detect vowel.

```
void main()
{
    char choice='e';
    clrscr();
    switch(choice)
    {
    case 'a':
    case 'A':
    printf("\n Entered letter is VOWEL
        %c",choice
    break;

    case 'e':
    case 'E':
    printf("\n Entered letter is VOWEL
        %c",choice);
    break;

    case 'i:
    case 'I':
    printf("\n Entered letter is VOWEL
        %c",choice);
    break;

    case 'o':
    case 'O':
    printf("\n Entered letter is VOWEL
        %c",choice);
    break;

    case 'u':
    case 'U':
    printf("\n Entered letter is VOWEL
        %c",choice);
    break;

    default:
    printf("Invalid case");
    }
    getche();
}
```

35. Program to calculate how many hours and minutes are there in a day.

```
void main()
{
int m,days=1,choice;
long p;
clrscr();
for(choice=1;choice<=2;choice++)

    switch(choice)
    {
    case 1:
    m=days*24;
    printf(" Hours are %d",m);
    break;

    case 2:
    m=days*24*60;
    printf("\n Minutes are %d",m);
    getche();
    break;

    default:
    printf("\n Invalid number");

    }
    getche();
}
```

36. Program to calculate number of seconds in a day. Use `switch()` statement.

```
void main()
{
    int choice=1;
    long m;
    clrscr();
    switch(choice)
    {
    case 1:
    m=(long)60*60*24;
    printf("\n Seconds are %ld",m);
    getche();
    break;

    default :
    printf("\n Invalid number");
    }
    getche();
}
```

37. Program to display names of a few months in a year.

```
void main()
{
        int month=3;
        clrscr();
        for(month=5;month<=7;month++)
    switch(month)
    {
```

```
case 1:
printf("\n%dst Month of Year is
    Janauary",month);
break;
case 2:
printf("\n%dnd Month of Year is
    Feburury",month);
break;
case 3:
printf("\n%drd Month of Year is
    March",month);
break;
case 4:
printf("\n%dth Month of Year is
    April",month);
break;
case 5:
printf("\n%dth Month of Year is
    May",month);
break;
case 6:
printf("\n%dth Month of Year is
    June",month);
break;
case 7:
printf("\n%dth Month of Year is
    July",month);
break;
case 8:
printf("\n%dth Month of Year is
    August",month);
break;
case 9:
printf("\n%dth Month of Year is
    September",month);
break;
case 10:
printf("\n%dth Month of Year is
    october",month);
break;
case 11:
printf("\n%dth Month of Year is
    November",month);
break;
case 12:
printf("\n%dth Month of Year is
    December",month);
break;
default:
printf("Invalid month");
break;
}
  getche();
}
```

38. Program to calculate number of months and balance days from number of days provided.

```
void main()
{
  int m,d=221,ch=0;
  clrscr();
  for(ch=1;ch<=2;ch++)
  switch(ch)
  {
  case 1:
  m=d/30;
  printf("\n Number of Months:- %d",m);
  break;
  case 2:
  d=d%30;
  printf("\n Number of days :- %d",d);
  break;
  }
  getche();
}
```

39. Program to calculate maturity amount with interest.

```
void main()
{
int ch,y,amount=5000;
float sum,r;
clrscr();
for(ch=1;ch<=5;ch++)
switch(ch)
{
  case 1:
  sum=amount+(amount*1*8.0/100);
  printf("\nMaturity amount for 1
    year:%.2f",sum);
  break;
  case 2:
  sum=amount*(1.0+(2*10.0)/100);
  printf("\nMaturity amount for 2
    years:%.2f",sum);
  break;
  case 3:
  sum=amount*(1.0+(3*12.0)/100);
  printf("\nMaturity amount for 3
    years:%.2f",sum);
  break;
```

```
    case 4:
    sum=amount*(1.0+(4*14.0)/100);
    printf("\nMaturity amount for 4
       years:%.2f",sum);
    break;

    case 5:
    sum=amount*(1.0+(5*16.0)/100);
    printf("\nMaturity amount for 5
       years:%.2f",sum);
    break;

    default:
    printf("Terminated by choice");
    }
      getch();
}
```

40. Program to calculate cost of petrol, diesel and kerosene.

```
void main()
{
  float p,d,k,I;
  clrscr();
  for(i=1;i<=3;i++)
  switch(i)
  {

  case 1:
  p=5*44.5;
  printf ("\n Total Cost of Petrol
     %.2f",p);
  break;

  case 2:
  d=5*31.2;
  printf("\n Total Cost of Diesel
     %.2f",d);
  break;

  case 3:
  p=5*22.3;
  printf("\n Total Cost of Kerosene
     %.2f",p);
  getche();
  break;

  default :
  printf("\n Invalid number");
  }
  getche();
}
```

41. Program to find total cost of BPL, Onida and LG TV.

```
void main()
{
int bc,ch,tot;
float oct,trans,pack,dis;
clrscr();
for(ch=1;ch<=3;ch++)
  switch(ch)
  {
  case 1:
  bc=6000;
  oct=bc*0.03;
  trans=bc*0.02;
  pack=bc*0.01;
  dis=bc*0.01;
  tot=(bc+oct+trans+pack)-(dis);
  printf("\nTotal cost of BPL 21
     inch TV is Rs %d",tot);
  break;

  case 2:
  bc=8000;
  oct=bc*0.04;
  trans=bc*0.05;
  pack=bc*0.03;
  dis=bc*0.01;
  tot=(bc+oct+trans+pack)-(dis);
  printf("\nTotal cost of Onida TV
     is Rs %d",tot);
  break;

  case 3:
  bc=6000;
  oct=bc*0.03;
  trans=bc*0.02;
  pack=bc*0.01;
  dis=bc*0.1;
  tot=(bc+oct+trans+pack)-(dis);
  printf("\nTotal cost of LG 21 TV
     Rs %d",tot);
  break;

  default:
  printf("Invalid case");

  getche();
  }
}
```

42. Program to use pow() and abs() function.

```
void main()
{
  int z,m;
  clrscr();
  for(m=1;m<=2;m++)
  switch(m)
  {
  case 1:
  z=pow(2,5);
  printf("\n %d",z);
  continue;
```

```
    case 2:
    z=abs(-4);
    printf("\n %d",z);
    break;

    default:
    printf("Invalid number");
    }
    getche();
}
```

43. Program to calculate number of days and hours from seconds.

```
void main()
{
    long seconds =5184000;
    float d;
    int i,h;
    clrscr();
    for(i=1;i<=2;i++)
        switch(i)
      {
    case 1:
    d=(float)seconds/(60*60);
    d=(float)d/24;
    printf("\n Total days %10.0f",d);
    break;

    case 2:
    h=d*24;
    printf("\n Total hours %d",h);
    break;

    default:
    printf("\n Invalid number");

     }
     getche();
}
```

44. Program to round down and up the given float numbers and compute logarithm value.

```
void main()
{
int z,m;
float p;
clrscr();
for(m=1;m<=3;m++)
  switch(m)

  {
  case 1:
  z=floor(2.5);
  printf("\n %d",z);
  continue;

  case 2:
  z=ceil(2.5);
  printf("\n %d",z);
  continue;

  case 3:
  p=log10(10);
  printf("\n %.2f",p);
  break;

  default:
  printf("Invalid number");
  }
  getch();
}
```

45. Program to calculate remainder, exponential and square root value of a entered number.

```
void main()
{
int z,m;
float p;
clrscr();
for(m=1;m<=3;m++)
  switch(m)
  {

  case 1:
  z=fmod(11,3);
  printf("\n %d",z);
  continue;

  case 2:
  p=exp(0);
  printf("\n %.2f",p);
  continue;

  case 3:
  p=sqrt(35);
  printf("\n %.2f",p);
  break;

  default:
  printf("Invalid number");
  }
}
```

46. Program to print value of sin(0), cos(0)and tan(45).

```
void main()
{
int z,choice;
float p;
clrscr();
for(choice=1;choice<=3;choice++)
  switch(choice)
```

```
{
case 1:
p= cos(0);
printf("\n %.2f",p);
break;

case 2:
p=sin(0);
printf("\n %.2f",p);
break;

case 3:
p=tan(45);
printf("\n %.2f",p);
break;

default:
printf("Invalid number");
}
getche();
}
```

47. Program to calculate factorial of a number, summation of a series and cubic summation of a series entered.

```
void main()
{
  int oper=3,x=1,y=5,z=10,i=0,p;
  clrscr();
  for(oper=1;oper<=3;oper++)
  switch(oper)
  {

  case 1:
  while(y>=1)
  {
  x=x*y;
  y=y-1;
  }
  printf("\nFactorial is %d ",x);
  break;

  case 2:
  while(z>=1)
  {
  i=i+z;
  z=z-1;
  }
  printf("\nSummation from 1 to 10
      is %d ",i);
  break;

  case 3:
  p=pow(1,3)+pow(2,3)+pow(3,3);
  printf("\nSeries summation is %d ",p);
  break;
  default:
  printf("Invalid oper");
  break;
  }
  getche();
}
```

48. Program to print 0 and 2. Use `static` keyword.

```
void main()
{
static int z,x=1;
clrscr();
for(z=0;z<3;z++)
{
switch(z)
{
case 1 : printf(" %s ","0");break;
case 2: printf(" %s ","2");break;
}
}
}
```

49. Program to print 501234 using `switch()` case statement.

```
void main()
{
int j=7;
clrscr();
switch(j)
{
 default: printf("5");
  case 0: printf("0");
  case 1: printf("1");
  case 2: printf("2");
  case 3: printf("3");
  case 4: printf("4");
}
}
```

50. Program to print entered letter. Use `putchar()` and `switch()` case statement.

```
void main()
{
char j='a'+32;
switch(j)
{
  case 'A' : putchar('A');
  case 'B' : putchar('B');
  default : putchar('D');
  case 'C' : putchar('C');
}
getch();
}
```

4.F Find the bug/s in the following program/s

if statements

1.
```
void main()
{
  int a,b,c,d,e,sum=0,i;
  printf("\n Enter Five Numbers: ");
  scanf("%d %d %d %d %d",&a,&b,&c,
     &d,&e);
  sum=a+b+c+d+e;
  for(i=sum;i<=sum;i--)
  {
     if(i==a || i==b || i==c ||
        i==d || i==e)
{
     printf("The largest Number is
        %d ",i);
     exit(0);
  }
}
```

2.
```
void main()
{
int a=3,b=2,c=2,x;
clrscr();
x=a-b-c;
if(x%=2)
{
  printf("\n Addition : %d",a+b+c);
}
  printf("\n Multiplication :
     %d", a*b*c);
}
```

if-else statements

3.
```
void main()
{
clrscr();
if(0)
printf("False");
else
printf("True");
}
```

4.
```
void main()
{
clrscr();
if(1);
else;
}
```

5.
```
void main()
{
clrscr();
if(3>2)
printf("2 is smaller than 3");
printf(" and ");
else
printf("3 is greater");
}
```

6.
```
void main()
{
clrscr();
if(3>2)
printf("3 is greater than 2");
else;
printf("\nIt's OK");
}
```

7
```
void main()
{
int m=10,n=15;
clrscr();
if(m!=n)
printf("\n Two numbers are equal.");
else
}
```

8.
```
void main()
{
  int x='C';
  clrscr();
  if(x='C')
  printf("%c",x);;
  else
printf("X is not equal to C");
}
```

9.
```
void main()
{
clrscr();
if(3>2)
```

```
printf("2 is smaller than 3");
else
printf(" Numbers are equal");
else
printf("3 is greater");
}
```

10.

```
void main()
{
clrscr();
if(3>2)
printf("2 is smaller than 3");
if(4==4)
printf("\nNumbers are equal");
else
printf("3 is greater");
}
```

Nested `if-else` statement

11.

```
void main()
{
int x=7,y=1,z=2;
clrscr();
printf("\nLargest out of Three
   Numbers is :");
  if(x>y)
   if(x>z)
  printf("x=%d\n",x);
  else
  printf("z=%d\n",z);
  if(z>y)
  printf("z=%d\n",z);
  else
  printf("y=%d\n",y);
}
```

`switch case` statements

12.

```
void main()
{
char c;
clrscr();
printf("Enter char : ");
scanf("%c",&c);
switch(c)
{
case 'x' :
printf("x entered");
case 'y' :
printf(" y entered");
break;
}
}
```

13.

```
void main()
{
char c;
printf("Enter char : ");
scanf("%c",&c);
switch(c)
{
default :
printf("Other char is entered");
exit(0);
case 'x' :
printf("x entered");
break;
}
}
```

14.

```
void main()
{
char x='X';
clrscr();

switch(x)
{
case 'C' : printf("%c",'C');
case 'D' : printf("%c",'D');
case 'A' : printf("%c",'A');
default:
}
}
```

15.

```
void main()
{
char x='X';
clrscr();

switch(x)
{
default :
case 'C' : printf("%c",'C');
case 'D' : printf("%c",'D');
case 'A' : printf("%c",'A');
}
}
```

16.

```
void main()
{
```

```
char x='X';
clrscr();

switch(x)
{
case 'C' : printf("%c",'C'); break;
case 'D' : printf("%c",'D');continue;
case 'A' : printf("%c",'A');
}
}
```

17.

```
void main()
{
char x='X';
clrscr();

switch(x)
{
    case x : printf("%c",'C'); break;
    case x : printf("%c",'D');continue;
    case x : printf("%c",'A');
}
}
```

18.

```
void main()
{
char x=0;
clrscr();

switch(x)
{
case 0 : printf("%c",'C'); break;
case 0 : printf("%c",'D');;
case 1 : printf("%c",'A');
}
}
```

4.G Attempt the following programming exercises

1. Write a program to calculate Electricity bill based on the consumption of units as follows
   (a) Rate per unit Rs 5 up to 100 units.
   (b) Rate per unit Rs 7 beyond 100 units.
2. Write a program to calculate the total salary based on the basic for different slabs.
   (a) If basic is more than 4000 and less than 6000 DA 40% HRA 20% Conveyance 10%
   (b) If basic is more than 6000 and less than 10000 DA 50% HRA 20% Conveyance 15%
   (c) If basic is more than 10000 and less than 20000 DA 70% HRA 40% Conveyance 35%
3. Write a program to calculate hotel bill. The conditions are given below.
   (a) Sale of eatables up to 100 Rs 11% discount.
   (b) Sale of eatables up to 1000 Rs 22% discount.
   (c) Sale of eatables up to 10000 Rs 33% discount.
4. Write a program to enter a letter through keyboard. Use `switch case` structure and print appropriate message. Recognize the entered letter is lower case or upper case.
5. Write a program to perform floating point addition, subtraction, multiplication and division using `switch case`.
6. Write a program to display the marks and status of students (A ,B C and Fail grades) based on the total marks scored in the various subjects in the annual examination.

ANSWERS

4.A Fill in the blanks

1. (a) relational
2. (a) true , false
3. (a) `if..else`
4. (a) equality
5. (a) constants
6. (a) identical constants
7. (b) integers
8. (a) program will run
9. (a) semicolon
10. (b) { }
11. (b) `case`
12. (b) colon

13. (a) `case` statements
14. (b) out of `switch()` block
15. (c) `goto`
16. (b) `switch`

4.B True or false

1.T 2.T 3.T 4.T 5.T 6.F 7.T 8.T 9.T 10.T
11.F 12.T 13.T 14.T 15.T 16.T 17.F 18.F
19.F 20.T

4.C Match the following correct pairs given in Group A with Group B

I 1. D, 2. A, 3. E, 4. B, 5. C
II 1. B, 2. A, 3. C
III 1. B, 2. A, 3. C
IV 1. D, 2. A, 3. B, 4. C
V 1. C, 2. A, 3. B.

4.D Select the appropriate option from the multiple choices given below

1. (a) the expression is always false
2. (b) the expressions is always true
3. (a) `if` block executed
4. (a) { }
5. (a) `if` statement
6. (a) unreachable code in function main
7. (c) selective structure
8. (a) keyword in C
9. (a) `switch` variable
10. (a) anywhere within the `switch`
11. (a) all the `cases` following it are executed
12. (a) 10
13. (a) pleasantmood
14. (a) Hai!
15. (c) I II III
16. (b) program error

4.E What will be the output/s of the following program/s?

1. Salary of an employee =Rs 1700
(Since years > 5, nets=1000+700)
2. Profit=Rs 50000.00
Incentive=Rs 12000.00
(100000−50000 & 2 decimal digits for float)
(50000*24/100 & 2 decimal digits for floating point number)
3. 1010101010
(Even though the loop is for 10 times, it is executed only for five times due to the satisfaction of a condition k=y. Increment of 'y' and decrement of 'k' are done within the loop and equality is checked between 'y' and 'k'. Exit operation from the loop happens when variables 'k' and 'y' are the same.)
4. 5 is smaller than 7
(n < b condition is satisfied)
5. Total bill will be Rs 1552.50
(differ=345 > 300 is satisfied and respective block instructions are executed)
6. Distinction class
(`percen > =70` condition is satisfied)
7. Hello How R U Sir?
(A has ASCII value 65 while B has 66, hence A < B and the concerned `printf()` statements are executed. Similarly, ASCII value of 'a' is 97 which is larger than 65. Hence, last `printf()` statement is executed.)
8. The Entered number 7 is odd
(7%2=1, hence odd number condition is satisfied)
9. Total bill for 300 units is Rs 750.00
(The consumed=300 which is greater than 200, and hence the statement in that block is executed.)
10. 4 8 − 9
(Since j > k && l > k condition is not satisfied, 'j' is decreased by 1.)
11. Numbers are equal
(Here, k==j & not j > k, hence the output is Numbers are equal)
12. Good Bye
if statement is executed. The `else` condition is satisfied.
13. Welcome
(since j=k=l=13, `if` condition is satisfied)
14. A=3 B=3 C=8
(The else condition is satisfied & the value of b is assigned to a i.e.3)
15. 2005 is a not a leap year
(In `goto` statement, program control is transferred to the `noleap` label and the above statement is displayed)
16. 9
(Since 'x' gets increased by 1 during the comparison `X=X++;`, the condition is not satisfied and the control goes to `else` and incremented value is decremented by 2, i.e. 11−2=9.)

17. 10
(In this example, 6 > 5 condition is satisfied and the displayed output as per `printf()` statement is 10.)
18. Person has incurred the loss of Rs 100
(200 < 300 condition is satisfied and the corresponding `printf()` statement is executed)
19. Answer out of three numbers (2 4 1)is 1
(Comparison is made between 2 ,4 and 1, and the smallest number 1 is displayed.)
20. y=9
(Comparison is made between three values and in this case z < y, hence the number 9 is displayed as per next statement followed by last `else`.)
21. 51
(Since hand=43 condition is satisfied, finally hand=43+7+1 is obtained.)
22. 1001
(Conditional statements are used and at last ×=1000+1=1001)
23. It is a digit
(In this case, `is`... function decides entered parameter's type, i.e. alphabet or number or neither or both, e.g. here `isalnum` function is used to detect p's type.)
24. It is a upper case character
(The `isupper` and `islower` functions are used to decide whether the given parameter is uppercase or lowercase.)
25. H
(Since `toupper` function converts the provided lowercase letter to uppercase)
26. Total Charges in Rs: 500 .
(Since `goto` statement transfers the control to specified label, here it is at charge2.)
27. × is even
(6%2=0 and corresponding `printf()` statement is executed)
28. L O V E
(Here, for loop is executed five times. Every time `for` loop gives new value of `ch` and corresponding `switch` statement is executed.)
29. 30 10 200 2
(Here, for loop is executed four times. Every time for loop gives new value of `ch` and corresponding `switch` statement is executed. Four operations are performed such as addition, subtraction, multiplication and division.)
30. 18
81
(The `continue` statement allows to execute `switch` statement twice which results in addition and multiplication of two numbers whose results are as above.)
31. Area of the square =25
Area of the Rectangle=24
Perimeter of the square =20
Perimeter of the Rectangle =20
(With `switch case` area and perimeters are calculated)
32. Area of a circle:- 28.26
Circumference of a circle:- 18.84
Diameter of a circle:- 6.00
(With `switch case` area, perimeter and diameters of a circle are calculated)
33. Volume of a Cylinder:- 226.08
Volume of a sphere:- 113.04
Volume of cone:- 75.36
Area of trapezium:- 44
(With `switch case` volume of a cylinder, sphere, cone and area of trapezium are calculated)
34. Entered letter is VOWEL e
(a,e,i,o,u and A,E,I,O,U are the vowels. With `switch case`, we have to detect entered letter is vowel or not)
35. Hours are 24
Minutes are 1440
(With `switch case`, number of hours and minutes of a day are calculated)
36. Seconds are 86400
(With `switch case`, number of seconds of a day is calculated)
37. 5th Month of Year is May
6th Month of Year is June
7th Month of Year is July
(With `switch case` three months (5th to 7th months) of a year are displayed)
38. Number of Months:- 7
Number of days :- 11
(With `switch case` the total months and days are calculated and displayed. `Mod` operation provides days and `divide` operation provides months.)
39. Maturity amount for 1 year: 5400.00
Maturity amount for 2 years: 6000.00
Maturity amount for 3 years: 6800.00
Maturity amount for 4 years: 7800.00

Maturity amount for 5 years: 9000.00
(With `switch case` the total maturity amount on Rs 5000 is calculated for various years with formulae and results are displayed)

40. Total Cost of Petrol 222.50
Total Cost of Diesel 156.00
Total Cost of Kerosene 111.50
(With `switch case` the total cost of Petrol, Diesel and Kerosene are calculated for the same quantity and the same have been displayed.)

41. Total cost of BPL 21 inch TV is Rs 6300
Total cost of Onida TV is Rs 8880
Total cost of LG 21 TV Rs 5760
(With `switch case` the total cost of different makes of TVs computed and the same have been displayed)

42. 32
4
(The `pow()` and `abs()` functions of C are used with `switch case`)

43. Total days 60
Total hours 1440
(With `switch case` the total days and hours are computed from the given numbers of seconds)

44. 2
3
1.00
(The library functions are used in `switch case` and values are computed)

45. 2
1.00
5.92
(The library functions `fmod()`, `floor()`, `log10()` and `ceil()` are used and `switch case` values are computed)

46. 1.00
0.00
1.62
(The library trigonometric functions are used and values are computed with `switch case`)

47. Factorial is 120
Summation from 1 to 10 is 55
Series summation is 36
(With `switch case` factorial of a number, summation of numbers between 1 and 10 and series summation have been performed)

48. 0 2
(With `switch case` and `static` keyword, 0 and 2 are displayed)

49. 501234
(With `switch case` numbers 501234 are displayed. After default all statements are executed.)

50. DC
(Refer ASCII table and using `swith cases`, the letters DC are displayed)

4.F Find the bug/s in the following program/s?

1. Curly brace is missing.
2. Warning message: Possibly incorrect assignment in function main.
3. No bug. `if(0)` is always false statement.
4. No Bug
5. Scope of `if()` block is not defined.
6. No Bug
7. `else` block is empty.
8. `printf()` in `if` block twice terminated.
9. `if` should not have multiple `else`.
10. Misplaced `else-if` structure.
11. No Bug
12. No Bug
13. No Bug
14. `default` block should have at least one statement.
15. No Bug
16. `continue` keyword.
17. Constant expressions are required.
18. Duplicate `case` defined, and double semicolon is present.

5 Loop Control Statements

CHAPTER OUTLINE

5.1 WHAT IS A PROGRAM LOOP?

A program loop is defined as a block of statements, which are frequently executed for certain number of times even though these statements come into view once in a program. This loop is also known as iterative structure or repetitive structure.

TABLE 5.1 Loops in C

for	*while*	*do-while*

for(expression-1;
expression-2;
expression-3)
statement;
	expression-1;
	while(expression-2)
	{
	statement;
	expression-3;
	}
		expression-1;
		do
		{
		statement;
		expression-3;
		}
		while(expression-2);

The C language supports three types of loop control statements and their syntaxes are described in Table 5.1.

`for` loop statement comprises of three actions. The three actions are placed in the `for` statement itself. The three actions initialize counter, test condition and re-evaluation parameters are included in one statement. The expressions are separated by semicolons (;).

The `for` statement is equivalent to `while` and `do-while` statement. The only difference between `for` and `do-while` is that in the former case, the logical condition is tested first and then the body of the loop is executed, whereas in the latter case test is performed after body of the loop.

Thus, in the `for` loop and `while` loop, the test is always performed at the beginning of the loop. The `for` and `while` loop fall under pre-test type. Whereas the `do-while` loop falls under post-test type. The `do-while` loop executes the body of the loop at least once regardless of the logical condition.

The body of the loop may not be executed at all times if the condition fails at the beginning. For example, in the following two statements, test condition is not proper at the beginning and hence no execution of statements.

```
for(a=10;a<10;a--)
printf("%d", a);
```

5.2 `for` LOOP

The `for` loop allows to execute a set of instructions until a certain condition is satisfied. Condition may be pre-defined or open-ended. The general syntax of the `for` loop will be as given in Figures 5.1, 5.2 and 5.3.

```
 for(initialize counter;test condition;
reevaluation parameter)
  {
  statement;
  statement;
  }
```

FIGURE 5.1 Syntax of `for` loop

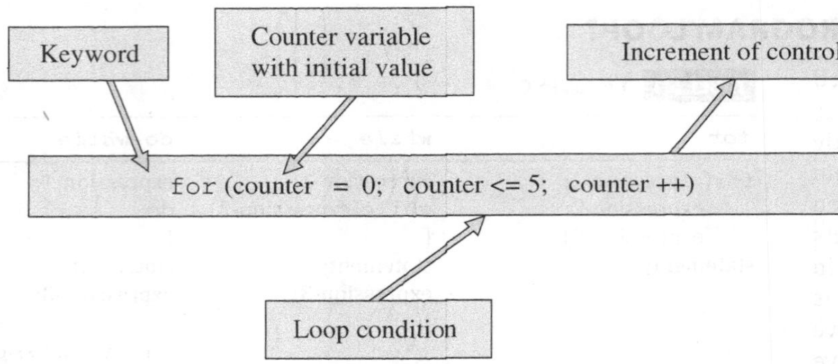

FIGURE 5.2 **`for` loop**

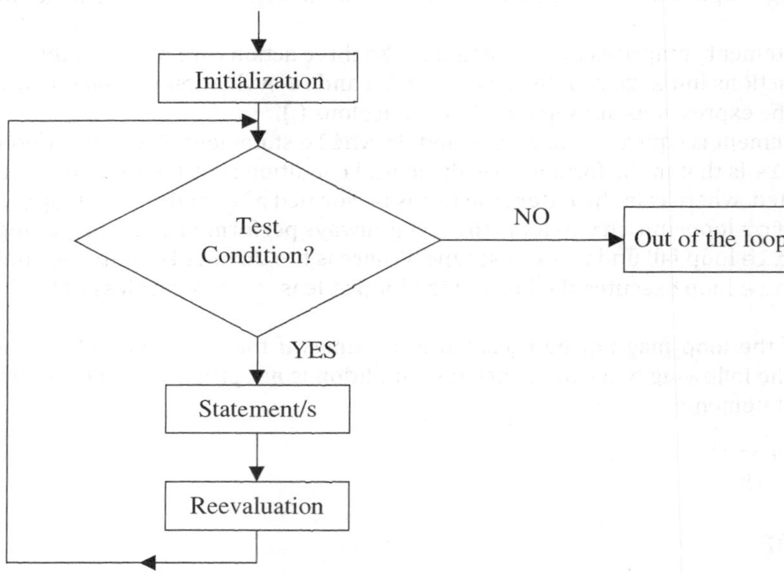

FIGURE 5.3 **Execution of `for` loop**

***Explanation*:**
The `for` statement contains three expressions which are separated by semicolons. Following actions are to be performed in three expressions.

The initialize counter sets a loop to an initial value. This statement is executed only once.

The test condition is a relational expression that determines the number of iterations desired or it determines when to exit from the loop. The `for` loop continues to execute as long as conditional test is satisfied. When the condition becomes false, the control of the program exits from the body of the `for` loop and executes next statement after the body of the loop.

The re-evaluation parameter decides how to make changes in the loop (quite often increment or decrement operations are to be used). The body of the loop may contain either a single statement or multiple statements. In case there is only one statement after the `for` loop, braces may not be necessary. In such a case, the only one statement is executed till the condition is satisfied. It is a good practice to use braces even for single statement following the `for` loop.

TABLE 5.2 Various formats of `for` loop

Serial No.	*Syntax*	*Output*	*Remarks*
1	`for(;;)`	Infinite loop	No arguments
2	`for(a=0; a<=20; )`	Infinite loop	'a' is neither incremented nor decremented
3	`for(a=0;a<=10;a++)` `printf("%d",a);`	Displays value from 0 to 10	'a' is incremented from 0 to 10. Curly braces are not necessary. Default scope of `for` loop is one statement after `for` loop
4	`for(a=10;a>=0;a--)` `printf("%d",a);`	Displays value from 10 to 0	'a' is decremented from 10 to 0

The syntax of `for` loop with only one statement will be shown in the third row of Table 5.2. The `for` loop can be specified by different ways, and it is as per Table 5.2.

5.3 NESTED `for` LOOPS

We can also use loops within a loop. In nested `for` loops, one or more `for` statements are included in the body of the loop. In other words, C allows multiple `for` loops in nested forms. There is no boundary on the number on nested loops. The number of iterations in this type of structure will be equal to the number of iterations in the outer loop multiplied by the number of iterations in the inner loop. The example given below is based on the nested `for` loops.

```
int i,j,a=0
for(i=0;i<=5;i++)
{
for(j=0;j<=5;j++)
      printf("%d",a++);
}
```

5.4 `while` LOOP

Another kind of loop structure in C is the `while` loop and the format is shown in Figure 5.4.

```
Syntax:

while(test condition)
{
  body of the loop
}
```

FIGURE 5.4 Syntax of `while` loop

The test condition is indicated at the top and it tests the value of the expression before processing the body of the loop. The test condition may be any expression. The loop statements will be executed till the condition is true, i.e. the test condition is evaluated and if the condition is true, then the body of the loop is executed. When the condition becomes false, the execution will be out of the loop.

The execution of the loop can be followed by the following flow chart (Figure 5.5).

The body of the loop may either contain single statement or number of statements. The same block can be repeated.

The braces are needed only if the body of the loop contains more than one statement. However, it is a good practice to use braces even if the body of the loop contains only one statement.

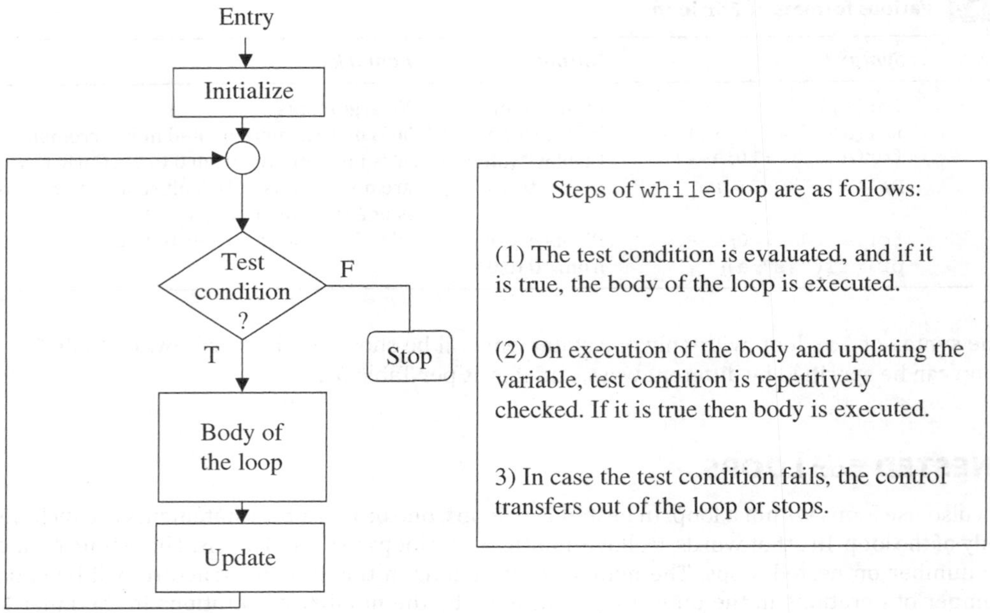

FIGURE 5.5 Steps of `while` loops

5.5 do-while

The format of `do-while` loop in C is given in Figure 5.6.

The comparison between the `while` and `do-while` loop is given in Table 5.3.

```
do
{
statement/s;
}
while(condition);
```

FIGURE 5.6 Syntax of `do-while` loop

TABLE 5.3 Comparison of the `while` and `do-while` loop

Serial No.	*while loop*	*do-while*
1	Condition is specified at the top	Condition is mentioned at the bottom
2	Body statement/s is/are executed when condition is satisfied	Body statement/s execute even when condition is false
3	No braces for a single statement	Braces are essential even when a single statement exits
4	It is entry controlled loop	It is exit controlled loop

5.6 do-while STATEMENT WITH while LOOP

The format of `do-while` with multiple `while` statements loop is given in Figure 5.7.

```
do
while(condition)
{
statement/s;
}
while(condition);
```

FIGURE 5.7 Syntax of `do-while` with multiple `while` statements

5.7 `break` STATEMENT

The keyword `break` allows the pro grammers to terminate the loop. The `break` skips from the loop or block in which it is defined. The control then automatically goes to the first statement after the loop or block. The `break` can be associated with all conditional statements.

We can also use `break` statements in the nested loops. If we use `break` statement in the innermost loop, then the control of the program is terminated only from the innermost loop.

The difference between the `break` and `exit()` is provided in Table 5.4.

TABLE 5.4 Difference between the `break` and `exit()`

Serial No.	*`break`*	*`exit()`*
1	It is a keyword	It is a function
2	No header file is needed	Header file `process.h` must be included
3	It stops the execution of the loop	Terminates the program

5.8 `continue` STATEMENT

The `continue` statement is exactly opposite to `break`. The `continue` statement is used for continuing the next iteration of loop statements. When it occurs in the loop, it dose not terminate, but it skips current iteration and control is transferred to the next iteration. It is useful when we want to continue the program without executing any part of the program. Table 5.5 gives the differences between `break` and `continue`.

5.9 `goto` STATEMENT

This statement does not require any condition. This is unconditional control jump. This statement passes control anywhere in the program, i.e. control is transferred to another part of the program without testing any condition. User has to define `goto` statement as follows.

TABLE 5.5 Difference between the `break` and `continue`.

`break`	*`continue`*
It is used to exit from current block or loop.	It is used to skip the current loop iteration and return the control to the next loop statement /iteration.
It terminates the loop.	It never terminates the loop/ program.
Control passes to the statement instantly following the body of the loop containing the break.	Control passes to the next statement.

```
goto label;
```

where the label name must start with any letter, label is the position where the control is to be transferred. Few examples are described in this chapter for the sake of understanding.

EXERCISES

5.A Fill in the blanks

1. A program loop is a ______ which are repeatedly executed for certain number of times.
   (a) defined block of statements
   (b) define sub-routine
   (c) none of the above

2. The default scope of any loop which is without ______ is one statement.
   (a) ()
   (b) { }
   (c) [ ]

3. The statements ______ of the `for` loop would keep on getting executed till the given condition is true.
   (a) inside the scope
   (b) outside the scope
   (c) none of the above

4. The initialize counter sets the counter to ______
   (a) starting value
   (b) final value
   (c) both (a) & (b)

5. Consider `int j=1`, the general syntax of `for` loop is `for(__; j<=9;_____)`.
   (a) `for(j=1;j<=9;j++)`
   (b) `for(;j<=9;)`
   (c) `for( j=1;j<=9)`

6. The general format of `for` statement is ________.
   (a) `for(`; test counter; increment/decremet counter)
   (b) `for(`initialise counter; test counter; increment/decremet counter)
   (c) `for(`initialise counter; test counter;)

7. Output of the following program is ________.

```
main()
{
  int i;
  clrscr();
  for(i=1;i<=printf("%d",i);)
  i++;
}
```

   (a) 12
   (b) 1
   (c) 112

8. In the `while()` loop, following one value makes the loop non-working.
   (a) −1
   (b) 1
   (c) 0

9. The loop ______-`while()`has two keywords.
   (a) `for`
   (b) `do`
   (c) `if`

10. The `while` statement must test condition that will finally become ______ otherwise the loop will run infinitely.
   (a) false
   (b) true
   (c) none of the above

11. The `while` loop is also referred to as ______.
   (a) entry controlled loop
   (b) exit controlled loop
   (c) middle controlled loop

12. In `do-while` loop, the statement `while` is terminated with ________.
   (a) , (comma)
   (b) ; (semicolon)
   (c) : (colon)

13. In ______ loop brackets are essential even if there is a single statement.
   (a) `while`
   (b) `do-while`
   (c) `for`

14. When it is needed to break the cycle of execution, ______ statement is used after satisfying the condition.
   (a) `exit();`
   (b) `break;`
   (c) `continue`

15. ______ is a library function.
   (a) `break`
   (b) `exit`
   (c) `continue`

16. The keyword ________ is used for transferring the control from one statement to other.
   (a) `switch`
   (b) `goto`
   (c) `struct`

17. The `for` loop structure is a ___ loop.
   (a) pre-test
   (b) post-test
   (c) none of the above

18. In the pre-tested loop, the body of the loop is executed ______ testing the logical condition.
   (a) before
   (b) after
   (c) none of the above

19. At least ____ time/s the body of the `do while` loop is executed.
    (a) one
    (b) two
    (c) none of the above

20. The keyword ______ is used to terminate the loop.
    (a) `break`
    (b) `goto`
    (c) none of the above

5.B. True or false

1. A loop repeatedly executes a block of statements for certain number of times.
2. The loop `for( ; ; )` is a non-working loop.
3. The `for( ; ; )` loop with no arguments can be executed.
4. The loop `for(a=1;a<20;a++)` will be executed for 20 times.
5. The `while(1)` is an infinite loop.
6. The loop cannot be nested.
7. Even if the condition is false, the `do-while` loop executes once.
8. The `do-while` loop must be terminated by semicolon.
9. The { } defines the block of the statement/s.
10. In case { } is not defined, following `for` statement, the default scope is one statement.
11. The `while` loop is a pre-test type of loop.
12. The `do-while` is a pre-test type of loop.
13. With `break` loop does not terminate.
14. The function of `continue` is the same as that of `break`.

5.C. Match the following correct pairs given in Group A with Group B

I

Group A		Group B	
Serial No.	**Loop**	**Serial No.**	**Number of Execution**
1.	`for(;;)`	A	Loop executes five times
2.	`for(j=1;j<=5;j++)`	B	Non-working loop
3.	`for(;;);`	C	Infinite loop

II

Group A		Group B	
Serial No.	**Loop**	**Serial No.**	**Number of Execution**
1.	`while(0)`	A	Wrong format of `while`
2.	`while(1)`	B	Non-working loop
3.	`while(a^10)`	C	Infinite loop

III

Group A		Group B	
Serial No.	**Expression**	**Serial No.**	**Output**
1.	`for(j=1; j<10;j++)`	A	10
2.	`for(j=1; j<=0;j--);`	B	987654321
3.	`for(j=9; j>0;j--)`	C	123456789

IV

Group A		Group B	
Serial No.	**Type of loop**	**Serial No.**	**Output**
1.	`while`	A	Condition is at the bottom
2.	`do-while`	B	Condition is at the top
3.	`for`	C	Initial and final values with step

V

Group A		Group B	
Serial No.	Types of Instruction	Serial No.	Output
1.	Control	A	Arithmetic instructions
2.	Arithmetic	B	Control the sequence of execution of instructions

Group A		Group B	
Serial No.	Types of Instruction	Serial No.	Output
3.	Declaration	C	Input/output operations
4.	Input output	D	Declaration of variable

5.D Select the appropriate option from the multiple choices given below

Problems on `for` loop

1. What will be the value of 'x' after the execution of the following program?

```
void main()
{
int k;
float x=1;
clrscr();
for(k=0;k<4;k++)
x*=.2;
printf("\nx=%g",x);
}
```

(a) x=0.0016
(b) x=0.0008
(c) x=1.6
(d) none of the above

2. What will be the value of 'f' after the execution of the following program?

```
void main()
{
  char k;
  float f=5;
  clrscr();
    for(k=1;k<=10;k++)
    {
    f-=.1;
    }
printf("\nf=%g",f);
}
```

(a) f=4
(b) f=-65
(c) f=66
(d) none of the above

3. What will be the value of variable 'sqsum' after execution?

```
void main()
{
 int i, sqsum=0;
 clrscr();
 for(i=1;i<=4;i++)
 {
  sqsum+=i*i;
 }
  printf("\nThe Sum of Squares %d",
   sqsum);
}
```

(a) sqsum=40
(b) sqsum=30
(c) sqsum= 20

4. In case the `for` loop statement is terminated by semicolon

(a) the compiler will flag error message and program will not compiled
(b) program will be executed, however, scope of the `for` loop will be NULL
(c) the termination will not affect the performance of the `for` loop

Problems on `while` loop

5. What will be the final value of 'c' after the execution of the following program?

```
void main()
{
int c=27,d=9;
clrscr();
while(d<=9)
{
```

```
d++;
printf("\n %d",++c);
}

}
```

(a) 28
(b) 27
(c) 26
(d) 9

6. How many times the `printf()`statement will be executed?

```
void main()
{
 int k;
 k=11;
 clrscr();
 while(k<10)
 {
 printf("Hi");
 --k;
 }
 }
```

(a) not a single time
(b) 11 times
(c) once
(d) 1

7. What will be the value of the variable 'sum'?

```
void main()
{
  int n=1245,k=1,sum=0;
  clrscr();
  while(n!=0)
  {
  k=n%10;
  sum=sum+k;
  k=n/10;
  n=k;
  }
printf("Sum %d ",sum);
}
```

(a) sum=13
(b) sum=12
(c) sum=10

8. What will be the output of the following program?

```
void main()
{
int x=11,y=40;
clrscr();
while(x!=0)
{
gotoxy(y--,3);
printf("%d",x%2);
x=x/2;
 }
 }
```

(a) 0011
(b) 1011
(c) 0010
(d) 0001

9. What will be the output of the following program?

```
void main()
{
 char c=48;
   clrscr();
   while(c!='5')
 {
   while(1)
   {
   printf("%c",c++);
   break;
   }
   }
}
```

(a) 012345
(b) 01234
(c) 1

10. What will be the output of the following program?

```
void main()
{
  char c=50;
  clrscr();
  while(c++!='5')
  {
  while(1)
  {
  printf("%c",c++);
  c+=2;
  break;
  }
  c--;
  printf("%c",c);
  break;
  }
}
```

(a) 45
(b) 35
(c) 25
(d) 50

Problems on `do-while` loop

11. What would be the final value of 'x' after the execution of the following program?

```
void main()
{
int x=1;
clrscr();
do    while(x<=7)
      {
      x++;
      } while(x<=5);
printf("\n x=%d",x);
}
```

(a) x=8
(b) x=6
(c) x=2
(d) none of the above

12. What will be the final values of 'x' and 'y'?

```
void main()
{
int x=1,y=1;
clrscr();
do    while(x<=8)
      {
      x++,y++;
      }  while(y<=5);
      printf("\n x=%d y=%d",x,y);
}
```

(a) x=9 y=9
(b) x=9 y=6
(c) x=6 y= 6
(d) none of the above

13.

```
void main()
{
int nm=0;
do
{
--nm;
printf("%d",nm);
nm++;
}
while(nm>=0);
}
```

In the above program

(a) the loop will run infinitely
(b) the program would not be compiled
(c) loop will not be executed

14. What will be the value of 's' after the execution of the following program?

```
void main()
{
int i=5,a=1;
int s=0;
clrscr();
do
{s=s+a++;
} while(a<=i);
printf("\b\bs=%d",s);
}
```

(a) s=15
(b) s=36
(c) s=40

15. How many `while` statements are possible in `do-while` loop?

(a) 2
(b) 1
(c) 3
(d) none of the above

16. The following one loop statement uses two keywords?

(a) `for` loop
(b) `do-while` loop
(c) `while` loop

17. Though the condition is false, the following loop statement executes once

(a) `for` loop
(b) `do-while` loop
(c) `while` loop

18. Of the following, only one loop statement is terminated by semicolon

(a) `for`
(b) `do-while`
(c) `while`

19. Which key you will use to terminate the infinite loop?

(a) `ctrl+alt+del`
(b) `ctrl+break`
(c) `ctrl+enter`

20. Which of the following one keyword you will apply to exit from the loop without increasing program code?

(a) `continue`
(b) `break`
(c) `goto`

21. The role of `continue` with loop is, it takes

(a) next iteration
(b) reduced iteration
(c) none of above

5.E What will be the output/s of the following program/s

Programs on `for` loop

1. Program to print numbers and their squares from 1 to 3 using `for` loop.

```
void main()
{
int i;
clrscr();
for(i=1;i<=3;i++)
{
printf("\n %2d %3d",i,i*i);
}
```

2. Program to print the numbers which are multiples of 5.

```
void main()
{
int i,x=5,j;
clrscr();
for(i=1;i<=10;i++)
{
      printf("%d ",i*x);
}
getche();
}
```

3. Program to print numbers and their square roots from 1 to 4 using `for` loop.

```
#include <math.h>
void main()
{
int i;
float a;
clrscr();
for(i=1;i<=4;i++)
{
printf("\n %d \t %.3f ",i,a=sqrt(i));
}
getche();
}
```

4. Program to print all integers up to 10 that are divisible by 10, using `for` and `if` loop.

```
void main()
{
int i,m=10;
clrscr();
for(i=1;i<=m;i++)
if(m%i==0)
printf("%d ",i);
getche();
}
```

5. Program to print the numbers from 1 to 5 in ascending and descending order.

```
void main()
{
int i=0;
clrscr();
for(;++i<=5;)
printf("%2d",i);
printf("\n\n");
for(;--i>=1;)
printf("%2d",i);
getche();
}
```

6. Program to print even numbers from 1 to 10.

```
void main()
{
int i,n=10;
clrscr();
for(i=1;i<=n;i++)
if(i%2==0)
printf("%d ",i);
getche();
}
```

7. Program to print even numbers which lie between 1 to 9. Using `for` loop and nested `if-else` with `break` and `continue` keywords.

```
void main()
{
int i=1;
clrscr();
for(;;)
    {
    if(i==9)
    break;
    else
    if(i%2==0)
    {
    printf("%d\t",i);
    i++;
    continue;
    }
    else
    {
    i++;
    continue;
    }
    }
    getche();
}
```

8. Program to print odd numbers from 1 to 10.

```
void main()
{
int i;
clrscr();
for(i=1;i<10;i++)
{
if(i%2==0)
continue;
printf("%d ",i);
}
getche();
}
```

9. Program to find factors of 45.

```
void main()
{
int i;
clrscr();
for(i=1;i<=45;i++)
{
      if(45%i==0)
    {
            printf("\t%d",i);
    }
}
getch();
}
```

10. Program to print factorial of 5 using `for` loop.

```
void main()
{
int i,m=5,fac=1;
clrscr();
for(i=1;i<=m;i++)
fac=fac*i;
printf("%d ",fac);
getche();
}
```

11. Some tricky program.

```
void main()
{
int x=0,y=1,z=1,sum,i,n=2;
clrscr();
for(i=1;i<=n;i++)
      {
      sum=x+y+z;
      printf(" %d %d %d %d ",
          x,y,z,sum);
          x=y,y=z,z=sum;
      }
getche();
}
```

12. Display ASCII values and corresponding characters.

```
void main()
{
char x;
int i;
clrscr();
for(i=65;i<=68;i++)
      {
      printf(" %d %c ",i,i);
      }
getche();
}
```

13. Program.

```
void main()
{
int i,c=5,d=2,x=1;
clrscr();
for(i=1;i<=c;i++)
x*=d;
printf("%d ",x);
getche();
}
```

14. Some mathematical problem.

```
void main()
{
int i,x=0;
float c;
clrscr();
for(i=1;i<=10;i++)
x=i+x;
c=(float)x/10;
printf("%.1f",c);
getche();
}
```

15. Some mathematical problem.

```
#include <math.h>
void main()
{
int i,n=2;
float x=0,y=0;
clrscr();
for(i=1;i<=n;i++)
{
x=x+(1/pow(i,2));
y=y+(1/pow(i,3));
}
printf("Value of x = %.2f",x);
printf("\nValue of y = %.2f",y);
getche();
}
```

16. Leap year program.

```
void main()
{
int y,x=0;
clrscr();
for(y=2000;y<=2007;y++)
     {
     if(y%4==0 && y%100!=0 ||
        y%400==0)
     {
     printf(" %d ",y);
     x++;
     }
     }
printf("\n\n%d",x);
getche();
}
```

17. Program on incrementaion and decrementation operators.

```
void main()
{
int n=2,a,b;
clrscr();
a=b=n;
printf("(++)       (--)\n");
printf("============");
for(;; a++,b--)
    {
    printf("\n%d\t%d",a,b);
    if(b==0)
    break;
    }
    getche();
}
```

18. Display numbers.

```
void main()
{
int i;
clrscr();
for(i=0;i<10;i++)
{
if(i%2==1)
continue;
printf("%d ",i);
}

for(i=4;i<10;i++)
{
if(i%2==0)
printf("\n%d",i);
break;
}
getche();
}
```

19. Cubes of 1 to 3 integers.

```
#include <math.h>
void main()
{
int i,x;
clrscr();
for(i=1;i<=10;i++)
      {
      printf("%d ",i*i*i);
      if(i==3)
      break;
      }
        getche();
}
```

20. Largest from an array.

```
void main()
{
int x[5]={5,15,3,10,7};
int i;
clrscr();

for(i=0;i<5;i++)
{
      if(x[i]>x[i+1])
      x[i+1]=x[i];
}
printf("%d\t",x[i]);
getche();
}
```

21. Program using few C functions.

```
#include <math.h>
void main()
{
int i,x;
float c;
clrscr();
printf("\n");
for(i=1;i<=25;i++)
{
c=sqrt(i);
x=floor(c);
if(c==x)
{
printf("\%4d",i);
}
}
getche();
}
```

22. Arrange numbers in ascending order.

```
void main()
{
int a=4,b=6,c=8,d=1,e=12,sum=0,i;
clrscr();
sum=a+b+c+d+e;
for(i=1; i<=sum;i++)
{
if(i==a || i==b || i==c || i==d || i==e)
printf("%4d",i);
}
getche();
}
```

23. Multiplication with repetitive addition method.

```
void main()
{
int a=3,b=4,c=0,d=0;
clrscr();
for(;;)
    {
    d=d+a;
    c++;
    if(c==b)goto stop;
    }
stop:printf(" %d * %d =%d",a,b,d);
getche();
}
```

24. Identify exact square numbers up to 100.

```
#include <math.h>
void main()
{
int i,x,count=0;
clrscr();
for(i=0;i<100;i++)
{
  x=sqrt(i);
  if(i==x*x)
  {
    printf("%d ",i);
    count+=1;
  }

}
getche();

}
```

25. Some mathematical problem.

```
void main()
{
int a=5,b=4,c=1,d=7,e=10,sum,i;
clrscr();
sum=a+b+c+d+e;
for(i=0; i<=sum;i++)
    {
if(i==a || i==b || i==c || i==d ||
   i==e)
    {
printf("\nThe Answer is : %d",i);
goto end;
    }
    }
    end:getche();
}
```

26. Prime number program.

```
void main()
{
int i=19,n;
clrscr();
    {
    for(n=2;n<i-1;n++)
    {
    if(i%n==0)
        {
        printf("\nThe number %d is
        not a prime ",i);
        getche();
        exit();
        }
    }
    printf("\nThe number %d is a
      prime ",i);
    getche();
    }
}
```

Programs on nested `for` loop

27. Some mathematical problem.

```
void main()
{
int i,j=0;
clrscr();
for(i=48;i<=49;i++)
    {
    for(j=49;j<=50;j++)
    printf( " %c%c",i,j);
    printf("\n");
    }
    getche();
}
```

28. Multiples of 1, 2 and 3.

```
#include <math.h>
void main()
{
```

```
int i,x,j;
clrscr();
for(i=1;i<=4;i++)
      {
      for(j=1;j<=3;j++)
      printf("%d ",i*j);
      printf("\n");
      printf("");

      }
         getche();
}
```

29. Prime number program.

```
#include<math.h>
void main()
{
int i,n=0,j,x;
clrscr();
printf("\n\n Prime numbers from 1 to
    15:-");
printf("");
for(i=1;i<=15;i++)
      {
       x=sqrt(i);
       for(j=2;j<=x;j++)
       {
       if(i%j==0)
       goto end;

       }
       printf("%d ",i);
       n++;
       end:;
 }
       printf("\n\n Total prime
         numbers from 1 to 15:- %d\n
         ",n);
      getche();
}
```

30. Display stars in specific order.

```
void main()
{
int x=3,i,j;
clrscr();
for(i=1;i<=x;i++)
      {
      for(j=1;j<=i;j++)
             {
             printf(" * ");
             }
      printf("\n");
      }
      getche();
}
```

31. Display numbers in ascending order.

```
void main()
{
int x[5]={5,15,3,10,7};
int i,j,temp;
clrscr();
for(i=0;i<5;i++)
         {
      for(j=i;j<4;j++)
      {
            if(x[i]>x[j+1])
            {
            temp=x[i];
            x[i]=x[j+1];
            x[j+1]=temp;
            }
      }
         }
for(i=0;i<5;i++)
printf("%d\t",x[i]);
getche();
}
```

32. Cube numbers up to 81.

```
#include<math.h>
void main()
{
int i, j, k=81;
clrscr();
for(i=1;i<k;i++)
{
for(j=1;j<=i;j++)
{
if(i==pow(j,3))
printf("\n %d",i);
}
}
getche();
}
```

33. Display symbols.

```
void main()
{
int x=2,i,j;
clrscr();
for(i=x;i>=1;i--)
```

```
        {
        for(j=1;j<=i;j++)
              {
              printf(" & ");
              }
        printf("\n");
        }
        getche();
}
```

34. Display symbols.

```
void main()
{
int x=3,i,j;
clrscr();
for(i=x;i>=1;i--)
      {
      for(j=1;j<=i;j++)
            {
            printf(" & ");
            }
      printf("\n");
      }
for(i=1;i<=2;i++)
      {
      for(j=i+1;j>=1;j--)
      {
      printf(" & ");
      }
      printf("\n");
      }
      getche();
}
```

35. Display numbers in some specific order.

```
void main()
{
int i,j;
clrscr();
for(i=1;i<=4;i++)
{
for(j=1;j<=i;j++)
{
 printf(" %d",i);
 }
 printf("\n");
}
printf("\n");
for(i=4;i>=1;i--)
{
 for(j=i;j>=1;j--)
{
 printf(" %d",i);
}
 printf("\n");
}
getche();
 }
```

36. Some tricky program.

```
void main()
{
int j,k;
clrscr();
for(j=0;j<1;j++)
for(k=j;k<=1;k++)
printf(" %d %d", j,k);
}
```

37. Some tricky program.

```
void main()
{
int j,k;
clrscr();
for(j=0;j<3;j++)
for(k=j;k<=2;k++)
printf(" %d", k+j);
}
```

38. Display numbers in some specific way.

```
void main()
{
int i,j;
clrscr();
          for(i=1;i<=3;i++)
          {
               for(j=i;j>=1;j--)
                {
                printf(" %d",j);
                }
                printf("\n");
          }
     for(i=3;i>=1;i--)
          {
               for(j=i;j>=1;j--)
                {
                 printf(" %d",j);
                }
                 printf("\n");
          }
 getche();
 }
```

39. Armstrong number program.

```
#include <math.h>
void main()
{
```

```
int n,d,x,j;
int k,cube;
clrscr();
     for(k=100;k<=300;k++)
     {
          cube=0;
          x=1;
          d=3;
          n=k;
          while(x<=d)
               {
               j=n%10;
               cube=cube+pow(j,3);
               n=n/10;
               x++;
               }
               if(cube==k)
               printf("\n%d",k);
     }
}
```

40. Program to display occurrence of numbers.

```
void main()
{
  int t,k,n=3,l,i;
  static int st[10];
  clrscr();
  for(l=1;l<=n;l++)
    {
     t=l;
     while(t!=0)
     {
     k=t%10;
     t=t/10;
     st[k]++;
     }
 }
 for(i=0;i<10;i++)
 if(st[i]>0)
 printf("\n %d Occurs %8d
   Times.",i,st[i]);
 getch();
 }
```

41. Display numbers in some specific way.

```
void main()
 {
 int i,j,x=3;
 clrscr();
 for(j=1;j<=x;j++)
     {
     for(i=1;i<=j;i++)
     printf("%3d",i);
     printf("\n");
     }
     printf("\n");
     for(j=x;j>=1;j--)
          {
            for(i=j;i>=1;i--)
               {
            printf("%3d",i);
               }
     printf("\n");
          }
     getche();
}
```

42. Display numbers in some specific way.

```
void main()
{
int k,l;
clrscr();
k=1;
while(k<=5)
{
        for(l=1;l<=k;l++)
        {
     printf("%d",k);
         }
printf("\n");
k++;
}
getche();
}
```

43. Display numbers in some specific way.

```
void main()
{
int k,l;
clrscr();
for(k=1;k<=5;k++)
{
    for(l=k;l>=1;--l)
     {
          printf(" %d",l);
     }
     printf("\n");
}
}
```

44. Display numbers in some specific way.

```
void main()
{
int k,l;
clrscr();
     for(k=1;k<=5;k++)
     {
       for(l=k;l<=5;l++)
```

```
        {
        printf(" %d ",l);
          }
            printf("\n");
    }
}
```

Programs on `while` *loop*

45. Program to display numbers from 1 to 9 using `while` loop.

```
void main()
{
int n=1;
clrscr();
while(n<10)
{
        printf("%d ",n);
        n+=1;
}
 getche();
}
```

46. Program to display odd numbers upto 10.

```
void main()
{
int n=1;
clrscr();
while(n<10)
{
        printf("%d ",n);
        n=n+2;
}
getche();
}
```

47. Count number of positives, negatives and zeros.

```
void main()
{
int i=-5,neg=0,pos=0,zer=0;
clrscr();
while(i<=5)
        {
        if(i<0)
        neg++;
        if(i==0)
        zer++;
        if(i>0)
        pos++;
        i++;
        }
        printf(" %d %d %d ",neg,zer,pos);
        getche();
}
```

48. Program on AND operation.

```
void main()
{
int j=2,k=3;
clrscr();
while(k>j)
 {
  printf(" %d ", k && j);
     k=k||j;
 }
}
```

49. Some numerical program.

```
void main()
{
int x[5]={1,1,1,1,1};
int y=x[0],i;
clrscr();
while(i<4)
{
y=y*2+x[i+1];
i++;
}
printf("%d\t",y);
getche();
}
```

50. Program to display string.

```
void main()
{
int i=0;
char a[5]={'A','s','h','o','k'};
clrscr();
printf("\nTransmitted
    information is:- ");
while(i<=4)
{
printf(" %c",a[i]);
i++;
}
printf(" \n Received information
    is:- ");
i=0;
while(i<=4)
{
printf(" %c",a[i]+3);
i++;
}
getche();
}
```

51. Program to display alphabets from a to z.

```
void main()
{
```

```
  char k='A';
  clrscr();
  while(k<='Z')
{
  printf("%c",k+32);
  k++
}
getche();
}
```

52. Program to calculate sum of first 10 numbers using static variable.

```
#include <math.h>
void main()
{
   static j,s;
   clrscr();
   j++;
   while(j<10;)
   {
     j--;
     s=s+abs(j);
     if(j==-10)
      break;
   }
   printf("%d",s);
}
```

53. Program to declare a character and find its ASCII value using `while` loop.

```
void main()
{
  char k='A';
  clrscr();
  while(k<=65)
{
  printf("%d ",k);
  k++;
}
gethe();
}
```

54. Program to display values from –1 to –5 using `while` loop.

```
void main()
{
int k=1;
clrscr();
while(k<5)
{
printf("%d",-k);
k++;
}
getche();
}
```

55. Program to display Fibonacci series upto 5.

```
void main()
{
int n=5,j=1,k=0;
clrscr();
while(k<=n)
{
printf(" %d ",k);
k=k+j;
printf("%d", j);
j=j+k;
}
getche();
}
```

56. Program to display even numbers from 0 to 8.

```
void main()
{
int n=0;
clrscr();
while(n<10)
{
     printf("%d ",n);
     n=n+2;
}
getche();
}
```

57. Program to display multiple of 5 upto 50.

```
void main()
{
int n=0;
clrscr();
while(n<50)
{
     printf("%d ",n);
     n+=5;
}
getche();
}
```

58. Program to display successive numbers which differ by 3 initiated from 1 upto 15.

```
void main()
{
int a=1,b=15;
clrscr();
while(b>a)
{
     printf("%d ",a);
     a+=3;
}
getche();
}
```

59. Program to display 10 to 1 numbers in descending order.

```
void main()
{
int a=1,b=10;
clrscr();
while(b>=a)
{
      printf("%d ",b);
      b-=1;
}
getche();
}
```

60. Program to display sum of first 10 numbers.

```
void main()
{
int a=0,b=10,sum;
clrscr();
sum=0;
while(a<=b)
{
      sum=sum+a;
      a=a+1;
}
printf("%d ",sum);
getche();
}
```

61. Armstrong number program.

```
void main()
{
int i,sum=0,n=370;
clrscr();
while(n>0)
      {
      i=n%10;
      n=n/10;
      sum=sum+i*i*i;
      }
      printf(" %d ",sum);
      getche();
}
```

62. Program on `static` keyword.

```
void main()
{
static k;
clrscr();
while(1)
{
k++;

while(1)
{
k++;

while(1)
{
if(k==8)
exit(0);
k++;
printf("\n %d",k);
}
}
}

}
```

63. Program to declare `static` variable.

```
void main()
{
static k;
clrscr();
while(k++)
{
printf("%d",k);
}
}
```

Programs on `do-while`

64. Program to display sum of first (1 to 9) 9 numbers.

```
void main()
{
int a=0,b=0,sum;
clrscr();
sum=0;
do
{
      sum=sum+a;
      a=a+1;
      b=b+1;
}
while(b<=9);

printf("%d ",sum);
getche();
}
```

65. Program to display separately the digits of an input number.

```
void main()
{
int n=123;
clrscr();
do
{
printf("%2d",n%10);
n=n/10;
}
```

```
while(n);
getche();
}
```

66. Program to display multiples of 15, which occurs up to 150.

```
void main()
{
int a=0,b=15;
clrscr();
do
{
      a=a+b;
      printf("%d ",a);
}
while(a<=135);
getche();
}
```

67. Program to display factorial of 6.

```
void main()
{
int a=6,b=1,fact=1;
clrscr();
do
{
      fact=fact*b;
      b=b+1;
}
while(b<=a);
printf("%d ",fact);
getche();
}
```

68. Program to display squares from 1 to 5.

```
#include<math.h>
void main()
{
int a=1,b=5,z;
clrscr();
do
{
      z=pow(a,2);
       printf("%d ",z);
      a=a+1;
}
while(a<=b);
getche();
}
```

69. Program to find cubes of numbers from 1 to 5 and arrange them in descending order.

```
#include<math.h>
void main()
{
int a=5,b=5,z;
clrscr();
do
{
      z=pow(a,3);
       printf("%d ",z);
      b=b-1;
      a-=1;
}
while(b>0);
getche();
}
```

70. Program to input binary number and find its decimal equivalent number.

```
void main()
{
int num=1111,rem,n,d,k=1,dec=0;
clrscr();
 n=num;
 do
 {
 rem=num%10;
 d=rem*k;
       dec=d+dec;
       k=2*k;
       num=num/10;
       }
 while(num>0);
 printf("Binary number =%d&
    corresponding it's decimal
    number=%d",n,dec);
}
```

71. Algebraic problem.

```
void main()
{
int a=11,b=5,sum=0;
clrscr();
do
{
      sum=sum+a;
      b--;
      a=a+11;
}
while(b>1);
printf("%d ",sum);

getche();
}
```

72. Program to display sum of first 9 numbers.

```
void main()
```

```
{
int a=9,b=10,sum=0;
clrscr();
do
{
      sum=sum+a;
      b--;
      a=a-1;
}
while(b>0);
printf("%d ",sum);

getche();
}
```

73. Program to display the series 1 3 7 13 21 31.

```
#include<math.h>
void main()
{
int a=1,b=2, c=42;
clrscr();
do
{
      printf("%d ",a);
      a=a+b;
      b=b+2;
 }
while(a<c);
getche();
}
```

74. Program to display sum of digits of 345.

```
void main()
{
int a,b,n=345,sum=0;
clrscr();
      do
      {
      a=n%10;
      sum=sum+a;
      n=n/10;
      }
      while(n>0);
      printf("%d",sum);
      getche();
}
```

75. Program to find multiplication of digits of number 567.

```
void main()
{
int a,n=567,mul=1;
clrscr();
      do
      {
      a=n%10;
      mul=mul*a;
      n=n/10;
      }
      while(n>0);
      printf("%d",mul);
      getche();
}
```

76. Program on AND operation.

```
void main()
{
int j=105,k=3;
j=j&k;
clrscr();
do
{
      printf("%d",j);
}
while(j==k);
}
```

77. Display numbers upto 7.

```
void main()
{
    static k;
    clrscr();
    do {
    printf(" %d ",k*-1);
    if(k==-7) k=1;
    }
    while(--k);
}
```

78. Use of static.

```
void main()
{
static k,j=0;
clrscr();
while(1)
    do {
    printf(" %d",k*-1);
    j++;
    if(j==7) exit(0);
    if(k==0) k=0;
    } while(k);
}
```

79. Some tricky program.

```
void main()
{
    int j=2,k=3,l=4;
```

```
clrscr();
 do
 {
 j=k=1;
 j++;
 printf("%d %d %d\n",
   j,k,l);
 k++;
 l++;
 }
while(l!=k);
 }
```

80. Program on Reversing.

```
void main()
{
char ch[]="1-May-2006",c,k=10;
clrscr();
  do
 {
putch(ch[k]);
k--;
}
while(k!=-1);
}
```

81. Numbers in some order.

```
void main()
{
int j=1;
clrscr();
do
{
printf("%d",++j);
++j;
}
while(j<12);
}
```

5.F Find the bug/s in the following program/s

Programs on `for` loop/s

1.

```
void main()
{
int x=7,y=0,z=7,i;
clrscr();
for(i=0;i<=x;i++);
      {
      y=x+i*z;
         printf(" %d",y);

      }
      getche();
}
```

2.

```
void main()
{
float i;
clrscr();
for(i=20;i>=19;i=i-0.25)
      {
      printf(" %2.2d",i);

      }
      getche();
}
```

3.

```
void main()
{
 int i;
  clrscr();
  for(i=1;i<5;)
  i++;
  printf("\nnumber: %5d   it's
    Square : %8d",i,i*i);
}
```

4.

```
void main()
{
int i,j=1,n=4;
float sum=1.0;
clrscr();

     for(i=1;i<=n;i++)
     {
     j=j*i;
     sum=sum+i/j;
     }
     printf("\n %.2f",sum);
     getche();
}
```

5.

```
void main()
{
 int i, sum=0,sqsum=0;
  clrscr();
  for(i=1;i<=5;i++)
 {
```

```
   printf("\nNumber: %5d it's
      Square : %8d",i,i*i);
}
 printf("\n========================
   ======");
  printf("\nThe Sum %6d Sum of
    Squares %9d",
sum,sqsum);
}
```

6.

```
void main()
{
int a=1,b=2,c=7,d=5,e=9,sum=0,i;
clrscr();
sum=a+b;
 for(i=sum; i<=sum;i--)
 {
   if(i==a || i==b || i==c || i==d
      || i==e)
{
printf("The Largest Number : %d",i);
exit();
}
 }
 }
```

7.

```
 #include <ctype.h>

 void main()
 {
 int c=1,i;
 char ch='z';
 clrscr();
 ch=toupper('ch');
for(i=65;i<=90;i++,c++)
if(ch ==i)
printf("\n'%c'is %dth Character in
Alphabetic. ",i,c);
 getche();
 }
```

8.

```
void main()
{
int i,fact=1;
clrscr();
    for(i=1;i<=4;i++);
    fact=fact*i;
    printf("\ Factorial of %d'
      is%d",i-1,fact);
getche();
}
```

9.

```
void main()
{
int i=1,fact=1,j;
clrscr();
    for(j=1;j<=4;j++)
    {
         while(i<=j);
           {
           fact=fact*i;
           i++;
           printf("\n Factorial of
                %d is:- %d",
                i-1,fact);
           }
    }
getche();
}
```

10.

```
void main()
{
int n,sum=0,number,R;
clrscr();
puts("Armstrong Numbers are as
   follows :");
for(n=1;n<=1000;++n)
{
while(number)
{
 R=number%10;
 sum=sum+R*R*R;
 number=number/10;
 }
 if(n==sum) printf(" %d ",n);
 sum=0;
 }
 }
```

11.

```
void main()
{
int h,m,s;
clrscr();
for(h=1;h<=12;h++)
{
 clrscr();
 for(m=1;m<=59;m++)
 {

   clrscr();
  for(s=1;s<=59;s++)
gotoxy(8,8);
```

```
printf("hh mm ss");
gotoxy(8,9);
printf("%d %d %d",h,m,s);
sleep(1);
}
 }
  }
```

12.

```
void main()
{
 char ch1,ch2,ch3;
 clrscr();
 for(ch1='A';ch1<='A';++ch1);
 for(ch2='A';ch2<='B';++ch2);
 for(ch3='A';ch3<='C';++ch3);
 printf("%c%c%c",ch1,ch2,ch3);
}
```

Programs on `while`

13.

```
void main()
{
int n=1;
clrscr();
while(n<10);
{
printf("%d ",n);
n=n+3;
}
getche();
}
```

14.

```
void main()
{
 int a=1,sum=0;
 clrscr();
while(a<10)
{
printf("%3d",a);
sum=sum+a;
a++;
}
printf("\n Sum of 10 numbers :%d",
    sum);
}
```

15.

```
void main()
{
  int a=5;
  long fact=1;
  clrscr();
    while(a>=1)
   {
      printf(" %d *",a);
      fact=fact*a;
      }
      printf(" = %d",fact);
 printf("\n Factorial of Given
    number is %ld",fact);
}
```

16.

```
void main()
{
int n;
clrscr();
printf("Enter the number up to 8:-");
scanf("%d",n);
while(n<9)
{
printf("%d ",);
n=n+1;
}
getche();
}
```

17.

```
void main()
{
int I=64;
char c='';
clrscr();
while(c=='Y')
{
printf("\t%c(%d)",i,i);
i++;
printf("\nPrint(Y/N)");
c=getch();
}
}
```

Programs on `do-while`

18.

```
void main()
{
int k=1;
clrscr();
do;
     {
     printf("\n %d",k);
     k=k+1;
     }
     while(k<=5);
```

```
        getche();
    }
```

19.

```
    void main()
    {
    chr i=65;
    clrscr();
    do
        {
        printf(" %c",i) i=i+1;
        }
        while(i<=90);
        getche();
    }
```

20.

```
    void main()
    {
    int num=678,sum=0,rev=0,digit;
    clrscr();
        do
        {
        digit=num-num\10*10;
        num=num/10;
        rev=rev*10+digit;
        sum=sum+digit;
        }
        while(num>0);
        printf("\n %d",rev);
        printf("\n");
        printf("\n %d",sum);
        getche();
    }
```

21.

```
    void main()
    {
    int i=10;
    clrscr();
    do
        {
        printf(" %d",i);
        i=i-1;
        }
        while(i>0 || i=5);
        getche();
    }
```

5.G Attempt the following programming exercises

1. Write a program to calculate sum of remainders obtained by dividing with modular division operations by 3 on 1 to19 numbers.
2. Write a program to display marks of a student in five subjects.
3. Write a program to find perfect square roots up to 100 starting from 1.
4. Write a program to find product of individual digits of a four digit number.
5. Write a program to display all characters from z to a with ASCII numbers.
6. Write a program to add all numbers which are divisible by 3 from 5 to 55.
7. Write a program to display numbers in multiples of 11.
8. Write a program to display three students' marks of three subjects and find total of individual students marks.
9. Write a program to find the prime numbers up to 35.
10. Write a program to find the leap years of 21st century.
11. Write a program to display stock market prices of 10 companies.

ANSWERS

5.A Fill in the blanks

1. (a) defined block of statements
2. (b) { }
3. (a) inside the scope
4. (a) starting value
5. (a) `for(j=1;j<=9;j++)`
6. (b) `for`(initialise counter; test counter;increment/ decremet counter)
7. (a) 12
8. (c) 0
9. (b) `do`

10. (a) false
11. (a) entry controlled loop
12. (b) ;(semicolon)
13. (b) `do-while`
14. (b) `break;`
15. (b) exit
16. (b) `goto`
17. (a) pre-test
18. (b) after
19. (a) one
20. (a) `break`

5.B True or false

1. T 2. F 3. T 4. F 5. T 6. F 7. T 8. T 9. T
10. T 11. T 12. F 13. F 14. F

5.C Match the following correct pairs given in Group A with Group B

I 1. C, 2. A, 3. B
II 1. B, 2. C, 3. A
III 1. C, 2. A, 3. B
IV 1. B, 2. A, 3. C
V 1. B, 2. A, 3. D, 4. C

5.D Select the appropriate option from the multiple choices given below

1. (a) x=0.0016
2. (a) f=4
3. (b) sqsum=30
4. (b) program will be executed however scope of the `for` loop will be NULL
5. (a) 28
6. (a) not a single time
7. (b) sum=12
8. (b) 1011
9. (b) 01234
10. (b) 35
11. (a) x=8
12. (a) x=9 y=9
13. (a) the loop will run infinitely
14. (a) s=15
15. (a) 2
16. (b) `do-while` loop
17. (b) `do-while` loop
18. (a) `do-while`
19. (b) `ctrl+break`
20. (b) `break`
21. (a) next iteration

5.E What will be the output/s of the following program/s

1. 1 1
2 4
3 9
(For each value of 'i', value of square of 'i' is printed. Since `for` loop is repeated for three times, the square of three numbers are printed.)

2. 5 10 15 20 25 30 35 40 45 50
(For each value of 'i' in the `for` loop, the corresponding number is obtained by multiplying 'i' with a constant 5. Here, 10 successive values are printed.)

3. 1 1.000
2 1.414
3 1.732
4 2.000
(Here, a `math.h` header file contains a function `sqrt()` which takes one parameter and returns square root of the parameter. The `for` loop is repeated for four times and `sqrt()` function is called with value of 'i' as a parameter and prints its square root.)

4. 1 2 5 10
(The % operator is used to check the remainder of the division operation. To enlist all numbers up to 10 that are divisible to 10, `if` statement is used within `for` loop. For each `if` with a condition 10 % num equals zero, value of the number gets printed.)

5. 1 2 3 4 5

5 4 3 2 1
(The variable 'i' is initialized to 0. Values of 'i' are printed by pre-incrementing first and then pre-decrementing in loops).

6. 2 4 6 8 10
(The % operator is used to enlist even numbers from 1 to 10. `If` statement is used within `for`loop.

For each `if` with a condition num % 2 equals zero, value of the number gets printed.)

7. 2 4 6 8
(All even numbers in the range 0 to 9 are printed using `continue` & `break` statement. With `continue` the current loop continues from beginning and `break` statement transfers control outside the current loop. Here, `for` loop is an infinite loop.)

8. 1 3 5 7 9
(All odd numbers between 0 through 10 are printed using `continue` statement only. For every even number, `for` loop is continued from first statement within `for` loop incrementing counter variable.)

9. Divisors of 45: 1 3 5 9 15 45
(In this programming example, `for` loop runs for 45 times. Each time 45 is divided by value of 'i'. The 'i' divides the number 45 with modulus operator (%) whose result would be exactly zero. Those 'i' which provide results zero after dividing are the divisors of 45.)

10. 120
(The factorial of 5 is calculated using `for` loop. The `for` loop is continued for five times. Each time 'fac' variable is multiplied by value of 'i' and result is stored in variable 'fac'.)

11. 0 1 1 2 1 1 2 4
(The `for` loop runs two times. First time, values of x, y, z, sum=x+y+z are printed. Further, value of y is assigned to x, z is assigned to y, sum is assigned to z. Next time, values of x, y, z, sum=x+y+z are printed.)

12. 65 A 66 B 67 C 68 D
(ASCII values of characters A, B, C, D are printed. When character variables are printed in integer form, their ASCII values are printed.)

13. 32
(x=x*d is calculated for five times. x=1 and d=2 are constants. With every execution of `for` loop, value of 'x' gets doubled. After five iterations value of 'x' becomes 32.)

14. 5.5
(Addition of numbers from 1 to 10 is calculated in `for` loop. Addition is an integer, i.e. 55. It is divided by an integer 10. Float typecast is used to convert the integer division into floating point number.)

15. Value of x = 1.25
Value of y = 1.12
(The `pow(x,y)` is a standard function defined in `math.h` header file and means 'x' to the power 'y'. values of 'x' and 'y' are calculated in `for` loop which runs twice.)

16. 2000 2004
2
(Leap years between 2000 through 2007 are determined using `for` loop. Values of 'x' are incremented each time. A leap year must be divisible by 4 and it should be divisible by 400 but not by 100.)

17. (++) (--)
============
2 2
3 1
4 0
(The `for` loop is terminated by `break` statement when value of variable 'b' becomes 0. The variables 'a' and 'b' are initialized to 2. With each execution of `for` loop, the variable 'a' is post incremented and 'b' is post decremented.)

18. 0 2 4 6 8
4
(Here, two `for` loops are used. Even numbers from 0 to 10 are enlisted in first `for` loop using `continue` statement. Second `for` loop starts from 4 to 10. With first occurrence of even number, `for` loop is terminated using `break` statement.)

19. 1 8 27
(Here, cube of first three numbers is calculated in `for` loop which terminates when value of 'i' becomes 3 due to `break` statement.)

20. 15
(Largest number from an array of five elements is to be detected and dispalyed. Two consecutive numbers are compared. If the first number is larger than the second number, they are interchanged. In this way, the last element is the largest in an array.)

21. 1 4 9 16 25
(The perfect square numbers from 0 to 25 are determined using `sqrt()` function defined in `math.h` header file. It is stored in floating point. The `floor()` function rounds off the floating point number to a lower integer, i.e. 4.5 is converted to 4.0.)

22. 1 4 6 8 12
(The numbers are arranged in ascending order. All numbers are added and addition is stored in variable 'sum'. The `for` loop runs for 'sum' number of times in

incrementing order. When variable 'i' equals any of the variables a,b,c,d,e in ascending order, value of 'i' is printed.)

23. 3 * 4 = 12
(Multiplication is performed with repetitive addition. First operand is added to other variable which is initialized to 0 and this step is repeated until for 'second operand' number of times.)

24. 0 1 4 9 16 25 36 49 64 81
(The perfect square numbers between 0 through 100 are enlisted. In the `for` loop, each number is checked for a perfect square by first taking its square root and then taking square of it. If both numbers are matched, the number is a perfect square.)

25. The Answer is :1
(The smallest number is determined using `for` loop. All numbers are added and addition is stored in the variable 'sum'. The `for` loop is executed for 'sum' number of times. The `for` loop is terminated with `goto` statement when variable 'i' equals to any of the numbers given in `for` first time.)

26. The number 19 is a prime
(A number 19 is checked for being a prime number. The `for` loop is used for checking the divisibility of number 19 starting from 2. If number is not divisible, it is a prime number.)

27. 01 02
11 12
(Refer ASCII table)

28. 1 2 3
2 4 6
3 6 9
4 8 12
(Example of nested `for`. Outer `for` loop is for the number to be multiplied by 1,2,3. Outer `for` loop here runs for four times.)

29. Prime numbers from 1 to 15:-1 2 3 5 7 11 13
Total prime numbers from 1 to 15: 7
(Prime numbers from 1 to 15 are checked by using nested `for` loop. Outer `for` loop is for total numbers to be checked (here 15). Inner loop runs 'square root' number of times. Here, `goto` statement is used for transferring the control.)

30. *
* *
* * *
(Two `for` loops are used, for displaying stars in particular order, one within the other. Outer `for` loop is for the number of rows. Inner `for` loop is for the number of columns. Inner loop runs for number of times equal to the current value of the variable in outer loop.)

31. 3 5 7 10 15
(Here, array elements are arranged in an ascending order using two `for` loops in nested form. Outer loop runs for number of times equal to array elements. Inner loop runs for array length –1 number of times. If 'i'th element is greater than 'i+1'th element, the elements are swapped, else next numbers are checked.)

32. 1
8
27
64
(The number of cubes from 1 to 81 is enlisted. Two `for` loops are used. Outer loop variable is to be checked for being cube. Inner loop is for the number whose cube is outer loop variable. The `pow()` function is used for finding cube of number.)

33. & &
&
(Two `for` loops are used, for displaying symbols in particular order, one within the other. Outer `for` loop is for the number of rows. Inner `for` loop is for the number of columns & is executed in decrementing order.)

34. & & &
& &
&
& &
& & &
(Two nested `for` loops are used for displaying symbols in particular order. Outer `for` loop is for the number of rows. Inner `for` loop is for the number of columns and is executed in decrementing order. The inner `for` loop in second nested `for` loop is incrementing order.)

35. 1
2 2
3 3 3
4 4 4 4

4 4 4 4
3 3 3
2 2
1
(Two nested `for` loops are used for displaying numbers in particular pattern. Outer `for` loop is

for the number of rows. Inner `for` loop is for the number of columns and runs `for` 'i' number of times in incrementing order. In second nested `for`, outer and inner `for` loop run in decrementing order. In each execution of `for` loop, value of 'i' is printed for 'j' number of times.)

36. 0 0 0 1
(Two `for` loops are used. Inner `for` loop is executed for two times. In the 1st execution, value of 'i' and 'j' are printed which are 0. In 2nd execution, the value of 'i' is 0 and 'j' is 1)

37. 0 1 2 2 3 4
(Two `for` loops are used. Outer `loop(j)` executes for 3 (0 to 2) times. Inner loop starts from (k=j) and runs upto k=2. With each execution, the value of (j+k) is printed.)

38. 1
2 1
3 2 1
3 2 1
2 1
1
(In the 1st nested `for` loop, outer loop(i) is for number of rows in ascending order. The inner `for` loop(j) is for number of columns and runs in decrementing order, printing values of 'j'. In 2nd nested `for` loop, outer loop(i) is for number of rows in descending order and inner `for` loop(j) is for number of columns and runs in decrementing order printing values of 'j'.)

39. 153
(Here, an Armstrong numbers 100 through 300 are detected and displayed. The `for` loop is used for checking each number, all digits are separated. Sum of cube of all digits is added. This number is checked with original number. If both numbers are equal, the number is Armstrong number.)

40. 1 Occurs 1 Times.
2 Occurs 1 Times.
3 Occurs 1 Times.
(Occurrence of 1, 2, 3 are checked between the numbers 1 to 3 and stored them in `array st []`.)

41. 1
1 2
1 2 3
3 2 1
2 1
1
(In the 1st nested `for` loop, outer loop(j) is for number of rows in ascending order (1 to 3) and inner `for` loop(i) is for number of columns and runs in incrementing order printing values of 'i'. In 2nd nested `for` loop, outer loop(j) is for number of rows in descending order (3 to 1) & inner `for` loop(i) is for number of columns and is run in decrementing order printing values of 'i'.)

42. 1
2 2
3 3 3
4 4 4 4
5 5 5 5 5
(Here, the numbers are printed in specific format using outer `while` loop and inner `for` loop. Variable 'k' is initialized to1. `while` loop is executed till 'k' is less than 5.The `for` loop is started from 1 and executed up to value of i=k.)

43. 1
2 1
3 2 1
4 3 2 1
5 4 3 2 1
(Two `for` loops are used. Outer(k) is in incrementing order (1 to 5). Inner is in decrementing order (l=k) to 1. Value of l is printed.)

44. 1 2 3 4 5
2 3 4 5
3 4 5
4 5
5
(Numbers from 1 to 5 are printed in a specific format. For each value of 'k' from 1 to 5, inner loop `for` is executed.)

45. 1 2 3 4 5 6 7 8 9
(The `while` loop is used to run the loop till the condition is true. In this, value 'n' is initialized to 1.The statements following the `while` condition n<10 are executed for nine times.)

46. 1 3 5 7 9
(The variable 'n' is initialized to 1, while the condition for n<10 is checked and loop is executed for each true. In loop, 'n' is printed and incremented by 2 to get the next odd number.)

47. 5 1 5
(The `while` condition i<=5 is checked and according to that corresponding actions are taken. In this example, the number of positives, negatives and zeros are to be counted from –5 to +5.)

48. 1
(Example is on logical AND operator. If the condition evaluated is true, then gives output 1 else 0.)

49. 31
(In this, till the `while` condition is true, arithmetic operation for evaluating the value of 'y' is performed.)

50. Transmitted information is:- A s h o k
Received information is:- D v k r n
(The `while` loop is executed for each true case and we get the entered data. In next `while`loop, entered character ASCII value is incremented by 3 and corresponding character is printed. This example is for encryption of the data.)

51. abcdefghijklmnopqrstuvwxyz
(The variable 'k' is assigned character A, then ASCII value of 'k' is incremented by 32 which gives lower case letter a .Thus, a to z are displayed with `while` loop.)

52. s=55
(Static variable preserves the value of variable. Default value of static variable is 0. Here, 'j' is declared as static variable whose value is preserved until the program is being executed.)

53. 65
(The variable 'k' is assigned a letter A. In `while` loop, ASCII value of 'k' is compared. If true, then ASCII value of character is printed.)

54. -1-2-3-4
(Here, 'k' is assigned equal to 1. In the `while` loop, negative of 'k' is printed and then 'k' is incremented. Loop is executed until the condition is true.)

55. 0 1 1 2 3 5
(Fibonacci series is obtained by adding previous two numbers. First two numbers are fixed 1 and 1. In the `while` loop, new element obtained is compared with number entered as limit of the series.)

56. 0 2 4 6 8
(This program displays even numbers from 0 to 8. Here, 'k' is assigned equal to 0 and then incremented to get next even number.)

57. 0 5 10 15 20 25 30 35 40 45
(This program displays numbers which are multiple of 5 up to 50. `while` condition n<50 is used here. In this, each number is incremented by 5 and printed.)

58. 1 4 7 10 13
(This program displays successive numbers differing by 3 from 1 to 15, 'a' is initialized to 1 and then incremented by 3 every time.)

59. 10 9 8 7 6 5 4 3 2 1
(This program is to display numbers from 1 to 10 in descending order. In this example, number 10 is assigned to a variable and then decremented by 1 for each true in the `while` loop.)

60. 55
(This program is to print the sum of numbers from 1 to 10. The 'sum' variable is assigned value 0 and the variable 'a' equal to 1. For each true of `while` loop condition, value of 'a' is added to 'sum' and incremented.)

61. 370
(Armstrong number is the number in which sum of individual digits cube is equal to the number itself. Each individual digit is obtained by taking modulo of number and then the number is divided by10.)

62. 3 4 5 6 7 8
(Static variable preserves the value of the variable. In this, 'k' is declared as static and last value of 'k' is used for further operations.)

63. NO OUTPUT GENERATED
(To declare a static variable, precede the variable definition with keyword `static`.)

64. 45
(This program displays the sum of numbers from 1 to 9 using `do-while` loop. In the `do-while` loop, loop is executed once compulsorily and then condition is checked. For each true, loop is then executed.)

65. 3 2 1
(This program is to display separately digits of an input number using `do-while` loop. Last digit is obtained by modulo operation and then dividing the number by 10.)

66. 15 30 45 60 75 90 105 120 135 150
(This program is to display numbers multiple of 15 up to 150 using `do-while` loop. The variable 'a' is equal to 0 and b=15.The 'b' is added to 'a' to get next multiple of 15.)

67. 720
(This program is to display the factorial of 6 using `do-while` loop. Here, fact=1, fact is multiplied by 'b' and 'b' is then incremented. For

each true of `do-while` loop condition, loop is executed.)

68. 1 4 9 16 25
(This program displays squares of numbers from 1 to 5 in ascending order using `do-while` loop. Header file `math.h` is included for `pow( , )` function. First parameter is number and second is the power of the number and here it is 2.)

69. 125 64 27 8 1
(This program displays cube of numbers from 1 to 5 in descending order using `do-while` loop. Header file `math.h` is included for `pow( , )` function. First parameter is number and second is the power of the number and here it is 3.)

70. Binary number =1111 & corresponding it's decimal number=15
(This program gives the decimal equivalent of input binary number.)

71. 110
(a=11, b=5, sum=0, a is incremented by 11 and added to sum. 'b' is then decremented and `do-while` loop condition b>=1 is checked.)

72. 45
(This program displays the sum of numbers from 1 to 9 using `do-while` loop. Here, values assigned to the different variables are a=9, b=10, sum=0.The variable 'a' is added to sum, b decremented, a decremented. The `do-while` loop condition b>0 is checked. If true, `do-while` loop is executed.)

73. 1 3 7 13 21 31
(This program displays series from 1 to 42 in a specific sequence. a=1, b=2, b added to a, b incremented by 2, if a<c, loop is executed again and again.)

74. 12
(This program performs the addition of individual digits of 345 using `do-while` loop, sum=0, last digit is obtained by modulo operation and then added to sum. The number then is divided by 10 and loop is executed for each true of `do-while` loop condition.)

75. 210
(This program performs the multiplication of individual digits of 567 using `do-while` loop, mul=1, last digit is obtained by modulo operation and then multiplied to mul. The number then divided by 10 and loop executed for each true of `do-while` loop condition.)

76. 1
(This program performs ANDing operation of two numbers bit by bit. Two input numbers are given. ANDing of these two numbers gives the output.)

77. 0 1 2 3 4 5 6 7
(This program displays the numbers up to 7 using `do-while` loop. 'k' is declared as static variable (which preserves the value of variable) and value of 'k' is printed. The default value of static variable is 0.)

78. 0 0 0 0 0 0 0
(The `do-while` loop is used inside a `while` loop. The 'k' and 'j' are declared as static variable. In `do-while` loop, value of 'k' is printed When j=7 or k=0, `do-while` loop is terminated.)

79. 5 4 4
(In `do-while` loop, j and k are made equal to 'l'. The 'j' is incremented, and their values are printed. 'k' and 'l' are then incremented. When l!=k condition fails, the loop is terminated.)

80. 6002-yaM-1
(The `do-while` loop is used to print the reverse of input data using `putch()`. When k!=-1 condition fails, the loop is terminated.)

81. 24681012
(This program prints the number in some order using `do-while` loop. The j=1.The 'j' is then pre-incremented and printed. When j<12 condition fails, loop is terminated.)

5.F Find the bug/s in the following program/s

1. Omit semicolon from `for` statement.
2. `%f` is needed instead of `%d` in `printf` statement.
3. Statements following `i++` should be enclosed within curly braces {} as scope of `for` loop.
4. `(float)i/j` is expected in sum statement.
5. Numbers are not added repetitively to the variables 'sum' and 'sqsum'.
6. All the five values of the variables should be added to variable 'sum' which is not done.
7. Replace 'z' in place 'ch' in ch= statement.
8. Semicolon is not needed in `for` statement.
9. Semicolon is not needed in `while`.
10. number=n should be placed before `while` in `for` loop.
11. Scope of `for` loop is not defined.

12. `for` statements are terminated by semicolon. `for` with semicolon does not carry meaning.
13. Semicolon at the end of `while` loop is not expected.
14. No Bug.
15. 'a' is not decremented in the while loop.
16. & is missing in `scanf` and 'n' variable in `printf`-statements.
17. Variable c should be initialized with 'Y'.
18. Semicolon is not expected in `do`.
19. `chr` should replace with `char`, and semicolon is missing in `printf`.
20. Instead of "\" division "/" is expected in digit statement.
21. i= =5 is expected.

6

Arrays

CHAPTER OUTLINE

6.1 DEFINITION OF AN ARRAY

An array is a collection of multiple elements which has same type of data. Array stores homogeneous (same data type) data contiguously in memory, and that too under one variable name, i.e. single name is assigned to the entire array elements. It stores either all integers or all floating point numbers or all characters.

Its data items can be called as element. One can access individual elements of an array using subscript, and subscript begins with at 0. Name of the array and subscript are associated. The subscript is to be enclosed within square brackets, and it is to be placed at the right of the array name. For example, in `num[0]`, `num` is the name of the array and 0 is the subscript. With this example, the first element of array can be accessed. Similarly, one can access the other elements of the array by changing the subscript.

6.2 DECLARATION OF ONE-DIMENSIONAL ARRAY

Array must be declared first and then values are to be assigned to its elements while writing the program in C. Values are not stored while declaration of the array. Memory is reserved depending on the number of elements specified in the array when the array is initialized. One-dimensional array elements are specified with one subscript. In other words, individual elements of a one-dimensional array are accessed by specifying a single subscript.

General syntax for declaration of one-dimensional array is as follows.

```
data_type name[length];
```

Here, in this case, `data_type` indicates the type of data elements to be stored in the array. Name of the array is `name`. Number of values to be stored in the array is indicated by the `length` and it is enclosed within the square bracket.

With this syntax, array of different data types can be declared as follows:

```
int num[5];
char ch[5];
float m[10];
```

The size of an array can be computed by knowing the number of memory locations needed to individual data and number of data elements in the `array(length)`. In the following examples, the arrays are declared. Their sizes can be computed.

The size of the array `int num [5];` is 10 because each integer needs two memory locations to store it, and length of the array is 5. Thus, the size of the array is 2*5=10. Similarly, one can compute size of character array, float arrays, etc.

5 memory locations are needed for `char ch[5];`

40 memory locations are needed for `float m [10];`

6.3 ONE-DIMENSIONAL ARRAY INITIALIZATION

The Array initialization can be done as follows:

```
int num[5]={5,4,3,2,1};
```

In this case, the array `num` with 5 elements is initialized. List of elements to be initialized is enclosed within the braces. Similarly, character array is initialized as follows:

```
char ch[2]={'a','b'};
```

Data in the array can be placed with the following program.

```
main()
{
int i=0,num[5];
clrscr();
printf("Enter the numbers:");
while(i<5)
{
scanf("%d",&num[i]);
i++;
}
getche();
}
```

In the above example, an array with the name num with a set of five elements is declared and elements of array are prompted by the user through the keyboard. The programmer can see the output of the above program on running it using C compiler.

One-dimensional array elements are stored contiguously in memory. The Figure 6.1 shows the memory locations and values stored in the array as cited above.

In Figure 6.1, array elements are 10, 20, 30, 25 and 50, and they can be stored in memory locations starting from 65516. Each element, in this case, requires two memory locations. Programmer may note that memory locations shown above may be different when the same program runs with the same compiler on other systems.

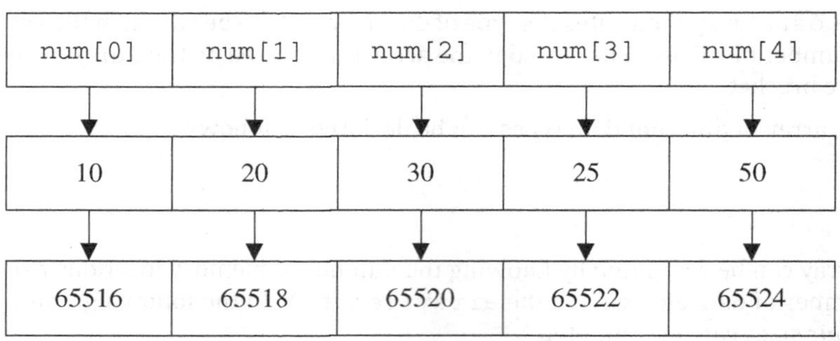

FIGURE 6.1 **Storage of one-dimensional array**

6.4 ACCESS TO ONE-DIMENSIONAL ARRAY ELEMENTS

Individual element of an array can be accessed by specifying the subscript number in the bracket following the array name. Array elements are numbered starting from 0. The first element of the array is num[0], second is num[1] and so on.

Subscript to the array specifies an exact element in the array.

***Example*:**

```
num[0]=1; /* First element*/
num[1]=2;
num[2]=4;
num[3]=2;
num[4]=5;
```

The number within the bracket represents the element position in array. First array element is `num[0]`, second `num[1]` and so on. The value of the array position is given on the right side of the above statements.

6.5 PRINTING ONE-DIMENSIONAL ARRAY ELEMENTS

Array elements can be printed on the screen using `printf` statement. Here, the loop is to be used.

Example:

```
for(i=0;i<10;i++)
{
printf("num[%d]=%d\n",i,num[i]);
}
```

6.6 INITIALIZATION OF TWO-DIMENSIONAL ARRAY

Two-dimensional array can be initialized as follows.

```
int empl[2][2] = {{1,2},{4,5}};
```

Here, in this example, the elements of two rows and two columns are initialized. The internal pairs of braces are not obligatory. The same array can be initialized as under.

```
int empl[2][2] = {1,2,4,5};
```

We can also read the elements of the array through the keyboard by using nested loops.

A simple program is illustrated on two-dimensional array.

```
void main()
    {
    int i,j;
    int num[3][3]={{1,2,3},{4,5,6},{7,8,9}};
    clrscr();
    printf("Elements of two-dimensional array:\n\n");
    for(i=0;i<=2;i++)
    {
    for(j=0;j<=2;j++)
    printf("%5d",num[i][j]);
    printf("\n");
    }
    getche();
    }
```

Output

Elements of two-dimensional array:

```
1 2 3
4 5 6
7 8 9
```

6.7 INITIALIZATION OF THREE-DIMENSIONAL ARRAYS

Three-dimensional array can be initialized as follows.

```
int num[3][3][3] =
                                    { 1,2,3,
4,5,6,
7,8,9,

1,4,7,
2,5,8,
3,6,9,
1,4,4,
2,4,7,
  8,8,5};
```

Here, we can also read the elements of the array through the keyboard by using nested loops.

An example on three-dimensional array is as follows.

```
void main()
{
int i,j,k;
int num[2][2][2]={1,2,3,4,5,6,7,8};
clrscr();
printf("Elements of three-dimensional arrays:\n\n");
for(i=0;i<=1;i++)
{
printf("\n");
for(j=0;j<=1;j++)
{
        for(k=0;k<=1;k++)
        printf("%5d",num[i][j][k]);
        printf("\n");
    }
}
getche();
}
```

Output

Elements of three-dimensional arrays:

```
1 2
3 4

5 6
7 8
```

6.8 ARRAYS AND POINTERS

In this chapter, so far we have seen the declaration and the initialization of an array. We can have array of integers or array of floating point numbers or array of characters. An individual element of any array can be accessed by the subscript to the array.

We can also access the individual elements by pointers. The compiler defines array name by itself an address or pointer. It points to the address of the first element (0th) of an array. The elements of the array together with their addresses can be displayed by using array name itself.

The following example explains the operation of array and pointer.

```
void main()
{
    int i,num[5]={10,20,30,40,50};
    int * ptr;
    clrscr();
    ptr=num;
    printf("Elements of an array with pointer:");
    for(i=0;i <=4;i++)
    printf(" %d",*&(ptr[i]));
    getche();
}
```

In the above program, an integer array `num` is declared and initialized. Here, `ptr` is an integer pointer. Pointer `ptr` points to the `num` by the statement `ptr=num;`. We can access every element of an array with the pointer.

One can see more programs given in the Section 6.E for detailed understanding.

6.8.1 Array and Function

We can pass elements of an array to the function from the `main`. Here, in the programming example given below, the total elements and array name are passed as argument to the function, and by invoking function one can display elements or one can make operations on the array elements.

```
void main()
{
    int i,num[5]={10,20,30,40,50};
    clrscr();
    printf("Elements of an array with pointer:");
    for(i=0;i<=4;i++)
    printf(" %d",num[i]);
    arry(5,num);
    getche();
}
    arry( int p,int q[5])
    {
    int j;
    printf("\nElements in the function: ");
    while(p>0)
    {
    for(j=4;j>=p;j--);
    printf(" %d",q[j]);
    p--;
    }
    }
```

Output
Elements of an array with pointer: 10 20 30 40 50
Elements in the function: 50 40 30 20 10

EXERCISES

6.A Fill in the blanks

1. In `int x[10];` the number 10 specified in the square bracket represents the ______.

   (a) 10 addresses
   (b) 10 values
   (c) 10 lines

2. Each array element is stored in eparate ______.

   (a) memory locations
   (b) pages
   (c) directory

3. The array `int x[5];` can hold values in between ______ to ______.

   (a) −32768 to 32767
   (b) 0 to 255
   (c) −32768 to 32768

4. In `int x[5]={2,3,4,5,6};` the base address is 65564, then the location of element 2 is ______.

   (a) 65564
   (b) 65566
   (c) 65568

5. In `int x[3]= {1,2,3};` the address of `x[2]` is 65498, i.e. e base address of the array is ______.

   (a) 65494
   (b) 65492
   (c) 65496

6. Output of the following program is ______.

```
void main()
{
  int x[]={1,2.2,3},i;
  clrscr();
  printf("%f",x[1]);
}
```

   (a) the program will not run
   (b) the program will run with warning messages
   (c) none of the above

7. The 1st element according to C compiler physically is a ______.

   (a) 2nd element
   (b) 0th element
   (c) 1st element

8. In `long k[4]` the total memory occupied by the array is ______.

   (a) 16
   (b) 8
   (c) 4

9. When in between two arrays of the same data type, if the values are interchanged then ______.

   (a) address of elements are also changed
   (b) only base address of the array is changed
   (c) none of the above

10. In `int x[3] if x[0]=12 and x[2]=26`, then `x[3]` is ______.

    (a) 0
    (b) 15
    (c) garbage value

11. Array element counting starts from zero, hence the statement `int x[0]` holds ______.

    (a) nothing
    (b) one integer value
    (c) one char value

12. If in `char c[]="Hello"` the H is stored at 65470, then the o is stored at ______.

    (a) 65474
    (b) 65475
    (c) 65480

13. Array element of two dimensions are stored in ______.

    (a) subsequent memory locations
    (b) alternate memory locations
    (c) any location

14. In ______, values of the array elements are passed to function.
    (a) call by value
    (b) call by reference
    (c) none of the above

15. In ______, addresses of the array elements are passed to function.
    (a) call by value
    (b) call by reference
    (c) none of the above

16. Fast access of array elements can be done using ______.
    (a) pointer
    (b) call by value
    (c) call by reference

17. One-dimensional array needs only ______ subscript.
    (a) one
    (b) two
    (c) both of the first two

18. An array is a collection of multiple elements of ______ data type.
    (a) dissimilar
    (b) same
    (c) none of the above

19. In `int x[5]`, the `x` represents a ______.
    (a) character
    (b) variable name of the array
    (c) none of the above

20. An array stores elements ______ in the memory.
    (a) randomly
    (b) non sequentially
    (c) contiguously

21. How many rows and columns are there in `int num[2][3]={ {1,2,3},{4,5,6} };`?
    (a) two rows and three columns
    (b) three rows and two columns
    (c) none of the above

22. What are the values of first row in `int num[2][3]={ 1,2,3,4 };`?
    (a) 1,2,3
    (b) 2,3,4
    (c) 1,2,4

23. What are the values of second row in `int num[2][3]={ 1,2,3,4 };`?
    (a) 1,2,3
    (b) 2,3,4
    (c) 4,0,0

24. What is the output of `int num[2][3]= { {1,2,3,4},{3,4,5,6} };`?
    (a) 1,2,3
    (b) 2,3,4
    (c) compilation error

25. What is the value of `a[1]` in static `int [3];`?
    (a) 1
    (b) 2
    (c) 0

6.B True or false

1. An array is a collection of elements of similar data type.
2. There is no boundary checking in C for arrays.
3. When an array is declared memory is reserved for it.
4. Array can be defined of any data type but not of `struct` data type.
5. Array elements are stored contiguously in memory locations.
6. The array name itself is an address.
7. The `stdin()` is a pre-defined stream.
8. Character array always ends with NULL char.
9. Array cannot be declared as `static`.
10. Array can be declared as constant.
11. Matrix operations can be easily manipulated using arrays.
12. The `scanf()` reads character from array.
13. If any array cannot be filled completely, the blank spaces turn to wastage of memory.
14. Array of pointers is collection of addresses.
15. Elements in array of pointers cannot be addresses of array components.
16. Default initial component values of an array are zeros when declared with `static` keyword.

6.C Match the following correct pairs given in Group A with Group B

I Group A / Group B

Serial No.	Declaration	Serial No.	Values
1.	`int x[3]`	A	{2.2,3.3,4.5}
2.	`float f[3]`	B	{1,2,3}
3.	`long [3]`	C	"CCC"
4.	`char[3]`	D	{30000, 258951, 45874}

II Group A / Group B

Serial No.	Element (`int x[4];`)	Serial No.	Address
1.	`x[0]`	A	65462
2.	`X[3]`	B	65466
3.	`X[2]`	C	65460
4.	`X[1]`	D	65464

III Group A / Group B

Serial No.	Element (`float x[4];`)	Serial No.	Address
1.	`x[0]`	A	65464
2.	`X[3]`	B	65468
3.	`X[2]`	C	65460
4.	`X[1]`	D	65472

IV Group A / Group B

Serial No.	Element (`char x[4];`)	Serial No	Address
1.	`x[0]`	A	65464
2.	`X[3]`	B	65463
3.	`X[2]`	C	65461
4.	`X[1]`	D	65462

V Group A / Group B

Serial No.	Element (`int x[4]={5,4,3,2};`)	Serial No.	Value
1.	`x[1]`	A	5
2.	`X[0]`	B	2
3.	`X[2]`	C	3
4.	`X[3]`	D	4

6.D Select the appropriate option from the multiple choices given below

1. What will be the value of `*x`?

```
void main()
{
  int *x;
  char in[10]="10";
  clrscr();
  sscanf(in,"%d",x);
  printf("\n Value of int x :
      %d",*x);
}
```

(a) 10
(b) 012
(c) "1"

2. What will be the output of the following program?

```
void main()
{
  int j[]={10,20,30,40,50};
  int m[]={2,4,6,1,3};
  int l[]={1,2,3,5,3},k;
  for(k=0;k<5;k++)
      l[k]=j[k]-m[k]+l[k];
        clrscr();
          for(k=0;k<5;k++)
        printf(" %d ", l[k]);
        getche();
}
```

(a) 9 18 27 44 50
(b) 11 22 33 36 50
(c) 9 18 27 42 50

3. What is the output of the following program?

```
void main()
{
  int j[]={5,4,3,2,1};
  int m[]={5,4,3,2,1};
```

```
  float l[]={2.0,2.2,2.2,2.2,2.2};
  float k;
  for(k=0;k<5;k++)
      l[k]=(float)((j[k]+m[k])/l[k]);
        clrscr();
          for(k=0;k<5;k++)
      printf(" %5.2f ", l[k]);
}
```

(a) 5.00 3.64 2.73 1.82 0.91
(b) 5.00 4.96 3.45 2.64 1.25
(c) 5.00 3.64 3.12 1.52 1.01

4. What is the output of the following program?

```
void main()
{
  char a[]={'A','B','C','D','E','F'};
  char b[]={'0','1','2','3','4','4'};
  char c[6],k;
      for(k=0;k<6;k++)
      c[k]=a[k]+b[k];
      clrscr();
      for(k=0;k<6;k++)
      printf("%c ", c[k]);
}
```

(a) q s u w y z
(b) Q S U W Y Z
(c) K J L M N O

5. What will happen if you enter (at run time) more values into an array than is its capacity?
(a) program will be terminated
(b) run time error message displayed
(c) array will be expanded

6. What will happen if you assign values in few locations of an array?
(a) rest of the elements will be set to 0
(b) compiler error message will be displayed
(c) possible system crash

7. When an array is passed to function, in real what gets passed ?
(a) address of the array
(b) Element numbers
(c) values of the array

8. Which is the correct statement to declare an array?
(a) `int x[]5;`
(b) `int x[5];`
(c) `int x{5}'`

9. The array name itself is pointer to
(a) 0th element
(b) 1st element
(c) last element

10. The array name itself is a
(a) constant pointer objet
(b) pointer
(c) address
(d) none of the above

11. If `int x[5],*p;` and `p=x;` then which of the following operation is wrong?
(a) `x++;`
(b) `p++;`
(c) `p=x;`

12. In `int x[3];` the base address of `x` is 65460, the elements are stored at
(a) 65460, 65462, 65464
(b) 65460, 65461, 65462
(c) 65460, 65464, 65468

13. In `int j[4]`, the `sizeof(j)` and `sizeof(int)` will display the value
(a) 8,2
(b) 2,8
(c) 2,2

6.E What will be the output/s of the following program/s?

One-dimensional array

1. Display few array elements.

```
#include <math.h>
void main()
{
  int i,marks[5]={55,56,67,
     78,64};
  clrscr();
  for(i=2;i<=4;i++)
  printf("\n %d",marks[i]);
  getche();
}
```

Explanation: Array elements from third position, i.e. 67, onwards are displayed on the screen.

2. Display characters defined in the array.

```
#include <math.h>
void main()
```

```
{
  char name []={'a','m','i','t'};
  int i;
  clrscr();
  for(i=0;i<=4;i++)
  printf(" %c",name[i]);
  getche();
}
```

Explanation: Contents of string array are displayed on the screen.

3. Use of %s for displaying array elements.

```
#include <math.h>
void main()
{
  char name []={'A','M','O','L'};
  int i;
  clrscr();
  for(i=0;i<=4;i++)
  printf(" %s",name);
  getche);
}
```

Explanation: Contents of string array are displayed on the screen 5 times.

4. Display characters together with ASCII (Decimal) and ASCII HEX.

```
void main()
{
char arr[6]={'H','e','l','l','o','!'};
int i;
clrscr();
  printf("Entered characters are:-");
  printf("\n Char ASCII ASCIIHEX ");
  printf("\n----------------------");

  for(i=0;i<6;i++)
  printf("\n \t%c \t%d \t%x",arr[i],
     arr[i],arr[i]);
    printf("\n--------------------");

  printf("\n");
  getche();
}
```

Explanation: Hello! is displayed. Equivalent ASCII numbers and HEX ASCII of each character of Hello! are displayed.

5. Sum of numbers from 1 to 10.

```
#include <math.h>
void main()
{
  int i,sum=0,num[]={1,2,3,4,5,6,7,
     8,9,10};
  clrscr();
  for(i=0;i<=9;i++)
  sum=sum+num[i];
  printf(" %d",sum);
  getche();
}
```

Explanation: Addition of 1 to 10 is performed in this program. Therefore, answer is 55.

6. Multiplication table of 6.

```
void main()
{
  int i,ans,num[5]={1,2,3,
     4,5};
  clrscr();
  for(i=0;i<=4;i++)
  {
  ans=num[i]*6;
  printf("\n %d*%d=%d",6,num[i],ans);
  }
}
```

Explanation: Multiplication table of 6 from 1 to 5 is displayed.

7. Factorial of 5.

```
void main()
{
  int i,m=1,num[5]={1,2,3,4,5};
  clrscr();
  for(i=0;i<=4;i++)
  m=m*num[i];
  printf("Total is %d ",m);
  getche();
}
```

Explanation: Program is for factorial of 5.

8. Arrange numbers in ascending order.

```
void main()
{
  int i,k,temp,num[6]={4,6,8,
     3,2,10};
  clrscr();

  for(i=0;i<=5;i++)
  {
  for(k=i+1;k<5;k++)
     {
        if(num[i]>num[k])
```

```
            {
              temp=num[i];
              num[i]=num[k];
              num[k]=temp;
            }
        }
    }
    for(i=0;i<6;i++)
    printf("\n %d",num[i]);
  getche();
  }
```

Explanation: Bubble sorting is used for arranging numbers in ascending order.

9. Reversing text and a number.

```
void main()
{
  char name[7]={'M','A','L','A','L'
      ,'A','M'};
  int i,rev[]={4,5,6};

  clrscr();
  for(i=6;i>=0;i--)
  {
  printf(" %c",name[i]);
  }
  printf("\n");
  for(i=2;i>=0;i--)
  {
  printf(" %d",rev[i]);
  }

getche();
}
```

Explanation: The text and numbers are reversed in this program.

10. Display array elements with pointer.

```
void main()
{
  int j[4]={2,3,4,5};
  int i;
  clrscr();
  for(i=0;i<=3;i++)
  printf(" %d",*(j+i));
  getche();
}
```

Explanation: With pointer, elements of array are displayed.

11. Show the memory locations where array elements are stored.

```
void main()
{
  int j[4]={2,3,4,5};
  int i;
  clrscr();
  for(i=0;i<=3;i++)
  {
  printf(" %d ",j[i]);
  printf("is stored at Location
      %u ", &j[i]);
  printf("\n");
  }

  getche();
}
```

Explanation: Elements with locations are displayed.

12. Passing array elements to a function.

```
void main()
{
  int i,numbers[5]={21,25,55,67,87};
  clrscr();
  for(i=0;i<5;i++)
  display(numbers[i]);
  getche();
}
  display(int m)
  {
  printf(" %d",m);
}
```

Explanation: Function is called from the `main()` five times and the elements are displayed.

13. Passing array elements to a function and to find their locations.

```
void main()
{
  int i,numbers[5]={11,22,33,
      44,55};
  clrscr();
  for(i=0;i<5;i++)
  display(&numbers[i]);
  getche();
}
  display(int *m)
  {
  printf(" %d %u",*m,*&(m));
  }
```

Explanation: Elements with locations are displayed using call by reference.

14. Passing all the array elements to a function.

```
void main()
```

```
{
  int i,numbers[5]={11,22,33,
     44,55};
  clrscr();
  for(i=0;i<5;i++)
  display(&numbers[i],5);
  getche();
}
  display(int *m,int p)
  {
  printf(" %d",*m);
}
```

Explanation: All the elements of array are passed to the function and are displayed using call by reference. Here, two parameters are used in the function.

15. Display few numbers of an array with pointer.

```
void main()
{
  int k,a[4]={1,2,3,4};
  int *ptr;
  clrscr();
  ptr=a;
  for(k=0;k<=3;k++)
  printf(" %d",*&ptr[k]+1);
  getche();
}
```

Explanation: Elements of array from second position are displayed using pointer.

16. Multiplication with array elements by some integer.

```
void main()
{
  int j,a[4]={5,10,15,20};
  int *pointer;
  clrscr();
  pointer=a;
  for(j=0;j<=3;j++)
  printf(" %d",pointer[j]*3);
  getche();
}
```

Explanation: Elements of array are multiplied with 3 and the result is displayed using pointer.

17. Store numbers in an array with pointers.

```
void main()
{
  int *arr[5];
  int a=31,b=19,k=40,l=71,c=32,z;
  clrscr();
  arr[0]=&a;
  arr[1]=&b;
  arr[2]=&k;
  arr[3]=&l;
  arr[4]=&c;
  for(z=0;z<=4;z++)
  {
  printf(" %d",*(arr[z]));
  }
  getche();
}
```

Explanation: Elements at different positions in array are stored and the same are displayed using pointer.

18. Find the smallest, largest and sum of their squares.

```
void main()
{
int a[4]={ 2, 4, 6, 1};
int i,big,little,sum;
clrscr();
  little=big=a[0];
  for(i=0;i<=3;i++)
  {
      if(a[i]>big)
      big=a[i];
      if(a[i]<little)
      little=a[i];
      }
      sum=big*big+little*little;
      printf("\n Largest=%d
         \n Smallest=%d \
         nSum of their squares
         =%d",big,little,sum);
      getche();
}
```

Explanation: Largest and smallest elements of an array are found and then their addition of squares are computed and results are displayed.

19. Searching a number in an array.

```
void main()
{
int a[7]={ 2,4,6,1,8,7,3};
int i,num=7;
clrscr();
  for(i=0;i<=6;i++)
{
if(num==a[i])
```

```
printf("\n The number %d is at
    %dth position in the array ",
    num,i+1);
}
getche();
}
```

Explanation: Element 7 is searched in the entire array and its position is found and displayed.

20. Searching a number in an array and its occurrence for number of times.

```
void main()
{
int a[7]={ 2,4,1,5,8,5,3};
int i,num=5,x=0;
clrscr();
  for(i=0;i<=6;i++)
  {
  if(num==a[i])
  {
printf("\n The number %d is at %dth
    position in the array",num,i+1);
  x=x+1;
  }
  }
printf("\n The number %d appeared %d
    times ",num,x);
getche();
}
```

Explanation: Element 5 is searched in the entire array and it is found at two positions and the same is displayed.

21. Sum of an array elements and their average.

```
void main()
{
int a[5]={17,12,15,14,18};
int i,sum=0;
float avg;
clrscr();

  for(i=0;i<=4;i++)
  {
  sum=sum+a[i];
  }
  avg=(float)sum/5;
  printf("Sum =%d \n
     Average=%.2f",sum,avg);
  getche();
  }
```

Explanation: Sum and average of five elements of array are calculated and results are displayed.

22. Addition of two array elements.

```
void main()
{
int i,array[]={2,3,4};
int array1[]={1,2,3};
clrscr();
printf("Element of first Array +
    Second Array= Addition\n");
  for(i=0;i<=2;i++)
  {
  printf("\n %d + %d = %d",array[i],
     array1[i],array[i]+array1[i]);
  }
getche();
}
```

Explanation: Addition of elements of two arrays is computed and results are displayed.

23. Display town name and its PIN code.

```
void main()
{
char town[6]={'N','A','N','D','E',
    'D'};
int j,pin[6]={4,3,1,6,0,3};
clrscr();
  for(j=0;j<6;j++)
  printf("%c",town[j]);
  printf(" - ");
  for(j=0;j<6;j++)
  printf("%d",pin[j]);
  getche();
}
```

Explanation: NANDED is displayed with its PIN code number.

24. Display number of days of different months.

```
void main()
{
int mont[12]={31,28,31,30,31,30,31,
    31,30,31,30,31};
int j;
clrscr();
  for(j=0;j<=3;j++)
  {
  printf("\n Month [%d] of a
     year contains %d days.
     ",j+1,mont[j]);
  printf("\n");
  }
getche();
}
```

Explanation: Number of days of four months is displayed.

25. Find even and odd numbers from an array.

```
void main()
{
  int a[5]={5,2,3,1,4};
  int i,even=0,odd=0;
  clrscr();
      for (i=0;i<=4;i++)
      if(a[i]%2==0)
      even++;
      else
      odd++;
      printf("\n %d even numbers and
          %d odd numbers ",even,odd);
      getche();
}
```

Explanation: Total even and odd numbers of an array are counted with counters and the same are displayed.

26. Find the number of negative, positive and zeros.

```
void main()
{
int a[6]={-5,-20,0,-11,40,0};
int i,neg=0,pos=0,zeros=0;
clrscr();

  for(i=0;i<=5;i++)
  {
  if(a[i]<0)
  neg++;
  if(a[i]>0)
  pos++;
  if(a[i]==0)
  zeros++;
  }
printf("\n%d negative numbers,
    %d positive and %d
    zeros",neg,pos,zeros);
  getche();
}
```

Explanation: Number of negative, positive and zero elements of an array are computed and the same is displayed.

27. Modular operation.

```
void main()
{
  int a[6]={1,3,9,12,18,6};
  int i,x=0,y=0;
  clrscr();
      for(i=0;i<=5;i++)
      {
      if(a[i]%3==0)
      x++;
      else
      y++;
      }
  printf("\n %d and %d ", x,y);
  getche();
}
```

Explanation: Number of array elements which are divisible by 3 and not divisible by 3 are found and the same are displayed.

28. Count number of characters of a string array.

```
#include <string.h>
void main()
{

  char name[7]={'V','A','I','B','H'
      ,'A','V'};
  int i,length;
  clrscr();
  length=strlen(name);
  printf("\n Length of the string
      is %d ",length-1);
  getche();
}
```

Explanation: Length of string array is calculated. Here, the total elements including null are 8. Instead of specifying 8 in the program, 7 is specified and because of this the result displayed is 7.

29. Logical thinking oriented problem and program.

```
void main()
{
  int x[]={1,2,3,4,5,6,7},k;
clrscr(); for(k=0;k<5;k++)
printf(" %d ",x[0]);
}
```

Explanation: First element is displayed for 5 times.

30. Program on determination of size of an array.

```
void main()
{
  int x[]={1,2,3,4,5,6,7};
  clrscr();
  printf(" %d ",sizeof(x));
}
```

Explanation: Size of array is determined. Since 7 integer numbers is specified, total size should be 14 (7*2).

31. Display some message using an array.

```
void main()
{
  char msg[]="C is Easy";
  int i=0;
  clrscr();
  while(msg[i])
  putc(msg[i++],stderr);
}
```

Explanation: Message "C is Easy" is displayed.

32. Display some message using an array.

```
void main()
{
char ch[]="System\0Programming";
char k=0;
clrscr();
while(ch[k]!=0)
  printf("%c",ch[k++]);
getch();
}
```

Explanation: Message "System" is displayed. Here, until 0 comes in the array, the characters are displayed.

33. Display some message using an array (tricky).

```
void main()
{
  char ch[]="System Programming";
  char j=0,k=strlen(ch);
  clrscr();
  while(j!=k)
  printf("%c",ch[j++]);
}
```

Explanation: System Programming is displayed.

34. Display the values of integer, char and float variables.

```
void main()
{
int a=100;
char c='C';
float p=3.14;
char spf[20];
clrscr();
sprintf(spf,"%d %c %.2f",a,c,p);
printf("\n%s",spf);
}
```

35. Display some message using an array.

```
void main()
{
char name[]="programming in c";
int x=0;
clrscr();
while(name[x]!=0)
{
printf("%c",name[x]-32);
x++;
}
}
```

Explanation: Message is displayed.

36. Display numbers in some specific pattern using an array.

```
void main()
{
int a[]={1,2,3,4,5,6},k;
int b[]={6,5,4,3,2,1};
clrscr();
for(k=0;k<6;k++)
printf(" %d ",a[k]+b[k]);
}
```

Explanation: Addition of two array elements is performed and the same are displayed.

37. Some typical program.

```
void main()
{
  int a[]={1,2,3,4,5,6,7},k=0,s=0;
  clrscr();
  for(;k<7;k++,s=s+a[k]);
  printf("\ns=%d",s);
}
```

38. Display some numbers using an array.

```
void main()
{
  int a[]={1,2,3,4,5,6,7};
  clrscr();
  printf("%d %d %d ",*a,*(a+1),*(a+3));
}
```

39. Some typical program.

```
void main()
{
  char c[2]={'C','A'};
  int x[3]={1,2,3};
  float f[3]={2.1,5.2,8.9};
  clrscr();
  printf("%c %d %g ",*
     (c+1),*(x+2),*(f+2));
}
```

40. Addresses of an array elements.

```
void main()
{
long j[]={1,2,3,4,5},*lp,
   k=0;
lp=j;
  clrscr();
  for(;k<5;k++)
  {
```

```
printf(" %u",lp);
lp++;
  }
}
```

Two-dimensional array

41. Program to print array elements in reverse order.

```
void main()
  {
  int i,j;
  int a[3][3]={{9,8,7},{6,5,4},
      {3,2,1}};
  clrscr();
  printf("Elements of an array in
      reverse order.\n\n");
      for(i=2;i>=0;i--)
      {
      for(j=2;j>=0;j--)
      printf("%5d",a[i][j]);
      printf("\n");
      }
getche();
}
```

Explanation: Elements of two-dimensional arrays in the reverse order are displayed.

42. Display odd numbers using two `for` loops.

```
void main()
{
  int j,k,x[4][2]={1,2,3,4,5,6,7,8};
  clrscr();
  for(j=0;j<4;j++)
  for(k=0;k<1;k++)
      printf(" %d",x[j][k]);
}
```

Explanation: Odd numbers of an array are displayed using two loops.

43. Display numbers in some sequence using two `for` loops.

```
void main()
{
  int j,k,x[4][2]={1,2,3,4,
      5,6,7,8};
  clrscr();
  for(j=0;j<3;j++)
  for(k=0;k<1;k++)
  printf(" %d",x[j][k]);
}
```

44. Display some numbers using an array.

```
void main()
{
  int x[3][3]={4,5,6,7,8,9,10,11,12};
  int j,k;
  clrscr();
  for(j=0;j<3;j++)
  for(k=0;k<3;k++)
  printf(" %d ",x[k][j]);
}
```

More than two-dimensional array

45. Display numbers using two `for` loops.

```
void main(){
  int
array[2][2][2][2]={1,2,3,4,5,
    6,7,8};
  int a,b,c,d;
  clrscr();
for(b=0;b<2;b++)
for(a=0;a<2;a++)
  printf(" %d ",array[a][b]
      [0][0]);
}
```

Explanation: Few elements of array are displayed.

46.

```
void main()
  {
      int a,b,c;
      int mat[3][3][3] ={ 1,2,3,
          4,5,6,
          7,8,9,
          1,4,7,
          2,5,8,
          3,6,9,
          1,4,4,
          2,4,7,
          8,8,5 };
  clrscr();
      for(a=0;a<3;a++)
      {
      printf("\n");
      for(b=0;b<3;b++)
  {
      for(c=0;c<3;c++)
      printf("%3d [%u] ",mat
          [a][b][c],&mat[a]
          [b][c]);
      printf("\n");
  }
  }
  }
```

Explanation: Elements of 3 *3 matrices and along with their locations are displayed.

6.F Find the bug/s in the following program/s

1.

```
void main()
{
  int a[5]={5,2,3,1,4};
  int i,result=1;
clrscr();

      for(i=0;i<=5;i++)
      result=result*a[i];
      printf("\nresult of multipli-
         cation =%d ",result);
      getche();
}
```

2.

```
void main()
{
int a[10]={5,6,7,8,9,3,4,5,4,6};
int i,sum=0;
float avg;
clrscr();
  for(i=0;i<=9;i++)
  {
  sum=sum+a[i];
  }
  avg=(float)sum/10;
  printf("\nSum of ten numbers
     =%d",&sum);
  printf("\nAverage of ten
     numbers=%.2f",&avg);
  getche();
}
```

3.

```
void main()
{
  char s[15];
  int i;
  clrscr();
  puts("Enter a String : ");
  gets(s);
  puts("Reverse Siring :");
  for(i=15;i>=0;i--)
  printf("%c",s[i]);
}
```

4.

```
void main()
{
  int i,num[]={24,34,12,44,56,17};
  int num1[]={12,24,35,78, 85,22};
  clrscr();
  printf("Array 1st - 2nd Array
     Addtion\n");
  for(i=0;i<=5;i++)
  {
     num[i]=num1[i]+ ++num[i];
     printf("\n %d ",num[i]);
  }
}
```

5.

```
void main()
{
  int i,num[]={24,34,12,44,56,17};
  clrscr();
  for(i=1;i<=5;i++)
  {
  printf(" %d ",num[i]);
  }
}
```

6.

```
void main()
{
  char msg[ ] = "C is\0Easy";
  int i = 0;
  clrscr();
  while(msg[i]!='\0')
  putc(msg[i++], stdout);
}
```

7.

```
void main()
{
  int i,j;
  int k[]={1,2,4,5,6,7,8,9};
  clrscr();
  clrscr();
  for(j=0;j<=8;j++)
  printf(" %u",*(k+j));
  }
```

8.

```
void main()
{
  int i,j;
  int k[]={1,2,4,5,6,7,8,9};
  clrscr();
  clrscr();
  for(j=0;j<8;j++)
  printf(" %u",&j[k]);
}
```

9.

```
void main()
{
```

```
   {
   int i;
   char city[5][8]={
   "Mumbai",
   "Chennai",
   "Kolkata"};

clrscr();
for(i=0;i<5;i++){
printf("Base Address = %u",
    &city[i]);
printf(" String = %s\n",
    city[i]);
}
}
}
```

10.

```
void main()
{
char name[]="Progr0ammin
    In C";
int x=0;
clrscr();
while(name[x++]!='\0');
putchar(name[x++]);
}
```

11.

```
void main()
{
  int a=10;
  char c='C';
  float p=3.14;
  char spf[6];
  clrscr();
  printf(spf,"%d %c %.2f",
     a,c,p);
  printf("\n%s",spf);
  getche();
}
```

12.

```
void main()
{
  int b[]={10,20,30,40,50};
  int i;
  for(i=0;i<=4;i++)
  printf(" %d ",(b+i));
}
```

13.

```
void main()
{
  int sub[10],i;
  clrscr();
  for(i=1;i<10;i++)
  {
  sub[i]=i;
  printf(" %d",sub[i]);
  }
}
```

14.

```
void main()
{
  long a[]={33000,20,30,
     40,50};
  int *j;
  j=a;
  clrscr();
  printf("%ld",*j);
}
```

15.

```
void main()
{
  int max=5;
  float arr[max];
  for(i=0;i<max;i++)
  scanf("%f",&arr[i]);
}
```

16.

```
void main()
{
int twod[][]={ 2,4,6,8};
printf("%d",twod);
}
```

17.

```
void main()
{
int thr[3][]= {2,4,3,6,8,2,
   2,3,1};
printf("%d",thr[1][1]);
}
```

18.

```
void main()
{
int a[5]={5,1,15,20,25};
int i,j,k=1,m;
i=++a[1];
j=a[1]++;
m=a[i+];
clrscr();
printf("\n %d %d %d",i,j,m);
}
```

6.G Attempt the following programming exercises

1. Write a program to read five elements from an array. Perform addition and multiplication of these elements.
2. Write a program to read a number containing three digits. Perform square roots of each digit. For example, the number is 149. Output should be square root of each digit, i.e. 1 2 3.
3. Write a program to read numbers of any lengths. Count odd numbers and display them in ascending order.
4. Write a program to find the total marks of three subjects Physics, Chemistry and Math of three students. Display their ids and marks with declaration and initialization of array.
5. Write a program to initialize two arrays having equal elements. Compute addition and subtraction of the respective elements of two arrays and display them.
6. Write a program to initialize and read 26 six alphabets in upper case and their ASCII values in reverse (Z to A).
7. Write a program to enter string in lower as well as upper case. Convert lower case to upper case and vice versa and display them in reverse order.
8. Read the marks of five subjects obtained by five students in an examination. Display the top two student codes and their marks.
9. Initialize two arrays and merge them. Display elements in descending order.
10. Write a program to perform the transpose of the matrix.
11. Program to check whether the given string is Palindrome or not.
12. Program to sort the numbers using Bubble sort method.
13. Program to sort the numbers using selection sort method.
14. Program to search the target element in an array and its position from the last element.
15. Program to merge two arrays.

ANSWERS

6.A Fill in the blanks

1. (b) 10 values
2. (a) memory locations
3. (a) −32768 to 32767
4. (a) 65564
5. (a) 65494
6. (a) the program will not run
7. (a) 0th element
8. (a) 16
9. (c) none of the above
10. (c) garbage value
11. (a) nothing
12. (a) 65474
13. (a) subsequent memory locations
14. (a) call by value
15. (b) call by reference
16. (a) pointer
17. (a) one
18. (b) same
19. (b) variable name of the array
20. (c) contiguously
21. (a) two rows and three columns
22. (a) 1,2,3
23. (c) 4,0,0
24. (c) compilation error
25. (c) 0

6.B True or false

1. T 2. T 3. T 4. F 5. T 6. T 7. T 8. T 9. F 10. T 11. T 12. T 13. T 14. T 15. F 16. T

6.C Match the following correct pairs given in Group A with Group B

I 1. B, 2. A, 3. D, 4. C
II 1. C, 2. B, 3. D, 4. A
III 1. C, 2. D, 3. B, 4. A
IV 1. C, 2. A, 3. B, 4. D
V 1. D, 2. A, 3. C, 4. B

6.D Select the appropriate option from the multiple choices given below

1. (a) 10
2. (a) 9 18 27 44 50
3. (a) 5.00 3.64 2.73 1.82 0.91
4. (a) q s u w y z
5. (a) program will be terminated
6. (a) rest of the elements will be set to 0
7. (a) address of the array
8. (b) int x[5];
9. (a) 0th element
10. (a) constant pointer objet
11. (a) x++;
12. (a) 65460, 65462, 65464
13. (a) 8,2

6.E What will be the output/s of the following program/s?

1. 67
   78
   64
2. m i t
3. AMOL AMOL AMOL AMOL AMOL
4. Entered characters are:
   Char ASCII ASCIIHEX

   H 72 48
   e 101 65
   l 108 6c
   l 108 6c
   o 111 6f
   ! 33 21
   ----
5. 55
6. 6*1=6
   6*2=12
   6*3=18
   6*4=24
   6*5=30
7. Total is 120
8. 2
   3
   4
   6
   8
   10
9. M A L A L A M
   6 5 4
10. 2 3 4 5
11. 2 is stored at Location 65518
    3 is stored at Location 65520
    4 is stored at Location 65522
    5 is stored at Location 65524
12. 21 25 55 67 87
13. 11 65516 22 65518 33 65520 44 65522 55 65524
14. 11 22 33 44 55
15. 2 3 4 5
16. 15 30 45 60
17. 31 19 40 71 32
18. Largest=6
    Smallest=1
    Sum of their squares=37
19. The number 7 is at 6th position in the array
20. The number 5 is at 4th position in the array
    The number 5 is at 6th position in the array
    The number 5 appeared 2 times
21. Sum =76
    Average=15.20
22. Element of first Array + Second Array= Addition
    2 + 1 = 3
    3 + 2 = 5
    4 + 3 = 7
23. NANDED - 431603
24. Month [1] of a year contains 31 days.
    Month [2] of a year contains 28 days.
    Month [3] of a year contains 31 days.
    Month [4] of a year contains 30 days.
25. 2 even numbers and 3 odd numbers
26. 3 negative numbers, 1 positive and 2 zeros
27. 5 and 1
28. Length of the string is 7
29. 1 1 1 1 1
30. 14
31. C is easy
32. System
33. System Programming
34. 1. 100 C 3.14
35. PROGRAMMING IN C
36. 7 7 7 7 7 7
37. s= −1
38. 1 2 4
39. A 3 8.9
40. 65476 65480 65484 65488 65492 (The output varies from system to system)

41. Elements of an array in reverse order
    1 2 3
    4 5 6
    7 8 9
42. 1 3 5 7
43. 1 3 5
44. 4 7 10 5 8 11 6 9 12
45. 1 0 5 0
46. Output:
    1 [65470] 2 [65472] 3 [65474]
    4 [65476] 5 [65478] 6 [65480]
    7 [65482] 8 [65484] 9 [65486]
    1 [65488] 4 [65490] 7 [65492]
    2 [65494] 5 [65496] 8 [65498]
    3 [65500] 6 [65502] 9 [65504]

    1 [65506] 4 [65508] 4 [65510]
    2 [65512] 4 [65514] 7 [65516]
    8 [65518] 8 [65520] 5 [65522]
    Addresses varies from system to system

6.F Find the bug/s in the following program/s

1. `for` loop should be from 0 to 4 instead up to 5.
2. & should be removed from the `printf` statements.
   Sum 57 and average 5.7
3. No bug. `char` array should be initialized or it should be declared static.
4. No bug.
5. Array elements counter should start from zero.
6. `NULL` character is present in between the string.
7. Attempt to read more elements than declared in array.
8. No Bug.
9. No bug.
10. The `while` loop is terminated.
11. `sprintf` is needed instead of `printf`.
12. statement `(b+i)` is invalid. It should be `*(b+i)`.
13. The last element is not initialized.
14. Array is of `long` type and pointer is `int`.
15. Variable i is not defined.
16. Size of the array is not defined.
17. Size of the array is not defined.
18. `m=a[i+]` main()

7

String Operations and Standard Functions

CHAPTER OUTLINE

7.1 DEFINITION OF STRING

String is defined as an array of characters. In the text, we find words and sentences and they are normally controlled by strings. Every string is terminated with `'\0'(NULL)` character.

An example of a string is as follows:

```
char name[ ]={'I','N','D','I','A','\0'};
```

In C, each character of the string occupies 1 byte of memory. The last character is always '\0'. It is not compulsory to write '\0' in a string. The compiler automatically puts '\0' at the end of a character array or string. The characters of string are stored in contiguous (neighbouring) memory locations.

7.2 DECLARATION AND INITIALIZATION OF A STRING

The syntax for declaration and initialization of a string is as follows.

```
char name[ ]="INDIA";
```

By declaring and initializing character arrays, the programmer can see the output as given below:

(i) `char` name[6] = { 'R', 'A', 'J', 'E', 'S', 'H'};

(ii) `char` name[7] = { 'R', 'A', 'J', 'E', 'S', 'H'};

In case of (i), the output will not be RAJESH, but it contains some garbage value at the end of RAJESH. Arguments in this example are initialized with [6], which is exactly equal to number of characters within the curly braces. The account of NULL character is not taken in this case. The NULL character must be included, and hence the argument must be [7] instead of [6] as given in statement (ii).

7.3 DISPLAY OF STRINGS WITH DIFFERENT FORMATS

The `printf()` function is used for displaying the various data types. The `printf()` function with `%s` format is to be used for displaying string on the screen. Various formats are shown in the Table 7.1.

TABLE 7.1 *String formats with different precision*

Serial No.	*Statement*	*Output*
1	`printf("%s\n",text);`	PRABHAKAR
2	`printf("%.5s\n",text);`	PRABH
3	`printf("%.8s\n",text);`	PRABHAKA
4	`printf("%.15s\n",text);`	PRABHAKAR
5	`printf("%-10.4s\n",text);`	PRAB
6	`printf("%11s",text);`	PRABHAKAR

Where the text is 'PRABHAKAR':

(i) The first statement displays the output 'PRABHAKAR'. The entire string can be displayed with the first statement.

(ii) We can also specify the precision with character string, which is to be displayed. The precision is (number of characters to be displayed) provided after decimal point. For instance, in the second statement in the above table, the first five characters are displayed. Here, the integer value 5 on the right side of the decimal point specifies the five characters to be displayed.

(iii) In the third statement, first eight characters are displayed.

(iv) The fourth statement displays the entire string.

(v) The fifth statement with –sign (e.g. `%-10.4s`) displays the string with left justified.

(vi) When the field length is less than the length of the string, the entire string is printed. When it is greater than the length of the string, blank spaces are initially printed followed by the string. This effect can be seen in the sixth statement.

(vii) When number of characters to be displayed are specified as zero after decimal point, then nothing will be displayed.

7.4 STRING STANDARD FUNCTIONS

Table 7.2 is a table that briefs about the string handling functions in C. They are frequently used for string manipulations. The string handling functions are given in `string.h` and they can be used as per programmers' need.

TABLE 7.2 *Standard C string library functions*

Functions	*Description*
`strlen()`	Determines the length of a string
`strcpy()`	Copies a string from the source to the destination.
`strncpy()`	Copies characters of a string to another string up to the specified length
`strcmp()`	Compares characters of two Strings (Function discriminates between small and capital letters)
`stricmp()`	Compares two strings (Function does not discriminate between small and capital letters
`strncmp()`	Compares characters of two strings up to the specified length
`strnicmp()`	Compares characters of two strings up to the specified length, And ignores case
`strlwr()`	Converts upper case characters of a string to lower case
`strupr()`	Converts lower case characters of a string to upper case
`strdup()`	Duplicates a string
`strchr()`	Determines first occurrence of a given character in a string
`strrchr()`	Determines last occurrence of a given character in a string
`strstr()`	Determines first occurrence of a given string in another string
`strcat()`	Appends source string to destination string
`strncat()`	Appends source string to destination string up to specified length
`strrev()`	Reversing all characters of a string
`strset()`	Set all characters of string with a given argument or symbol
`strnset()`	Set specified numbers of characters of string with a given argument or symbol
`strspn()`	Finds up to what length two strings are identical
`strpbrk()`	Searches the first occurrence of the character in a given string and then it displays the string starting from that character

EXERCISES

7.A Fill in the blanks

1. The _____ character also occupies memory space.

   (a) NULL
   (b) '^'
   (c) ?

2. When a string is reversed, the NULL character will be at the _____.

   (a) beginning of the string
   (b) end of the string
   (c) within the string

3. "B" is a _____ and 'B' is a _____.

   (a) string constant, `char` constant
   (b) `char` constant, string constant
   (c) string constant, string constant

4. The `char name[8]` means array `name` holds maximum _____ characters excluding NULL.

   (a) 8
   (b) 7
   (c) 6

5. For the declaration such as `char x[ ]= "abcd";` the size of the array is determined by _____.

   (a) compiler
   (b) OS
   (c) linker

6. The library function `strncpy()` requires _____ arguments.

   (a) 1
   (b) 2
   (c) 3

7. The `strlen()` function requires _____ arguments.

   (a) 1
   (b) 2
   (c) 3

8. The string function _____ compares characters of two strings up to the given length.

   (a) `strcmp()`
   (b) `strncmp()`
   (c) `strrcmp()`

9. The string function `strupr()` converts _____.

   (a) lower case characters of a string to upper case
   (b) lower case characters of a string to title case
   (c) lower case characters of a string to sentence case

10. The string function `strncpy()` copies _____.

    (a) all characters of a string to another string
    (b) characters of a string to another string up to the specified length
    (c) none of the above

11. _____ function finds second string in the first string.

    (a) `strstr()`
    (b) `strnstr()`
    (c) `strsearch()`

12. _____ function appends the target string to the source string. Concatenation of two strings would be done using this function.

    (a) `strcat()`
    (b) `strncat()`
    (c) `strrcat()`

13. 'A' + _____ = 'a'

    (a) 33
    (b) 32
    (c) 12

14. The ASCII equivalent of 32 is _____

    (a) ?
    (b) –
    (c) space

15. The statement `printf("%d",' ')` will print _____.

    (a) 34
    (b) 32
    (c) 31

16. The `atoi(string)` converts a string of digits into _____.

    (a) integers
    (b) floating number
    (c) characters

7.B True or false

1. In C, a group of characters within double quotation mark enclosed in bracket is called a string.
2. Every string ends with a NULL character.
3. The declaration `char name[ ] = "India";` is valid.
4. The `strlen()` function returns the length of the given string.
5. The `strdup()` is used to copy the string.
6. The `sricmp()` and `strncmp()` are exactly the same.

7. While reversing the string, address in memory also gets changed.
8. If pre-existing string is replaced with new, memory addresses remain the same.
9. If the string is reversed, the NULL character appears first.
10. The length of the string includes NULL character.
11. "12345" is a valid string.
12. 'A' is a valid string.
13. If two strings are merged, the string contains two NULL characters.
14. The string is declared as character array.
15. The string is not stored in successive memory locations.
16. The `character` constant C ends with NULL character.
17. The format string `%c` is used to display a string.
18. The NULL `character` and 0 are treated as same by a compiler.
19. 'A'> 'a'
20. 'A'=65 (Letter A is equivalent to as Decimal 65)

7.C Match the following pairs given in Group A with Group B

I

Group A		Group B	
Serial No.	**Output**	**Serial No.**	**Statement**
If `char text[] = "PRABHAKAR"`			
1.	`printf("%s\n", text);`	A	PRABHAKAR
2.	`printf("%.5s\n",text);`	B	PRAB
3.	`printf("%.8s\n",text);`	C	PRABHAKAR
4.	`printf("%.15s\n",text);`	D	PRABHAKA
5.	`printf("%-10.4s\n",text);`	E	PRABH
6.	`printf("%11s", text);`	F	PRABHAKAR

II

Group A		Group B	
Serial No.	**Functions**	**Serial No.**	**Working**
1.	`strlen()`	A	Duplicate the string
2.	`strcpy()`	B	Copies the string
3.	`strdup()`	C	Returns length of the string
4.	`Strrev()`	D	Reverse the string

III

Group A		Group B	
Serial No.	**Functions**	**Serial No.**	**Header File/ Operation**
1.	`strlen()`	A	`math.h`
2.	`abs()`	B	`System function`
3.	`main()`	C	`stdio.h`
4.	`printf()`	D	`string.h`

IV

Group A		Group B	
Serial No.	**Functions**	**Serial No.**	**Meaning/ Operation**
1.	`strupr()`	A	Converts a string to lower case
2.	`strlwr()`	B	Comparison of two strings
3.	`strcmp()`	C	Concatenation of strings
4	`strcat`	D	Converts a string to upper case

V

Group A		Group B	
Serial No.	**Functions**	**Serial No.**	**Operation**
1.	`gets()`	A	Prints as many strings
2.	`puts()`	B	Reads one string
3.	`scanf()`	C	Writes one string
4.	`printf()`	D	Reads as many strings

7.D Select the appropriate option from the multiple choices given below

1. The string is declared as
   (a) character array
   (b) string array
   (c) `long char` array

2. The string always ends with
   (a) NULL character
   (b) `\ char`
   (c) `! char`

3. To duplicate the string, one of the following functions is appropriate.
   (a) `strdup()`
   (b) `strupr()`
   (c) `strspn()`

4. Which function will you use for copying string from source to destination?
   (a) `strcpy()`
   (b) `strrev()`
   (c) `strlwr()`

5. All the string functions are defined in
   (a) `string.h`
   (b) `math.h`
   (c) `iostream.h`

6. One of the following is not a string constant.
   (a) "string"
   (b) "C"
   (c) 'C"

7. To read a string through the keyboard, following unformatted function is used.
   (a) `scanf()`
   (b) `gets()`
   (c) none of the above

8. The NULL character at the end of the string is put by
   (a) compiler
   (b) operating system
   (c) user

9. The NULL character is useful for compiler to
   (a) detect the end of the string
   (b) detect the beginning of the string
   (c) search in the memory

10. `c[ ]="CPLUSPLUS";` in order to print the "CPP". the statement will be
    (a) `printf("%c %c %c", c[0],c[1],c[5]);`
    (b) `printf("%s %s %s", c[0],c[1],c[5]);`
    (c) `printf("%s %s %s", c[1],c[2],c[6]);`

11. Which of the following function is more appropriate for reading string with spaces?
    (a) `printf()`
    (b) `gets()`
    (c) `scanf()`

12. The `strlen()` function returns the length of the string including
    (a) all characters, spaces and symbols, numbers excluding NULL character
    (b) all characters, spaces and symbols, numbers and NULL character
    (c) characters, numbers and excluding spaces

13. `char x[ ]="Program";` the `sizeof(x)` will return
    (a) 7
    (b) 8
    (c) 9

7.E What will be the output/s of the following program/s?

Programs to display string and string operations

1. Display a string "MAHARASHTRA".

```
#include <string.h>
void main()
{
char *a1[12]={"MAHARASHTRA"};
clrscr();
printf("%s ",*a1);
getche();
}
```

2. Display a string "NAGPUR".

```
#include <string.h>
void main()
{
char a1[6]={"NAGPUR"};
```

```
int j;
clrscr();
for(j=0;j<6;j++)
printf("%c ",a1[j]);
++j;
getche();
}
```

3. Display strings "MAHARASHTRA" and "MADHYA-PRADESH" with and without pointer.

```
#include <string.h>
void main()
{
char a1[12]="MAHARASHTRA";
char *a2[13]={"MADHYAPRADESH"};
clrscr();
printf("%s ",a1);
printf("%s ",*a2);
getche();
}
```

4. Display strings "KOLHAPUR" and "NAGPUR" with and without pointer.

```
#include <string.h>
void main()
{
char a1[7]={"NAGPUR"};
char *n="SOLAPUR";
clrscr();
n="KOLHAPUR",
printf("%s %s ",*&(n),a1);
getche();
}
```

5. Display text with different formats.

```
void main()
{
char text[15]="MOUNTAIN";
clrscr();
printf("%.5s\n",text);
printf("%.8s\n",text);
getche();
}
```

6. Program on encryption of a string.

```
void main()
{
char text[15]="MOUNTAIN";
int i;
clrscr();
for(i=0;i<=7;i++)
printf("%c ",text[i]+2);
getche();
}
```

7. Program on string characters to ASCII values.

```
void main()
{
char text[15]="ZYX";
int i;
clrscr();
for(i=0;i<=2;i++)
printf("%d ",text[i]-2);
getche();
}
```

8. Arithmetic operation on character.

```
#include <string.h>
void main()
{
char alpha='z';
int number=67;
char text1[20]="Discovery";
clrscr();
alpha='z'-1;
printf("\n%c %d", alpha,'z'+1);
printf("\n%d %c",
    number+2,number-2);
printf("\n%s ", text1+5);
getche();
}
```

9. Arithmetic operation on character.

```
#include <string.h>
void main()
{
char alpha='z';
int number=50;
char text1[20]="Pleasent";
clrscr();
alpha='z'-25;
printf("\n%c %d", alpha,'z'+1);
printf("\n%d %c", number,
    number*2);
printf("\n%s ", text1+4);
getche();
}
```

10. String and pointer.

```
#include <string.h>
void main()
{
char word[]="Capital Delhi";
int integer=65;
char *string="1234";
clrscr();
printf("\n%s ", *&(word));
printf("\n%d %c %d",integer,integer,
    sizeof(word));
```

```
printf("\n%s ", *&(string));
getche();
}
```

11. Number of words in a sentence.

```
void main()
{
char sentence[30]="You too can be
    expert in C";
int count=0,i=0;
clrscr();
while(sentence[i]!='\0')
  {
  if(((sentence[i]>=97)&&(sentence
      [i]<=122))||((sentence [i]>=65)&&
      (sentence[i]<=90)))
    {
    i++;
    if(sentence[i]==32)
    {
    count++;
    i++;
    }
    }
}
if(sentence[i]=='\0')
count++;
printf(" %d\n",count);
getche();
}
```

12. Count number of spaces in the sentence using while loop and if statement.

```
void main()
{
char sentence[20]="Hello! How R U?";
int count=0,i=0;
clrscr();
printf("\n%s",sentence);
while(sentence[i++]!='\0')
if(sentence[i]==32)
count++;
printf("\n%d",count);
getche();
}
```

13. Sorting the list of places without using string functions.

```
void main()
{
char place[5][20]={"Delhi","Chennai",
   "Bangalore","Mumbai","Nanded"};
int i,j;
clrscr();
printf("Sorted List of Cities.\n");
for(i=65;i<=122;i++)
{
for(j=0;j<5;j++)
{
if(place[j][0]==i)
printf("\n%s",place[j]);
}
}
getche();
}
```

14. Characters and ASCII values.

```
void main()
{
char s;
clrscr();
for(s=97;s<=122;s++)
{
if(s>100 && s<123)
continue;
printf("\n%c %d",s,s);
}
getch();
}
```

15. Display numbers.

```
void main()
{
char a;
clrscr();
for(a=49;a<=60;a++)
{
if(a>57 && a<61)
continue;
printf(" %c %d ",a,a);
}
getch();
}
```

16. Program to remove of vowels.

```
void main()
  {
  char line[5],line2[5];
  int i,j=0;
  clrscr();
  printf("\n Enter Text ");
  gets(line);
  for(i=0;i<5;i++)
    {
if(line[i]=='a' || line[i]=='e' ||
   line[i]=='i' || line[i]=='o' ||
   line[i]=='u')
```

```
    continue;
    else
      {
      line2[j]=line[i];
      j++;
      }
    }
printf("\n Text With Vowels -: %s",
   line);
printf("\n Text Without Vowels -:
   %s",line2);
getche();
}
```

17. Hamming distance.

```
void main()
{
int a[4]={1,0,1,0},b[4]={1,0,0,1},
   i,j,count=0;
clrscr();

for(i=0;i<=3;i++)
    {
    j=a[i]^b[i];
    if(j==1)
    count=count+1;
    }
printf("\n Hamming Distance is
   =%d",count);
getche();
}
```

String copy with and without `strcpy()` function

18. Program to copy a string using `strcpy()` function.

```
#include <string.h>
void main()
{
char name1[10]={'P','r','i','y','a'},
   name2[10];
clrscr();
printf("\n Original name=%s",name1);
strcpy(name2,name1);
printf("\n Copied name is=%s",name2);
getch();
}
```

19. String copy and size of strings.

```
#include <string.h>
void main()
{
char a[55]={"Software people are
   intelligent"};
char b[60]={"Highly knowledgeable people
   can design hardware circuits"};
clrscr();
strcpy(a,b);
printf("\n%s ",a);
printf("\n%d
   %d",sizeof(a),sizeof(b));
getche();
}
```

20. Copying without `strcpy()`.

```
void main()
{
char main[10]="abcd",dup[10];
int i;
clrscr();
for(i=0;i<10;i++)
dup[i]=main[i];
printf("Original String : %s",main);
printf("\nDuplicate String : %s",dup);
getche();
}
```

21. Copying a string.

```
#include <string.h>
void main()
{
char text1[20]="Deepawali",*text2;
clrscr();
text2=text1;
printf("\n%s ", *&(text2));
getche();
}
```

Copy of string up to certain length with `strncpy()` function

22. Copy of string up to certain length.

```
#include <string.h>
void main()
{
char main[20]="Amit", photocopy[20];
int n =3;
clrscr();
strncpy(photocopy,main,n);
printf("Original String : %s", main);
printf("\nDuplicate String : %s",
   photocopy);
getche();
}
```

23. Copy of string up to certain length.

```
#include <string.h>
void main()
{
char str1[15]="wonderful",
   str2[15]="beautiful";
int n=6;
clrscr();
```

```
printf("\n Source String-:%s", str1);
printf("\n Destination String-:%s",
   str2);
strncpy(str2,str1,n);
printf("\nDestination String -:%s",
   str2);
getche();
}
```

Programs on different string functions: strcpy() , strlwr() , strupr() , etc.

24. Use different string functions: strcpy(), strlwr(), strupr()

```
#include <string.h>
void main()
{
char a[50]={"Computer Education leads
   to Prosperity and fame"};
char b[50]; clrscr(); strcpy(b,a);
   printf("%s \n%s",a,b);
strupr(b);
printf("\n%s",b);
strlwr(b);
printf("\n%s",b);
strrev(b);
printf("\n%s",b);
getche();
}
```

String length with and without strlen() function

25. Program to find the length of the string.

```
#include <string.h>
void main()
{
char text[20];
int len;
clrscr();
printf("type text below.\n");
gets(text);
len=strlen(text);
printf("length of the string
   is=%d",len);
}
```

26. Length of a string without function.

```
void main()
{
char group[15]={'I','n','d','i','a'};
int len=0,i;
clrscr();
for(i=0;group[i]!='\0';i++)
len++;
printf("Length of the string
   is=%d",len);
getch();
}
```

27. Program to find the length of the strings without function.

```
void main()
{
char str1[20]={'M','U','T','H','A'},
str2[20]={'M','U','L','H','A'};
int diff,i=0,j=0;
clrscr();
while(str1[i]!='\0')
i++;
printf("\n Length of the first
   string =%d",i);

while(str2[j]!='\0')
j++;
printf("\n Length of the second
   string =%d",j);

if(i==j)
printf("\n Lengths of the strings
   are same");
else
printf("\n Lengths of the strings
   are not same ");
getch();
}
```

String comparison with and without strcmp() function

28. Program on comparison of two strings.

```
#include <string.h>
void main()
{
char str1[20]={'C','o','m','p','u',
   't','e','r'},
str2[20]={'C','o','m','p','u','t',
   'e','r'};
clrscr();
if((strcmp(str1,str2))==0)
printf("Strings are same \n");
else
printf("Strings are not same \n");
getch();
}
```

29. Program to compare the two strings.

```
#include <string.h>
void main()
{
char
str1[20]={'G','o','d','a','w','a',
   'r','i'},
```

```
str2[20]={'S','a','r','a','s','w',
    'a','t','i'};
int diff;
clrscr();
diff=(strcmp(str1,str2));
if(diff==0)
printf(" strings are same \n");
else
printf(" strings are not same \n");
getch();
}
```

30. Progrm on `stricmp()` function.

```
#include <string.h>
#include <process.h>
void main()
{
char ans[8];
int i;
clrscr();
for(i=1;i<=3;i++)
{
printf("\nWhat is the currency of
    India?");
scanf("%s",ans);
fflush(stdin);
if(stricmp(ans,"Rupees")==0)
{
printf("\nAnswer is Correct.");
exit(1);
}
else
if(i<3)
printf("\n Try Again !\n");
}
clrscr();
printf("\n Currency of India is
    Rupees.");
}
```

31. Comparison of strings and use of `strlen()` function.

```
#include <string.h>
void main()
{
char str1[15]="clever",
    str2[15]="Intelligent";
int x,y,z;
clrscr();
printf("\n Source String:-%s",str1);
printf("\n Destination String:-
    %s",str2);
y=strcmp(str2,str1);
if(y==0)
{
  z=strlen(str1)=strlen(str2);
  printf("\nLength of both the
      strings:- %d" ,z);
}
else
{
  y=strlen(str1);
  x=strlen(str2);
  printf("\nLength of the first
      string:- %d" ,y);
  printf("\nLength of the second
      string:- %d" ,x);
}
getche();
}
```

32. Use of functions such as `strcmp`, `strcat` and `strlen`.

```
#include <string.h>
void main()
{
char str1[20]="C is",
    str2[20]="easy language";
int x,y,z;
clrscr();
printf("\n Source String:-%s",str1);
printf("\n Destination String:-
    %s",str2);
y=strcmp(str2,str1);
if(y==0)
{
  z=strlen(str1)==strlen(str2);
  printf("\nLength of both the
      strings:- %d" ,z);
}
else
{
  strcat(str1,str2);
  printf("\n Final string is :-%s",str1);
  x=strlen(str1);
  printf("\nLength of the final
      string:- %d" ,x);
}
getche();
}
```

33. Sorted list of places with string functions.

```
#include <string.h>
void main()
{
char place[5][20]={"Nanded","Latur",
    "Aurangabad","Jalna","Beed"},
    temp[20];
```

```
int i,j;
clrscr();
printf("\nSorted List of Cities");
for(i=1;i<5;i++)
{
for(j=1;j<5;j++)
{
  if(strcmp(place[j-1],place[j])>0)
  {
  strcpy(temp,place[j-1]);
  strcpy(place[j-1],place[j]);
  strcpy(place[j],temp);
  }
}
}
for(i=0;i<5;i++)
printf("\n%s",place[i]);
getche();
}
```

34. Use of `strcmp()`and a program on it for ASCII difference.

```
#include <string.h>
void main()
{
char a1[]={"M"},a2[]={"M"},a3[]={"C"},
    a4[]={"B"};
int c1,c2,c3;
clrscr();
c1=strcmp(a1,a2);
c2=strcmp(a3,a4);

printf("%s %s=%d\n",a1,a2,c1);
printf("%s %s=%d\n",a3,a4,c2);
getche();
}
```

Use of memcmp() function

35. Find the length of strings with `memcmp ()` function

```
#include <string.h>
void main()
{
char text[30]="LATUR",text1[20]=
    "UDGIR",chp;
clrscr();
printf("\nFirst text is:-%s", text);
printf("\nSecond text is :-%s",
    text1);

chp=memcmp(text,text1,5);
if(chp!=0)
printf("\nText length of first
    string is same as of second");
else
printf("\nText length of the
    strings are not same ");
getche();
}
```

36. Concatenation of two strings with function

```
#include <string.h>
void main()
  {
    char str1[30]="Those who see
        invisible ", str2[30]="they
        are valuable ";
    clrscr();
    printf("\n Source String:-%s",
        str1);
    printf("\n Destination String:-
        %s",str2);
    strcat(str1,str2);
    printf("\n Final string is
        :-%s",str1);
        getche();
}
```

37. Concatenation of two strings without function.

```
#include <string.h>
void main()
{
char str[20], str1[20]=
    {'M','U','T','H','A'},
str2[20]={'M','U','L','H','A'};
int i,j;
clrscr();

for(i=0;str1[i]!='\0';i++)
str[i]=str1[i];
str[i]=' ';

for(j=0;str2[j]!='\0';j++)
str[i+j+1]=str2[j];
str[i+j+1]='\0';
printf("\n\n");
printf("Final name is=%s",str);
getch();
}
```

Program on lower case to upper case using `strupr()` function

38. Lower case to upper case.

```
#include <string.h>
void main()
{
char str[50]={"failure is the first
    step of success"};
clrscr();
strupr(str);
```

```
printf("\n%s",str);
getche();
}
```

39. Program on lower case to upper case using strupr.

```
#include<string.h>
void main()
{
  char name[10]={'h','e','l','l',
      'o','!','h','a','i'};
  clrscr();
  printf("\n string characters %s
      ",strupr(name));
  getche();
}
```

Conversion of a string from upper case to lower case with `strlwr()` function and without function

40. Program on conversion of a string from upper case to lower case.

```
#include<string.h>
void main()
{
  char name[8]={'V','A','I','B','H'
      ,'A','V'};
  clrscr();
  printf("\n string characters %s ",
      strlwr(name));
  getche();
}
```

41. Conversion from upper case to lower case without the use of function.

```
void main()
{
char group[15]={'A','B','C','D'};
int i;
clrscr();
for(i=0;i<=4;i++)
printf(" %c ",group[i]+32);
getch();
}
```

42. Display text with `while` loop.

```
void main()
{
char a1[]={'M','U','M','B','A','I'};
int i=0;
clrscr();
while(a1[i]!='\0')
{
printf("%c ",a1[i]+32);
i++;
}
getche();
}
```

Program to search a character

43. Program to search a character in a string and count its occurrence.

```
void main()
{
  int count=0,i;
  char name[10]={'h','e','l','l','o',
      '!','h','a','i'};
  char s='l';
  clrscr();
  count=0;
  for(i=0;i<10;i++)
  {
  if(name[i]==s)
  count++;
  }
  printf("\n %d ",count);
  getche();
}
```

Reversing the string with and without `strrev()` function

44. Reversing the string.

```
#include<string.h>
void main()
{
  char name[10]={'H','E','L','L',
      'O','!','H','A','I'};
  clrscr();
  printf("\n string characters %s",
      strrev(name));
  getche();
}
```

45. Reversing the string.

```
#include <string.h>
void main()
{
char group[15]={'V','i','s','h',
    'a','l'};
int len=0,i;
clrscr();
for(i=0;group[i]!='\0';i++)
len++;
printf("\nLength of the string is:-
    %d",len);
printf("\n");
printf("\nReverse of the string:- ");
```

```
for(group[i]='\0';i>=1;i--)
printf("\n%c",group[i-1]);
getch();
}
```

Duplication of a string with strdup() function

46. Duplication of a string.

```
#include <string.h>
void main()
{
char text1[20]="Global",*text2;
clrscr();
text2=strdup(text1);
printf("Original String=%s\nDuplicate
String = %s",text1,text2);
getche();
}
```

Occurrence of a character in a string with strchr() function

47. Occurrence of a character in a string.

```
#include <string.h>
void main()
{
char string[30]="AMERICA",ch,*chp;
clrscr();
  printf("\nString is:-%s",string);
  printf("\nCharacter to find :");
  ch=getchar();
  chp=strchr(string,ch);
  if(chp)
  printf("Character %c found in
     string.",ch);
  else
  printf("Character %c not found in
     string.",ch); }
```

48. Address of each character.

```
#include <string.h>
void main()
{
char string1[30]="Splendid",string2,
    *chp;
int i;
clrscr();
printf("\nstring1 is:- %s",string1);

puts("\nEnter Character to find from
    the text :");

string2=getche();
for( i=0;i<strlen(string1);i++)
printf("\n%c %u",string1[i],
    &string1[i]);
chp=strchr(string1,string2);
if(chp)
{
printf("\nAddress of first %c
    returned by strchr() is %u ",
    string2,chp);
getche();
}
else
printf("'%c' String is not present
    in Given String",string2);
getche();
}
```

Occurrence of a given string in another string with strstr() function

49. Use of strstr() function.

```
#include<string.h>
void main()
{
char sentence[30]="India is a
    democratic country",sentence2[20]
    ="country",*chp;
clrscr();
chp=strstr(sentence,sentence2);
if(chp!=0)
printf("'%s' String is present in a
    given sentence .",sentence2);
else
printf("'%s' String is not present
    in given sentence.",sentence2);
getche();
}
```

Set all characters of a string with a given argument or symbol with strset() function

50. Use of strset().

```
#include <string.h>
void main()
{
char string[15]="Innovation";
char smbol='I';
clrscr();
printf("Before strset(): %s\n",
    string);
strset(string,smbol);
printf("After strset(): %s\n",string);
getche();
}
```

Use of strset() function

51. Use of strnset().

```
#include <string.h>
```

```
void main()
{
char sentence[20]="Knowledgeable
   world";
char target='x';
clrscr();
printf("Before strset(): %s\n",
   sentence);
strnset( sentence,target,13);
printf("After strset(): %s\n",
   sentence);
getche();
}
```

Length of two strings identical with `strspn()` function

52. Use of strspn().

```
#include <string.h>
void main()
{
char string[20]="Hello!World",string
   2[10]="Hello!";
int length;
clrscr();
length=strspn(string,string2);
printf("After %d Characters there
   is no match.\n",length);
getche();
}
```

Searches the first occurrence of the character in a given string `strpbrk()` function

53. Use of strpbrk().

```
#include <string.h>
void main()
{
char *ptr;
char text1[20]="Discovery",text2
   [20]="v";
clrscr();
ptr=strpbrk(text1,text2);
puts("String from given Character
   is:-");
printf(ptr);
getche();
}
```

7.F Find the bug/s in the following program/s

String operations and display

1.

```
void main()
{
char
name[6]={'S','A','N','J','A','Y'};
clrscr();
puts(name);
}
```

2.

```
void main()
{
char
name[7]={'S','A','N','J','A','Y'};
clrscr();
printf("\n %.0s",name);
}
```

3.

```
void main()
{
char *name={"Have a Nice Day"},c;
clrscr();
for(c=0;c<15;c++)
printf("%s",name[c]);
}
```

4.

```
void main()
{
char a1[]={"KOLKATTA"};
int i;
clrscr();
while(a1[i++]!='\0')
printf("%c ",a1[i]);
getche();
}
```

5.

```
void main()
{
char a1[6]={'NAGPUR'};
clrscr();
printf("%c ",a1);
getche();
}
```

6.

```
void main()
{
char *a[]="ROYAL";
clrscr();
printf("%s %u",*(a),&*a);
getche();
}
```

7.

```
void main()
{
char a1[6]={"CHENNAI"};
int i;
clrscr();
for(i=0;i<7;i++)
printf("%c ",a1[i]);
++i;
getche();
}
```

8.

```
void main()
{
char text[15]="MOUNTAIN";
int i;
clrscr();
for(i=7;i>=0;i--)
printf("%.8d",text[i]);
getche();
}
```

9.

```
void main()
{
char *a2[10]={"MADHYAPRADESH"};
clrscr();
printf("%s",*&(a2));
getche();
}
```

***strcpy()* function**

10.

```
#include <string.h>
void main()
{
char str1[15]='snowy',
   str2[15]='sunny';
clrscr();
printf("\n Source String-:%s", str1);
printf("\n Destination String-:%s", str2);
strncpy(str2,str1,3);
printf("\nDestination String -:%s",
   str2);
getche();
}
```

11.

```
#include <string.h>
void main()
{
char a[40]={"Software people are
   intelligent"};
char b[40];
clrscr();
strcpy(b,&a);
printf("%s \n %s",a,b);
getche();
}
```

***strchr()* function**

12.

```
#include <string.h>
void main()
{
char text[30]="SINGAPUR",cha,*chp;
clrscr();
  printf("\nString is:-%s",text);
  printf("\nCharacter to find :");
  cha=getchar();
  chp=strchr(text[],cha);
  if(chp!=0)
  printf("Character %d found in
     text.",cha);
  else
  printf("Character %d not found in
     text.",cha);
  getche();
}
```

***strset()* function**

13.

```
#include <string.h>
void main()
{
char text[20]="Great Sea";
char target='I';
clrscr();
printf("Before strset(): %s\n", text);
strset(target, text);
printf("After strset(): %s\n", text);
getche();
}
```

String operations

14.

```
#include <string.h>
void main()
{
char alpha='a';
int number=50;
char text1[20]="Happy";
clrscr();
alpha=a+25;
printf("\n%c %d",'calpha',alpha-1);
printf("\n%d %c", number*2,number*2);
printf("\n%s ", text1+1);
```

```
getche();
}
```

15.

```
void main()
{
char text[30]={"Programming needs
    Patience"};
int count=0,i=0;
clrscr();
  do
  {
  if(text[i]==32 || text[i]=='\0')
  count++;
  }
  while(text[i++]!='\0')

  printf(" %d\n",count);
  getche();
}
```

16.

```
void main()
{
char a[]="C needs skills";
clrscr();
printf("%c %u",a,&a);
getche();
}
```

strcmp() function

17.

```
#include <string.h>
void main()
{
char a[40]={"Software people are
    intelligent"};
char b[60]={"Highly knowledge-
    able people can design hardware
    circuits"};
clrscr();
printf("\n%s ",a);
printf("\n%d",sizeof(a));
if(strcmp(b,a)==0);
printf("\n Lengths of Strings are
    identical ");
else
printf("\n Lengths of Strings are
    dissimilar ");
getche();
}
```

18.

```
#include <string.h>
void main()
{
char static a[10]="Smily";
char static b[10]="Smily";
char c[70];
int x;
clrscr();
printf("\n%s ",a);
printf("\n%s ",b);
x=strcmp(a,b);
if(x!=0);
{
printf("\nString lengths are
    dissimilar");
strcat(a,b);
printf("\n%s",a);
getche();
}
else
{
printf("\nString lengths are
    similar");
x=strlen(a);
printf("\n%d",x);
getche();
}
}
```

String operations

19.

```
void main()
{
char a[5];
clrscr();
a[0]='v';
a[1]='i';
a[2]='j';
a[3]='a';
a[4]='y';
a[5]='\0';
printf("\n%s ",a);
printf("\n%d %d",size of(a));
getche();
}
```

20.

```
void main()
{char *am={"Amol"};
char *at={"Amit"};
```

```
char *st;
clrscr();
st=at;
at=am;
am=at;
printf("%s and %s",at,am);
}
```

21.

```
void main()
{
char a[]='A';
char b[]='B';
char c[]='C';
char d[3];
d[0]=a[0];
d[1]=b[0];
d[2]=c[0];
}
```

22.

```
void main()
{
char a[]={'A'};
char b[]={'B'};
char c[]={'C'};
char d[4];d[0]=a[0];
d[1]=b[0];
d[2]=c[0];
printf("%s",d);
}
```

23.

```
void main()
{
char a[][]="abcdefdf";
clrscr();
printf("%s",a);
}
```

24.

```
#include <string.h>
void main()
{
char a[]="abcdefdf";clrscr();
printf("%c",strlan(a));
}
```

`strdup()` function

25.

```
#include <string.h>
void main()
{
char text1[]="ORIGIONAL";
char text2[10];
text2=strdup(text1);
printf("%s",text2);
}
```

`strrev()` function

26.

```
void main()
{
char text1[]="ORIGIONAL";
char *text2;
clrscr();
text1=strrev(text1);
printf("%s",text2);
}
```

7.G Attempt the following programming exercises

1. Write a program to enter the names of three subjects and display them.
2. Write a program to enter the names of four metros. Display them in ascending order.
3. Write a program to enter some text. Display each sentence with first character to be the capital one.
4. Write a program to enter text in lower case through the keyboard. Convert characters into ASCII.
5. Write a program to enter some text through the keyboard. Count the occurrence of a particular word in it.
6. Write a program to print the entered word with all possible combinations of letters.
7. Write a program to encrypt the text "Beautiful." Shift each character by three positions on higher side.
8. Write a program to enter some text and find the number of spaces in it.
9. Write a program to enter state and their capitals and display both in descending order of capitals.
10. Write a program to enter the text and count the character 'e' that appears at the end of each word in the text.

ANSWERS

7.A Fill in the blanks

1. (a) NULL
2. (b) end of the string
3. (a) string constant, `char` constant
4. (b) 7
5. (a) compiler
6. (c) 3
7. (a) 1
8. (b) `strncmp()`
9. (a) lower case characters of a string to upper case
10. (b) characters of a string to another string up to the specified length
11. (a) `strstr()`
12. (a) `strcat()`
13. (b) 32
14. (c) space
15. (b) 32
16. (a) integers

7.B True or false

1. T 2. T 3. T 4. T 5. T 6. F 7. F 8. T 9. F 10. F 11. T 12. F 13. F 14. T 15. F 16. F 17. F 18. T 19. F 20. T

7.C Match the following correct pairs given in Group A with Group B

I 1. F, 2. E, 3. D, 4. C, 5. B, 6. A
II 1. C, 2. B, 3. A, 4. D
III 1. D, 2. A, 3. B, 4. C
IV 1. D, 2. A, 3. B, 4. C
V 1. B, 2. C, 3. D, 4. A

7.D Select the appropriate option from the multiple choices given below

1. (a) character array
2. (a) NULL `character`
3. (a) `strdup()`
4. (a) `strcpy()`
5. (a) `string.h`
6. (c) 'C'
7. (b) `gets()`
8. (c) user
9. (a) detect the end of the string
10. (a) `printf("%c %c %c",c[0],c[1],c[5]);`
11. (a) `gets()`
12. (a) all characters, spaces and symbols, numbers excluding NULL `character`
13. (b) 8

7.E What will be the output/s of the following program/s?

1. MAHARASHTRA
   Here, in this program, the contents of character array are printed. Character pointer variable 'a' and string format specifier `%s` are used in the program.
2. N A G P U R
   Here, in this program, the contents of the character array are displayed using character array index and character format specifier `%c`. Character by character are taken and displayed using `for()` loop.
3. MAHARASHTRA MADHYAPRADESH
   Output of the program is printed using character pointer only, but the method of representation is different. Also, initialization of both the arrays is done in different ways.
4. KOLHAPUR NAGPUR
   Here, in this program, the output is printed using pointer to character array like `*(&n)`, which means pointer to address of variable 'n'.
5. MOUNT
   MOUNTAIN
   The program shows the way to print desired number of characters of the given string using `printf()` function.
6. O Q W P V C K P
   It is a small example of encryption, where ASCII values of characters are used to encrypt the given string like expression `text[i]+2`. It prints the character whose ASCII values are shifted by 2 than the character in the array.
7. 88 87 86
   The program shows the ASCII values of characters which are two places behind the actual ASCII values of characters. Here, remember that to print ASCII value format specifier used is `%d` and not `%c`.
8. y 123
   69 A
   very
   First two outputs are the same like above two programs. In the third output, we have set address of

character pointer to location where 'v' is stored, hence `printf` has printed the string starting from 'v'.

9. a 123
50 d
sent
The same concept as of the above program, with different arithmetic operations.

10. Capital Delhi
65 A 14
1234
Here, in the second line of the output, it is observed that the printed size of the array using the `sizeof` function and the other two output lines are different representations of character pointer variable.

11. 7
To calculate the number of words in a given statement, we are comparing each character present in an array to ASCII values of alphabets (lower and upper letters), and then identified the spaces (ASCII 32) and counted them in a statement until NULL character is observed.

12. Hello! How R U?
3
To calculate number of spaces in a statement, every character is compared with space ASCII 32 and this process is done till NULL character appears in the statement. Counting spaces in the statement gives number of words.

13. Sorted List of Cities.
Bangalore
Chennai
Delhi
Mumbai
Nanded
Here, checking for first character of each one-dimensional array with ASCII values of 'A TO Z' is done and they are printed accordingly.

14. a 97
b 98
c 99
d 100
It is a program for getting ASCII values of different alphabetical characters using format specifiers `%c` and `%d`.

15. 1 49 2 50 3 51 4 52 5 53 6 54 7 55 8 56 9 57
Here, we are finding ASCII values of numbers in character format using the same method as in the previous program.

16. Enter Text abcd
Text With Vowels -: abcd
Text Without Vowels -: bcd
This is a sample program of comparison of `char` variables with `char` constants, where we are comparing array contents with vowels and storing non-vowels in different array and printing the array with vowels and non-vowels.

17. Hamming Distance is =2
Hamming Distance is calculated by XORing each bit of a binary array with respective bit of second one, and then counting number of times the output is '1'.

18. Original name=Priya
Copied name is=Priya
Simple example of string copy function
`strcpy()` in `string.h` header file.

19. Highly knowledgeable people can design hardware circuits
55 60
Simple example of string copy function `strcpy()` and length of strings are calculated with size of().

20. Original String : abcd
Duplicate String : abcd
Here, we are copying the contents of one character array into another array until NULL character appears using `for` loop.

21. Deepawali
The string Deepawali is copied to the address pointed by pointer `text2`. Then, the string is printed.

22. Original String : Amit
Duplicate String : Ami
The string up to specified length, i.e. 'n' is copied using `strncpy();` function. The original and duplicate strings are displayed.

23. Source String-:wonderful
Destination String-:beautiful
Destination String -:wonderful
One string is copied into another string using `strncpy();` function.
Here, n=6 so "wonder" is replaced by "beauti".

24. Computer Education leads to Prosperity and fame
Computer Education leads to Prosperity and fame
COMPUTER EDUCATION LEADS TO PROSPERITY AND FAME
computer education leads to prosperity and fame
emaf dna ytirepsorp ot sdael noitacude retupmoc
String is displayed in upper case as well as in lower case using functions `strupr();` and `strlwr();`
String is reversed using function `strrev();`

25. Romali length of string is=6
Number of characters in the word is calculated using `strlen();` function.

26. Length of the string is=5
Length of the string is calculated without the `strlen();` function.

27. Length of the first string =5
Length of the second string =5
Lengths of the strings are same
Lengths of the strings are calculated and compared without using function.
The result is displayed accordingly.

28. Strings are same
`strcmp()` function compares character by character of two strings. Two strings are same and hence the output of the program is 'strings are same'.

29. Strings are not same

30. What is the currency of India?Rupee
Try Again !
What is the currency of India?Ruppea
Try Again !
What is the currency of India?Rupees
Answer is Correct. Currency of India is Rupees.
The answer given by the user is stored in `ans` string and compared with 'Rupees' which is correct answer. The result is displayed accordingly.

31. Source String:-clever
Destination String:-Intelligent
Length of the first string:- 6
Length of the second string:- 11
Two strings are compared using `strcmp();` if strings are of the same length, both the strings will be displayed in one line, otherwise differently. Length of the string is calculated using `strlen();` function.

32. Source String:-C is
Destination String:-easy language
Final string is :-C iseasy language
Length of the final string:- 17
Concatenation of two strings is done using function `strcat();`

33. Sorted List of Cities
Aurangabad
Beed
Jalna
Latur
Nanded
Names of different places are taken in one array and they are placed in alphabetical order using `strcmp();` function. Bubblesort algorithm is used to place the names in order.

34. M M=0
C B=1
The function `strcmp();` compares ASCII values of the characters.

35. First text is:-LATUR
Second text is :-UDGIR
Text length of the first string is the same as of second.
Text lengths of the strings is compared using `memcmp();` function.

36. Source String:-Those who see invisible
Destination String:-they are valuable
Final string is :-Those who see invisible they are valuable
Concatenation of two strings is done using `strcat();` function.

37. Final name is=MUTHA MULHA
Concatenation of two strings is done by simply displaying one after the other string. Three strings are taken in this example.

38. FAILURE IS THE FIRST STEP OF SUCCESS
Text in the string is fully converted to upper case using function `strupr();`

39. string characters HELLO!HAI
String is taken in the lower case which is then converted into upper case using `strupr();` function.

40. vaibhav
String is taken in the upper case which is then converted into lower case using `strlwr();` function.

41. a b c d
The upper case string is converted into lower case string by simply adding 32. (ASCII table)

42. m u m b a i
Upper case string is converted into lower case string.

43. 2
The program is on searching the character. How many times one specific character is encountered in the string can be found out by comparing that character with the string 'character-by-character'.

44. string characters IAH!OLLEH
Similar example as cited in Q 43. String reverse function `strrev()`in header file `string.h`.

45. Length of the string is:- 6
Reverse of the string:-
I
a
h
s
i
V

Array of the string is operated in the reverse so as to get the reverse of the original string "Vishal".

46. Original String = Global
Duplicate String = Global
Duplication of string is done with pointer operation. Text2 points to text and the duplication of the string is obtained with `strdup()` function.

47. String is:-AMERICA
Character to find :M
Character M found in string.
The presence of one specific character in the given string is tested.

48. string1 is:- Splendid
Enter Character to find from the text :
S
S 65494
p 65495
l 65496
e 65497
n 65498
d 65499
i 65500
d 65501
Address of first S returned by strchr()is 65494
Occurrence of a character S and its address location are displayed with `strchr();` string function.

49. 'country' String is present in a given sentence .
Here, in this case `strstr()` function is used.

50. Before strset(): Innovation
After strset(): IIIIIIIII
All the characters of a string are replaced by I with string function `strset();`

51. Before strset(): Knowledgeable world
After strset(): xxxxxxxxxxxxx world
One specific character is assigned to specified length of string (in this case '13') using `strset();` function.

52. After 6 Characters there is no match.
Two strings are compared using function `strspn()` which returns the number of identical characters in two strings.

53. String from given Character is:-
very
First string is broken from a specific character passed to the function as a second parameter. Here, `strpbrk()` function is used, which returns string starting from that character.

7.F Find the bug/s in the following program/s

1. String is larger than the array capacity.
2. The zero before 's' restricts the output.
3. Format string `%c` is required.
4. 'i'is to be initialized with some value say i=−1.
5. Array initialization is incorrect and `%s` is to be used instead of `%c`.
6. ROYAL must be enclosed within curly braces.
7. `char` array is to be initialized with 7 instead of 6.
8. Replace 'c' instead of 'd' in `printf` statement.
9. '&' operator to be deleted.
10. Double quotation mark is needed in `char` statement.
11. `*&a` instead of `&a`.
12. [ ] is not needed in `chp` line and `%c` is to be placed in place of `%d` in `printf` statements.
13. Exchange target and text in `strset` statement.
14. A character should be enclosed with single quotation mark in alpha statement, and instead of `cal-pha`, it should be alpha in `printf()`.
15. ';'(Semicolon is missing in while statement)
16. `%s` instead of `%c`.
17. If statement never terminates with ; (semicolon).
18. ; is not expected in `if` statement.
19. Place `sizeof` instead of `size of` in the `printf` statement.
20. The swapping statement would be am=st;
21. The initializing of array elements is without curly brace.
22. String is not terminated by NULL `char`.
23. `char` array cannot be multi-dimensional.
24. `strlan()` is not existing.
25. text2 should be `char` pointer.
26. Copying not possible onto itself.

8

Pointers

CHAPTER OUTLINE

8.1 POINTER DEFINITION

With pointers we can perform lot many operations by using memory addresses. It is possible to access and display the memory location of a variable using '&' operator. A pointer variable holds the memory address of any type of variable. The pointer variable and normal variable should be of the same type. The pointer is denoted by asterisk (*) symbol.

Pointer: A pointer is a variable that holds a memory address. A pointer can have any name that is legal for other variable, and it is declared in the same fashion like other variables but it is always declared by * operator.

8.2 FEATURES OF POINTERS

(i) Pointers save the memory space.

(ii) Execution time with pointer is faster because data is manipulated with the address, i.e. direct access to memory location.

(iii) The memory is accessed efficiently with the pointers. The pointer assigns the memory space and also it releases. The memory is dynamically allocated.

(iv) Pointers are used with data structures. They are useful for representing two-dimensional and multi-dimensional arrays.

(v) We can access elements of any type of array irrespective of its subscript range.

(vi) Pointers are used in file handling.

(vii) Pointers are used to allocate memory dynamically.

8.3 POINTERS AND ADDRESSES

When a variable of any data type is declared, according to its data type the memory is reserved.

As shown in Figure 8.1, the memory locations are reserved for the variables x, y and c. Integer variables require two bytes each and for character variable one byte is reserved. The locations 65550 and 65551 are used to store 'x', 65552 and 65553 are used to store 'y' and so on. The starting address for 'x' is 65550 and 'y' is 65552. The character needs only one byte and its location shown in Figure 8.1 is 65554.

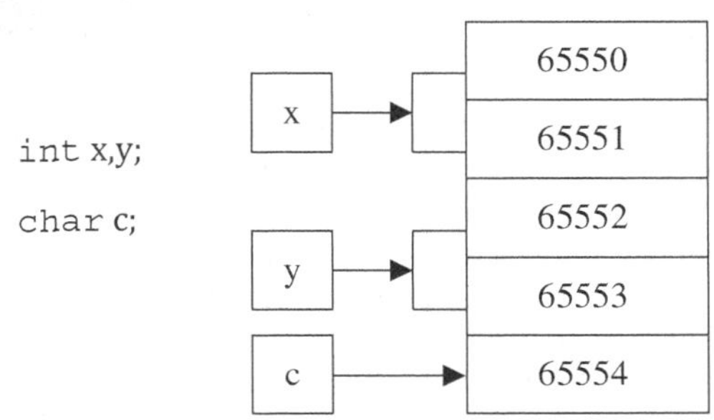

FIGURE 8.1 **Memory allocated**

8.4 POINTER DECLARATION

The pointer variables can be declared as follows.

Example:

```
int *x;
float *f;
char *y;
```

(i) In the first statement, 'x' is an integer pointer and it tells to the compiler that it holds the address of any integer variable. In the same way, 'f' is a float pointer which stores the address of any float variable and 'y' is a character pointer that stores the address of any character variable.

(ii) The indirection operator (*) is also called the dereferencing operator. When a pointer is dereferenced, the value at that address stored by the pointer is retrieved.

(iii) Normal variable provides direct access to their own values, whereas a pointer provides indirect access to the values of the variable whose address it stores.

(iv) The indirection operator (*) is used in two distinct ways with pointers, declaration and dereference.

(a) When a pointer is declared, the asterisk(*) indicates that it is a pointer, not a normal variable.

(b) When the pointer is dereferenced, the indirection operator indicates that the value at that memory location stored in the pointer is to be accessed rather than the address itself.

(c) Also note that the indirection operator (*) is the same operator that can be used for multiplication. The compiler knows which operation to be performed, based on the context.

(d) The '&' is the address operator and it represents the address of the variable. The '`%u`' is used with `printf()` function for printing the address of a variable. The address of any variable is a whole number.

8.5 ARITHMETIC OPERATIONS WITH POINTERS

Arithmetic operations on pointer variables are also possible. Increment, decrement, prefix and postfix operations can be performed with the pointers. The effect of these operations is shown in Table 8.1 given below.

From the above table, we can observe that on the increment of pointer variable for integers, the address is incremented by 2, i.e. 4046 is the original address and on increment its value will be 4048, because integers require two bytes.

Similarly, for characters, floating point numbers and long integers require 1, 4 and 4 bytes, respectively. After the effect of increment and decrement, the memory locations are shown in Table 8.1. Refer program number 14 under 8.E for detail understanding.

TABLE 8.1 Pointer and arithmetic operation

Data Type	*Initial Address*	*Operation*		*Address After Operations*		*Required Bytes*
`int` i=2	4046	++	--	4048	4044	2
`char` c='x'	4053	++	--	4054	4052	1
`float` f=2.2	4058	++	--	4062	4054	4
`long` l=2	4060	++	--	4064	4056	4

8.6 POINTERS AND ARRAYS

The array name itself is an address or pointer. It points to the address of the first element(0th) element of an array). The elements of the array together with their addresses can be displayed by using array name itself. The array elements are always stored in contiguous memory locations.

8.7 POINTERS TO POINTERS

A pointer is known as a variable containing address of another variable. The pointer variables also have an address. The pointer variable containing address of other pointer variables is called as pointer to pointer. This chain can be continued to any extent.

8.8 DYNAMIC MEMORY ALLOCATION

There is a technique by which program can obtain space in the main memory which is called dynamic allocation. Dynamic allocation is a technique in which a program can acquire storage space in the main memory. In this method, the space for the program is allocated during execution of the program. The free region of the memory is called the heap.

8.9 MEMORY ALLOCATION FUNCTIONS

(i) malloc( ): This function is used to allocate memory space in bytes to the variables of different data types. This function reserves bytes of determined size and returns the base address to the pointer variable. The prototypes are declared in `alloc.h` and `stdlib.h`. The format of the `malloc()` function is as under.

```
pnt=(data type*)malloc(given size);
```

Here, from the data type, compiler understands the pointer type, and given size is the size to reserve the memory.

```
pnt=(int *)malloc(20);
```

Here, in this declaration, 20 bytes are allocated to pointer variable `pnt` of type `int` and base address is returned to pointer `pnt`.

(ii) calloc( ): This function is useful for allocating multiple blocks of memory. It is declared with two arguments. The prototypes are declared in `alloc.h` and `stdlib.h`. The format of the `calloc()` function is as follows.

```
pnt=(int *)calloc(4,2);
```

The above declaration allocates four blocks of memory; each block contains 2 bytes. The base address is stored in the integer pointer. This function is usually used for allocating memory for array and structure. The `calloc()` can be used in place of `malloc()` function. The programs illustrated with `malloc()` function can be executed using `calloc()` function.

(iii) free( ): The `free()` function is used to release the memory allocated by memory allocating functions. Thus, using this function wastage of memory is prevented. The declaration of the function is given below.

```
free(pnt);
```

In the above declaration, `pnt` is a pointer. The `free()` function releases the memory occupied by the pointer variable `pnt`.

(iv) realloc( ): This function reallocates main memory. The prototypes are declared in `alloc.h` and `stdlib.h`. Attempts are made to shrink or enlarge the previously allocated memory by `malloc()` or `calloc()` functions. It returns the address of the reallocated block, which can be different than the original address. If the block cannot be reallocated or size = 0, `realloc()` returns NULL. The syntax of this function is as below.

```
pnt=realloc(pnt,newsize);
```

This function reallocates new memory of new size to the pointer variable `pnt`.

EXERCISES

8.A Fill in the blanks

1. A pointer is a memory variable that stores a ________.
   (a) memory address
   (b) value
   (c) none of the above

2. Pointer can have any name that is legal for other ________.
   (a) variable
   (b) keyword
   (c) header file

3. Pointer is declared in the same fashion like other variable, but it is always denoted by ________ operator.
   (a) *
   (b) &
   (c) #

4. Pointers save the ________.
   (a) memory space
   (b) value
   (c) none of the above

5. The execution time with pointer is faster because ________.
   (a) data is manipulated with the address
   (b) data is manipulated with the values
   (c) none of the above

6. Pointers are used with data structures. They are useful for representing ________ and multi-dimensional arrays.
   (a) two-dimensional
   (b) multi-dimensional
   (c) none of the above

7. In the statement `int *x` is an ________.
   (a) `integer` pointer
   (b) `float` pointer
   (c) `unsigned` pointer

8. Declaration of `int *x;` tells the compiler that it holds the ________.
   (a) address of any integer variable
   (b) address of any `float`variable
   (c) address of any `char` variable

9. The indirection operator (*) is used for ________.
   (a) declaration and dereference
   (b) declaration
   (c) dereference
   (d) none of the above

10. When the pointer is dereferenced, the indirection operator indicates that the ________.
    (a) value at that address stored can be accessed
    (b) address of variable can be accessed
    (c) none of the above

11. Fill in the columns after ++ and -- operations.

Data Type	*Initial Address*	*Operation*		*Address after Operations*	
`int i=2`	4046	++	--	4048	4044
`char c='x'`	4053	++	--		
`float f=2.2`	4058	++	--		
`long l=2`	4060	++	--		

12. The array name by itself is an address or ________.
    (a) pointer
    (b) value
    (c) identifier

13. The array of pointers is nothing but ________.
    (a) a collection of addresses
    (b) a collection of values
    (c) all the above

14. The pointer variables also have an ________ which is stored in another pointer.
    (a) name
    (b) address
    (c) value

15. The pointer variable containing address of another pointer variables is called as ________.
    (a) pointer to pointer
    (b) pointer
    (c) double pointer

16. The memory address of the variable is ________.
    (a) constant
    (b) pointer constant
    (c) integer

8.B True or false

1. A pointer saves the memory space.
2. A pointer is a memory variable that stores memory address.
3. Pointers can be used to represent arrays.
4. The indirection operator asterisk (*) is used to identify the pointer variable.
5. The & is address operator and represents the address of the variable.
6. The physical memory locations of the variable is system dependent.
7. The user can predict the address of the memory variable.
8. The pointer of any data type requires only four bytes.
9. A pointer cannot point to another pointer variable.
10. The address of pointer variable for integer is 4044, after incrementing the pointer variable its address becomes 4066.
11. The pointer variable holding address of another pointer is pointer to pointer.
12. `p**` is a pointer to pointer.
13. `*p` is a pointer.
14. `char **q` is pointer to pointer.

8.C Match the following correct pairs given in Group A with Group B

I

Group A		Group B	
Serial No.	**Data type**	**Serial No.**	**Required bytes**
1.	`int i=2`	A	4
2.	`char c='x'`	B	8
3.	`float f=2.2`	C	1
4.	`double l=2`	D	2

II

Group A		Group B	
Serial No.	**Declaration**	**Serial No.**	**Declaration**
1.	`int *x;`	A	Array
2.	`float **x;`	B	Pointer to pointer
3.	`long *x`	C	Integer pointer
4.	`int x[5]`	D	Long pointer

III

Group A		Group B	
Serial No.	**Data type**	**Serial No.**	**Required bytes**
1.	`double`	A	10
2.	`long double`	B	2
3.	`unsigned char`	C	8
4.	`signed int or int`	D	1

IV

Group A		Group B	
Serial No.	**Operator**	**Serial No.**	**Meaning**
1.	`*`	A	Address value
2.	`&b`	B	Value at address of 'b'
3.	`*(&b)`	C	Address of variable 'b'
4.	`% u`	D	Pointer operator

V

Group A		Group B	
Serial No.	**Functions**	**Serial No.**	**Meaning**
1.	`calloc()`	A	Allotment of memory space
2.	`realloc()`	B	Freeing memory space
3.	`free()`	C	Allotment of many blocks of memory
4.	`malloc()`	D	Changing the size of memory block

8.D Select the appropriate option from the multiple choices given below

1. Following one operation with which addresses are not possible.
   (a) Addition of two addresses (pointers).
   (b) ++
   (c) –
2. Following one operation is possible with address holding (pointers).
   (a) multiplication of addresses or multiplication of address with a constant
   (b) division of address with a constant
   (c) ++
   (d) none of the above
3. The declaration `int *arrp[3]` is nothing but
   (a) integer array
   (b) integer pointer array
   (c) one of the above
4. Pointer to pointer can be denoted as
   (a) **p
   (b) p**
   (c) *p
5. The following program will show the error message

```
int p=2;
char *c=&p;
```

   (a) expression syntax in function main
   (b) non-portable assignment
   (c) suspicious pointer conversion
   (d) none of the above
6.
```
int p=2,*k;
int *c=&p;
k=c;
```
   we can say that
   (a) pointer 'c' and 'k' are pointing to 'p'
   (b) pointer 'k' pointing to 'p' and 'c'
   (c) only pointer 'c' pointing to 'p'
7.
```
int s,*j,**kk;
j=&s;
kk=&j;
```
   we can say that
   (a) kk is pointer of pointer
   (b) j is pointer of pointer
   (c) k is only pointer

8.E What will be the output/s of the following program/s?

1. Use pointer and display value and address of an integer element.

```
void main()
{
   int num=10,*p;
   p=&num;
   clrscr();
   printf(" %d",*p);
   printf(" %d",num);
   printf(" %u",&num);
   printf(" %u",p);
   getche();
}
```

Explanation: Pointer 'p' points value stored at address of num. To access the value of num, we use pointer. Value of num=10. In the first two `printf()` statements, the variable value 10 is printed. Also, in the third and fourth `printf()` statements, the addresses of num are displayed.

2. Use pointer and display a number.

```
void main()
{
   int p=10;
   void *pt=&p;
   clrscr();
   *(int*)pt=12;
   printf("%d",p);
}
```

Explanation: Void pointer holds the address of any data type such as `int`, `float`, `char` and by assigning the address, we can typecast it, i.e. which data type. The `*(pt)` points the value stored at the address held by pt. The next value assigned to the pointer is 12 and the same is displayed.

3. Use pointer and display number by different ways.

```
void main()
{
int t=10,*p;
clrscr();
p=&t;
printf("\n t = %d t = %d t = %d",
    t,*(&t),*p);
}
```

Explanation: In the above program, it displays the value of the variable 't'. Three different syntaxes are used in the `printf()` statement.

4. Use pointers and display long integers and floating point numbers.

```
void main()
{
long int a,*pa;
float b,*pb;
clrscr();
printf("Enter Integer & float
   Value :");
scanf("%ld %f",&a,&b);
pa=&a;
pb=&b;

printf("\n Address of a=%u",pa);
printf("\n Value of a=%ld",a);
printf("\n Value of a=%ld",*(&a));
printf("\n Value of a=%ld",*pa);
printf("\nAddress of b=%u",pb);
printf("\n Value of b=%.2f",b);
printf("\n Value of b=%.2f",*(&b));
printf("\n Value of b=%.2f",*pb);
}
```

Explanation: Integer value 2345 and float value 2.345 are prompted through the keyboard. The same values and their addresses are printed on the screen.

5. Display the memory requirement for character, integer and float number and their pointers.

```
void main()
{
clrscr();
printf("char %d byte & its pointer %d
   bytes\n",sizeof(char),
   sizeof(char*));
printf("int %d byte & its pointer %d
   bytes\n",sizeof(int),sizeof
   (int*));
printf("float %d byte & its pointer %d
   bytes\n",sizeof(float),sizeof
   (float*));
}
```

Explanation: Pointer of any data type requires two bytes. This is shown in all the three `printf()` statements.

6. Program to display a string using pointer.

```
void main()
{
   char c[]="India";
   char *p;
   p=c;
   clrscr();
   printf("%s",p);
}
```

Explanation: Here, the address of 0th element is assigned to character pointer 'p'. In other words, base address of the string is assigned to 'p'. After every increment of 'p', the pointer goes to the next character of the string. The displayed string on the screen is India.

7. Display two strings.

```
void main()
{
   char *c="India";
   char *p ="Bharat";
   char *k;
   k=p;
   p=c;
   clrscr();
   printf("%s",p);
   printf(" %s",k);
}
```

Explanation: Here, the address of the 0th element is assigned to character pointers 'c' and 'p'. In other words, base addresses of a string are assigned to 'k' and 'p'. The displayed string on the screen is India and Bharat.

Arithmetic operations with pointers

8. Use pointers and display addition of two numbers with and without pointers.

```
void main()
{
   int a=5,b=7,c,d,*ap,*bp;
   clrscr();
   ap=&a;
   bp=&b;
   c=a+b;
   d=*ap+*bp;
   printf("\n Sum of A & B :%d",c);
   printf("\n Sum of A & B : %d",d);
}
```

Explanation: Here, sum of A and B is 12 .With simple arithmetic addition a+b, which is stored in 'c', is displayed sum of A & B =12, i.e. addition of value pointed by pointer ap & bp is 12.

9. Use pointers and display addition, subtraction, multiplication and division of two numbers with pointers.

```
void main()
{
int a=25,b=10,*p,*j;
p=&a;j=&b;
clrscr();
printf(" %d %d %d %d %d",*p+b,
    *p-b,*p * *j,*p / *j,*p % *j);
}
```

Explanation: Execution of printf() always starts from right to left, so in following sequences operation will be performed:
∗p%∗j = 25 % 10 = 5
∗p / ∗j = 25 /10 = 2
∗p ∗ ∗j = 25 ∗ 10= 250
∗p-b= 25- 10 =15
∗p+b=25+10=35
Thus, the output will be as 35, 15, 250, 2, 5

10. Multiplication and addition of pointers.

```
void main()
{
  int num=10,*p;
  p=&num;
  clrscr();
  num=*p**p+*p+*p;
  printf(" %d",num);
  getche();
}
```

Explanation: Here, in this program *p = 10 & num = 10, hence num=*p * *p + *p + *p=10*10+ 10+10= 120

11. Use pointer increment operation to display characters.

```
void main()
{
  char name[15]="He",*ch;
  ch=name;
  clrscr();
  while(*ch!='\0')
  {
   printf("%c",(*ch)+1);
   ch++;
  }
}
```

Explanation: *ch points character stored in name array and gives its value in ASCII by %c, thus it will print "He". But (*ch) +1 indicates ASCII value added by 1 every time, hence instead of He it will print If [(I= (ASCII of H) +1) & (f=(ASCII of e) +1)]

12. Use pointer increment operation to display characters.

```
void main()
{
  char name[15]="Good",*ch;
  ch=name;
  clrscr();
  while(*ch!='\0')
  {
  printf("%c",(*ch)-1);
  ch++;
  }
}
```

Explanation: The answer is also similar to previous one.

13. Use pointer increment operation and display addresses of an array element.

```
void main()
{
int x[5]={3,4,6,8,10},t=0;
clrscr();
printf("\nElement No. Element
   Address");
while(t<5)
{
printf("\n x[%d] = \t%8d
   %9u",t,*(x+t),x+t);
t++;
}
}
```

Explanation: In this program, initially t=0 & * (x+t) => x[t] && x+t=>&x increments with positions indicated by 't'. Thus, elements and addresses are displayed.

14. Pointer incrementation and decrementation operations.

```
void main()
{
  int num=10,*p;
  clrscr();
  p=&num;
  printf(" %u",p);
  printf(" %u",p+4);
  printf(" %u",p-2);
```

```
  printf(" %d",++(*p));
  getche();
}
```

Explanation: The 'p' prints the address of num and it is 65498. p+4 mean base address added by 8 bytes, i.e. (65498+8=65506) and p-2 becomes (65498-4=65494) and at last ++((*p))=++(10)=11.

Array operations and display

15. Display elements of an array without pointer.

```
void main()
{
int x[]={1,2,3,4,5,6,7},k=1;
clrscr();
while(k<=5)
{
  printf("%2d",k[x-1]);
  k++;
 }
}
```

Explanation: Initially k=1 & k[x-1] indicates & [(base address)–one location]= first address, now 'k' will increment the position of base address by particular location, but 'k' will increment up to 5 only, the output will print up to 5 value from 0th location to 4th location.

16. Perform operation on array elements and display them.

```
void main()
{
   int a[]={15,20,40},b[3],j=0,k=2;
   clrscr();
   for(j=0;j<3;j++)
  {
    b[j]=a[k];
    k--;
  }
    j=0;
   while(j<3)
   printf(" %d ",b[j++]);
}
```

Explanation: Inner for loop will assign value as
b[0]=a[2]=>b[0]=40
b[1]=a[1]=>b[1]=20
b[2]=a[0]=>b[2]=15
thus output will of b[0],b[1],b[2] as 40,20,15.

17. Display numbers with an array with and without pointer.

```
void main()
{
int arr[]={10,20,30},p=0;
clrscr();
 for(p=0;p<3;p++)
 {
  printf("\n%d %d %d",
    p[arr],*(arr+p),arr[p]);
}
}
```

Explanation: In this program p[arr]=>arr[p]. *(arr+p)=> pointer points the base address and holds the value stored in it and position increments by 'p' value.
arr[p] will print
0[arr]=*(arr+0)=arr[0]=10
1[arr]=*(arr+1)=arr[1]=20
2[arr]=*(arr+2)=arr[2]=30

18. Use pointer and display addition of array elements.

```
void main()
{
 int arr[]={15,20,40},sum=0,j=0;
 clrscr();
 while(j<3)
 sum=sum+*(arr+j++);
 printf("\n sum %d",sum);
}
```

Explanation: Initially j=0 and the loop will execute thrice as
sum=0+*(arr+0)=0+15=15
sum=15+*(arr+1)=15+20=35
sum=35+*(arr+2)=35+40=75

19. Use pointer and display array elements.

```
void main()
{
 int *arr[3];
 int ar[]={5,10,15},k;
 for(k=0;k<3;k++)
 arr[k]=ar+k;
 clrscr();
 for(k=0;k<3;k++)
 printf("%d ",*(arr[k]));
}
```

Explanation: *arr[ ] is array of pointer. The arr[k]=ar+k holds the address and pointer points the value stored in that address.

20. Sum of squares and cubes of array elements.

```
#include <math.h>
void main()
```

```
{
int k[]={1,2,3,4,5},t,sumsq=0,
    sumc=0;
clrscr();
for(t=0;t<5;t++)
{
sumsq=sumsq+pow(*(t+k),2);
sumc=sumc+pow(k[t],3);
}
printf("\nSum of Squares of array
    elements : %d", sumsq);
printf("\nSum of Cubes of array ele-
    ments : %d",sumc);
}
```

Explanation:

- Power function is used to calculates x raise to y i.e. pow(x,y).
- *(t+k) takes the value stored in k[] array and finds square and cubes according to the functions.
- And recursive addition is performed.
- For square
  pow(k[0],2)+pow(k[1],2)+pow(k[2],2)+pow(k[3],2)+pow(k[4],2)=pow(1,2)+pow(2,2)+pow(3,2)+pow(4,2)+pow(5,2)=1+4+9+16+25=55
- For cube
  pow(k[0],3)+pow(k[1],3)+pow (k[2],3)+pow(k[3],3)+pow(k[4],3)=pow(1,3)+pow(2,3)+pow(3,3)+pow(4,3)+pow(5,3)=1+8+27+64+125=225

21. Three by three matrix and printout its numbers.

```
void main()
{
int i,j=1,*p;
int a[3][3]={{1,2,3},{4,5,6},
    {7,8,9}};
clrscr();
printf("\tElements of An Array with
    their addresses\n\n");
p=&a[0][0];
for(i=0;i<9;i++,j++)
{
printf("%5d [%5u ]",*(p),p);
p++;
if(j==3)
{
printf("\n");
j=0;
}}
}
```

Explanation:
%5d indicates identifier for integer value with 4 blank spaces.
%5u indicates identifier for integer address.
p holds the base addresses which are always indicated by a[0][0] and pointer points value at that address.
Thus, *p gives pointed values after incrementing its location as p++ by 2 bytes.
Elements and their addresses are displayed.

22. Display original array and duplicate array elements.

```
void main()
{
int so[]={1,2,3,4,5},*pb,ds[5],i;
pb=so;
clrscr();
for(i=0;i<5;i++)
{
  ds[i]=*pb;
  pb++;
}
printf("Original Array Duplicated
    Array");
for(i=0;i<5;i++)
printf("\n\t%d\t\t %d", so[i],ds[i]);
}
```

Explanation: In this program, 'pb' holds the address of 'so', and *pb points value at that address which is assigned to 'ds'.

23. Print addresses and element values of an array.

```
void main()
{
int *arrp[3];
int arrl[3]={5,10,15},k;
for(k=0;k<3;k++)
arrp[k]=arrl+k;
clrscr();
printf("\n\tAddress Element\n");
for(k=0;k<3;k++)
{
  printf("\t%u",arrp[k]);
  printf("\t%7d \n",*(arrp[k]));
 }
 }
```

Explanation: The arrp is array of pointer, i.e. arrp[0], arrp[1], arrp[2] will give address of each element.
arrl is integer array which has value 5 10 15.
"arrp[k]=arrl+k" indicates assigning the address to array pointer which points the value stored at that address.

Pointer to pointer

24. Use pointer to pointer and display values of element.

```
void main()
{
 int a=2,*p,**q;
 p=&a;
 q=&p;
 clrscr();
 printf("%d %d %d",a,*p,**q);
}
```

Explanation:

- `p=&a` means 'p' holds the address of 'a'.
- `q=&p` means 'q' holds the address of 'p'.
- `*p` points value at the address of 'a'.
- `**q` points to the pointer which contains value stored at the address of 'a' `**q=>*(*(q))=>*(*(&p))=>*(*(&(&a))=>*(&a)=>2`

25. Use pointers to pointers and display numbers.

```
void main()
{
int k;
int a[]={1,2,3};
int *b[3];
int **c[3];
int ***d[3];
int ****e[3];
int *****f[3];
clrscr();
for(k=0;k<3;k++)
{
    b[k]=a+k;
    c[k]=b+k;
    d[k]=c+k;
    e[k]=d+k;
    f[k]=e+k;
}
for(k=0;k<3;k++)
{
printf("%3d",*b[k]);
printf("%3d",**c[k]);
printf("%3d",***d[k]);
}
}
}
printf("%3d",****e[k]);
printf("%3d\n",*****f[k]);
}
}
```

Explanation:
`*b[3]` is array pointer of size 3.
`**c[3]` is array pointer to pointer of size 3.
`***d[3]` is array pointer to pointer to pointer of size 3.
`****e[3]` is array pointer to pointer to pointer to pointer of size 3.
`*****f[3]` is array pointer to pointer to pointer to pointer to pointer of size 3.
`b[k]=a+k;` 'b' holds the address of 'a'.
`c[k]=b+k;` 'c' holds the address of 'b'.
`d[k]=c+k;` 'd' holds the address of 'c'.
`e[k]=d+k;` 'e' holds the address of 'd'.
`f[k]=e+k;` 'f' holds the address of 'e'.

Double pointers

26. Print element values and their addresses using pointers and double pointers.

```
void main()
{
 int a=2,*p,**q;
 p=&a;
 q=&p;
 clrscr();
 printf ("\n Value of a= %d Address
    of a=%u",a,&a);
 printf ("\n Through *p Value of
    a= %d Address of a=%u",*p,p);
 printf ("\n Through **q Value of a=
    %d Address of a=%d",**q,*q);
}
```

Explanation:
The address of a becomes –40.
It takes value within the range –128 to +127, thus `*q` holds the address of a=65496–65536= –40.
If we take `%u`, then it prints the address of a=65496.

8.F Find the bug/s in the following program/s

1.

```
void main()
{
char *c;
float x=10;
c=&x;
printf("%d",*c);
}
```

2.

```
void main()
{
float x=10.25,*f;f=x;
clrscr();
printf("%g",*f);
}
```

3.

```
void main()
{
float x=10.25,*t,*f;
t=&x;
f=&t;
clrscr();
printf("%g",**f);
}
```

4.

```
void main()
{
char sa[]="How are you ?";
char t,*f;f=&sa;
clrscr();
printf("%s",f);
}
```

5.

```
void main()
{
int *t,x;t=&x;x=11;
*t++;
clrscr();
printf("%d",*t);
}
```

6.

```
void main()
{
int t[]={1,2,3,4,5};
int *p,*q,*r;p=t;q=p[1];
r=p[2];
clrscr();
printf("%d %d %d",*p,*q,*r);
}
```

7.

```
void main()
{
int num[2][3]={1,2,3,4,5},*k;
k=&num;
clrscr();
printf("%d",*k);
}
```

8.

```
void main()
{
int x=5,y=8,z;
int *px,*py,*pz;px=&x;py=&y;pz=&z;
   pz=*px+*py;
clrscr();
printf("%d",z);
}
```

9.

```
void main()
{
int x=5;
int *px=&x,*py;
clrscr();
printf("%d",px);
}
```

10.

```
void main()
{
 int x,*px;
 *px=5;
 px=&x;
 clrscr();
 printf("%d",x);
}
```

11.

```
void main()
{
 int *p,*q,a=2;
 p=&a;
 q=p;
 clrscr();
 printf("%d %d", p ,q);
}
```

12.

```
void main()
{
 int *p,*q,**t,a=2;
 p=&a;
 q=p;
 t=p;
 clrscr();
 printf("%d %d %d", *p ,*q,**t);
}
```

13.

```
void main()
{
```

```
 int y[]={1,2,3},*p;
 p=&y[1];
 clrscr();
 printf("%d %d",(1+y),*p);
}
```

14.

```
void main()
{
 unsigned y[]={65555,65550,65543};
 clrscr();
 printf("%u",y[2]);
}
```

15.

```
void main()
{
int p[]={1,2,3,4};
char *c;
c=p;
clrscr();
printf("%d",*c);
}
```

8.G Attempt the following programming exercises

1. Write a program to allocate memory for 10 integers and 5 floating point numbers.
2. Write a program to display all the elements of a character array using pointer.
3. Write a program to access unsigned integers using pointer and display them.
4. Write a program to calculate area and circumference of a circle using pointer.
5. Write a program to demonstrate the use of `realloc ()` and `calloc ()` functions.

ANSWERS

8.A Fill in the blanks

1. (a) memory address
2. (a) variable
3. (a) *
4. (a) memory space
5. (a) data is manipulated with the address
6. (a) two-dimensional
7. (a) integer pointer
8. (a) address of any integer variable
9. (a) declaration and dereference
10. (a) value at that address stored can be accessed
11.

4054	4052
4062	4054
4064	4056

12. (a) pointer
13. (a) a collection of addresses
14. (b) address
15. (a) pointer to pointer
16. (b) pointer constant

8.B True or false

1. T 2. T 3. T 4. T 5. T 6. T 7. F 8. F 9. F 10. F
11. T 12. F 13. T 14. T

8.C Match the following correct pairs given in Group A with Group B

I 1. D, 2. C, 3. A, 4. B
II 1. C, 2. B, 3. D, 4. A
III 1. C, 2. A, 3. D, 4. B
IV 1. D, 2. C, 3. B, 4. A
V 1. C, 2. D, 3. B, 4. A

8.D Select the appropriate option from the multiple choices given below

1. (a) addition of two addresses (pointers)
2. (c) ++
3. (a) integer pointer array
4. (a) **p
5. (a) expression syntax in function main
6. (a) pointer 'c' and 'k' are pointing to 'p'
7. (a) kk is pointer of pointer

8.E What will be the output/s of the following program/s?

1. 10 10 65498 65498
2. 12
3. t=10 t=10 t=10
4. Enter Integer & float Value :2345 2.345
   Address of a=65492
   Value of a=2345
   Value of a=2345
   Value of a=2345
   Address of b=65496
   Value of b=2.35
   Value of b=2.35
   Value of b=2.35
5. char 1 byte & its pointer 2 bytes
   int 2 byte & its pointer 2 bytes
   float 4 byte & its pointer 2 bytes
6. India
7. India Bharat
8. Sum of A & B : 12
   Sum of A & B : 12
9. 35 15 250 2 5
10. 120
11. If
12. Fnnc
13. Element No. Element Address
    x[0] = 3 65490
    x[1] = 4 65492
    x[2] = 6 65494
    x[3] = 8 65496
    x[4] = 10 65498
14. 65498 65506 65494 11
15. 1 2 3 4 5
16. 40 20 15
17. 10 10 10
    20 20 20
    30 30 30
18. sum=75
19. 5 10 15
20. Sum of Squares of array elements : 55
    Sum of Cubes of array elements : 225
21. Elements of An Array with their addresses
    1[65482] 2[65484] 3[65486]
    4[65488] 5[65490] 6[65492]
    7[65494] 8[65496] 9[65498]
22. Original Array Duplicated Array

Original Array	Duplicated Array
1	1
2	2
3	3
4	4
5	5

23. Address Element

Address	Element
65494	5
65496	10
65498	15

24. 2 2 2
25. 1 1 1 1 1
    2 2 2 2 2
    3 3 3 3 3
26. Value of a= 2 Address of a=65496
    Through *p Value of a= 2 Address of a=65496
    Through **q Value of a= 2 Address of a=−40

8.F Find the bug/s in the following program/s

1. Pointer and variable should be of the same data type.
2. & is missing in assignment statement.

3. `**f` should be declared as pointer to pointer.
4. & is not needed.
5. `t++` does not work, `(++*t)` works.
6. & is required in `q=p[1];` and `r=p[2];`
7. `k=#` would be `k=&num[0][0];`
8. In the assignment statement `*pz` is required.
9. `%u` is required for formatting address.
10. The statement `*px=5;` should appear after `px=&x;`
11. * is missing `(*p,*q)`
12. In the statement `t=p`, & is missing.
13. * missing at `(1+y)`.
14. Array values are beyond range.
15. Pointer type does not match with the array type.

9

Functions

CHAPTER OUTLINE

9.1 INTRODUCTION

It is laborious to prepare and maintain a large size program. Moreover, identification of flow of data is difficult to understand. The best way to prepare a programming application is to divide the bigger program into small pieces or modules, and the same modules can be repeatedly called from the `main()` function as and when required. These small modules or subprograms are easily manageable. This process is called divide and conquer. In C, such small modules are called functions. Figure 9.1 describes the method of developing a program.

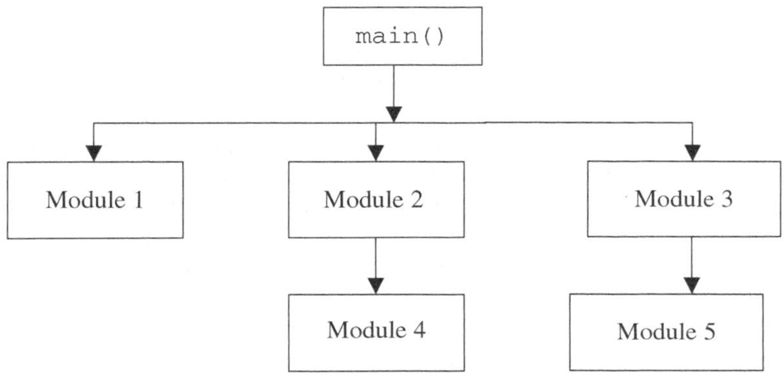

FIGURE 9.1 A program divided into multiple functions

The programs written in C language highly depends upon functions. The C program is nothing but a combination of one or more functions. Every C program starts with user-defined function `main()`. Each time when a new program is written, `main()` function must be defined. The `main()` calls another function to share the work. The main program to each function can supply data. A specific operation is performed on the data and value is returned to the calling function.

The C language supports two types of functions (i) library functions and (ii) user-defined functions. The library functions are pre-defined set of functions. Their task is limited. User should not worry to understand the internal working of these functions. User can only use the functions but cannot change or modify them. For example `sqrt(81)` gives result 9. Here, the user need not worry about its source code, but the result should be provided by the function.

The user-defined functions are totally different. The functions defined by the user according to his/her requirement are called as user-defined functions. User can modify the function according to the requirement. User certainly understands the internal working of the function. User has full scope to implement his/her own ideas in the function. Thus, the set of such user-defined functions can be useful to another programmer. One should include the file in which the user-defined functions are stored to call the function in the program. For example, let `square(9)` is a user-defined function that gives the result 81. Here, user knows the internal working of the `square()` function, as its source code is visible. This is the major difference between the two types of functions.

9.2 DEFINITION OF FUNCTION

A function is a self-contained block or a sub-program of one or more statements that performs a special task when called.

9.2.1 Why Use Functions?

(i) If we want to perform a task repetitively, then it is not obligatory to rewrite the particular block of the program again and again. Shift the particular block of statements in an user-defined function. The function defined can be called any number of times depending upon the requirement to perform the task.

(ii) Using functions, large size programs can be reduced to smaller ones. It is easy to debug and find out the errors in it. It also increases readability.

9.2.2 How Function Works?

(i) Once a function is defined and called, it takes some data from the calling function and returns a value to the called function.

(ii) The detail of inner working of a function is unknown to the rest of the program. Whenever a function is called, control passes to the called function and working of calling function is paused. When the execution of called function is completed, control returns back to the calling function and executes the next statement.

(iii) The values of actual arguments passed by the calling function are received by the formal arguments of the called function. The number of actual and formal arguments should be the same. Extra arguments are discarded if they are defined. If the formal arguments are more than the actual arguments, then the extra arguments appear as garbage. Any mismatch in the data type will produce the unexpected result.

(iv) The function operates on formal arguments and sends back the result to calling function. The `return` statement performs this task.

9.3 FUNCTION DEFINITION SYNTAX

Function definition syntax is as follows:

```
return type
function_name (argument/ parameter
list)
{
local variable declaration;
Statement1;
Statement2;
return(value);
}
```

Table 9.1 simulates the working of a function with its necessary components.

TABLE 9.1 Working of function

```
void main()
{
  int x,y,z;
  -------------
  -------------
abc(x,y,z);                     Function Call
    |
    └──────────────────────► Actual arguments
  -------------
  -------------
}
int abc(int l, int k, int j)   Function definition
{
           |
           └─────────────────► Formal arguments
  -------------
  -------------
return(value);                  return value
}
```

(i) The return type of the function can be `int`, `float`, `double`, `char`, `void`, etc., depending upon what is to be returned from called function to the calling function. By default in C, function returns `int`, if return type is not mentioned.

(ii) *Actual argument*: The arguments of calling functions are actual arguments. In Table 9.1, variables 'x', 'y' and 'z' are actual arguments.

(iii) *Formal argument*: The arguments of called function are formal arguments. In Table 9.1, variable 'l', 'k' and 'j' are formal arguments.

(iv) *Function name*: A function must follow the same rule as we use for variable naming.

***Example*:**

```
sum(int a, int b);
```

where `sum()` is a user-defined function and 'a' and 'b' are integer variable arguments. The function name must be ended by a semicolon (;).

(v) *Argument/parameter list*: The argument list means variable names enclosed within the parentheses. They must be separated by comma (,). These formal arguments (consignment) are to receive values from actual argument, and for performing this, a communication between consignee and consignor functions is made.

(vi) *Function call*: A compiler executes the function when a semicolon (;) is followed by the function name. A function can be called simply using its name like other C statement, terminated by semicolon (;). The called function should not be terminated with semicolon(;).

Consider the following example.

9.1 Write a program to show how user-defined function is called.

```
void main()
{
 int x=1,y=2,z;
 z=add(x,y); /* Function Call */
 printf("\nz=%d",z);
}
/* Function Definition */
add(int a, int b) /* Called Function*/
{
return(a+b);
}
```

Output

```
z=3
```

***Explanation*:**

In the above program, values of 'x' and 'y' are passed to function `add()`. Formal argument 'a' and 'b' receive the values. The function `add()` calculates addition of both the variables and returns result. The result is collected by the variable 'z' of the `main()` function which is printed through the `printf()` statement. By default, called function returns integer to the calling function, hence return type is not mentioned in the called function at the beginning.

9.2 Write a program to define user-defined function. Call them at different places.

```
void y();
void y()
{
printf("Y");
}

void main()
{
void a(),b(),c(),d();
clrscr();
        y();
        a();
        b();
        c();
        d();
}

void a()
{
printf(" A");
y();
 }

void b()
{
  printf(" B");
  a();
 }

void c()
{
  a();
  b();
   printf(" C");
}

void d()
{
printf(" D");
c();
b();
a();
}
```

Output

```
Y A Y B A Y A Y B A Y C D A Y B A Y C B A Y A Y
```

Explanation:

From the above program, we derive the following:

(a) The `main()` function can call any other function defined before or after `main()` function.

(b) Any other user-defined function can call the `main()` function.

(c) The user-defined function can call only those user-defined functions which are defined before it, i.e. the function `a()` can call only `y()` and not `b()`, `c()` and `d()`. The function `b()` cannot call function `c()` and `d()`. The function `d()` can call all the functions because it is the last function.

(vii) *Local and global variables*: There are two kinds of variables: (a) local and (b) global.

(a) *Local variable*: The local variables are defined within the body of the function or block. The variable defined is local to that function or block only. Other functions cannot access these variables. The compiler shows errors in case other functions try to access the variables.

In the following example, 'b' and 'c' are the local variables, which are defined within the body of the function `fun()`. The same variable names may be defined in different functions. They are local to that particular function.

Programs on local and global variables are illustrated below.

9.3 Write a program to show how same variable names can be used in different functions.

```
void main()
{
int b=10,c=5;
clrscr();
printf("\n In main() B=%d C=%d",b,c);
fun();
}
fun()
{
int b=20,c=10;
printf("\nIn fun() B=%d C=%d",b,c);
}
```

Output

```
In main() B=10 C=5
In fun() B=20 C=10
```

Explanation:
In the above program two functions are used. One is `main()` and other user-defined `fun()`. The variables 'b' and 'c' are defined in both the functions. Their effect is only within the function in which they are defined. Both the functions print local values of 'b' and 'c' assigned in their functions.

We can also declare the same variable names for actual and formal arguments. The compiler does not confuse them as same variables. The scope of every auto variable is local to the block in which they are defined.

(b) *Global variables*: Global variables are defined outside the `main()` function. Multiple functions can use them. The example is illustrated below for understanding.

9.4 Write a program to show the effect of global variables on different functions.

```
int b=10,c=5;
void main()
```

```
{
clrscr();
printf("\nIn main() B=%d C=%d",b,c);
fun();
b++;
c--;
printf("\n Again In main() B=%d C=%d",b,c);
}

fun()
{
b++;
c--;
printf("\nIn fun() B=%d C=%d",b,c);
}
```

Output

```
In main() B= 10 C=5
In fun() B=11 C=4
Again In main() B= 12 C=3
```

***Explanation*:**
In the above program, variables 'b' and 'c' are defined outside the `main()`, hence they are global. They can be called by any other function. The same variables 'b' and 'c' are used throughout the program. In `main()`, values of 'b' and 'c' are printed.

The function `fun()` is called, 'b' is incremented and 'c' is decremented. The values of 'b' and 'c' are printed. The control then returns to the function `main()`.

Again 'b' is incremented and 'c' is decremented. The values of 'b' and 'c' are printed. Here, both the functions use the same variables.

(viii) *Return value*: It is the outcome of the function. The result obtained by function is sent back to the calling function through the `return` statement. The `return` statement returns one value per call. The value returned is collected by the variable of the calling function.

9.4 THE RETURN STATEMENT

The user-defined function uses `return` statement to return the value to the calling function. Exit from the called function to the calling function is done by the use of return statement. When `return` statement is executed, it returns always 1.

9.5 Write a program to use return statement in different ways.

```
main()
{
int pass(int);
int x,y;
clrscr();

printf("Enter value of x : ");
```

```
scanf("%d",&x);
if(x==1 || x<0)
return 0;

y=pass(x);
switch(y)
{
case 1:
printf("The value returned is %d",y);
break;
default :
printf("The Cube of %d is : %d",x,y);
}

return NULL;
}

int pass(a)
{
if(a==0)
return 1;
else
return(a*a*a);
}
```

Output

```
Enter value of x : 5
The Cube of 5 is :125
```

(i) `return 0`: This statement returns zero to the operating system if the value entered by the user is 1 or negative.

(ii) `return 1`: The value of 'x' is passed to the function `pass()`. If the value is zero, then the `return` statement returns 1. The `return` statement is used to exit from the function `pass()`.

(iii) `return(a*a*a)`: In a function `pass()`, when the `if` statement finds the value of 'x' as non-zero, then `else` block is executed and the `return` statement returns cube of entered number.

(iv) `return` NULL: This statement returns NULL.

The return statement can be used in following ways.

(i) `return(expression);`

***Example*:**
`return(a+b+c);`

If such statement is executed, the expression within the parentheses is first solved and the result obtained is returned.

(ii) A function may use one or more `return` statements. It is used when we want to return a value depending upon certain conditions.

9.5 TYPES OF FUNCTIONS

Depending on the arguments present, the return value sends the result back to the calling function. Based on this, the functions are divided into four types.

9.5.1 Without Arguments and Return Values

(i) Neither data are passed through the calling function nor are the data sent back from the called function (Table 9.2).

TABLE 9.2 Function without arguments and return values

Calling Function	*Analysis*	*Called Function*

void main()
{
------------------ 	
------------------ 	
abc();
------------------ 	
------------------ 	
}
	No arguments are passed
	
	No values are sent back
		abc()
		{
		------------------ 	
		------------------ 	
		------------------ 	
		}

(ii) There is no data transfer between calling and called functions.

(iii) The function is only executed and nothing is returned.

(iv) If such functions are used to perform any operation, they act independently. They read data values and prints result in the same block.

(v) Such functions may be useful to print some message, draw a line or spilt the line, etc.

Example:

9.6 Write a program to display message using user-defined function with no actual and formal parameters and no return value.

```
void main()
{
void message(void);
message();
}
void message(void)
{
puts("Have a nice day");
}
```

Output

```
Have a nice day
```

***Explanation*:**
This program contains a user-defined function named `message()`. It requires no arguments and returns nothing. It displays only a message when called.

9.5.2 With Arguments But Without Return Values

(i) In the above functions, the arguments are passed through the calling function. The called function operates on the values. But no result is sent back (Table 9.3).

TABLE 9.3 With arguments but without return values

Calling Function	*Analysis*	*Called Function*

`void main()`
`{`
`------------------`
`------------------`
`abc(x);`
`------------------`
`------------------`
`}`
	Argument(s) are passed
	
	No values are sent back
		`void abc(y)`
		`{`
		`------------------`
		`------------------`
		`------------------`
		`}`

(ii) Such functions are partly dependent on the calling function. The result obtained is utilized by the called function and there is no gain to the `main()`.

***Example*:**

9.7 Write a program to send value to user-defined function and display the results.

```
main()
{
void dat(int ,int ,int);
int d,m,y;
clrscr();
printf("Enter Date dd/mm/yy");
scanf("%d %d %d",&d,&m,&y);
dat(d,m,y);
return 0;
}

void dat(int x, int y, int z)
{
printf("Date = %d/%d/%d",x,y,z);
}
```

Output

```
Enter Date dd/mm/yy 12 12 2001
Date = 12/12/2001
```

***Explanation*:**
In this program, three value are passed to `dat()` function. The `dat()` function receives argument form `main()` and displays date. But it returns nothing.

9.5.3 Function With Passing Arguments and Return Values

(i) In the above example, the copy of actual argument is passed to the formal argument, i.e. value of 'x' is assigned to 'y' (Table 9.4).

TABLE 9.4 Function with passing arguments and return values

Calling Function	*Analysis*	*Called Function*

void main()
{
int z;
------------------- 	
z=abc(x);
------------------- 	
------------------- 	
}
	Argument(s) are passed
	
	Values are sent back
		int abc (int y)
		{
		------------------- 	
		y++;
		------------------- 	
		------------------- 	
		return(y);
		}

(ii) The return statement returns the incremented value of 'y'. The returned value is collected by 'z'.

(iii) Here, data is transferred between calling and called functions, i.e. communication between functions is made.

9.8 Write a program to pass values to user-defined function. Collect and display the values returned by the called function.

```
main()
{
int dat(int ,int ,int);
int d,m,y,t;
clrscr();
printf("Enter Date dd/mm/yy : ");
scanf("%d %d %d",&d,&m,&y);
t=dat(d,m,y);
printf("\nTomorrow = %d/%d/%d",t,m,y);
return 0;
}

int dat(int x, int y, int z)
{
printf("\nToday = %d/%d/%d",x,y,z);
return(++x);
}
```

Output

```
Enter Date dd/mm/yy : 12 12 2001
Today = 12/12/2001
Tomorrow = 13/12/2001
```

***Explanation*:**
In the above program, three values date, month and year are passed to function `dat()`. The function displays date. The function `dat()` returns next date. The next date is printed in function `main()`. Here, the function `dat()` receives arguments and returns values.

9.5.4 Function Without Passing Arguments, But With Return Values

(i) In the above type of function no argument(s) are passed through the `main()` function. But the called function returns values (Table 9.5).

TABLE 9.5 Function without arguments and but with return values

Calling Function	*Analysis*	*Called Function*
void main()		int abc(void)
{	No argument(s) are passed	{
int z;		int y=5;
----------------		----------------
z=abc();		----------------
----------------		----------------
----------------	Values are sent back	return(y):
}		}

(ii) The called function is independent. It reads values from keyboard or generates from initialization and returns the values.

(iii) Here, both the calling and called function partly communicate with each other.

9.9 Write a program to receive values from user-defined function without passing any value through `main()`.

```
main()
{
 int sum(void),a,s;
 clrscr();
 s=sum();
 printf("Sum = %d",s);
 return 0;
 }

 int sum(void)
 {
 int x,y,z;
 printf("\n Enter Three Values :");
 scanf("%d %d %d",&x,&y,&z);
 return(x+y+z);
}
```

Output

```
Enter Three Values : 3 5 4
Sum = 12
```

Explanation:

The user-defined function sum() is independent function. The function sum() reads three values through the keyboard and returns their sum to function main(). The main() only prints the sum.

9.6 CALL BY VALUE AND REFERENCE

There are two ways in which we can pass arguments to the function. They are (i) call by value and (ii) call by reference.

(i) *Call by value*: In this type, value of actual arguments is passed to the formal arguments and operation is done on the formal arguments. Any change made in the formal argument does not affect the actual arguments because formal arguments are photocopy of actual arguments. Hence, when function is called by call by value method, it does not affect the actual contents of the actual arguments. Changes made in the formal arguments are local to the block of called function. Once the control returns back to the calling function, changes made vanish. The below example illustrates the use of call by value.

9.10 Write a program to send values by call by value.

```
main()
{
int x,y,change(int , int);
clrscr();
printf("\n Enter Values of X & Y :");
scanf("%d %d",&x,&y);
change(x,y);
printf("\n In main() X=%d Y=%d",x,y);
return 0;
}

change(int a, int b)
{
int k;
k=a;
a=b;
b=k;
printf("\n In Change() X=%d Y=%d",a,b);
}
```

Output

```
Enter Values of X & Y : 5 4
In Change() X=4 Y=5
In main() X=5 Y=4
```

Explanation:

In the above program, we are passing values of actual arguments 'x' and 'y' to the function change(). The formal arguments 'a' and 'b' of function change() receive these values(). The values are interchanged, i.e. value of 'a' is assigned to 'b' and vice versa and printed. When the control returns back to the main(), the changes made in function change() vanishes. In the main(), the values of 'x' and 'y' are printed as they read from the keyboard. In the call by value method, the formal argument acts as photocopy of the actual argument. Hence, changes made in them are temporary.

(ii) *Call by reference*: In this type, instead of passing values, addresses (reference) are passed. Function operates on addresses rather than values. Here, the formal arguments are pointers to the actual argument. In this type, formal arguments point to the actual argument. Hence, changes made in the argument are permanent. The below example illustrates the call by reference.

9.11 Write a program to send a value by reference to the user-defined function.

```
main()
{
int x,y,change(int* , int*);
clrscr();
printf("\n Enter Values of X & Y :");
scanf("%d %d",&x,&y);
change(&x,&y);
printf("\n In main() X=%d Y=%d",x,y);
return 0;
}

change(int *a, int *b)
{
int *k;
*k=*a;
*a=*b;
*b=*k;
printf("\n In Change() X=%d Y=%d",*a,*b);
}
```

Output

```
Enter Values of X & Y : 5 4
In Change() X= 4 Y=5
In main() X=4 Y=5
```

Explanation:

In the above example, we are passing addresses of formal arguments to the function `change()`. The pointers in the `change()` receive these addresses, i.e. pointer points to the actual argument. Here, the `change()` function operates on the actual argument through the pointer. Hence, the changes made in the values are permanent. In this type of call, no `return` statement is required.

9.7 FUNCTION RETURNING MORE VALUES

So far we know that the function can return only one value per call. We can also force the function to return more values per call. It is possible by call by reference method. The example given below illustrates this fact.

9.12 Write a program to return more than one value from user-defined function.

```
main()
{
int x,y,add,sub,change(int* , int*, int*, int*);
```

```
clrscr();
printf("\n Enter Values of X & Y :");
scanf("%d %d",&x,&y);
change(&x,&y,&add,&sub);
printf("\n Addition : %d ",add);
printf("\n Subtraction : %d ",sub);
return 0;
}

change(int *a, int *b,int *c,int *d)
{
*c=*a+*b;
*d=*a-*b;
}
```

Output

```
Enter Values of X & Y : 5 4
Addition : 9
Subtraction : 1
```

***Explanation*:**
In this program, return statement is not used. Still function returns more than one value. Actually, no values are returned. Once the addresses of variables are available, we can directly access them and modify their contents. Hence, in the call by reference method, it is possible to directly modify the contents of the variable. The memory addresses of the variables are unique. There is no scope rule for memory address. If we declare the same variable for actual and formal arguments, their memory addresses will be different from each other.

9.8 FUNCTION AS AN ARGUMENT

Till now, we passed values or address through the functions. It is also possible to pass a function as an argument.

9.13 Write a program to pass a user-defined function as an argument to another function.

```
main()
{
int doub(int);
int squar(int);
int y=2,x;
clrscr();
x=doub(squar(y));
printf("x=%d",x);
}
int doub(m)
{
int p;
p=m*2;
```

```
return(p);
}
int squar(k)
{
int z;
z=k*k;
return(z);
}
```

Output

```
x=8
```

***Explanation*:**
In the above example, instead of passing a variable or its address, a function is passed as an argument. The innermost function `square()` is executed first and completed. Its return value is collected by the `double()` function. The double function uses the `square()` function as an argument. It operates on the return value of `square()` function and makes the returned value double and returns to the `main()` function.

9.9 FUNCTION WITH OPERATORS

The program given below illustrates the use of various operators with function.

The assignment operator (=): The use of this operator is to assign some value to the variable. To assign return value of function to the variable, following syntax is used.

***Syntax*:**
`x=sqr(2);`

where 'x' is a variable and `sqr()` is a user-defined function. The value returned by the `sqr()` function is assigned to the variable 'x'.

9.14 Write a program to assign return value of a function to another variable.

```
void main()
{
int input(int);
int x;
clrscr();

x=input(x);
printf("\nx=%d",x);
}
input(int k)
 {
  printf("\nEnter Value of x = ");
  scanf("%d",&k);
  return(k);
}
```

Output

```
Enter Value of x = 5
X=5
```

Explanation:
In the above program, the user-defined function `input()` reads integer value through the keyboard. The read value is returned to `main()` function. The variable 'x' in `main()` function collects the returned value. The `printf()` statement prints the value of 'x'.

9.10 FUNCTION AND DECISION STATEMENTS

There are two ways to use decision-making statements in C.

Use of `if-else` *statement*: For syntax see Table 9.6.

TABLE 9.6 Function and `if` statement

Without Function	***With Function***

`if(condition)`
`Statement1;`
`else`
`Statement1;`
`}`
	`if(fun())`
	`statement1;`
	`else`
	`statement2;`
	
	where `fun()` is a function.

The `if-else` statement is used to make the decision in the program at run time. It decides which statement to execute and which statement to skip, depending upon certain condition.	Here, in this example, instead of writing condition directly, we are passing function. Here, when the `if()` statement executes, control is passed to the function `fun()`. The return value of function is used for condition.

The above syntax is used commonly in the program.

9.15 Write a program to call user-defined function through `if` statement.

```
void main()
{
int a();
clrscr();
if(a()%2==0)
printf("\n The number is even.");
else
printf("\n The Number is odd.");
}
      a()
      {
      int a;
      printf("\n Enter value of a : ");
      scanf("%d",&a);
      return(a);
      }
```

Output

```
Enter value of a : 5
The Number is odd.
```

Explanation:
In the above program, `a()` reads number from the terminal and sends it to the `main()` function. The `modulus` operation is done on the return value. If the result of `mod` operation is zero, then the message printed is "The number is even" otherwise "The Number is odd". Thus, in this example the returned value of the function is directly used for modulus operation.

9.11 FUNCTION AND LOOP STATEMENTS

Loop statements are used to repeat program code repetitively for a given number of times or based on certain conditions:

1. The `for` loop.
2. The `while` loop.
3. The `do-while` loop.

(i) *Working with for loop* (Table 9.7):

TABLE 9.7 Function and `for` loop

Without Function	*With Function*

`for(starting value; stop value; step)`
or
`for(initial value; condition, increment/decrement)`
	`for(fun(); fun1(); fun2())`
	where `fun()`, `fun1()` and `fun2()` are user-defined functions.

These are common syntaxes of the for loop statement.	In the above example, at every step of `for` loop, we are using user-defined function, i.e. when such statement executes, iterations are completed calling the functions.

9.16 Write a program to call function through the for loop.

```
#include <process.h>
void main()
{
int plus(int),m=1;
clrscr();
for(;plus(m);m++)
{
printf("%3d",m);
}
}
plus(int k)
```

```
{
if(k==10)
{
exit(1);
return NULL;
}
else
return(k);
}
```

Output

```
1 2 3 4 5 6 7 8 9
```

Explanation:
In the above example, in each iteration of the `for` loop, the function `plus()` gets called. The function `plus()` checks value of the formal argument 'k'. If the variable 'k' contains 10, the program is terminated, otherwise value of 'k' is returned as it is. Thus, the function `plus()` checks the value of loop variable.

9.12 FUNCTIONS WITH ARRAYS AND POINTERS

9.12.1 Initialization of Array Using Function

User always initializes the array using statement like `int d [ ]={1,2,3,4,5}`, instead of this, function can also be directly called to initialize the array. The program given below illustrates this point.

9.17 Write a program to initialize an array using functions.

```
main()
{
 int k,c(),d[]={c(),c(),c(),c(),c()};
 clrscr();
 printf("\n Array d[] elements are :");
 for(k=0; k<5; k++)
 printf("%2d",d[k]);

 return(NULL);
 }

 c()
 {
 static int m,n;
 m++;
 printf("\nEnter Number d[%d] : ",m);
 scanf("%d",&n);
 return(n);
}
```

Output

```
Enter Number d[1]  : 4
Enter Number d[2]  : 5
Enter Number d[3]  : 6
Enter Number d[4]  : 7
Enter Number d[5]  : 8
Array d[] elements are : 4 5 6 7 8
```

***Explanation*:**
Function can be called in the declaration of array. In the above program, `d[]` is an integer array and `c()` is a user-defined function. The function `c()` when called reads value through the keyboard. The function `c()` is called from an array, i.e. the value returned by the function is assigned to the array.

Tip: Compile and execute this program in C++.

9.12.2 Passing Array Elements to Function

Arrays are collection of one or more elements of the same data type. Array element can be passed to the function by value or reference. The programs given Below explain both the ways.

9.18 Write a program to pass array element to the function. Use call by value method.

```
void main()
{
int k, show(int,int);
int num[]={12,13,14,15,16,17,18};
clrscr();

for(k=0; k<7; k++)
show(k,num[k]);
}

show(int m,int u)
{
printf("\nnum[%d] = %d ",m+1,u);
}
```

Output

```
num[1]=12
num[2]=13
num[3]=14
num[4]=15
num[5]=16
num[6]=17
num[7]=18
```

***Explanation*:**
The show() is a user-defined function. The array num[] is initialized with seven elements. Using for loop, the show() function is called for seven times and one element is sent per call. The function show() prints the element.

9.13 RECURSION

So far we have seen functions calling one another. In programming, there might be a situation where a function needs to invoke itself. The C language supports recursive feature, i.e. a function is called repetitively by itself. The recursion can be used directly or indirectly. The direct recursion function calls to itself till the condition is true. In indirect recursion, a function calls another function, then the called function calls the calling function.

When a function calls itself, until the last calls is invoked till that time the first call also remains open. At every time a function is invoked, the function returns result of its previous call. The sequence of return ensues all the way up to the line until the first call returns the result to the caller function.

9.19 Write a program to call main() function recursively and perform sum of 1 to 5 numbers.

```
#include <process.h>

int x,s;
void main(int);

void main(x)

{
      s=s+x;
      printf("\n x = %d s = %d",x,s);

      if(x==5)
      exit(0);
      main(++x);
}
```

Output

```
x = 1 s = 1
x = 2 s = 3
x = 3 s = 6
x = 4 s= 10
x = 5 s= 15
```

***Explanation*:**
In the above program, variable 'x' and 'y' are declared outside main() function. Initially, their values are zeros. Followed by it, prototype of function main() is defined. The variable 'x' is passed through the main() function. The variable 'x' is added to variable 's' till the value of 'x' reaches to 5. Every time function main() is called repeatedly and 'x' is incremented. The result of the program is displayed at the output. The value of 'x' in main() is 1 because it is a command line arguments.

The recursive function `main()` is called as the Table 9.8. The analysis of each step is given for understanding.

TABLE 9.8 Steps of recursive function

Function Call	*Value of 'x'*	*Value of 's' (sum)*		
main(1)	x=1	s=1	(1 + 0)	=1
main(2)	x=2	s=3	(2 + 1 + 0)	=3
main(3)	x=3	s=6	(3 + 2 + 1 + 0)	=6
main(4)	x=4	s=10	(4 + 3 + 2 + 1 + 0)	=10
main(5)	x=5	s=15	(5 + 4 + 3 + 2 + 1 + 0)	=15

9.14 LIBRARY FUNCTIONS (TABLE 9.9)

TABLE 9.9 Library function

Serial No.	*Function*	*Description*
1.	`sqrt(j)`	Calculates square root of 'j'
2.	`log(j)`	Natural logarithm of j base 'e'
3.	`ceil(j)`	Rounds 'j' to the smallest integer >= j
4.	`pow(j,k)`	j raised to power 'k'
5.	`rand()`	Generates random number

9.20 Write a program to demonstrate the use of functions given in Table 9.8.

```
#include <math.h>
void main()
{
   clrscr();
   printf("\n Square root of 9 is %g",sqrt(9));
   printf("\n log of 5 is : %g",log(5));
   printf("\n 10.3 after ceil() : %g",ceil(10.3));
   printf("\n power 3 raised to 4 is : %g",pow(3,4));
}
```

Output

```
Square root of 9 is 3
log of 5 is : 1.60944
10.3 after ceil() : 11
power 3 raised to 4 is : 81
```

***Explanation*:**
In the above program, `sqrt()` function returns square root of 9. `log()` gives result 1.60944, the `ceil()` promotes 10.3 to 11 and `pow()` calculates 3^4. All the above functions are defined in `math.h` header file.

9.21 Write a program to demonstrate the use of `rand()` function.

```
#include <stdlib.h>
void main()
{
    int j;
    clrscr();
    for(j=0;j<=15;j++)
    {
      printf("%10d",1+(rand()%6));
      if(j%5==0)
      printf("\n");
}}
```

Output

```
5
5  3  5  5  2
4  2  5  5  5
3  2  2  1  5
```

***Explanation*:**
In the above program, the `rand()` function produces random number which is modular divided by 6 and added to 1. The obtained number is displayed. The last `printf()` inserts a line.

EXERCISES

9.A Fill in the blanks

1. The library function ________ returns absolute value.

   (a) `pow()`
   (b) `abs()`
   (c) `sum()`

2. The header file ________ contains all the mathematical functions.

   (a) `stdio.h`
   (b) `math.h`
   (c) `conio.h`

3. The functions defined by user are ________.

   (a) user-defined functions
   (b) standard functions
   (c) library functions

4. The user cannot change the definition of ________.

   (a) user-defined functions
   (b) system functions
   (c) library functions

5. When a function executes itself, it is called ________.

   (a) iteration
   (b) recursion
   (c) looping

6. The ________ function cannot be used for recursion.

   (a) user-defined functions
   (b) system functions
   (c) library functions

7. While defining recursion function, a provision should be made to ________.

   (a) storing the value
   (b) tracing the program
   (c) to stop the program

8. The result obtained by function is sent back to the calling function through the ________ statement.

   (a) exit
   (b) return
   (c) array

9. Whenever a function is called, __________ passes to the called function.

   (a) arguments
   (b) control
   (c) data

10. A keyword ________ is used for a function not returning any value.

   (a) `int`
   (b) `void`
   (c) `avoide`

11. A function can return a value as well as ________.

   (a) address
   (b) integer
   (c) float

12. The function operates on __________ and sends back the result to the calling function.

   (a) actual arguments
   (b) formal arguments
   (c) addresses

13. `void sum(void)` means __________.

   (a) function neither sends any argument nor returns any result
   (b) function sends argument but not return result
   (c) function returns results but not required any input

14. `float sum()` means ________.

   (a) it returns `float` value
   (b) it returns `int` value
   (c) it is a `void`

15. `int avg(float,float, float)` means ________.

   (a) returns `float` value and passes three float values
   (b) returns `int` value and passes three float values
   (c) returns `longint` value and passes three float values

16. `int sum(int *)` means ________.

   (a) address is passed
   (b) value is passed
   (c) no value is passed

17. In call by address, call from arguments are pointer to ________.

   (a) `main()` function
   (b) actual arguments
   (c) itself

18. A function can return more values by the method called ________.

   (a) call by value
   (b) call by address
   (c) call by parameter

9.B True or false

1. Every C Program starts with the function `main()`.
2. Library function can be defined by the user.
3. User-defined functions have serious limitations.
4. `sum()` is a standard library function.
5. The `abs()` is a standard library function.
6. The `abs()` gives absolute value.
7. Mathematical library functions are defined in `math.h`.
8. Functions not returning any value are known as void.
9. The `return` statement can return more than one value at a time.
10. The arguments of calling function are called actual arguments.

11. A user-defined function cannot call another user-defined function.
12. A user-defined function cannot call the `main()` function.
13. The scope of local variables is limited to the block in which they are defined.
14. Actual and formal arguments can have same variable name.
15. In call by value, values are passed to formal arguments.
16. In call by address, formal arguments are pointers to actual arguments
17. A change made in formal arguments can change the value of variable permanently.
18. A function prototype gives information in advance to the compiler.
19. A function can be passed as an argument to another function.
20. The data type before the function name indicates the type of value the function will return.
21. By default, function returns integer value.
22. When a function calls itself, the process is called recursion.
23. Like variables, functions also have address in the memory.
24. Functions can be invoked using pointers to function.
25. Function prototype is not necessary to match with actual function definition.

9.C Match the following correct pairs given in Group A with Group B

I

Group A		Group B	
Serial No.	**Data Type**	**Serial No.**	**Meaning**
1.	`abs()`	A	Clear the screen
2.	`sqrt()`	B	Quit from the program
3.	`clrscr()`	C	Gives square root of the value
4.	`exit()`	D	Absolute value
		E	Gives square of the number

II

Group A		Group B	
Serial No.	**Data Type**	**Serial No.**	**Header file/ Operation**
1.	`abs()`	A	`process.h`
2.	`sqrt()`	B	`conio.h`
3.	`clrscr()`	C	`math.h`
4.	`exit()`	D	`stdio.h`

III

Group A		Group B	
Serial No.	**Data Type**	**Serial No.**	**Header file/ Operation**
1.	`delay()`	A	`alloc.h`
2.	`ceil()`	B	`dos.h`
3.	`circle()`	C	`math.h`
4.	`malloc()`	D	`graphics.h`

9.D Select the appropriate option from the multiple choices given below

1. The arguments of caller function are called
   (a) actual arguments
   (b) formal arguments
   (c) memory variable
2. Following one keyword is used for function not returning any value
   (a) `void`
   (b) `int`
   (c) `auto`
3. Function prototype is not compulsory when function definition is given
   (a) before caller function
   (b) after caller function
   (c) at the end of program
4. The limitation of return statement is
   (a) it can return only one value
   (b) it is critical to use
   (c) it consumes more memory space

5. The recursion of the function can be stopped
   (a) using conditional statement
   (b) by pressing `ctrl+break`
   (c) using keyword return

6. In C functions, return statement is not compulsory because the return address is
   (a) stored on the stack
   (b) stored into the pointer
   (c) stored in register variable of the CPU

7. The use of return statement is to
   (a) return value
   (b) inform compiler the end of program
   (c) push back the control of the program

8. When a user-defined function is invoked, values are passed
   (a) on the stack
   (b) into ROM
   (c) to memory variables

9. When a function returns value 0 (zero), it indicates
   (a) normal termination
   (b) erroneous termination
   (c) none of the above

10. Arrays are passed to the function by
    (a) value
    (b) address
    (c) none of the above

11. It is necessary to declare the type of function in the calling program if
    (a) the function returns non integer value
    (b) the function returns an integer
    (c) the function is defined in the same file

12. By default, function returns
    (a) integer
    (b) float
    (c) NULL

13. The function name itself is an
    (a) address
    (b) value
    (c) definition

14. The main is a
    (a) keyword
    (b) system user-defined function
    (c) library function

15. Which is the correct statement for finding the cube of 5 ?
    (a) `pow(5,3);`
    (b) `pow(3,5);`
    (c) `pow(3);`
    (d) none of the above

16. The `floor()` function returns
    (a) round down value
    (b) round up value
    (c) absolute value
    (d) zero value

17. Recursion is a process in which the function calls
    (a) itself
    (b) another function
    (c) `main()` function
    (d) none of the above

18. The meaning of keyword `void` before a function name means
    (a) function should not return any value
    (b) function should return any value
    (c) no arguments are passed
    (d) none of the above

19. A global pointer can access variable of
    (a) all user-defined functions
    (b) only `main()` function
    (c) only library functions
    (d) none of the above

20. The `if(fun())` transfers the control to
    (a) the function `fun()`
    (b) the condition specified followed by `if(fun)` statements
    (c) the statements specified followed by `if(fun)`
    (d) none of the above

21. The arguments in a function are provided
    (a) within the parenthesis
    (b) within the braces
    (c) within angle bracket angles

22. Global variables appear
    (a) outside the `main()`
    (b) within the `main(_)`
    (c) above the header files
    (d) none of the above

9.E What will be the output/s of the following program/s?

Functions without arguments and return values

1. Use function and display some message.

```
void main()
{
clrscr();
printf("\n India is ");
sub();
getche();
}
sub()
{
printf(" my Country");
}
```

2. Use two functions and display some message.

```
void main()
{
clrscr();
printf("\n India is ");
sub();
secondsub();
printf("\n I love my country");
getche();
}
        sub()
        {
        printf(" my Country");
        }
secondsub()
{
    printf(" ");
}
```

3. Program to add numbers from 1 to 7.

```
void main()
{
clrscr();
sum();
getche();
}

sum()
    {
    int a=7,f=0,d;
    while(a>=1)
    {
    f=f+a;
    a=a-1;
    }
    printf("\n%d",f);
    }
```

4. Program to find factorial of 5.

```
void main()
{
clrscr();
fact();
getche();
}
fact()
        {
        int a=5,f=1,d;
        while(a>=1)
        {
        f=f*a;
        a=a-1;
        }
        printf("\n%d",f);
        }
```

5. Program to add and multiply numbers.

```
void main()
{
int a=3,b=4,c=5,d;
clrscr();
mul();
d=a+b+c;
printf("\n%d",d);
getche();
}

mul()
        {
        int a=2,b=3,c=4,d;
        d=a*b*c;
        printf("\n%d",d);
        }
```

6. Program to see the effect of the same variables used in main and in other functions.

```
void main()
{
int a=10,b=20;
clrscr();
printf("\n a=%d b=%d",a,b);
fun();
}
fun()
{
int a=30,b=40;
printf("\n a=%d b=%d",a,b);
}
```

7. Addition of cubes of 1, 2 and 3.

```
#include<math.h>
void main()
{
void cube();
cube();
clrscr();
}
void cube()
    {
    int i,x=0;
    for(i=0;i<4;i++)
    x=x+pow(i,3);
    printf("\n%d",x);
    getch();
    }
```

8. Program on multiplication and division.

```
void main()
{
int a=20,b=30 ,c;
clrscr();
printf("\n%d %d",a,b);
mul();
div();
getche();
}
    mul()
    {
    int a=20,b=20,c;
    c=a*b;
    printf("\n%d",c);
    }
    div()
    {
    int a=200,b=10,c;
    c=a/b;
    printf("\n%d",c);
    }
```

9. Program on display of ASCII characters in specific format

```
void main()
{
void alpha();
alpha();
clrscr();
}
void alpha()
    {
    int i;
    for(i=97;i<=101;i++)
    printf("%c%c ",i,i+2);
    getch();
    }
```

10. Program to display combination of ASCII numbers and characters.

```
void main()
{
void caps();
caps();
clrscr();
}
void caps()
{
int i=65;
while(i<70)
{
printf("%c%d ",i+1,i+1);
i++;
}
getche();
}
```

11. Display cubes of numbers from 1 to 4.

```
void main()
{
int j=0;
void cube(int);
   clrscr();
   for(j=1;j<5;j++)
   cube(j);
}
void cube(j)
{
   printf(" %d ",j*j*j);
}
```

12. Display some message with function.

```
void main()
{
int show();
int(*p)();
clrscr();
p=show();
}
show()
{
 puts("In function show()");
}
```

With arguments but without return values

13. Program to find the leap year.

```
void main()
{
void leapyear(int);
```

```
int year= 2004;
leapyear(year);
getche();
}

 leapyear(x)
   {
   clrscr();
   if(x%4==0&&x%100!=0||x%400==0)
   printf("\nThe year %d is a leap
      year ",x);
   else
   printf("\nThe year %d is a not a
      leap year ",x);
   }
```

14. Display numbers from 0 to 15.

```
void main()
{
void display(int);
int x,i;
clrscr();
for(i=0;i<=5;i++)
   printf("%d ",i);
display(i);
for(i=11;i<16;i++)
   printf("%d ",i);
getche();
}
 void display(int a)
   {
   for(a=6;a<=10;a++)
      printf("%d ",a);
   }
```

15. Program to reverse the number.

```
void main()
{
void rever(int);
int x=54;
clrscr();
printf("\n%d",x);
rever(x);
getche();
}

 void rever(int a)
   {
   int y;
   y=a%10;
   a=a/10;
   printf("\t%d%d ",y,a);
   }
```

16. Program to multiply the digits of 2345.

```
#include<math.h>
void main()
{
void mul(void);
mul();
clrscr();
}
void mul()
    {
    int x=2345,b,t,s=1;
    do
    {
    t=x%10;
    x=x/10;
    s=t*s;
    }
    while(x>0);
    printf("\n%d",s);
        getch();
    }
```

17. Program to display the date.

```
void main()
{
 void dat(int,int,int);
 int d=5,m=9,y=2005;
 dat(d++,m,y);
 }
 void dat(x,y,z)
 {
 clrscr();
 printf("%d-%d-%d",x,y,z);
 }
```

18. Program to generate the Hamming code.

```
static int q=0,a[7];
void main()
{
int i,b[4];
void hamming(int *);
clrscr();
printf("Enter the 4-bit
   binary no.\n\n");
for(i=0;i<4;i++)
scanf("%d",& b[i]);
hamming(b);
getch();
}

void hamming(int *p)
{
a[0]=p[0];
```

```
a[1]=p[1];
a[2]=p[2];
a[4]=p[3];
a[3]=a[0]^a[1]^a[2];
a[5]=a[0]^a[1]^a[4];
a[6]=a[0]^a[2]^a[4];
printf("Generated hamming
    code = ");
while(q<7)
{
printf("%d",a[q]);
q++;
}
}
```

With arguments and return values

19. Program on factorial of 4.

```
void main()
{
int fact(int);
int a=4,fac;
clrscr();
fac=fact(a);
printf("\n%d",fac);
getche();
}

int fact(x)
int x;
    {
    int f=1,d;
    while(x>=1)
    {
    f=f*x;
    x=x-1;
    }
    return(f);
    }
```

20. Program of cube of 5.

```
void main()
{
float cb(int);
int num=5,result;
clrscr();
result=cb(num);
printf("\n Result of function
    is= %.2d",result);
getche();
}
    float cb(int x)
    {
    float y;
    y=x*x*x;
    return(y);
    }
```

21. Program on square of float number 4.3.

```
void main()
{
float num=4.3,s;
float sqr(float);
clrscr();
s=sqr(num);
printf("\n Square of (%.2f)
    is (%.2f)",num,s);
getche();
}

float sqr(float x)
{
float y;
y=x*x;
return(y);
}
```

22. Program on doubling the float number 4.5.

```
#include<math.h>
void main()
{
float c=4.5,z;
float fun(float);
clrscr();
z=fun(c);
printf("\n%f",z);
getche();
}
float fun(float x)
 {
 return(x*2);
 }
```

23. Find the larger out of two numbers.

```
void main()
{
int fun(int,int);
int x=5,y=8,result;
result=fun(x,y);
printf("\nResult of this program
    is %d ",result);
getche();
}

fun(int a,int b)
  {
```

```
clrscr();
if(a>b)
return(a);
else
return(b);
}
```

24. Program to find the largest out of three numbers.

```
void main()
{
int fun(int,int,int);
int x=12,y=10,z=8,p;
clrscr();
p=fun(x,y,z);
printf("\n%d",p);
getch();
}
fun(int a,int b,int c)
    {
    if(a>b && a>c)
    return(a);
    if(b>c && b>a)
    return(b);
    if(c>a && c>b)
    return(c);
    }
```

25. Program to find square of largest out of three numbers.

```
void main()
{
int fun(int,int,int);
int a=1,b=2,c=3,p;
clrscr();
p=fun(a,b,c);
printf("\n%d",p);
getch();
}
fun(int x,int y,int z)
    {
    if(x>y && x>z)
    return(x*x);
    if(y>z && y>x)
    return(y*y);
    if(z>x && z>y)
    return(z*z);
    }
```

26. Program to reverse the number.

```
void main()
{
int rev(int);
int a=46,p;
clrscr();
p=rev(a);
printf("\n%d",p);
getch();
}
rev(int x)
    {
    int b,c;
    while(x>0)
    {
    b=x%10;
    x=x/10;
    c=b*10+x;
    return(c);
    }
}
```

27. Summation from 1 to 10.

```
void main()
{
int sum(int);
int a=10,p;
clrscr();
p=sum(a);
printf("\n%d",p);
getch();
}
sum(int x)
    {
    int b,s=0;
    while(x>0)
    {
    s=x+s;
    x--;
    }
    return(s);
    }
```

28. Addition of individual digits of 2345.

```
void main()
{
int sum(int);
int a=2345,p;
clrscr();
p=sum(a);
printf("\n%d",p);
getch();
}
sum(int x)
    {
    int b,p,s=0;
    while(x>0)
    {
    p=x%10;
    x=x/10;
```

```
    s=p+s;
    }
    return(s);
    }
```

29. Addition of squares of individual digits of 1234.

```
#include<math.h>
void main()
{
int square(int);
int a=1234,t;
clrscr();
t=square(a);
printf("\n%d",t);
getch();
}
square(int x)
    {
    int b,t,s=0;
    do
    {
    t=x%10;
    x=x/10;
    s=pow(t,2)+s;
    }
    while(x>0);
return(s);
}
```

30. Average of three float numbers.

```
void main()
{
float ave(float,float,float);
float av;
clrscr();
av=(float)ave(4.0,3.0,6.0);
printf("%2.2f",av);
getche();
}
float ave(float j,float k,float l)
    {
      return(j+k+l)/3;
    }
```

31. Average of three integers.

```
void main()
{
float ave(int,int,int);
float av;
clrscr();

av=(float)ave(2,3,5);
printf("%g",av);
 }
 float ave(int j,int k, int l)
 {
 return((float)(j+k+l)/3);
 }
```

32. To study the effect of postfix addition operators on two variables.

```
void main()
{
   int add(int,int);
   int x=1,y=2,z;
   z=add(x,y);
   clrscr();
   printf("\nz=%d",z);
}
add(int a, int b)
{
a++;
b++;
return(a+b);
}
```

33. Use pointers and add three numbers.

```
void main()
{
 int *sum(),*s;
 clrscr();
 s=sum();
 printf("Sum=%d",*s);
}
*sum()
{
 int x=2,y=4,z=5,k; k=x+y+z;
 return(&k);
}
```

34. To see the effect of postfix addition operator.

```
int j=3;
void main()
{
int plus(int),k;
k=plus(j);
clrscr();
printf("k=%d j=%d",k,j);
}
int plus (int j)
{
j++;
return j;
}
```

35. Display some number with pointer and address.

```
void main()
{
void plus(int*);
```

```
int j=3;
plus(&j);
clrscr();
printf("j=%d",j);
}
void plus(int *k) {return ++*k;}
```

36. Function as an argument.

```
void main()
{
int input(int);
int sqr(int);
int x;
clrscr();
x=sqr(1-input(x)+1);
printf("\nSquare =%d",x);
}
input(int k)
{
k=5;
return k;
}
sqr(int m) {return(m*m);}
```

37. Function as an argument.

```
void main()
{
int input(int);
int sqr(int);
int x;
clrscr();
x=sqr(5*input(x)/2);
printf("\nSquare =%d",x);
}
input(int k)
{
k=8;
return k;
}
sqr(int m) {return(m*m);}
```

38. Function as an argument.

```
void main()
{
 int b(),x=3,y=7,z=0,n=3,a;
clrscr();
while(z++!=n) {
y=y+pow(x,b());
printf("%d+",y);
 if(z==n){ printf("\b y=%d",y);
}}}
b(){ static int m; return ++m; }
```

39. Identify the given number whether even or odd.

```
void main()
{
int a();
clrscr();
if(a()%2==0)
printf("\n The Number is Even");
else
printf("\n The Number is Odd");
 }
 a()
 {
 int a=4;
 return(a);
}
```

Without arguments but with return values

40. Square of two numbers.

```
void main()
{
int sq(void);
int result;
clrscr();
result=sq();
printf("\n Result of function
    is= %.2d",result);
getche();
}
    sq()
    {
    int x=2,y=3;
    return(x*x+y*y);
    }
```

41. Display some message.

```
void main()
{
 int y();
 clrscr();
 while(y()!=0)
{
 printf("Value is non-zero");
 break;
}
}
y()
{
int x=1;
return x;
}
```

42. Display integer, float and a character.

```
void main()
{
```

```
int x;
float p;
char q;
clrscr();
display();
getche();
}
display()
{
int z=12;
float y=12.5;
char s='A';
printf("\n%d \t%2.2f\t %c",z,y,s);
return;
}
```

Call by value

43. Display numbers before and after calling function.

```
void main()
{
void fun(int,int);
int x=5,y=8;
clrscr();
printf("\nBefore execution of
    function x and y are %d %d ",
    x,y);
fun(x,y);
printf("\nAfter execution of
    function x and y are %d %d ",
    x,y);
getche();
}
 fun(int a,int b)
   {
   int temp;
   temp=a;
   a=b;
   b=temp;
   printf("\nx and y values in
      function are %d %d ",a,b);
   }
```

44. Display swapping operations before and after calling function.

```
void main()
{
void swap(int,int);
int x=5,y=10;
clrscr();
printf("\n%d %d",x,y);
swap(x,y);
printf("\t\t%d %d",x,y);
getche();
}
 swap(int a,int b)
   {
   int temp;
   temp=a;
   a=b;
   b=temp;
   printf("\t\t%d %d ",a,b);
   }
```

Call by reference

45. See the effect of call by reference.

```
void main()
{
int swap(int*,int*);
int x=10,y=20;
clrscr();
swap(&x,&y);
printf("\nx= %d y=%d",x,y);
getche();
}
swap(int *a,int*b)
   {
   int y;
   y=*a;
   *a=*b;
   *b=y;
   }
```

46. To follow the mathematical operations.

```
void main()
{
int display(int*,int*);
int x=10;
int p=20;
clrscr();
display(&x,&p);
getche();
}
display(int *z,int *y)
{
*z=*z**z;
*y=(*y**y)+(*z+*z);
printf("\n%d \t%d\t ",*z,*y);
return;
}
```

47. To understand the pointer operator.

```
void main()
{
int z=5;
int *p;
int *fun();
```

```
clrscr();
p=&z;
printf("\nAddress of z= %u ",p);
p=fun(&p);
printf("\nAddress of z= %u ",p);
getche();
}
int *fun(y)
int **y;
    {
    *y=*y+1;
    return(*y);
    }
```

Function as an argument

48. Function as an argument.

```
void main()
{
int input(int);
int sqr(int);
int y;
clrscr();
y=sqr(2*input(y)/2);
printf("\nSquare =%d",y);
getche();
}
input(int m)
{
m=20;
return m;
}
sqr(int k)
{
return(k*k);
}
```

49. Argument as a function.

```
void main()
{
 int mult(int,int);
 int add(int,int);
 int a,b,c,ans;
 a=5;
 b=8;
 c=4;
 clrscr();
 ans = mult(c,add(a,b));
 printf(" Answer = %d\n", ans);
 getche();
 }
 add(int x, int y)
 {
 return(x+y);
 }
 mult(int p, int q)
 {
 return(p*q);
}
```

50. Argument as a function.

```
void main()
{
int a(),b(),c();
clrscr();
a(b(c(a())));
}
int a()
{
printf("A");
}
int b()
{
printf("B");
}
int c()
{
printf("C");
}
```

Recursive function

51. Use recursive function and display from 4 to 1.

```
void main()
 {
 void rec(int);
   int x;
   x=4;
   clrscr();
   rec(x);
 }
 rec(int y)
 {
 if(y >0)
 {
 printf("%d ",y);
 rec(y-1);
 }
 }
```

Programs on library functions

52. Program on power() and abs() functions.

```
#include<math.h>
void main()
{
int x=2,y=3,z,p;
float q=-2.167;
clrscr();
z=pow(x,y);
```

```
p=abs(q);
printf("%d%d ",z,p);
getch();
}
```

53. Program on sqrt() and abs() functions.

```
#include<math.h>
void main()
{
int x=9,y=3,l,p;
float q=-2.9,m;
clrscr();
m=sqrt(x);
p=abs(q);
l = pow10(y);
printf("\n%f\n%d ",m,p);
printf("\n%d",l);
getch();
}
```

54. Program on log() and log10() functions.

```
#include<math.h>
void main()
{
int x=1000,p,q;
clrscr();
p=log(x);
q=log10(x);
printf("\n%d",p);
printf("\n%d",q);
getch();
}
```

55. Program on fmod() function.

```
#include<math.h>
void main()
{
float x=32,y=5,q;
clrscr();
q=fmod(x,y);
printf("\n%g",q);
getch();
}
```

56. Program on cos() and sin() functions.

```
#include<math.h>
void main()
{
int x=0,q,r;
clrscr();
q=sin(x);
r=cos(x);
printf("\n%d\n%d",q,r);
getch();
}
```

57. Program on floor() and ceil() functions.

```
#include<math.h>
void main()
{
float x=10.96,q,r;
clrscr();
q=ceil(x);
r=floor(x);
printf("\n%f\n%f",q,r);
getch();
}
```

58. Program on exp() Function.

```
void main()
{
int x=1;
float q;
clrscr();
q=exp(x);
printf("\n%f",q);
getch();
}
```

59. Function as an argument.

```
#include<math.h>
void main()
{
    int x,y;
    x= -64;
    clrscr();
    y = sqrt(abs(x));
    printf("Answer =%d\n",y);
    getche();
}
```

9.F Find the bug/s in the following program/s?

1.

```
void main()
{
sum(int f);
int f=2;
clrscr();
sum(f);
}
```

```
sum(int j)
{
 printf("%d",j);
}
```

2.

```
void main()
{
int a=0, B();
a=a+ +-B();
printf("%d",a);
}
B()
{
 int x;
 printf("Enter a Number ");
 scanf("%d",&x)
 return x
}
```

3.

```
void main()
{
int sum(int j, k,l);
clrscr();
sum(1,2,3);
}
 sum(int j,int k, int l)
 {
  printf("%d %d %d",j,k,l);
 }
```

4.

```
void main()
{
void show(void);
clrscr();
show();
 }
 show()
 {
  puts("Hello");
  }
```

5.

```
void main()
{
float ave(int,int,int);
float av;
clrscr();
av=ave(2,3,5);
printf("%g",av);
 }
 float ave(int j,int k, int l)
 {
 float x= j+k+l/3.0;
 }
```

6.

```
void A()
{
 clrscr();
 printf("\n in A");
}
void main()
{
   A('x','x');
}
```

7.

```
void main()
{
int B();
B(5.5);
}
B(float a)
{
clrscr();
printf(" %f",a);
}
```

8.

```
void main()
{
int B();
B();
}
C()
{
 printf("In C");
}
B()
{
 printf("In B");
 C();
 B();
}
```

9.

```
void main()
{
int b=10;
float c=5.5;
clrscr();
```

```
printf("\n In main() B=%d C=%d",b,c);
fun(b,c);
}

fun(int b, int c)
{
printf("\nIn fun() B=%d C=%d",b,c);
}
```

10.

```
int b=10,c=5;
void main()
{
clrscr();
printf("\nIn main() B=%d C=%d",b,c);
fun();
b++;
c--;
printf("\n Again In main() B=%d
    C=%d",b,c);
}

fun()
{
b++;
c--;
printf("\nIn fun() B=%d C=%d",b,c);
}
```

11.

```
int b=10,c=5;
void main()
{
  int pass(int);
  int x=3,y;
  clrscr();

  if(x==1 || x<0)
  return 0;

  y=pass(x);
switch(y)
{
case 1:
printf("The value returned is
    %d",y);
break;
default :
printf("The Cube of %d is :
    %d",x,y);
}

return NULL;
}

pass(a)
{
if(a==0)
return;
else
return(a*a*a);
}
```

12.

```
void main()
{
int sum(),a,s;
clrscr();
sum();
printf("Sum = %d",s);
return 0;
}

sum()
{
int x=4,y=5,z=7;
return(x+y+z);
}
```

13.

```
void main()
{
int *sum(),*s;
clrscr();
s=sum();
printf("Sum = %d",*s);
return 0;
}

sum()
{
int x,y,z,k;
printf("\nEnter Three Values :");
scanf("%d %d %d",&x,&y,&z);
k=x+y+z;
return(&k);
}
```

14.

```
void main()
{
int x,y,change(int* , int*);
clrscr();
printf("\n Enter Values of X & Y :");
scanf("%d %d",&x,&y);
change(&x,&y);
printf("\n In main() X=%d Y=%d",x,y);
return 0;
}
```

```
change(int a, int b)
{
int *k;
*k=*a;
*a=*b;
*b=*k;
printf("\n In Change() X=%d
    Y=%d",*a,*b);
}
```

15.

```
void main()
{
if(1)
printf("1"),
printf("0");
else
printf("2");
}
```

9.G Attempt the following programing exercises

1. Write a program to display "Test in C " 10 times. Create user-defined function `message()`.
2. Write a user-defined function for the following tasks.
   (a) Clearing the screen
   (b) Display character at specified row and column number
   (c) Display horizontal line with given symbol
3. Write a program in which the following user-defined functions can be invoked for performing the appropriate tasks.
   (a) Cube of a number
   (b) Square of a number
   (c) Area of a square
   (d) Conversion of decimal number to binary
   (e) Reverse the number
4. Write a program to calculate average rainfall of 10 days. Create `rain()` function.
5. Write a program to count for how many times a function is called. Create a user-defined function.
6. Write a program to return the result of addition and multiplication of three float numbers.
7. Write a program to increment the number in a function and display the return value of the function.
8. Write a program to display numbers in multiples of 5 up to 100 with a user-defined function.
9. Write a program to calculate square of float values and display it.
10. Write a program to find prime factors of entered number. For example, prime factors of 32 are 2,2,2,2 and 2.

9.H Answer the following questions

1. Write the definition of a function. Indicate types of functions available in C.
2. How do functions help to reduce the program size?
3. Differentiate between library and user-defined functions.
4. How does a function works? Explain how arguments are passed and results are returned?
5. List any five-library functions and illustrate them with suitable examples.
6. What are actual and formal arguments?
7. What are the uses of `return` statements?
8. What does it mean if there is no return statement in the function?
9. What are the void functions?
10. Why is it possible to use same variable names for actual and formal arguments?
11. What is the `main()` function in C? Why is it necessary in each program?
12. Explain the different formats of `return()` statements. How many values does the return statement return at each call?
13. What is a global pointer? Illustrate with a suitable example.

14. Why the return statement is not necessary when a function is called by reference?
15. Distinguish between function prototype and function definition?
16. Does the function prototype match with the function definition?
17. Can we define a user-defined function with the same library function name?
18. What is recursion? Explain its advantages.
19. Explain types of recursions.
20. Is it possible to call library a function recursively?

ANSWERS

9.A Fill in the blanks

1. (b) `abs()`
2. (b) `math.h`
3. (a) user-defined functions
4. (c) library functions
5. (b) recursion
6. (c) library functions
7. (a) storing the value
8. (b) return
9. (b) control
10. (b) void
11. (a) address
12. (b) formal arguments
13. (a) function neither sends any argument nor returns any result
14. (a) it returns `float` value
15. (b) returns `int` value and passes three float values
16. (a) address is passed
17. (b) actual arguments
18. (b) call by address

9.B True or false

1. T 2. F 3. F 4. F 5. T 6. T 7. T 8. T 9. F 10. T 11. F 12. F 13. T 14. T 15. T 16. T 17. F 18. T 19. T 20. T 21. T 22. T 23. T 24. T 25. F

9.C Match the following correct pairs given in Group A with Group B

I 1. D, 2. C, 3. A, 4. B
II 1. C, 2. C, 3. B, 4. A
III 1. B, 2. C, 3. D, 4. A

9.D Select the appropriate option from the multiple choices given below

1. (a) actual arguments
2. (a) `void`
3. (a) before caller function
4. (a) it can return only one value
5. (a) using conditional statement
6. (a) stored on the stack
7. (a) return value
8. (a) on the stack
9. (a) normal termination
10. (b) address
11. (a) the function returns non integer value
12. (a) integer
13. (a) address
14. (b) system user-defined function
15. (a) `pow(5, 3);`
16. (a) round down value
17. (a) itself
18. (a) function should not return any value
19. (a) all user-defined functions
20. (a) the function `fun()`
21. (a) within the parentheses
22. (a) outside the `main()`

9.E What will be the output/s of the following program/s?

1. India is my Country
2. India is my Country
   I love my country
3. 28
4. 120
5. 24
   12
6. a=10 b=20
   a=30 b=40
7. 36
8. 20 30
   400
   20
9. ac bd ce df eg
10. B66 C67 D68 E69 F70
11. 1 8 27 64
12. In function `show()`
13. The year 2004 is a leap year
14. 0 1 2 3 4 5 6 7 8 9 10 11 12 13 14 15
15. 54 45
16. 120
17. 5-9-2005
18. Enter the 4-bit binary no.
    1 0 1 0
    Generated hamming code = 1010010
19. 24
20. Result of function is= 125
21. Square of (4.30) is (18.49)
22. 9.000000
23. Result of this program is 8
24. 12
25. 9
26. 64
27. 55
28. 14
29. 30
30. 4.33
31. 3.33333
32. z=5
33. Sum=11
34. k=4 j=3
35. j=4
36. Square=9
37. Square=400
38. 443+879+1315 y=1315
39. The Number is Even
40. Result of function is= 13
41. Value is non-zero
42. 12 12.50 A
43. Before execution of function x and y are 5 8
    x and y values in function are 8 5
    After execution of function x and y are 5 8
44. 5 10 10 5 5 10
45. x= 20 y=10
46. 100
    600
47. Address of z= 65522
    Address of z= 65524
48. Square =400
49. Answer = 52
50. ACBA
51. 4 3 2 1
52. 82
53. 3.000000
    2
    1000
54. 6
    3
55. 2
56. 0
    1
57. 11
    10
58. 2.718282
59. Answer =8

9.F Find the bug/s in the following program/s?

1. Expression syntax. `sum(int f)` not needed.
2. ;`(semicolon)` missing in `scanf()`.
3. Function prototype error.
4. In function definition, void is not mentioned.
5. Return statement is not mentioned.
6. No error.
7. Function prototype error.
8. Infinite recursion.
9. In main, 'c' is float but in `fun()` formal argument is `int`.
10. No bug.
11. Compiler error.
12. Return value is not assigned to variable.
13. Function should be declared as pointer.
14. Formal arguments should be pointers.
15. Infinite recursion, no breaking statement.

10

Storage Class

CHAPTER OUTLINE

10.1 INTRODUCTION

The variables declared in C programs are different from the ones in other languages. We can use the same variable names in the C program in separate blocks. When we declare a variable, it is available only to the specific part or block of the program. The remaining block or other function cannot access the variable. Variables declared within the function are called as internal variables and those declared outside the function are called as external or global variables.

The area or block of the C program from where the variable can be accessed is known as the 'scope of the variables'. The area or scope of the variable depends on its storage class, i.e. where and how it is declared. There are four scope variables:

(i) Function
(ii) File
(iii) Block
(iv) Function prototype

The storage class of a variable tells the compiler

(i) The storage area of the variable
(ii) The initial value of the variable if not initialized
(iii) The scope of the variable
(iv) The life of the variable, i.e. how long the variable would be active in the program

Any variable declared in C can have any one of the four storage classes:

(i) Automatic variables
(ii) External variables
(iii) Static variables
(iv) Register variables

The storage class determines the storage duration, scope and linkage. The variable's storage duration is the period during which the variable exists in the memory. Some kinds of variables are repeatedly created in the memory, and some exist throughout the program execution.

Another important aspect is scope, i.e. the area in which the variable can be accessed. Some variables are global and can be accessed anywhere in the program. On the other hand, some variables are limited in scope in the block where they are defined. The above declared four kinds of storage classes can be further divided in two types depending on the storage duration. They are automatic storage duration and static storage duration. Generally, local variables have automatic storage where the use of keyword `auto` is optional. Static variable belongs to static storage class defined by static and external keyword. From the above discussion, we can state that there are two types of storage classes: (a) local and (b) global and storage class specifiers are `auto`, `register`, `static` and `extern`.

Lifetime of variable: Every variable has life time, i.e. the time duration during which its status is active in the program. We can also say that the lifetime of a variable is the time gap between its declaration and cleanup. The lifetime depends upon the storage class. For example, `auto` variable gets destroyed immediately when the function execution is over, whereas the `static` variable remains in the memory.

Visibility of variable: Visibility of variable is another property. It defines its scope. Scope is of two types: local and global. Global is recognized throughout the program, whereas local variable scope is limited to declaration block.

10.2 AUTOMATIC VARIABLES

`auto` variables are defined inside a function. A variable declared inside the function without storage class name is, by default, an `auto` variable. These functions are declared on the stack. The stack provides temporary storage. The scope of the variables is local to the block in which they are defined. These variables are available only to the current block or program. Once the executions of the function take place and the return turns off the function, the contents and existence of the `auto` variables or local variables vanish. Whenever a function is executed, all `auto` variables are allocated memory, and deallocated when the execution of function ends. The `auto` variables are safe, i.e. they cannot be accessed directly by other functions.

A keyword `auto` is used for declaration of automatic variables. By default, every variable pertains to auto storage class.

Below a program is given on `auto` storage class.

10.1 Write a program to show the working of auto variable.

```
void main()
{
auto float p=5.5;
clrscr();
call2();
printf("\nP=%2.2f",p);
}

void call1()
{
auto float p=10.54;
printf("\nP=%2.2f",p);
}

 call2()
 {
 auto float p=20.50;
 call1();
 printf("\nP=%2.2f",p);
 }
```

Output

```
P=10.54
P=20.50
P=5.50
```

Explanation:

In the above program, the variable 'p' is declared and initialized in three different functions. Each function, when called, prints the local values of variables 'p', which are shown in the output. When a function is called, it declares its own variable 'p' and when a function terminates, the local variable 'p' is destroyed. Here, every function has its own variable 'p' with different value. The three different variables 'p' have their own unique memory locations. Even after the removal of `auto` word from the program, there will not be any error thrown by the compiler. The reader can verify this fact.

10.2 Write a program to show the working of auto variables in different blocks.

```
void main()
{
int p=100;
clrscr();
printf("\n P=%d",p);
{
int p=50;
printf("\n P=%d",p);
}
{
int p=40;
printf("\n P=%d",p);
}
printf("\n P=%d",p);
}
```

Output

```
P=100
P=50
P=40
P=100
```

Explanation:
In the above program, the declaration of 'p' is made at three places with different values. In the first block, the value of 'p' is 100 and the same is displayed on the screen first. In the second block, the value of 'p' is 50. The control passes to the second block and 'p' is assigned a new value 50 and the same is displayed. When the control goes to third block, 'p' is 40 and the displayed value is 40. After it exits from the third block, the value of 'p' vanishes, which is initialized in the third block. In the last `printf()` statement, the value of 'p' is 100 which is declared in the first block.

10.3 EXTERNAL VARIABLES

The external storage class indicates that the variable has been defined at other place other than the place where it is declared. It can be declared in another source file. The variable declaration generally appears before the `main()` and use of keyword `extern` is optional. Initialization cannot be done because its value is defined in another source file. Memory is not allotted in the source program, and it is allotted where it is defined.

The variables that are available to all the functions, i.e. from the entire program, can be accessed. These variables are called external or global variables. External variables are declared outside the function body. In case, in a program both external and `auto` variables are declared with the same name, the first priority is given to the `auto` variable. In this case, the external variable is hidden. If we declare external variables in the program, there is no need to pass these variables to other function. The compiler does not allocate memory for these variables. It is already allocated for it in another module where it is declared as global variable.

10.3 Write a program to demonstrate the use of external variables.

```
float p=11.06;
void main()
{
  extern float p;
  clrscr();
  p=p*3;
  printf("p=%2.2f",p);
  fun();
  printf("\np=%2.2f",p);
}
  fun()
  {
  p=p*p;
  }
```

Output

```
p=33.18
p=1100.91
```

Explanation:

In the above program, variable 'p' is declared and initialized with 11.06. The second declaration inside the `main()` with keyword `extern` indicates that it has been declared already. The expression p=p*3 gives result 33.18, i.e. value of 'p' considered is 11.06. In function `fun()`, the value of 'p' is considered 33.18, and hence the final result is 1100.91 . We can also declare the statement `float` p=11.06 in another file. The file must be included in the main program. Consider the program below.

File `abc.c` contains as given below (give the proper path).

```
float p=11.06;
```

10.4 Write a program to demonstrate the use of external variables.

```
#include "abc.c"
void main()
{
  extern float p;
  clrscr();
  p=p*3;
```

```
    printf("p=%2.2f",p);
    fun();
    printf("\np=%2.2f",p);
}
    fun()
    {
    p=p*p;
    }
```

Output

```
p=33.18
p=1100.91
```

Explanation:
This program is the same as the last one. Only the statement `float` p=11.06 is stored in the file `abc.c`. The file is included in the main program. The output is the same.

10.4 STATIC VARIABLES

The static variable may be an internal or external type, depending upon where it is declared. If declared outside the function body, it will be `static` global. In case declared within the body or block, it will be `auto` variable. When a variable is declared as `static`, its garbage value is removed and initialized to NULL value. The contents stored in these variables remain constant throughout the program execution. A static variable is initialized only once; it is never reinitialized. The value of static variable persists at each call and the last change made in the value of static variable remains throughout the program execution. Using this property of static variable, we can count how many times a function was called.

The following program illustrates the working of static variables.

10.5 Write a program to show the use of static variable.

```
void main()
{
clrscr();
for(;;)
print();
}

print()
{
int static m;
m++;
printf("\nm=%d",m);
if (m==3)
exit(1);
}
```

Output

```
m=1
m=2
m=3
```

***Explanation*:**
In the above program, `print()` function is called. The variable 'm' of `print()` function is static variable. It is increased and printed in each call. Its contents persist at every call. In the first call, its value is changed from 0 to 1, in second call 1 to 2 and in the third call 2 to 3.

10.5 REGISTER VARIABLES

We can also keep some variables in the CPU registers instead of memory. The keyword `register` tells the compiler that the variable list followed by it is kept in the CPU registers, since register access is much faster than the memory access. If the CPU fails to keep the variables in CPU registers, in that case the variables are assumed as `auto` and stored in memory. CPU registers are limited in numbers. Hence, we cannot declare more variables with register variables. However, compiler automatically converts register variables into non-register variables once the limit is reached. User cannot determine the success or failures of the register variables. We cannot use register class for all types of variables. The CPU registers in a microcomputer are 16 bit registers. The data type `float` and `double` need space more than 16 bits. If we define variables of these data type with register class, no errors will be shown. The compiler treats them as variables of `auto` class.

Syntax:
```
register int k;
```

10.6 Write a program to declare and use variables of register class.

```
void main()
{
        register char m='a';
        clrscr();

        for(;m<=101;m++)
        printf("\t%c",m);
}
```

Output

```
a b c d e
```

***Explanation*:**
In the above program, variable 'm' is declared and initialized to 'a'. The `for` loop displays values from 'a' to 'e'. The register class variable is used as loop variable.

EXERCISES

10.A Fill in the blanks

1. Data type of register variable can be _______.

   (a) `float`
   (b) `char`
   (c) `double`

2. _______ variables are made available to all the functions declared in the program.

   (a) local
   (b) global
   (c) none of above

3. The address of _______ variable cannot be printed.

   (a) `static`
   (b) `register`
   (c) `auto`

4. The variable static c=400 is of _______ type.

   (a) `integer`
   (b) `long`
   (c) `char`

5. The static variable may be of internal or _______ type.

   (a) external
   (b) local
   (c) global

6. The values of register variables are kept in _______.

   (a) CPU registers
   (b) stack
   (c) queue

7. The CPU registers are _______.

   (a) limited
   (b) unlimited

8. The `long` type of variables cannot be of _______ type.

   (a) static
   (b) external
   (c) register

9. We cannot declare pointer to _______ .

   (a) register variable
   (b) static variable
   (c) external variable

10. Though declared in the program, the storage class of _______ is decided at run time.

    (a) register variable
    (b) static variable
    (c) external variable

11. When compiler fails to put the value of register variable in CPU, the register variables are treated as _______.

    (a) auto variable
    (b) static variable
    (c) external variable

12. The local static variable's scope is _______.

    (a) global to that function
    (b) local to that function
    (c) none of the above

13. The scope of _______ variables is inside the block in which they are declared or in the function where it is declared.

    (a) static
    (b) auto
    (c) register
    (d) none of the above

14. The scope of _______ variable is global.

    (a) register
    (b) auto
    (c) external

10.B True or false

1. Auto variables are defined inside the function.
2. An auto variable must be prefixed with keyword `auto`.
3. Auto functions are defined on the stack.
4. Auto variables are global variables.
5. The external variables are available to the entire program.
6. The external variables are global in access.

7. The external variables are defined outside the function.

8. In case both external and auto variable are defined with the same name, the external variables get identified (assume that only `main()` function exists).

9. A static variable can be of external and auto type.

10. The value of static variables persists.

11. A static variable must be initialized explicitly.

12. We can place value of variable in the CPU register using keyword `register`.

13. We can confirm whether the values are placed or not in the CPU register.

14. If the register variables are not kept in the CPU register, they are treated as auto variables.

10.C Match the following correct pairs given in Group A with Group B

I

Group A		Group B	
Serial No.	**Item**	**Serial No.**	**Meaning**
1.	Default storage	A	Auto
2.	Static storage	B	Global scope
3.	External storage	C	Local scope
4.	Auto storage	D	CPU register
5.	Register	E	Value persists

II

Group A		Group B	
Serial No.	**Item**	**Serial No.**	**Meaning**
1.	Automatic	A	External data type
2.	Static	B	Auto
3.	Register	C	Register
4.	External	D	Static

III

Group A		Group B	
Serial No.	**Item**	**Serial No.**	**Meaning**
1.	Global variables	A	CPU Register
2.	Local variables	B	Initial value is zero
3.	Static	C	Outside the `main()` function
4.	Register	D	Scope of the value is within the block or local to the block

IV In regard to `register` storage class

Group A		Group B	
Serial No.	**Item**	**Serial No.**	**Meaning**
1.	Life time of variable	A	Initial value is zero
2.	Initial value	B	Local to that block where it is defined
3.	Storage of variable	C	Register
4.	Scope of the variable	D	Within the block

10.D Select the appropriate option from the multiple choices given below

1. A static variable is the one that

   (a) retains its value throughout the program
   (b) cannot be initialized
   (c) same as automatic variable

2. An external variable is the one

   (a) which is accessible by all functions
   (b) which is declared outside all the functions
   (c) both (a) and (b)

3. If a storage class is not defined, then the default storage class is

   (a) auto
   (b) static
   (c) external

4. Even if not initialized, this type of variable does not hold garbage value

   (a) auto variable
   (b) external variable
   (c) register variable

5. The auto variable can be of
   (a) static
   (b) external
   (c) pointer
6. The storage class of the variable tells the compiler
   (a) storage area of the variable
   (b) the scope of the variable
   (c) both (a) and (b)
7. The storage class of local variable can be
   (a) auto
   (b) external
   (c) none of the above
8. If external and auto variables are declared with the same name, the priority is given to
   (a) auto variable
   (b) external variable
   (c) none of the above
9. Following one keyword is not related to C storage classes
   (a) `static`
   (b) `auto`
   (c) `case`
10. The register variables are by default
   (a) `int`
   (b) `long`
   (c) `float`

10.E What will be the output/s of the following program/s?

Programs on automatic variables

1.

```
void main()
{
    auto float p=2.2;
    clrscr();
    {
    {
    { printf("%2.2f",p);
    }
    printf(" %2.2f",p);
    }
    printf(" %2.2f",p);
    }
}
```

Explanation: In the above program, the variable 'p' is declared and initialized with 2.2. This value remains the same throughout the program, hence the result displayed is the same for each `printf()` statement.

2.

```
void main()
{
 auto int j=1;
 clrscr();
 {
 auto int j=2;
 {
 auto int j=3;
 printf("%d",j);
 }
 printf("%d",j);
 }
 printf("%d",j);
 }
```

Explanation: In the above program, the declaration of 'j' is made at three places with different values. First, 3 is displayed, then 2 and at last 1.

3.

```
void main()
{
auto int x=20;
clrscr();
printf("\nx=%d",x);
  {
  auto int x=30;
  printf("\nx=%d",x);
  }
  printf("\nx=%d",x);
getche();
}
```

Explanation: In the above program, the initialization of 'x' is made at two places with different values. Immediately following the `main()`, the value of 'x' is 20 and the same is displayed on the screen first. In the second block, the value of 'x' is 30. The control passes to the second block, and 'p' is assigned a new value 30 and the same is displayed. When the control goes to the third `printf()`, 'x' is 20 and the displayed value is 20.

4.

```
void main()
{
    int v=5;
    clrscr();
  {
    int v=4;
    printf(" %d ",v);
  }
  printf(" %d ",v);
  {
    int v=9;
    printf("%d ",v);
  }
  printf("%d ",v);
}
```

Explanation: In the above program, the initialization of 'v' is made at three places with different values. All variables are with `auto`, but it is not mentioned, by default the variables declared are `auto` type. Immediately following the `main()`, the value of 'v' is 5. In the second block, the value of 'v' is 4. The control passes to the second block and 'v' is assigned a new value 4 and the same is displayed. When the control goes to second `printf()`, 'v' is 5 and the displayed value is 5. In the third `printf()` , 'v' is 9 and at last the `printf()` displays 5.

5.

```
void main()
{
    int x=11;
    clrscr();
    printf("\n x=%d",x);
    {
    float x=2.5;
    printf(" x=%g",x);
    }
    {
    char *x="Auto Storage Class";
    printf(" x=%s",x);
    }
}
```

Explanation: Refer to earlier program explanation.

Programs on external variables

6.

```
int v;
void main()
{
    extern int v;
    clrscr();
    printf("%d ",v);
    call1();
    call2();
    printf("%d ",v);
    getche();
}
      call1()
      {
      int v=20;
      printf("%d ",v);
      }
      call2()
      {
    int v=10;
    printf("%d ",v);
    }
```

Explanation: In the above program, variable 'v' is declared as external. First time the variables value is uninitialized, hence the value should be 0. The same value is passed in the last `printf()` statement. In the `call1()`, the variable's value is 20 and in the next `call2()` the value displayed is 10.

7.

```
int v=10;
void main()
{
    extern int v;
    clrscr();
    printf("%d ",v);
    fun1();
    printf("%d ",v);
    fun2();
    getche();
}
      fun1()
      {
      fun2();
      printf("%d ",v);
      }
      fun2()
      {
      int v=20;
      printf("%d ",v);
      }
```

Explanation: In the above program, variable 'v' is declared and initialized with 10. Observe the functions invoked carefully and see the outputs.

8.

```
int v=10;
void main()
{
    clrscr();
    call1();
    call2();
    printf("In main()");
}
call1(){ printf(" In call1()"); }
call2(){ printf(" In call2()"); }
```

Explanation: Same as earlier.

9.

```
int v=10;

void main()
{
    clrscr();
    call1();
    call2();
    printf(" In main( )");
}
call1(){ printf(" In call1()v=%d",v); }
call2(){ printf(" In call2()v=%d",v); }
```

10.

```
int v=10;
void main()
{
clrscr();
printf ("\n%d",v);
for(;;)
print();
}
print()
 {
  v++;
  printf(" %d",v);
  if (v==13)
  exit(0);
}
```

Explanation: This program illustrates the impact of global variable. Global variable v is accessible for both functions `main()` and `print()`. Value of variable v is incremented and printed till it becomes 13.

11.

```
int v=5;
 void main()
{
 clrscr();
 while(v<=10)
 print();
 }
   print()
    {
    ++v;
    printf(" %d",v);
    if (v==8)
    exit(0);
    }
```

Explanation: 'v' is initialled to 5. Then, in the loop, the value updates and three values displayed are 6, 7 and 8.

12.

```
int x=12;

void main()
  {
  int x=25;
  clrscr();
  printf("%d\n",x);
  show();
  }
show()
{
printf("%d",x);
}
```

Programs on static variables

13.

```
void main()
{
 clrscr();
 increment();
 increment();
 increment();
 }
 increment()
 {
   static int j=1;
   printf("\n%d",j);
   j++;
   }
```

Explanation: In the above program, `increment ()` function is called three times. The static variable 'j' is 1. It is increased and printed in each call. Its contents persist at every call. In the first call, its value is changed from 0 to 1, in second call 1 to 2 and in the third call 2 to 3.

14.

```
int x=10;
void main()
```

```
{
   static int x;
   clrscr();
   printf("%d\n",x+4);
   show();
}
      show()
      {
      static int x;
      printf("%d",x*2+ ++x);
      }
```

Explanation: Variable x is declared at three places. Impact of external variable is not prevalent in this program. The `main` has static variable x. Hence, scope of local static variable x is observed in the `main()` and hence the value to be printed is x+4=0+4=4. Its scope is over after terminating `main()`. In the function `show()`, static variable x is defined. Hence, its default value is 0. As per `printf()` statement in the function output becomes 1. Hence the output of the program is 4 and 1.

15.

```
void main()
{
static int count =5;
printf("\n%d",count--);
if (count!=0)
main();
 }
```

Explanation: In the above program, the variable 'count' is initialized to 5. It is displayed from 5 to 1 with decrementing each time by 1.

16.

```
void main()

{
auto int x=2;
register
int i;
static int y=50;
clrscr();
for(i=0;i<4;i++)
printf("% d",i);
printf("% d",x);
printf("% d",y);
getche();
}
```

Programs on static and auto variables

17.

```
void main()
{
static int i;
clrscr();
while(i<=5)
 {
 printf("% d",i);
 i++;
 }
   {
   auto int i=5;
   printf("% d",i);
   }
   {
   static int p=7;
   printf("% d",p);
   }
   getche();
   }
```

18.

```
static int i=5;
void main()
{
auto int i;
clrscr();
for(i=3;i>0;i--)
printf(" % d",i);
   {
   auto int i=5;
   printf("% d",i);
   }
   {
   static int p=7;
   printf("% d",p);
   }
getche();
}
```

Program on static, register and auto variables

19.

```
void main()
{
clrscr();
{
 register int j=100;
  {
  register int j=20;
   {
```

```
        register int j=30;
        printf("% d",j);
    }
    {
        register int j=20;
        printf("% d",j);
    }
  printf("% d",j);
   }
  printf("% d",j);
}
 getche();
}
```

Explanation: Refer to register variables.

20.

```
static int y=50;

void main()
{
static int y=20;
register int i=0;
auto int x= 2;
clrscr();
for(i=3;i>0;i--)
printf("% d",i);
printf("% d",x);
printf("% d",y);
getche();
}
```

21.

```
void main()
{
clrscr();
{
 static int j=10;
   {
   register int j=20;
```

```
   {
      register int j=30;
      printf(" % d",j);
   }
   {
      auto int j=40;
      printf(" % d",j);
   }
 printf(" % d",j);
   }
 printf(" % d",j);
}
 getche();
}
```

22.

```
void main()
{
clrscr();
{
 static int j=40;
 {
static int j=10;
   {
      static int j=15;
      printf("% d",j);
  }
  {
      auto int j=25;
      printf("% d",j);
  }
 printf("% d",j);
  }
 printf("% d",j);
}
 getche();
}
```

10.F Find the bug/s in the following program/s

1.

```
Auto int x=20;
void main(){
auto int x=10;
clrscr();
printf("\nx=%d",x);
}
```

2.

```
void main()
{
register x=10;
printf("\nx=%d",x);
}
```

3.

```
void main()
{
clrscr();
value();}
static value()
{
 printf("Hi");
}
```

4.

```
void main()
 {
   int x=25;
   clrscr();
   printf("%d\n",x);
   show();
 }
 show(){ printf("%d",x); }
```

5.

```
void main()
{
int count =5;
printf("\n%d",count--);
if (count!=0) main();
}
```

6.

```
float x=5.5;
main()
{
  float y,f();
  clrscr();
  x*=4.0;
  y=f(x);
  printf("%g %g",x,y);
  }
  float f(float a)
  {
     a+=1.3;
     x-=4.5;
   return a+x;
   return 0;
   }
```

7.

```
register int i;
void main()
{
clrscr();
for(i=3;i>0;i--)
printf("% d",i);
getche();
}
```

8.

```
auto int i=10;
void main()
{
clrscr();
for(i=4;i>1;i--)
printf(" % d",i);
 {
 auto int i=5;
 printf(" % d",i);
 }
 getche();
}
```

10.G Attempt the following programming exercises

1. Write a program to calculate the multiplication and sum of the digits of entered number. Create user-defined function `muld()` and `sumd()`. Use the static variable and calculate the multiplication and sum of digits.
2. Write a program to call function `main()` recursively. The program should be terminated when the `main()` function is called during the 5th time. Take help of the static variable.
3. Write a program to factorial of a number. Use static variable with user defined function.
4. Write a program to create the `for` loop from 1 to 10000. Declare the loop variable of class register and `auto`. Observe the time required for completing the loop for both type of variables. Find out in which class the execution time is minimum.

10.H Answer the following questions

1. List and explain the four scope variables in brief.
2. What are the automatic variables?
3. Distinguish between static and external variables.
4. Briefly explain register variables.
5. List the limitations of register variables.
6. Why does the register storage class not support all data types?
7. Can we declare a variable in different scopes with different data types? Answer in detail.
8. Explain lifetime and visibility of a variable.

ANSWERS

10.A Fill in the blanks

1. (b) `char`
2. (b) global
3. (b) register
4. (a) integer
5. (a) external
6. (a) CPU register
7. (a) limited
8. (c) register
9. (a) register variable
10. (a) register variable
11. (a) auto variable
12. (b) local to that function
13. (b) auto
14. (c) external

10.B True or false

1. T 2. F 3. T 4. F 5. T 6. T 7. T 8. F
9. T 10. T 11. F 12. T 13. F 14. T

10.C Match the following correct pairs given in Group A with Group B

I 1. A, 2. E, 3. B, 4. C, 5. D
II 1. B, 2. D, 3. C, 4. A
III 1. C, 2. D, 3. B, 4. A
IV 1. D, 2. A, 3. C, 4. B

10.D Select the appropriate option from the multiple choices given below

1. (a) retains its value throughout the program
2. (d) both (a) and (b)
3. (a) auto
4. (b) external variable
5. (a) static
6. (c) both (a) and (b)
7. (a) auto
8. (a) auto variable
9. (c) case
10. (a) `int`

10. E What will be the output/s of the following program/s?

1. 2.20 2.20 2.20
2. 321
3. x=20
   x=30
   x=20
4. 4 5 9 5
5. x=11 x=2.5 x=Auto Storage Class
6. 0 20 10 0
7. 10 20 10 10 20
8. In `call1()` In `call2()` In `main()`
9. In `call1()` v=10 In `call2()` v=10 In `main()`
10. 10 11 12 13
11. 6 7 8
12. 25
    12
13. 1
    2
    3
14. 4
    1
15. 5 4 3 2 1
16. 0 1 2 3 2 50
17. 0 1 2 3 4 5 5 7
18. 3 2 1 5 7
19. 30 20 20 100
20. 3 2 1 2 20
21. 30 40 20 10
22. 15 25 10 40

10.F Find the bug/s in the following program/s

1. Automatic variables cannot be defined outside functions.
2. No Bug
3. No Bug
4. Variable 'x' should be defined.
5. Count should be static.
6. Return 0 should be removed.
7. Incompatible storage class.
8. Incompatible storage class.

11 Preprocessor Directives

CHAPTER OUTLINE

11.1 INTRODUCTION

You are now aware of the execution of C programs. For refreshing the knowledge of the reader, lets look at certain steps the program execution needs. These are: (a) the C program is written in editor, (b) compilation, (c) linking and (d) the executable code generation. In between these stages, one more stage also involves, i.e., the preprocessor. The preprocessor is a program that processes the source program before it is passed onto the compiler.

The program typed in the editor is the source code to the preprocessor. The preprocessor then passes the source code to the compiler. It is not necessary to write the program with preprocessor facility. But it is a good practice to use it preferably at the beginning. The preprocessor reduces the execution time of a program because it is similar to a function call.

One of the most important features of C language is to offer preprocessor directives. The preprocessor directives are always preferably initialized at the beginning of the program before the `main()` function. It begins with a # (hash) symbol. It can be placed anywhere, but quite often it is declared at the beginning before the `main()` function or any particular function. In traditional C, # (hash) must begin at the first column.

11.2 #define DIRECTIVE

The syntax of `#define` directive is as follows.

```
#define identifier substitute
```

OR

```
#define identifier (argument 1... argument N) substitute
```

Example:

```
#define PI 3.14
```

This statement defines PI as macro template and 3.14 as macro substitute. During preprocessing, the preprocessor replaces every occurrence of PI (identifier) with 3.14 (substitute value). Here, PI is a macro template and 3.14 is its macro expansion. The macro templates are generally declared with capital letters for quick identification. One can also define macros with small letters. The macro templates and their expansions must be separated with at least one blank space. It is not necessary to provide space between # and `define` . It is optional to the programmer. To increase readability programmer should provide space.

The macro definition should not be terminated with semicolon. The words followed by # are not keywords. Programmer can use these words for variable names.

A few examples are illustrated below for understanding macros.

11.1 Use the identifier for 3.14 as PI and write a program to find the area and perimeter of a circle.

```
#define PI 3.14
void main()
{
float r,area,perimeter;
clrscr();
printf("\n Enter radius of circle in cms:-");
scanf("%f",&r);
area=PI*r*r;
```

```
perimeter=2*PI*r;
printf("Area of a Circle = %.2f cm2",area);
printf("\nPerimeter of a Circle = %.2f cm",perimeter);
getche();
}
```

```
Output
Enter radius of circle in cms:-5
Area of a Circle = 78.50 cm²
Perimeter of a Circle = 31.40 cm
```

Explanation:
In the above program, PI replaces 3.14 during the program execution. In the program, instead of writing the value of PI as 3.14, we define directly the value of PI as 3.14. The term PI is replaced by 3.14 and used for calculating the area of a circle and perimeter.

11.3 UNDEFINING A MACRO

A macro defined with `#define` directives can be undefined with `#undef` directive.

Syntax:
`#undef` macro_template substitute

It is useful when we do not want to allow the use of macros in any portion of the program.

11.2 Write a program to undefine a macro.

```
#undef x 2
void main()
{
int k;
clrscr();
for(k=1;k<=5;k++)
printf("%d\t",k*x);
}
```

Explanation:
In the above program, 'x' is undefined in place of 2 with macro. The macro `#undef` directive undefines the same macro. Hence, the compiler flags an error message 'undefined symbol 'x' in function main'. In case, one more statement `#define x 2` is written after `for` loop, then the compiler does not show any error and the output displayed on the screen would be '2 4 6 8 10'.

11.4 TOKEN PASTING AND STRINGIZING OPERATORS

Stringizing operation: In this operation, a macro argument is converted into string. The sign # carries the operation. It is placed before the argument.

11.3 Write a program to carry out stringizing operation.

```
#define identical(m) printf(#m)
void main()
{
  clrscr();
  identical(Imagination beyond vision);
  getche();
}
```

Output

```
Imagination beyond vision
```

***Explanation*:**

In the above program, after conversion the statement `identical(Imagination beyond vision)` is treated as `printf("Imagination beyond vision")`. It is not essential to enclose the text with quotation marks in the stringizing operator. If # is removed from the macro definition, user has to enclose the text in double quotes.

11.5 #include DIRECTIVE

The `#include` directive loads the specified file in the current program. The macros and functions of the loaded file can be called in the current program. The included file also gets complied with the current program. The syntax is as given below:

(i) `#include "filename"`

(ii) `#include <fileame>`

where # is a symbol used with directives.

(i) The file name is included in the double quotations marks indicates that the search for the file is made in the current directory and in the standard directories.

***Example*:**

`#include "stdio.h"`

(ii) When the file name is enclosed within angle brackets without double quotation marks, the search for file is made only in the standard directories.

***Example*:**

```
#include <stdio.h>
#include <udf.h>
```

A programming example is given below on include file.

```
#include<math.h>
main()
{
```

```
int p=5,q;
clrscr();
#include "c:\turboc2\amit\undefine.c"
printf("\nSquare of 5 is: ");
q=pow(p,2);
printf("%d",q);
getche();
}
```

Output

```
Hello ! How R U
Square of 5 is: 25
```

Contents of `c:\turboc2\amit\undefine.c` file.

```
printf("Hello ! How R U");
```

***Explanation*:**
In the first program, the "`c:\turboc2\amit\undefine.c`" is included. It is a user defined function file. The complete program along with the included one are executed. The output of the program is displayed.

11.6 CONDITIONAL COMPILATION

Quite often one can use conditional compilation directives in the programs. The most frequently used conditional compilation directives are `#ifdef`, `#if`, `#else`, `#endif`, `#elif`, etc. These directives allow the programmer to include the portions of the codes based on the conditions. The compiler compiles selected portion of the source codes based on the conditions. The syntax of the `#ifdef` directive is given below.

***Syntax*:**

```
#ifdef identifier
{
      Statement1;
      statement2;
}
#else
{
      statement3;
      statement4;
}
#endif
```

The `#ifdef` preprocessor tests whether the identifier has defined substitute text or not. If the identifier is defined, then `#if` block is compiled and executed. The compiler ignores `#else` block even if errors are intentionally made. Error messages will not be displayed. If identifier is not defined, then `#else` block is compiled and executed.

11.5 Write a program to use conditional compilation statement as to whether the identifier is defined or not.

```
#undef DEPT 1
void main()
{
clrscr();
#if DEPT
printf("This is ELECTRONICS department. ");
#else
printf("This is COMPUTER department.");
#endif
getche();
}
```

Output

```
This is COMPUTER department.
```

Explanation:
In the above program, out of the `main()`, `#undef` macro is defined. `#if` checks whether the `DEPT` identifier is defined or not. If defined, the `#if` block is executed else `#else` block. In this example, `#else` bock is executed. On execution, the output of the program is "This is COMPUTER department.". In case, the identifier is defined, the `#if` block is executed and output is "This is ELECTRONICS department.".

11.7 `#ifndef` DIRECTIVE

The syntax of the `#ifndef` directive is given below.

Syntax:

```
#ifndef identifier
      {
      statement1;
      statement2;
      }
#else
      {
      Statement3;
      Statement4;
      }
#endif
```

The `#ifndef` works exactly opposite to that of `#ifdef`. The `#ifndef` preprocessor tests whether the identifier has defined substitute text or not. If the identifier is defined, then the `#else` block is compiled and executed and the compiler ignores the `#if` block even if errors are intentionally made. Error Messages will not be displayed. If identifier is not defined, then the `#if` block is compiled and executed.

11.6 Write a program to check conditional compilation directives #ifndef. If it is observed, display one message otherwise another message.

```
#define VISION 1
void main()
{
clrscr();
#ifndef VISION
printf("\n Non Visionary people.");
#else
printf("\n Visionary people.");
#endif
getche();
}
```

Output

```
Visionary people.
```

Explanation:
In the above program, `#ifndef` checks for the identifier VISION. If it is defined, then the `#else` block is executed. On execution of the block, the output of the program is "Visionary people.". In case, the identifier is undefined, the `#ifndef` block is executed and output is "Non Visionary people."

11.8 `#error` DIRECTIVE

The `#error` directive is used to display user defined message during compilation of the program. The syntax is as given below.

```
#if !defined(identifier)
#error <ERROR MESSAGE>
#endif
```

11.7 Write a program to display user-defined error message using `#error` directive.

```
#define B 1
void main()
{
clrscr();
#if !defined(A)
#error MACRO A IS NOT DEFINED.
#else
printf("Macro found.");
#endif
}
```

Explanation:
In the above program, an identifier 'B' is defined. In the absence of the identifier, an error is generated and the `#error` directive displays the error message. The error message is user defined and displayed in the message box at the bottom of the editor.

11.9 #line DIRECTIVE

In order to renumbering the source text, this directive is used. The syntax of line directive is as follows:

```
#line <constant> [ <identifier> ]
```

This causes the compiler to renumber the line number of the next source line as given by `<constant>`, and `<identifier>` gives the current input file. If `<identifier>` is absent, then the current file name remains unchanged.

Example:

```
#line 15 pragma.c
```

11.10 inline DIRECTIVE

This reports the compiler that the source code has in line `asm` statements. It is important to know in advance that the source code contains assembly code.

11.11 #pragma SAVEREGS

This assure that a huge function will not alter the value of any of the registers when it is entered. Place this directive instantly prior to the function definition.

11.12 THE PRE-DEFINED MACROS IN ANSI AND TURBO C

11.12.1 ANSI C Pre-Defined Macros

The lists of pre-defined macros according to ANSI standard are as per Table 11.1. There are five pre-defined macros and are always available to the programmer for use. They cannot be undefined. Every macro name is defined with two underscores as prefix and suffix. These macros are useful for finding the system information such as date, time, file name and line number. A program is illustrated for testing these macros.

TABLE 11.1 Pre-defined macros in ANSI C

Pre-Defined Macros	*Function*
__DATE__	Displays system date in string format
__TIME__	Displays system time in string format
__LINE__	Displays line number as an integer
__FILE__	Displays current file name in string format
__STDC__	In ANSI C the value returned will be non-zero.

11.8 Write a program to use pre-defined macros of ANSI C.

```
#include <stddef.h>
void main()
{
clrscr();
printf("\nDATE : %s",__DATE__);
printf("\nTIME : %s",__TIME__);
printf("\nFILE NAME : %s",__FILE__);
printf("\nLINE NO. : %d",__LINE__);
printf("\nANSI Keywords? : %d",__STDC__);
}
```

```
Output
DATE : Mar 13 2009
TIME : 14:28:32
FILE NAME : AMIT\COND.C
LINE NO. : 11
ANSI Keywords? : 1
```

***Explanation*:**
In the above program, five macros are used in the `printf()` statements. On its execution, the output of the program is displayed as shown above. The program displays system date, time, program file name and total lines in the program. The STDC indicates whether the version of C compiler follows ANSI C standard. Here, the result is one. Hence, the compiler follows ANSI C standards. The programmer should set ANSI keyword on option by selecting option menu of the editor – compiler-source-ANSI keywords only on.

11.12.2 Turbo C Pre-Defined Macros

The pre-defined macros in Turbo C are listed in Table 11.2. The programmer can use the macro __TURBOC__ to find the version of Turbo. By setting option of code generation in option menu, one can test next two macros. For more information, the user is advised to view options in option menu.

TABLE 11.2 Pre-defined macros in Turbo C

Pre-Defined Macros	*Function*
__TURBOC__	Displays current Turbo C version
__PASCAL__	1 if "Calling convention...Pascal" option is chosen, otherwise undefined.
__CDECL__	1 if "Calling convention...C" option is chosen, otherwise undefined.
__MSDOS__	The integer constant 1.

11.9 Write a program to use few pre-defined macros indicated in Table 11.2.

```
#include <stddef.h>
void main()
{
clrscr();
printf("\nMSDOS : %d",__MSDOS__);
printf("\nCALLING CONVENTION : %d",__CDECL__);
getche();
}
```

```
Output
MSDOS : 1
CALLING CONVENTION : 1
```

11.13 THE PRE-DEFINED MARCOS IN `ctype.h`

The header file `ctype.h` contains a set of macros that check character. Table 11.3 describes all the macros. These macros take an argument of integer type and return an integer.

TABLE 11.3 Pre-defined macros in `ctype.h`.

Serial No.	*Macro*	*Returns* `true (!0)` *Value If*
1	`isalpha(d)`	d is a letter
2	`isupper(d)`	d is a capital letter
3	`islower(d)`	d is a small letter
4	`isdigit(d)`	d is a digit
5	`isalnum(d)`	d is a letter or a digit
6	`isxdigit(d)`	d is a hexadecimal digit
7	`isspace(d)`	d is a space
8	`ispunct(d)`	d is a punctuation symbol
9	`isprint(d)`	d is a printable character
10	`isgraph(d)`	d is printable, but not a space
11	`iscntrl(d)`	d is a control character
12	`isascii(d)`	d is an ASCII code

11.10 Write a program to identify whether the entered character is a letter or a digit or capital or small using pre-defined macros.

```
#include <ctype.h>
void main()
{
char d;
int f;
clrscr();
printf("\n Enter any character : ");
d=getche();
  f=isalpha(d);
  if(f!=0)
  {
    printf("\n%c is a letter in",d);
    f=isupper(d);
      if(f!=0)
      printf(" Capital case");
      else
      printf(" Small Case");
}
else
{
f=isdigit(d);
    if(f!=0)
    printf("\n %c is a digit",d);
    else
    {
    f=ispunct(d);
    if(f!=0)
    printf("\n %c is a punctuation symbol",d);
    }
}
    getche();
}
```

Output
```
Enter any character : C
C is a letter in upper case
```

Explanation:
In the above program, a character is entered through the keyboard. The macro `isalpha()` checks whether it is a digit or a letter. It returns true or false value to the variable 'd'. The `if` condition checks the value of variable 'd'. If the entered character is a letter, the `if` block is executed and again the macro `isupper()` checks whether the character is upper or small case. Thus, appropriate messages are displayed.

If the entered character is not a letter, `else` block of the first `if` statement is executed. The macro `isdigit()` checks whether the character is a digit or any other symbol. If it is a digit, `if` block is executed otherwise `else` block is executed. In the `else` block, macro `ispunct()` checks whether the entered character is a punctuation symbol. If so, the message is displayed.

EXERCISES

11.A Fill in the blanks

1. The program typed in the editor is the ______ to the preprocessor.
   (a) source code
   (b) object code
   (c) ASCII code

2. The preprocessor passes the source code to the C ______.
   (a) compiler
   (b) assembler
   (c) interpeter

3. The preprocessor directives are always initialized at the ______.
   (a) beginning of the program
   (b) run time
   (c) compile time

4. The preprocessor begins with a symbol ______.
   (a) //
   (b) #
   (c) $

5. A macro defined with ______ directives can be undefined with `#undef` directive.
   (a) `#define`
   (b) `#include`
   (c) `#ifdef`

6. In ______ operation macro argument is converted to string.
   (a) string concatenation
   (b) stringizing operation
   (c) string coping

7. The ______ loads specified file in the current program.
   (a) `#include`
   (b) `#define`
   (c) `#ifndef`

8. The ______ is used to display user defined message during compilation of the program.
   (a) `#error`
   (b) `#pragma`
   (c) `#stderr`

9. Inline directive reports the compiler that the source code has in line ______ statements.
   (a) bsm code
   (b) asm code
   (c) c++ code

11.B True or false

1. The preprocessor is a program that processes the source code before compilation.
2. The program typed in the editor is the source code for the preprocessor.

3. The `#define` defines the macro templates.
4. The macro definition must be terminated by a semicolon.
5. The `define` is a keyword.
6. The `#undef` undefines the macro.
7. The `#include` loads the specified file.
8. With `#include "stdio.h"`, the compiler searches the file in the entire system.
9. With `# include <stdio.h>` , the compiler searches the file in the standard directory.
10. The conditional compilation means that few statements can be skipped from the compiler.
11. The `#ifdef` and `#ifndef` works exactly the same way.
12. The `#error` flags user defined messages.
13. The `#pragma` sets off/on warning and error messages.
14. The `#ninclude` closes the file loaded by `#include`.
15. The macro template and its macro expansion are separated by blanks or tabs.
16. A space between # and `define` is compulsory.
17. Compiler generates faster code for variables than constants.
18. There should be space between macro template and its argument, i.e. AREA (x).
19. We can split the macros into multiple lines with a back slash.
20. In a macro, call controls are passed on to a macro function.

11.C Match the following correct pairs given in Group A with Group B

I

Group A		Group B	
Serial No.	**Pre-defined macros**	**Serial No.**	**Function**
1.	_DATE_	A	Displays current file name in a string format
2.	_TIME_	B	Displays line number as an integer
3.	_LINE_	C	In ANSI C, the value returned will be non-zero
4.	_FILE_	D	Displays system date in a string format
5.	_STDC_	E	Displays system time in a string format

II

Group A		Group B	
Serial No.	**Directive**	**Serial No.**	**Function**
1.	`#define`	A	Specifies the alternative when `#if` fails
2.	`#else`	B	Tests a compile time condition
3.	`#include`	C	Tests whether the macro is not defined
4.	`#ifdef`	D	Specifies the end of `#if`
5.	`#endif`	E	Tests for a macro definition
6.	`#ifndef`	F	Specifies the file to be included

II

Group A		Group B	
Serial No.	**Directive**	**Serial No.**	**Function**
7.	`#if`	G	Undefines a macro
8.	`#undef`	H	Defines a macro substitute value

III

Group A		Group B	
Serial No.	**Macros**	**Serial No.**	**Function**
1.	`stdin`	A	Standard output device
2.	`stdout`	B	Standard printer
3.	`stderr`	C	Standard input device
4.	`stdaux`	D	Standard error output device
5.	`stdprn`	E	Standard auxiliary device

IV

Group A		Group B	
Serial No.	**Macros**	**Serial No.**	**Function**
1.	COMPILER	A	Translates the assembly program
2.	PREPROCESSOR	B	A program can be typed
3.	LINKER	C	Compiles the source code
4.	ASSEMBLER	D	Supplies source code to the compiler
5.	EDITOR	E	Relocatable object code

11.D Select the appropriate option from the multiple choices given below

1. What will be the value of 'y' after execution of the following program?

```
#define plus(x) x;
#define minus(x) --x+ plus(x);
void main()
{
int x=8,y;
clrscr();
y=minus(x)
printf("\n y = %d",y);
}
```

(a) y=14
(b) y=15
(c) y=13
(d) none of the above

2. What will be the values of variables 'x' and 'y' after the execution of the following program?

```
#define P x++;
#define plus(x) P
void main()
{
  int x=2,y;
  clrscr();
  y=plus(x)
  printf("\nx = %d y = %d",x,y);
}
```

(a) x=3 y=2
(b) x=3 y=3
(c) x=2 y=2
(d) none of the above

3. In the following example, whether the macro is treated as

```
#define S "This Book Teaches C"
void main()
{
  printf("\n %s",S);
}
```

(a) macro as well as array
(b) only macro
(c) only array
(d) none of the above

4. What will be the output after the execution of the following program?

```
#define S "This Book Teaches C"
void main()
{
clrscr();
  printf("\n %c",*(S+3));
}
```

(a) s
(b) h
(c) i
(d) T

5. What will be the value of the variable 'z' after execution of the following program?

```
#define ROW 2
#define COL 3
int a[ROW][COL]={8,6,4,2,0,-2};
void main()
{
  int x,y,z=0;
  clrscr();
  for(x=0;x<ROW;x++)
  for(y=0;y<COL;y++)
  if(a[x][y]>z)
  z=a[x][y];
  printf("\nz = %d",z);
}
```

(a) z=8
(b) z=−2
(c) z=0
(d) z=2

6. What will be the value of the variable 'k' and 'm' after the execution of the following program?

```
#define product(k) k*k
void main()
{
int k=3,m;
m=product(k++);
clrscr();
printf("\t k=%d m=%d",k,m);
}
```

(a) k=5 m=9
(b) k=4 m=16
(c) k=5 m=25
(d) k=4 m=9

7. The following program will display

```
#define P &x
void main()
{
int x=2;
clrscr();
printf("\t %u",P);
}
```

(a) address
(b) value
(c) error message
(d) none of the above

8. The following program will display the output

```
void main()
{
int x=2,*p=5;
p=&x;
#define P &p
clrscr();
printf("\t %d",**P);
}
```

(a) 2
(b) 5
(c) 65500
(d) none of the above

9. Consider the statement `#define` PI 3.14, it means

(a) every occurrence of PI (identifier) is replaced with 3.14 (substitute value)
(b) occurrence of only PI in expressions is replaced with 3.14
(c) none of the above

10. A macro defined with `#define` directives can be undefined with

(a) `#undef` directive
(b) `#ifndef`
(c) `#!def`

11. The file name is included in the double quotations marks indicates that

(a) the search for the file is to be made in the current directory and in the standard directories
(b) the search for the file is to be made in the current directory
(c) the search for the file is to be made in the entire system
(d) bad file name format in include directory

12. When the file name is included without double quotation marks and when the program is executed, the message that appears on the screen will be

(a) the search for the file is made only in the standard directories
(b) the search for the file is made only in the current directory
(c) the search for the file is to be made in the entire system
(d) bad file name format in `include` directory

13. Generally the standard directories for header file and library files are

(a) include and lib
(b) turboc2 and include
(c) tc2 and Lib

14. The standard directory called `include` contains

(a) header files
(b) library file
(c) program file

15. The standard directory called lib contains

(a) header files
(b) library file
(c) program file

16. The conditional compilation directives allow the programmer to

(a) compile a part of the program
(b) compile entire program
(c) compile the program excluding header files

17. In the statement `#ifdef` , `#else` , `#endif`, the compiler ignores `#else` block

(a) when the macro is not defined
(b) when the macro is defined
(c) none of the above

18. What is the output of the following program?

```
#define SQUARE X*X*X
void main()
{
int X=10;
printf("%d",SQUARE);
getche();
}
```

(a) 100
(b) 1000
(c) 10

19. What is the output of the following program?

```
#define PI 3.14
void main()
{
float x;
clrscr();
for(x=PI*2;x<=7.28;x++)
printf("%g",x);
getche();
}
```

(a) 7.28
(b) 6.28
(c) 6.28 7.28

11.E What will be the output/s of the following program/s?

Programs on define directive

1.

```
#define PI 3.14
void main()
{
    float r=2.2,area;
      area=PI*r*r;
      clrscr();
      printf("Area of a Circle =
       %.2f cm2",area);
}
```

Explanation: Here, PI is used as macro and its value is 3.14. In this program r (a variable) is assigned value 2.2. Using area = PI*r*r;, area is calculated.

2.

```
#define N 5
#define say printf
void main()
{
int k;
clrscr();
for(k=1;k<=N;k++)
say(" %d ",k);
}
```

Explanation: Here, two macros, 'N' and 'say', are used. 'N' and 'say' are assigned 5 and `printf`, respectively. In `for` loop, 'k' varies from 1 to 5. Instead of `printf`, we are using 'say' so we get the output as the value of 'k' every time the loop is executed.

3.

```
#define DOUBLE(a) a*2
void main()
{
int a=1;
clrscr();
for(;a<=5;a++)
printf(" %d",DOUBLE(a));
}
```

Explanation: Here, DOUBLE is used as a macro which has assigned the value as 2*a. When we execute `for` loop, it takes values from 1 to 5. We get output as multiple of 2 every time the loop is executed.

4.

```
#define MAX(x,y) if (x>y) c=x; else c=y;
void main()
{
    int x=3,y=5,c;
    clrscr();
    MAX(x,y);
    printf("\n Largest of two
       numbers = %d",c);
}
```

Explanation: Here, MAX function is used as macro. MAX function has two variables. In that, the variable which has the largest value that is assigned to variable 'c', and it is displayed as output.

5.

```
#define RANGE (j> 30 && j<51)
  void main()
  {
  int j=31;
  clrscr();
  if (RANGE)
  printf("Within range");
  else
  printf("Out of Range");
}
```

Explanation: Here, RANGE is used as a macro. It holds the values in from 30 to 51. User prompts the data through the keyboard, and if(RANGE) is between 30 to 51, we get the output "Within range" otherwise we get the output "Out of Range".

6.

```
#define FUN(k) k+3.14
void main()
{
{
int x=2;
clrscr();
printf("%g",x*FUN(FUN(x)));
}
}
```

Explanation: Here FUN(k) is used as a macro. It holds equation k + 3.14. 'x' is assigned value as 2 and we are calculating 2*FUN(FUN(x)), i.e. (2+3.14)*2 = 10.280000, and `%g` removes unwanted zeros, i.e. we get output as 10.28.

7.

```
#define PRINT(a) printf("%c",a)
void main()
{
int a=2;
```

```
clrscr();
for(a=48;a<55;a++)
PRINT(a);
}
```

Explanation: Here, PRINT(a) is used as a macro. `PRINT(a)` replaces `printf("%c",a)`. When `for` loop runs from 48 to 54, corresponding ASCII values of 48 to 54 are displayed, i.e. 0 to 6 are displayed.

8.

```
# include<math.h>
# define P a*2
#define X P/4
void main()
{
int a=20,z;
clrscr();
printf("\n %d ",P);
printf(" %d ",X);
getche();
}
```

Explanation: Here, two macros are used, i.e. P and X. P and X are assigned to 2*a and P/4, respectively. The user input a = 20 is present. So, we get P = 2*a = 2*20 = 40 and X = P/4 = 40/4 = 10.

9.

```
#define con(x,y) x##y
void main()
{
int xy=20;
clrscr();
printf("\n %d ",con(x,y));
getche();
}
```

Explanation: Here, `con(x, y)` is used as macro which has value x##y which means xy. The user input xy =20 is present, so we get the output = `con(x, y)` = xy = 20.

Program on undefining macro

10.

```
#include <stdio.h>
#include <conio.h>
#define say(m) printf(#m)
void main()
{
  #undef say(m) printf(#m)
  #define say(m) printf(#m)
clrscr();
  say(Great thoughts come from crea-
     tive people);
  getche();
}
```

Explanation: Here, `say(m)` is used as a macro which replaces `printf(#m)`. By using `#undef say(m) printf(#m)`, we remove assignment of `say(m)` to `printf(#m)`. Again, we define `#define say(m) printf(#m)`, and due to this we get the output 'Great thoughts come from creative people'.

Programs on token pasting and stringizing operators

11.

```
#define say(m) printf(#m)
void main()
{
clrscr();
say(C is portable );
}
```

Explanation: Here, `say(m)` is used as a macro which replaces `printf(#m)`. As we are using operator in `printf(#m)`, whatever is present in the `say` bracket will get printed at output. If inverted commas are inserted, then they will also get printed.

Programs on conditional compilation

12.

```
#define else
void main()
{
  clrscr();
  #ifdef LINE
  printf("This is line number one. ");
  #else
  printf("This is line number two.");
  #endif
}
```

Explanation: Here, `else` is used as a macro. The `#ifdef` (identifier) becomes true if the symbol specified by (identifier) has been previously defined with `#define` directive.

13.

```
#define K 1
void main()
{
clrscr();
```

```
#ifndef K
printf("\n Macro is not defined.");
#else
printf("\n Macro is defined.");
#endif
}
```

Explanation: Here, `K` is used as a macro. The `#ifndef`(identifier) becomes true if the symbol specified by (identifier) has not been previously defined with `#define` directive. No output is obtained.

Program on `include` directive

14.

```
#include "udf.c"

void main()
{
clrscr();
factorial();
getche();
}
/* New File*/
Content of udf.c file are as follows.

factorial()
{
int x=4,i=1;
while(x>0)
{
i=x*i;
x--;
}
printf("\n %d",i);
}
```

Explanation: Here, two programs are present. The name of the second program is udf and in that factorial of 4 is calculated, i.e. 24. In the first program, second program is included by `#include "udf.c"` and factorial function is called, so that in the first program we get output as factorial of 4, i.e. 24.

Programs on pre-defined macros

15.

```
#include <stddef.h>
void main()
{
clrscr();
printf("\nDATE      : %s",__DATE__);
printf("\nTIME      : %s",__TIME__);
printf("\nFILE NAME : %s",__FILE__);
printf("\nLINE NO.  : %d",__LINE__);
}
```

Explanation: Here, in this example, pre-defined macros are used. The date of the system, present time, file name in which the program is written and line numbers are displayed.

16.

```
void main()
{
clrscr();

#ifdef __TINY__
printf("\nTINY %d",__
   TINY__);
#else
#ifdef __SMALL__
printf("\nSMALL %d",__
   SMALL__);
#else
#ifdef __MEDIUM__
printf("\nMEDIUM %d",__MEDIUM__);
#endif
#endif
#endif
}
```

Explanation: The memory model is selected at the time of compilation. In our case, 'small' is selected and hence the answer 'small' is displayed.

Program on pre-defined macros used in `ctype.h`

17.

```
#include <ctype.h>
void main()
{
int d=5;
int f;
clrscr();
  f=isalpha(d);
  if(f!=0)
  printf("\n%c is a letter ",d);
  else
  printf("\n%d is an Integer",d);
  getche();
}
```

Explanation: In this program, the `isalpha` function is used which becomes true if the variable is a character. Here, d=5, and so f = `isalpha (d)` = `isalpha (5)`. As 5 is not a character, 'f' becomes false. Due to this, f=0. So we get the output as 5 which is an integer.

11.F Find the bug/s in the following program/s

1.
```
#include <stdio.h>
#define 3.14 PI
void main()
{
printf("%f",PI);
}
```

2.
```
#include <stdio.h>
#define DOUBLE(a) a*2#define
TRIPLE(a) a*3
void main()
{
int a=1;
clrscr();
    for(;a<=5;a++)
    printf("\n %d \t%d\t
%d",a,double(a), TRIPLE(a));
}
```

3.
```
#include <stdio.h>
#define wait getche()
void main()
{
int k;#undef wait()
getche();
clrscr();
for(k=1;k<5;k++)
printf(" %d ",k);
wait;
}
```

4.
```
#include <stdio.h>
#define say(m) printf(m)
#define show(m) printf(#m)
void main()
{
clrscr();
say(Hello);
show(Hello);
}
```

5.
```
#include <stdio.h>
#define T 8
void main()
{
clrscr();
#ifndef T
printf("\n Macro is not defined");
#else
printf("\n Macro is defined");
}
```

6.
```
#include <stdio.h>
define T 8
void main(){
clrscr();
printf("\n %d",T);
}
```

7.
```
#include <stdio.h>
void main()
{
clrscr();
printf("\n TIME : %s",__TIME__);
}
```

8.
```
#include <stdio.h>
void main()
{
char d='1';
int f;
f=isalpha(1);
clrscr();
if (f!=0)
printf("%c is a letter",d);
else
printf("\n %c is not a letter",d);
}
```

9.
```
#include <stdio.h>
#include <conio.h>
#define B 1
void main()
{
clrscr();
#if !defined(A)
#error MACRO A IS NOT DEFINED.
#else
printf("Macro found.");
#endif
}
```

10.
```
#include <stdio.h>
#include<conio.h>
define FUN(k) k+3.14

void main()
{
{
int x=2;
```

```
clrscr();
printf("%d",x*FUN(x));
}
}
```

11.

```
#include <stdio.h>
#include<conio.h>
#define PRINT (a) printf("%c",a)
void main()
{
int a=2;
clrscr();
for(a=48;a<55;a++)
PRINT(a);
}
```

12.

```
#include <stdio.h>
#include <conio.h>
#pragma warn +aus
#pragma warn +def
#pragma warn +rvl
#pragma warn +use
void main()
{
int x=2,y,z;
clrscr();
printf("\n y= %d",y);
}
```

11.G Attempt the following programing exercises

1. Write a program to check whether the entered character is digit or letter. Display appropriate messages. Use macros defined in `ctype.h` header file.
2. Write a program to calculate the average of five numbers. Define macro for number five.
3. Write a program to define macros for opening and closing curly braces with BEGIN and END, respectively. Use these macros in C program in place of opening and closing curly braces.
4. Write a program to undefine a macro defined in `#define` directive. Observe the result.
5. Write a program to explain conditional compilation.
6. Write a program to display user-defined error message using `#error` directive.
7. Write a program to define macro for function `main()`. Call the function using the macro.
8. Write a program to find smallest and largest out of three numbers using macros with arguments.
9. Write programs to use macros as array and pointer.

11.H Answer the following questions

1. What is a preprocessor directive?
2. What is the `#include` directive? How does it help the programmer?
3. Distinguish between function and preprocessor directive.
4. What do you mean by token pasting and stringizing operators?
5. List pre-defined macros according to ANSI standard together with their uses.
6. Elaborate on conditional compilation.
7. What is `#pragma` directive? How do you set different warnings on and off?
8. Can we undefine a pre-defined macro?

ANSWERS

11.A Fill in the blanks

1. (a) source code
2. (a) compiler
3. (a) beginning of the program
4. (b) #
5. (a) `#define`
6. (b) stringizing operation
7. (a) `#include`
8. (a) `#error`
9. (b) asm code

11.B True or false

1. T 2. T 3. T 4. F 5. F 6. T 7. T 8. F 9. T 10. T
11. F 12. T 13. T 14. F 15. T 16. F 17. F 18. F
19. T 20. F

11.C Match the following correct pairs given in Group A with Group B

I 1 D, 2. E, 3. B, 4. A, 5. C
II 1. H, 2. A, 3. F, 4. E, 5. D, 6. C, 7. B, 8. G
III 1. C, 2. A, 3. D, 4. E, 5. B
IV 1. C, 2. D, 3. E, 4. A, 5. B

11.D Select the appropriate option from the multiple choices given below

1. (a) y=14
2. (a) x=3 y=2
3. (a) macro as well as array
4. (a) s
5. (a) z=8
6. (a) k=5 m=9
7. (a) address
8. (a) 2
9. (a) every occurrence of PI (identifier) is replaced with 3.14 (substitute value)
10. (a) `#undef` directive
11. (a) the search for the file is to be made in the current directory and standard directories
12. (d) bad file name format in `include` directory
13. (a) include and lib
14. (a) header files
15. (b) library file
16. (a) compile a part of program
17. (b) when macro is defined
18. (b) 1000
19. (b) 6.28

11.E What will be the output/s of the following program/s?

1. Area of a Circle =15.20 cm^2
2. 1 2 3 4 5
3. 2 4 6 8 10
4. Largest of two numbers = 5
5. Within range
6. 10.28
7. 0123456
8. 40 10
9. 20
10. Great thoughts come from creative people
11. C is portable
12. This is line number two.
13. Macro is defined
14. 24
15. DATE : Aug 31 2005
    TIME : 14:04:54
    FILE NAME : ANK.C
    LINE NO. : 10
16. SMALL 1
    Based on the memory model selection the answer will be different.
    Here, small memory model is selected. Hence, the output small 1
17. 5 is an Integer

11.F Find the bug/s in the following program/s

1. The statement defining macro would be `#define` PI 3.14
2. The macro DOUBLE is typed as double
3. The macro `wait` is undefined
4. The text 'Hello' should be enclosed in double quotes in `say` macro
5. `#endif` is missing
6. # is missing
7. `No Bug`
8. Header file `<ctype.h>` to be included
9. No bug
10. Format string should be `%g` or `%f`
11. The gap between PRINT and (a) should be removed
12. There is no bug. Warning errors are set

12

Structure and Union

CHAPTER OUTLINE

12.1 BASICS OF STRUCTURE

A structure is a collection of one or more variables of different data types, grouped together under a single name. It is a derived data type to be arranged in a group of related data items of different data types. It is a user-defined data type because the user can decide the data types to be included in the body of a structure. By using structures, we can make a group of variables, arrays and pointers.

12.2 FEATURES OF STRUCTURES

It is possible to copy the contents of all structure elements of different data types to another structure variable of its type using assignment (=) operator. It is possible because the structure elements are stored in successive memory locations.

Comparison between array and structure is shown in Table 12.1.

TABLE 12.1 Comparison between array and structure

Serial No.	*Points for Comparison*	*Array*	*Structure*
1.	Collection of data	Same data type	Different data types
2.	Keyword	Array is not a keyword	`struct` is a keyword
3.	Declaration and definition of data types	Only declaration	Both declaration and definition
4.	Bit fields	Does not have bit fields	May contain bit fields
5.	Accessing elements by	Subscript	Dot(.) operator or -> operator
6.	Process of adding/deleting an element	Difficult	Easy

The nesting of structures is possible, i.e. one can create structure within the structure. Using this feature, one can handle complex data types. It is also possible to pass structure elements to a function. This is similar to passing an ordinary variable to a function. One can pass individual structure elements or entire structure by value or address.

It is also possible to create structure pointers. In the pointer, we have studied pointing a pointer to an `integer`, a pointing to a `float` and a pointing to a `char`. In the similar way, we can create a pointer pointing to structure elements. For this it requires -> operator.

12.3 DEFINITION AND DECLARATION OF STRUCTURE

Structure is defined as

```
struct struct_type
{
type1 variable1;
type2 variable2;
------------------
------------------
};
```

Structure definition always starts with `struct` keyword. Here, `struct_type` is known as tag. The members of the structure are enclosed within a pair of curly braces. A closing brace is terminated with a semicolon.

After defining structure, we can declare structure variables as follows.

```
struct struct_type v1,v2,v3;
```

Here, `v1`, `v2` and `v3` are variables of structure `struct_type`. This is similar to declaring variable of any data type.

```
int v1, v2,v3;
```

Here, `v1`, `v2` and `v3` are variables of integer data type.

Example:
Defining a structure and declaration of structure variables is done as given below.

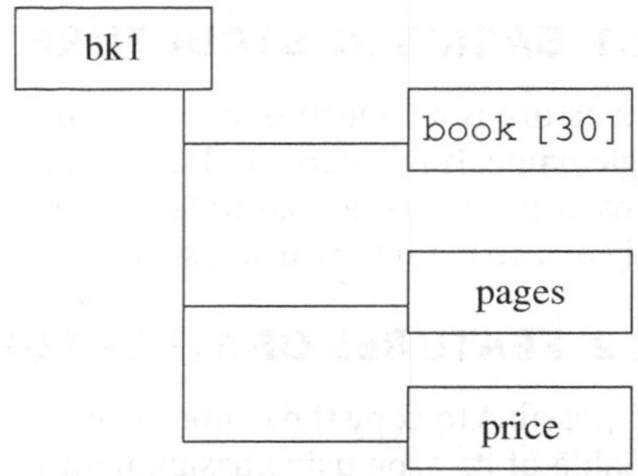

FIGURE 12.1 Block diagram of structure

```
struct book1
{
char book[30];
int pages;
float price;
};
struct book1 bk1;
```

In the above example, a structure of type `book1` is defined. It consists of three members book [30] of `char` data type, pages of `int` type and price of `float` data type. Figure 12.1 explains various members of a structure.

```
struct book1 bk1;
```

The above line creates variable `bk1` of type `book1` and it reserves total 36 bytes (30 bytes for book [30], 2 bytes for `integer` and 4 bytes for `float`). Through `bk1` all the three members of the structure can be accessed.

In order to initialize structure elements with certain values, following statement is used:

```
struct book1 bk1 = { "shrinivas",500,385.00};
```

All the members of structure are related to variable `bk1`.

```
structure_variable.member or bk1.book
```

The period (.) sign is used to access the structure members.

We can directly assign values to members as given below:

```
bk1.book ="shrinivas";
bk1.pages=500;
bk1.price=385.00;
```

12.4 STRUCTURE WITHIN A STRUCTURE

Thus, a structure within a structure can be used to create complex data applications. The syntax of the structure within the structure is as follows.

```
struct time
{
int second;
```

```
int minute;
int hour;
};
struct t
{
int carno;
struct time st;
struct time et;
};
struct t player;
```

Figure 12.2 explains structure within structure.

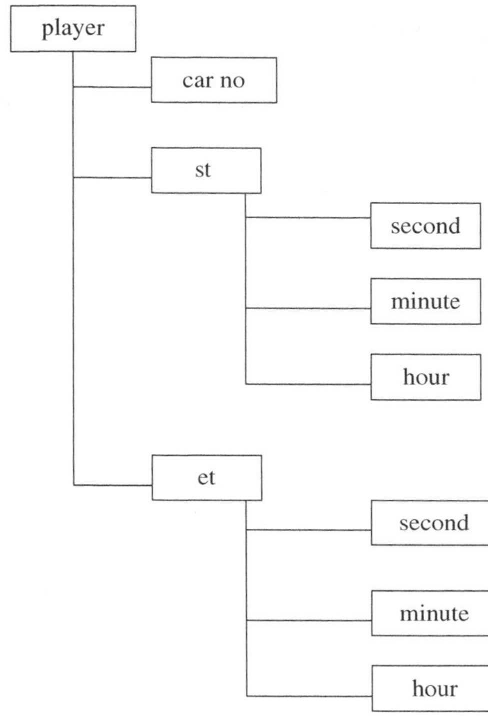

FIGURE 12.2 **Structure within structure**

12.5 ARRAY OF STRUCTURES

As we know, array is a collection of same data types. In the same way, we can also define array of structure. In such type of array, every element is of structure type. Array of structure can be declared as follows.

```
struct time
{
int second;
int minute;
int hour;
} t[3];
```

In the above example, `t[3]` is an array of three elements containing three objects of time structure. Each element of `t[3]` has structure of time with three members that are second, minute and hour.

12.6 POINTER TO STRUCTURE

We know that pointer is a variable that holds the address of another data variable. The variable may be of any data type, i.e. `int`, `float` or `double`. In the same way, we can also define pointer to structure. Here, starting address of the member variables can be accessed. Thus, such pointers are called structure pointers.

Example:

```
struct book
{
char name[25];
char author[25];
int pages;
};
struct book *ptr;
```

In the above example, `*ptr` is pointer to `structure book`. The syntax for using pointer with the member is as given below.

(1) `ptr->name` (2) `ptr->author` and (3) `ptr->pages`

By executing these three statements, starting address of each member can be estimated.

12.7 STRUCTURE AND FUNCTIONS

Like variables of standard data type, structure variables can be passed on to the function by value or address. The syntax of the same is as given below.

```
struct book
{
char name[35];
char author[35];
int pages;
} b1;
void main()
{
------------
------------
show(&b1);
-------------
-------------
}
show(struct book *b2)
{
------------
------------
}
```

Whenever a structure element requires to be passed on to any other function, it is essential to declare the structure outside the `main()` function, i.e. global.

In the above example, `structure book` is declared before `main()`. It is a global structure. Its member elements are `char` name [35], `char` author [35] and `int` pages. They can be accessed by all other functions.

12.8 `typedef`

We can create new data type by using `typedef`. The statement `typedef` is to be used while defining the new data type. The syntax is as given below.

```
typedef type dataname;
```

Here, `type` is the data type and `dataname` is the user-defined name for that type.

```
typedef int hours;
```

Here, hours is another name for `int` and now we can use hours instead of `int` in the program as follows.

```
hours hrs;
```

12.9 BIT FIELDS

Bit field provides exact amount of bits required for storage of values. If a variable value is 1 or 0, we need a single bit to store it. In the same way, if the variable is expressed between 0 and 3, then the two bits are sufficient for storing these values. Similarly, if a variable assumes values between 0 and 7, then three bits will be sufficient to hold the variable and so on. The number of bits required for a variable is specified by non-negative integer followed by colon.

To hold the information, we use the variables. The variables occupy minimum one byte for `char` and two bytes for `integer`. Instead of using complete integer if bits are used, space of memory can be saved. For example, to know the information about the vehicles, following information has to be stored in the memory:

(i) Petrol vehicle

(ii) Diesel vehicle

(iii) Two-wheeler vehicle

(iv) Four-wheeler vehicle

(v) Old model

(vi) New model

In order to store the status of the above information, we may need two bits for type of fuel as to whether vehicle is of petrol or diesel type. Three bits are needed for its type as to whether the vehicle is a two- or a four-wheeler. Similarly, three bits are required for model of the vehicle. Total bits required for storing the information would be 8 bits, i.e. 1 byte. It means that the total information can be packed into a single byte. Eventually, bit fields are used for conserving the memory. The amount of memory saved by using bit fields will be substantial, and this is proved from the above example.

However, there are restrictions on bit fields when arrays are used. Arrays of bit fields are not permitted. Also, the pointer cannot be used for addressing the bit field directly, although use of the member access operator (- >) is acceptable.

The unnamed bit fields could be used for padding as well as for alignment purposes.

The structure for the above problem would be as follows.

```
struct vehicle
{
unsigned type : 3;
unsigned fuel : 2;
unsigned model : 3;
};
```

The colon (:) in the above declaration tells to the compiler that bit fields are used in the structure and the number after it indicates how many bits are required to allot for the field.

12.10 ENUMERATED DATA TYPE

The `enum` is a keyword. It is used for declaring enumeration types. The programmer can create his/her own data type and define what values the variables of these data types can hold. This enumeration data type helps in reading the program.

Consider the example of 12 months of a year.

```
enum month {Jan, Feb, Mar, Apr, May, June, July, Aug, Sep, Oct, Nov, Dec};
```

This statement creates a user-defined data type. The keyword `enum` is followed by the tag name `month`. The enumerators are the identifiers Jan, Feb, Mar, Apr, May and so on. Their values are constant `unsigned integers` and starts from 0. The identifier January refers to 0, February refers to 1 and so on. The identifiers are not to be enclosed with quotation marks. Also, note that the integer constants are not permitted as identifier.

12.11 union

union is a variable, which is similar to the structure. It contains number of members like structure but it holds only one object at a time. In the structure, each member has its own memory location, whereas members of union have same memory locations. It can accommodate one member at a time in a single area of storage. union also contains members of types int, float, long, arrays, pointers, etc. It allocates fixed specific bytes of memory for access of data types irrespective of any data type.

The union requires bytes that are equal to the number of bytes required for the largest members. For example, the union contains char, int and long int, then the number of bytes reserved in the memory for the union is 4 bytes. Examples are illustrated under 12.E for understanding.

12.12 CALLING BIOS AND DOS SERVICES

We can access BIOS and DOS services through C language. Few simple examples are illustrated by making use of BIOS and DOS services. The programmer does not have direct access to the CPU registers. However, the C language provides an interface that allows the programmer to access any BIOS or DOS service. The C language defines a union type called REGS and structure type called SREGS in the file dos.h which escorts the C compiler. These data types are used to pass parameters to the CPU registers. In order to have access to these definitions, the programmer has to include dos.h header file.

The union type REGS contains the CPU registers. These registers are used for holding the data temporarily. The microprocessors 8086, 8088, 80186, 80286, and 80386 use a variety of registers for arithmetic and logical operations. Also, they are used to receive instructions and pass data to and from memory.

The 8086 CPU registers are 16 bits in size. They are AX, BX, CX, DX, SI, DI and CFLAG, which is a carry flag. The size of CFLAG also is 16 bits. The structure that defines these 16 bits registers is called 'X'. The 'X' stands for a register pair. Size of each register is 8 bits. Thus, the size of paired registers 'X' is 16 bits.

The union also allows us to refer 8 bit registers of above type processors. These 8 bits registers are AL, AH, BL, BH, CL, CH, DL and DH. The structure that defines these 8 bit registers is called 'h'. Here, 'h' stands for a half register, i.e. 8 bit register.

There are also segment registers in the above processors. The size of segment registers is 16 bits. These segment registers are DS, ES, CS and SS. The structure type SREGS defines these segment registers.

The C language provides functions such as intdos(), intdosx() and segread() to access DOS services. The intdos() is used for calling DOS interrupt. The intdos() invokes a DOS function by issuing software interrupt INT 21H.

We can also invoke BIOS services by using C functions such as int86() and int86x(). The int86() stands for 8086 interrupt. The int86() functions invokes a BIOS functions by issuing a software interrupt. The int86() function can be invoked with the following three arguments:

Interrupt type number corresponding to ROM-BIOS service and two arguments of union type REGS, they are "x" and "h".

The int86() function takes the values of input registers from one REGS union and returns to the output registers in another. The int86x() function is similar to int86(). The difference is int86x() requires an input argument in DS or ES register.

12.13 UNION OF STRUCTURES

We know that one structure can be nested within another structure. It the same way, a union can be nested within another union. We can also create structure in a union or vice versa.

EXERCISES

12.A Fill in the blanks

1. A structure is a ______.
   (a) collection of one or more variables of same or different data types
   (b) collection of one or more variables of different data types
   (c) collection of one or more variables of similar data types

2. By using structures, we can make a group of variables, ______ , pointers.
   (a) arrays
   (b) classes
   (c) functions

3. If objects 'b' and 'c' are of structure data type, then the contents of 'b' can be copied to 'c' using ______.
   (a) =
   (b) ==
   (c) copying

4. Structure elements are stored in ______.
   (a) contiguous memory locations
   (b) random memory locations
   (c) in CPU registers

5. The `typedef` ______.
   (a) gives new name to existing data type
   (b) gives new definition to existing data type
   (c) none of the above

6. Bit field provides exact amount of ______ required for storage of values.
   (a) bits
   (b) bytes
   (c) words

7. The values of enumerated data types are ______.
   (a) constant unsigned integers
   (b) constant signed integers
   (c) unsigned integers

8. We can access ______ and ______ services through C language.
   (a) BIOS & DOS
   (b) DOS & Windows
   (c) BIOS

9. The 8086 CPU registers are ______ bits in size.
   (a) 16 bits
   (b) 8 bits
   (c) 4 bits

10. We can also invoke BIOS services by using C functions such as ______ .
    (a) `int86()`
    (b) `intx()`
    (c) `intdos()`

11. Union is a variable, which is similar to the structure. It contains number of members like structure but ______.
    (a) it holds only one object at a time
    (b) it holds two objects at a time
    (c) it holds values exactly like structure

12. Union members ______.
    (a) share same memory locations
    (b) have different memory locations
    (c) none of the above

13. The union requires bytes that are equal to the number of bytes required for______.
    (a) the largest type members
    (b) the smallest type members
    (c) size of object

12.B True or false

1. A structure is a set of different data type.
2. A `struct` is a keyword.
3. Structure elements can be accessed directly.
4. The dot operator can be used to access the `struct` variable.
5. The structure definition must be terminated by semicolon.
6. The declaration and initialization of structure variable can be done at once.
7. Structure can be defined inside another structure (nested).

8. It is possible to pass structure elements to function.
9. The array of structure elements cannot be declared.
10. The `ptr` is pointer to the structure and it can access elements using -> operator.
11. Bit fields provide exact amount of bits required for storage.
12. Bit fields are always defined of `signed` type.
13. The `enum` keyword is used to define enumerated data type.
14. The value of enumerated data type starts from 1.
15. The structure elements are stored in separate memory locations.
16. The `union` elements are stored at random memory locations.
17. The `union` has common storage space for all its variables.
18. The `union` requires more space as compared to structure.

12.C Match the following correct pairs given in Group A with Group B

I

Serial No.	Group A	Serial No.	Group B
1.	Structure	A	Collection of same data types
2.	Array	B	Collection of one or more variables of similar or different data types, but holds only one object at a time
3.	Enum	C	Collection of one or more variables of different data type
4.	Union	D	Collection of user defined data types

II

Serial No.	Group A	Serial No.	Group B
1.	Structure	A	Subscript
2.	Array	B	. or -> operators

III

Serial No.	Group A	Serial No.	Group B
1.	Structure	A	2 bytes
2.	Union	B	Memory equal to addition of sizes of all elements declared
3.	Enumerated	C	Memory that is equal to largest size element

12.D Select the appropriate option from the multiple choices given below

1. Various members of the structure are specified
   (a) within the curly braces separated by semicolons
   (b) within the curly braces separated by comma
   (c) within the square brackets
   (d) within the angle brackets
2. Memory is reserved when
   (a) structure is defined
   (b) structure variables are declared
   (c) ampersand (&) operator is used
3. The members of a structure are
   (a) dissimilar data types
   (b) signed data types
   (c) unsigned data types
4. The structure is a
   (a) user-defined data types
   (b) system defined variables
   (c) keyword
5. The `typedef` is a
   (a) variable
   (b) system defined file
   (c) keyword
6. Struture elements are stored
   (a) contiguously
   (b) continuous memory locations
   (c) randomly
7. The size of a structure is decided by
   (a) its members
   (b) one of its member
   (c) none of the above
8. Number of bytes required for enumerated data type in memory is
   (a) 2 bytes
   (b) 1 bytes
   (c) 3 byte

9. Memory allocation in `union` is decided by
   (a) largest variable type
   (b) all variable types
   (c) none of the above

10. The `int86()` function invokes
   (a) DOS function
   (b) BIOS function
   (c) user-defined function

11. The `intdos()` function invokes
   (a) user-defined function
   (b) DOS function
   (c) both (a) and (b)

12. `Int 33` is a
   (a) software interrupt
   (b) hardware interrupt
   (c) both (a) and (b)
   (d) none of the above

13. The structure holds the memory of
   (a) one element at a time
   (b) elements defined in structure
   (c) both (a) and (b)
   (d) none of the above

14. Bit fields are used only with
   (a) `unsigned int` data type
   (b) `float` data type
   (c) `char` data type
   (d) `int` data type

15. Observe the following program neatly and choose the appropriate `printf()` statement from the options.

```
  struct company
  {
  char *company ;
  };
void main()
{
struct company m={"Dorling"};
----
}
```

   (a) printf("\n company : %s",m.company);
   (b) printf("\n company : %s",m->company)
   (c) printf("\n company : %s",m.*company)
   (d) printf("\n company : %s",*m.company)

16. What will be the value of 'm' displayed on execution of the following program?

```
struct bit
  {
  unsigned int m :3;
  };
void main()
{
struct bit b={7};
clrscr();
printf("\n m = %d",b.m);
}
```

   (a) m= 7
   (b) m=1
   (c) m=3
   (d) none of the above

17. The size of structure in bytes occupied in the following program will be

```
struct bit
  {
  unsigned int m :4;
  unsigned int x :4;
  int k;
  double f;
  };
  struct bit b;
void main()
{
clrscr();
printf("\n Size of structure in
   Bytes = %d",sizeof(b));
}
```

   (a) 8
   (b) 11
   (c) 7
   (d) 4

18. `struct month j,m,k={"August"};` in this statement, string is assigned to
   (a) object j
   (b) object m
   (c) object k

19. The union contains `char`, `integer` and `double`, then the number of bytes reserved in the memory for the union is _______ bytes.
   (a) 8
   (b) 1
   (c) 2

12.E What will be the output/s of the following program/s?

Programs on declaration and initialization of structures

1. Program on display information of a student.

```
void main()
{
struct emp
{
char name[30];
int age;
int sal;
};
struct emp e={"Satish",28,20000};
clrscr();
printf("\n Name : %s",e.name);
printf("\n Age : %d",e.age);
printf("\n Salary : %d",e.sal);
getche();
}
```

Explanation: In the above program, the structure `emp` is defined with its member variables `char name [30]`, `int age` and `int sal`. The 'e' is an object of the structure `emp`. The statement `struct emp e = {"Satish",28,20000};` defines object 'e' and initializes the variables with the values enclosed in the curly braces. Using `printf()` statement, contents of individual fields are displayed.

2. Program to display time.

```
void main()
{
struct time
    {
    int second;
    int minute;
    int hour;
    } t;
  t.second=45;
  t.minute=15;
  t.hour=11;
  clrscr();
  printf("%d:%d:%d",t.hour,t.
     minute,t.second);
}
```

Explanation: This program is similar to 12.E(1). Initilization of variables is different. Variables are different and 't' is the object.

3. Program to display the information of a book 't'.

```
void main()
{
struct book
{
 char *book;
 int pages;
 float price;
};
struct book bk;
bk.book="Programming in C";
bk.pages=300;
bk.price=250.00;
clrscr();
printf("\n Book : %s",bk.book);
printf("\n Pages : %d",bk.pages);
printf("\n Price : %g",bk.price);
}
```

Explanation: This program is similar to 12.E(2).

4. Program to display total size of variables.

```
void main()
{
struct emp
{
char name[30];
int age;
int sal;
};
struct emp e={"Santosh",28,7000};
clrscr();
printf("\n SIZE OF e :
    %d",sizeof(e));
}
```

Explanation: This program calculates the total size of variables declared in structure. The characters are 30 and two integers are there. Each character needs 1 byte and integer needs 2 bytes. Thus, total should be 34 bytes memory.

5. Program to display numbers.

```
void main()
{
struct emp
{
int k;
int a;
int s;
};
struct emp e={1,2,4};
e.k++;
clrscr();
```

```
printf("%d %d %d",e.k,e.a,e.s);
}
```

Explanation: In this program, the value of 'k' is incremented by post increment operator.

6. Program to display authors information.

```
void main()
{
struct emp
{
char book_name[40];
char author[20];
int pages;
int cost;
};

struct emp e={"Programming
    with ANSI and Turbo
    C","Ashok",594,195};
clrscr();
printf("\n Book Name : %s",e.book_
    name);
printf("\n Author's Name : %s",
    e.author);
printf("\n Pages : %d",e.pages);
printf("\n Cost : %d",e.cost);

getche();
}
```

Explanation: This program is the same as that of 12. E(1). The variables are different.

7. Some tricky problem.

```
void main()
{
struct emp
{
int a;
int b;
int c;
};
struct emp e={10,20,40};
e.a++;
e.b++;
e.c=e.a+e.b;
clrscr();
printf("%d %d %d",e.a,
    e.b,e.c);
getche();
}
```

Explanation: In this program, the value of 'a' and 'b' are incremented, and on incrementing their values are added and result 32 is displayed.

8. Program on display book information.

```
void main()
{
 struct book
 {
   char *book;
   int pages;
   float price;
 };
  struct book bk,ck;
  bk.book="Data Structure
    through C";
  bk.pages=400;
  bk.price=215.00;
  ck=bk;
  clrscr();
  printf("\n Book : %s",ck.book);
  printf("\n Pages : %d",ck.pages);
  printf("\n Price : %g",ck.price);
}
```

Explanation: No explanation is needed if earlier programs are followed.

Program on structure within structure

9. Program to display information of an officer and his date of joining.

```
void main()
{
struct name
{
char first[7];
char second[7];
};

struct j_date
{
int day;
int month;
int year;
};

struct data
{
struct name nm;
struct j_date bt;
};
struct data r1={"Thomas","Rajesh",1
    0,01,2005};
clrscr();
printf("Name : %s %s \n",r1.
    nm.first,r1.nm.second);
```

```
printf("Joining Date : %d.%d.%d",r1.
    bt.day,r1.bt.month,r1.bt.year);
getche();
}
```

Explanation: One can refer to structure within structure program. In the above program, two structures are defined. The first structure is name that contains member fields `char` first and `char` second. The second structure is `j_date` whose member fields are day, month and year. The variable `nm` and `bt` are the objects of the two structures. Using these two variables, it is possible to access the member variables of the first structure as well as second structure elements.

Programs on pointer to structure

10. Program to display numbers with pointers.

```
void main()
{
int *p;

    struct num
    {
    int a;
    int b;
    int c;
    };
struct num d;
d.a=2;
d.b=3;
d.c=4;

p=&d.a;

clrscr();

 printf("\n a=%d",*p);
 printf("\n b=%d",*(++p));
 printf("\n c=%d",*(++p));
}
```

Explanation: In this program, one can access the variables of structure using pointers. The pointer variable 'p' points to the location of 'a'. 'p' is incremented two times pointing to the address of 'b' and 'c'.

11. Program on display time.

```
void main()
{
    struct time
    {
    int second;
    int minute;
    int hour;
    };
    struct time *t;
    t->second=50;
    t->minute=20;
    t->hour=12;
    clrscr();
    printf("%d:%d:%d",t->hour,t->
      minute,t->second);
}
```

Explanation: In `printf()` statement, to print the structure elements using pointer an arrow operator → (- and > together) is used instead of `dot(.) operator`. Using the array pointer, member variables are displayed.

12. Program to display information of a student.

```
#include <string.h>
void main()
{
    struct boy
    {
    char *name;
    int *age;
    float *height;
    };
  struct boy b;

    char nm[10]="Somesh";
    int ag=20;
    float ht=5.40;

    strcpy(b.name,nm);
    b.age=&ag;
    b.height=&ht;

    clrscr();
    printf("\n Name = %s",
      b.name);
    printf("\n Age = %d",*b.age);
    printf("\n Height = %g",*b.height);
}
```

Explanation: Using `dot operator`, the contents of the structure elements are displayed.

Program on structure and function

13. Program to display information of a boy.

```
void main()
{
struct boy
{
char name[25];
int age;
int wt;
};
```

```
struct boy b1={"Sachin",27,55};
print(b1.name,b1.age,b1.wt);
}
print(char *s, int t, int n)
{
clrscr();
printf("\n %s %d %d",s,t,n);
return 0;
}
```

Explanation: In the above example, structure name has member variables like a character array name [25], age and weight of integer type. We have passed the base address of `name`, but values of `age` and `wt`. Thus, here values are passed using call by reference and call by value methods.

14. Program to display information of a book.

```
struct book
{
 char name[35];
 int pages;
 float price;
 };
 void main()
 {
  struct book bk={"Programming in
   C",350,400};
 clrscr();
 show(&bk);
}
show(struct book *b2)
{
printf(" Book : %s \n Pages :%d
    \n Price :%g",b2->name,b2-
    >pages,b2->price);
}
```

Explanation: In the above program, structure `book` is defined outside the `main()`. So it is global and every function can access it. The object defined on structure `book bk` is passed to function. Thus, using -> operators the contents of individual elements of structure are displayed.

Program on union and structure

15. Program to display numbers with `structure` and `union`.

```
void main()
{
struct x
{
float f;
char p[];
};
union y
{
struct x s;
};
union y st;
st.s.f=10.9;
st.s.p[0]=90;
st.s.p[1]=89;
clrscr();
printf("\n %g",st.s.f);
printf("\n %c",st.s.p[0]);
printf("\n %c",st.s.p[1]);
}
```

Explanation: In the above program, structure 'x' is defined. The union 'y' contains structure member as its member variable. The variable 's' is an object of structure 'x' and 'st' is an object of union 'y'. The member variables of structure 'x' are assigned with certain values. Using objects of structure and union with dot operator, member contents of member variables are displayed.

Programs on `typedef`

16.

```
#define H 60
void main()
{
 typedef int hours;
 hours hrs=2;
 clrscr();
 printf("\n Minutes : %d",hrs*H);
 printf("\n Seconds : %d",hrs*H*H);
}
```

Explanation: In the above example, `typedef` declared hours as an integer data type. Immediately after the `typedef` statement, 'hrs' is a variable of hours data type which is similar to `int`. This is initialized with 2. Further, the program calculates minutes and seconds using 'hrs' variable. The preprocessor macro definition is also used.

17.

```
void main()
{
  typedef char string [20];
  string a="Hello";
  clrscr();
  printf("\n %s",a);
}
```

Explanation: The `typedef` user defined data type is declared, and `string[]` is a synonym for the type `char`. The string "Hello" is displayed.

18. Program to display information of an employee.

```
void main()
{
 typedef struct
 {
   char name[20];
   char sex[2];
   int acno;
 } info;
 info empo={"Sanjay","M",1452};
 clrscr();
 printf("\n %s %s %d", empo.name,
    empo.sex, empo.acno);
}
```

Explanation: In the above program, `info` is another user-defined name for defining the structure. Here, `info` is used for defining the structure variables such as employee's name, sex, and age, etc.

Programs on enumerated data type

19. Program to display the values of some months with enum data.

```
void main()
{
 enum {Jan,Feb,March,Apr,May};
 clrscr();
 printf("Jan=%d",Jan);
 printf("\nFeb=%d",Feb);
}
```

Explanation: In the above program, enumerated data type is declared with 5-month names within two curly braces. The compiler assigns 0 value to the first identifier Jan, 1 for Feb, etc. Using `printf()` statement, the constants are displayed for different identifiers.

20. Day of weeks.

```
void main()
 {
 enum day {Sunday=1, Monday, Tues-
    day, Wednesday, Thrusday, Fri-
    day, Saterday};
 clrscr();

 printf("\nTuesday = %d",Tuesday);
 printf("\nFriday = %d",Friday);
 printf("\nSunday = %d",Sunday);
 getche();
 }
```

Explanation: Concept is similar to previous program.

21. String function in enumerated data type.

```
#include <string.h>
void main()
{
enum capital
{
MUMBAI,HYDERABAD, BANGALORE
};

struct state
{
char name[15];
enum capital c;
};
struct state s;
strcpy(s.name,"MAHARASHTRA");
s.c=MUMBAI;
clrscr();
printf("\n State : %s",s.name);
if(s.c==MUMBAI)
printf("\n MUMBAI is Capital of
   %s",s.name);
getche();
}
```

Explanation: In the above program `enum` data type `capital` is defined and initialized with three identifiers. They are Mumbai, Hyderabad, and Bangalore. The structure `state` is declared with two members such as `name` and `capital`. The structure variables are assigned with values MAHARASHTRA and MUMBAI. The `printf()` statement displays the contents of structure variables. If the structure variable `s.c` contains value, a MUMBAI message is displayed, otherwise not.

Program on union

22. Sizes of union and structure.

```
void main()
{
union result
{
int marks;
char grade;
};
struct res
{
char name[15];
int age;
union result perf;
} data;
clrscr();
```

```
clrscr();
printf("%s",m->month);
}
```

12.

```
struct month
{
char *month;
};
void main()
{
static struct month j,m,k={"August"};
clrscr();
printf("%s",m.month);
printf("\n%s",m.month);
printf("\n%s",k.month);
}
```

12.G Attempt the following programming exercises

1. Write a program to define a structure with city as tag with fields such as city_name, population, district_name, total_engineering colleges, medical_colleges. Read and display the same data.
2. Attempt the Q 1 using pointer to structure.
3. Define a structure with exam as tag name. Define different fields such as name, last_name, gender, age, marks_Phy, marks_chem., marks_math, total. Create array of structure variables. Read and display the 5 records.
4. Define a structure with player as tag name. The members of this structure should be name, age, weight, height, tot_medals_win. Read and display the data of 5 players.
5. Write a program to create structure within a structure. The outer structure should contain members such as nation, no_sat launched and inner structure should contain weight, height, cost, launch_station, etc. Read and display the data of 3 nations. Assume suitable data.
6. Create a structure that should include members hotel_name, tot_rooms, room_rent, tot_employee. Assume suitable data of five hotels. Display the hotel name having largest number of rooms with minimum room rent.
7. Write a program to accept records of different districts using array of structures. The structure should contain name, population, medical collages, management colleges, compu_literacy rate, tot_food-prod, etc. Display the district, which is having highest literacy rate.

ANSWERS

12.A Fill in the blanks

1. (a) collection of one or more variables of same or different data types
2. (a) arrays
3. (a) =
4. (a) contiguous memory locations
5. (a) gives new name to existing data type
6. (a) bits
7. (a) constant unsigned integers
8. (a) BIOS & DOS
9. (a) 16 bits
10. (a) `int86()`
11. (a) it holds only one object at a time.
12. (a) shares same memory locations
13. (a) The largest type members.

12.B True or false

1.T 2.T 3.F 4.T 5.T 6.F 7.T 8.T 9.F 10.T
11.T 12.F 13.T 14.F 15.T 16.F 17.T 18.F

12.C Match the following correct pairs given in Group A with Group B

I 1. C, 2. A, 3. D, 4. B
II 1. B, 2. A
III 1. B, 2. C, 3. A

12.D Select the appropriate option from the multiple choices given below

1. (a) within the curly braces separated by semi-colons
2. (a) structure is defined
3. (a) dissimilar data types
4. (a) user-defined data types
5. (c) keyword
6. (a) contiguously
7. (a) its members
8. (a) 2 bytes
9. (a) largest variable type
10. (b) BIOS function
11. (b) DOS function
12. (a) software interrupt
13. (b) elements defined in structure
14. (a) `unsigned int` data type
15. (a) `printf("\n company : %s",m.company);`
16. (a) m=7
17. (b) 11
18. (c) object k
19. (a) 8

12.E What will be the output/s of the following program/s?

1. Name : Satish
   Age : 28
   Salary : 20000
2. 11 : 15 : 45
3. Book : Programming in C
   Pages : 300
   Price : 250
4. SIZE OF e : 34
5. 2 2 4
6. Book Name : Programming with ANSI and Turbo C
   Author's Name : Ashok
   Pages : 594
   Cost : 195
7. 11 21 32
8. Book : Data Structure through C
   Pages : 400
   Price : 215
9. Name : Thomas Rajesh
   Joining Date : 10.1.2005
10. a=2
    b=3
    c=4
11. 12 : 20 : 50
12. Name = Somesh
    Age = 20
    Height = 5.40
13. Sachin 27 55
14. Book : Programming in C
    Pages :350
    Price :400
15. 10.9
    Z
    Y
16. Minutes : 120
    Seconds : 7200
17. Hello
18. Sanjay M 1452
19. Jan=0 Feb=1
20. Tuesday = 3
    Friday = 6
    Sunday = 1
21. State : MAHARASHTRA
    MUMBAI is Capital of MAHARASHTRA
22. Size of union : 2
    Size of Structure : 19
23. Y
24. Total Memory = 488 KB
25. A

12.F Find the bug/s in the following program/s

1. `*b1` is a pointer and hence operator `->` is to be used in place of dot.
2. Structure should be terminated by semicolon.

3. Variable 'b2' is not pointer and hence use of `->` is invalid.
4. Structure should be defined outside all functions.
5. `typedef int` hours.
6. Bit held too large in `int` type. Replace 32 by 4.
7. The `enum` data type name month and dot operator are not required in `printf()` statement.
8. No Bug.
9. Header file `<dos.h>` is not defined.
10. Object cannot be used for post increment operation.
11. Use of -> operator for non-pointer object.
12. Object 'j' and 'm' are not initialized.

13

Files

CHAPTER OUTLINE

13.1 INTRODUCTION OF A FILE

A file is nothing but a collection of records and each line of the data is recorded in the file. The record is a group of related data items. All data items related to students, employees, customers, etc. are nothing but records. In other words, file is a collection of numbers, symbols and texts placed onto the secondary devices like hard disk, pen drive and compact disk. Files are stored permanently onto the disk, and one can access them for further monitoring/processing if needed. In the next few paragraphs or sections, we will learn how files can be read and modified as per requirements.

13.1.1 Definition of a File

A file can be considered as a stream of characters, spaces, tabs etc. Also it can be a set of records that can be accessed through a set of library functions. These functions are available in `stdio.h`.

13.2 STREAMS AND FILE TYPES

The reading and writing of data is done with streams. The streams are designed to allow the user to access files efficiently. A stream is a file and using physical device like keyboard information is stored in the file. Printer and monitor are used to display the stream. The FILE object uses these devices.

The FILE object contains all the information about a stream like current position, pointer to any buffer, error and end of file (EOF). Using this information of object, C program uses pointer, which is returned from the stream function `fopen()`. A function `fopen()` is used for opening a file.

13.2.1 File Types

There are two types of files.

(i) *Sequential file*: In this type of file, the data are kept sequentially. If we want to read last record of the file, it is expected to read all the records before that particular record. It takes more time for accessing the records.

(ii) *Random access file*: In this type, the data can be read and modified randomly. If it is desired to read the last record of a file, directly the same record can be read. Due to random access of data, it takes less access time as compared to the sequential file.

13.3 STEPS FOR FILE OPERATIONS

The following operations can be performed on files in C.

(i) Opening a file

(ii) Reading or writing a file

(iii) Closing a file

Most of the compilers support file handing functions. Few file-handling functions that are available in standard library are listed in the Table 13.1. The library functions supported by ANSI compilers are very exhaustive and hence all functions are not provided. One should check the ANSI C library functions before using them.

TABLE 13.1 File functions

Function	*Operation*
fopen()	Creates a new file for read/write operation
fclose()	Closes a file associated with file pointer
closeall()	Closes all files opened with fopen()
fgetc()	Reads the character from current pointer position and advances the pointer to next character
getc()	Same as fgetc()
fprintf()	Writes all types of data values to the file
fscanf()	Read all types of data values from a file
putc()	Writes character one by one to a file
fputc()	Same as putc()
gets()	Reads string from the file
puts()	Writes string to the file
putw()	Writes an integer to the file
getw()	Reads an integer from the file
fread()	Reads the structured data written by fwrite() function
fwrite()	Writes block of structured data to the file
fseek()	Sets the pointer position anywhere in the file
feof()	Detects the end of the file
ferror()	Reports error occurred while read/write operations
perror()	Prints compiler's error messages along with user defined messages
ftell()	Returns the current pointer position
rewind()	Sets the record pointer at the beginning of the file
unlink()	Removes the specified file from the disk
rename()	Changes the name of the file

13.3.1 Opening of File

A file has to be opened before read and write operations. Opening of a file creates a link between the operating system and the file functions. The name of the file and its mode of operation are to be indicated to the operating system. This important task is carried out by the structure FILE that is defined in stdio.h header file. So, this file must be included.

When a request is made to the operating system for opening a file, it does so by granting the request. If request is granted, the operating system points to the structure FILE. In case the request is not granted, it returns NULL. That is why the following declaration before opening of the file is to be made.

```
FILE *fp
```

where fp is file pointer.

Each file that we open has its own FILE structure. The information in the file may be its current size and its location in the memory. The only one function to open a file is fopen().

***Syntax*:**

```
FILE *fp;
fp=fopen("data.txt","r");
```

Here, fp is a pointer variable that contains address of the structure FILE that has been defined in the header file stdio.h. It is necessary to write FILE in upper case. The function fopen() will open a file data.txt in read mode. The C compiler reads the contents of the file because it finds the read mode ("r"). Here, "r" is a string and not a character. Hence, it is enclosed with double quotes and not with single quotes.

The fopen() performs four important tasks:

(i) It searches the disk for opening of the file.

(ii) In case the file exists, it loads the file from the disk into the memory. If the file is found with huge contents, then it loads the file part by part.

(iii) If the file does not exist this function returns a NULL. NULL is a macro defined in the header file stdio.h. This indicates that it is unable to open the file. There may be following reasons for the failure of fopen() function.

  (a) when the file is in protected or in hidden mode or

  (b) the file may be in use by another program.

(iv) It locates a character pointer, which points the first character of the file. Whenever a file is opened, the character pointer points to the first character of the file.

13.3.2 Text Modes

(i) w (write)

This mode opens a new file on the disk for writing. If the file already exists, its contents will be overwritten without confirmation. If the concerned file is not found, a new file is created.

Syntax:

```
fp=fopen("data.txt","w");
```

Here, data.txt is the file name and "w" is the mode.

(ii) r(read)

This mode searches a file and if the file is found the same is loaded into the memory for reading from the first character of the file. The file pointer points to the first character and the reading operation begins. If the file does not exist, then the compiler returns NULL to the file pointer. Using pointer with if statement, we can prompt the user regarding failure of operation. The syntax of read mode is given below.

Syntax:

```
fp=fopen("data.txt","r");

if(fp==NULL)
printf("File does not exist");
      OR
if(fp=(fopen("data.txt","r"))==NULL)
printf("File does not exist");
```

Here, data.txt is opened for reading only. If the file does not exist, the fopen() returns NULL to file pointer fp. Using the NULL value of fp with if statement, we can prompt the user for failure of fopen() function.

(iii) a (append)

This mode opens a pre-existing file for appending data. The data appending process starts at the end of the opened file. The file pointer points to the last character of the file. If the file does not exist, then new file is opened, i.e. if the file does not exist, then the mode of "a" is same as "w". Due to some or other reasons, if the file is not opened, in such a case NULL is returned. File opening may be impossible due to insufficient space in the disk, etc. Syntax for opening a file with append mode is as follows.

***Syntax*:**

```
fp=fopen("data.txt","a");
```

Here, if `data.txt` file already exists, it will be opened. Otherwise, a new file will be opened with the same name.

(iv) `w+ ( write + read )`

This mode is used for file search operation in the disk. In case the file is found, its contents are destroyed. If the file does not find, a new file is created. Returns NULL, if failed to open the file. In this file mode, new contents can be written and thereafter programmer can read them.

***Example*:**

```
fp=fopen("data.txt", "w+");
```

In the above example, `data.txt` file is open for reading and writing operations.

(v) `a+ (append + read)`

In this file operation mode, the contents of the file can be read and records can be added at the end of the file. A new file is created in case the concerned file does not exist. Due to some or other reasons, if file is unable to open, then NULL is returned.

***Example*:**

```
fp=fopen("data.txt","a+");
```

Here, `data.txt` is opened and records are added at the end of the file without affecting the previous contents.

`(a+)`: If file does not exist, a new file is created. Write operation is performed first and the contents are read thereafter. Before reading character, the pointer is set to begin the file using `rewind()`.

(vi) r+ (read + write)

This mode is used for both reading and writing. We can read and write the record in the file. If the file does not exist, the compiler returns NULL to the file pointer. It can be written as follows.

***Example*:**

```
fp=fopen("data.dat","r+");

if(fp==NULL)
printf("File not found");
```

In the above example, `data.dat` is opened for read and write operation. If `fopen()` failed to open the file, it returns NULL. The `if` statement checks the value of file pointer `fp`, and if it contains NULL, a message is printed and program terminates.

13.3.3 Binary Modes

When numerical data is to be transferred to disk from RAM, the data occupies more memory space on disk. For example, a number 234567 needs 3 bytes memory space in RAM, and when transferred to the disk, it requires 6 bytes memory space. For each numerical digit, one byte space is needed. Hence, total requirement of memory space for the number 234567 would be 6 bytes. Thus, text mode is inefficient for storing large amount of numerical data because space occupation by it is large. Only solution to this inefficient memory use is to open a file in binary mode, which takes lesser space than text mode. Few binary modes are described below.

(i) `wb(write)`

This mode opens a binary file in write mode.

Example:

```
fp=fopen("data.dat","wb");
```

Here, `data.dat` file is opened in binary mode for writing.

(ii) `rb(read)`

This mode opens a binary file in read mode.

Example:

```
fp=fopen("data.dat","rb");
```

Here, `data.dat` file is opened in binary mode for reading.

(iii) `ab(append)`

This mode opens a binary file in append mode, i.e. data can be added at the end of the file.

Example:

```
fp=fopen("data.dat","ab");
```

Here, `data.dat` file is opened in append mode.

(iv) `r+b(read + write)`

This mode opens a pre-existing file in read and write mode, i.e. file can be read and written.

Example:

```
fp=fopen("data.dat","r+b");
```

Here, the file `data.dat` is opened for reading and writing in binary mode.

(v) `w+b(read + write)`

This mode creates a new file in read and write mode.

Example:

```
fp=fopen("data.dat","w+b");
```

Here, the file `data.dat` is created for reading and writing in binary mode.

(vi) `a+b(append + write)`

This mode opens a file in append mode, i.e. data can be written at the end of the file. If the file does not exist, a new file is created.

Example:

```
fp=fopen("data.dat","a+b");
```

Here, the file `data.dat` is opened in append mode and data can be written at the end of the file.

13.3.4 Reading a File

Once the file is opened using `fopen()`, its contents are loaded into the memory (partly or wholly). The pointer points to the very first character of the file. The `fgetc()` function is used to read the contents of the file. The syntax for `fgetc()` is as follows:

```
ch=fgetc(fp);
```

where `fgetc()` reads the character from current pointer position and advances the pointer position so that the next character is pointed. The variable 'ch' contains the character read by `fgetc()`.There are also other functions to read the contents of the file, which are explained in the coming pages.

13.3.5 Closing a File

The file that is opened from the `fopen()` should be closed after the work is over, i.e. we need to close the file after reading and writing operations. In other words, the file must be closed after operations. Also, whenever a opened file needs to be reopened in another mode, in such a case also the opened file must be closed first. Closing the file enables to wash out all its contents from the RAM buffer, and further the link is disconnected from the file.

Example:
The function to close a file is

```
fclose(fp);
```

This statement closes the file associated with file pointer `fp`. This function closes one file at a time. In order to close all files, the following function syntax is used:

```
fcloseall();
```

This function closes all the opened files and returns the number of files that have been closed. It does not require any argument.

13.4 FILE I/O

(i) `fprintf()`

This function is used for writing characters, strings, integers, floats, etc. to the file. The `fprint()` function is used for writing characters in various formats. Hence, this function is called formatted function. It contains one more parameter that is file pointer, which points the opened file.

The operation of `fprintf()` and `fscanf()` functions are identical to that of `printf()` and `scanf()` except that the former function works with files .

The format of `fprintf()` is as follows:

```
fprintf(fp,"control string",text);
```

where `fp` is file pointer associated with an opened file in write mode. The text can be variables, constants or strings.

(ii) `fscanf()`

This function reads characters, strings, integers, floats, etc. from the file pointed by file pointer. This is also a formatted function. The syntax of this function is as follows.

```
fscanf(fp,"control string",text);
```

With this statement, reading operations from the designated file is done.

(iii) `getc()`

This function reads a single character from the opened file and moves the file pointer. It returns EOF, if end of the file is reached.

For example in the statement `c=getc(f);`, a character is read from the file whose file pointer is 'f'. A program is illustrated under 13.E(1) based on this function.

(iv) `putc()`

This function is used to write a single character into a file. If an error occurs, it returns EOF.

For example, in the statement `putc(c,fp);`, a character contained in character variable 'c' is written in the file whose file pointer is `fp`.

(v) `fgetc()`

This function is similar to `getc()` function. It also reads a character and increments the file pointer position. If any error or end of file is reached, it returns EOF.

(vi) `fputc()`

This function writes the character to the file shown by the file pointer, and also increments the file pointer.

Syntax:

```
fputc(c,fp);
```

where `fp` is the file pointer and 'c' is a variable written to the file pointed by file pointer.

(vii) `fgets()`

This function reads string from a file pointed by file pointer. It also copies the string to a memory location referenced by an array.

(viii) `fputs()`

This function is useful when we want to write a string into the opened file.

(ix) `putw()`

This function is used to write an integer value to the file pointed by file pointer. This function deals with integer data only.

(x) `getw()`

This function returns the integer value from a file and increments the file pointer. This function deals with integer data only.

13.5 OTHER FILE FUNCTIONS

13.5.1 fseek() Function

The `fseek()` can be used to access the part of the file. The file pointer can be moved to any position in a file. It positions the file pointer on the stream. The format of `fseek()` is as follows.

```
fseek(filepointer,offset,position);
```

Thus, three arguments are to be passed through this function. They are

(i) File pointer.

(ii) Offset: Offset may be positive (moving in forward from current position) or negative moving backwards. The offset being a variable of type `long`.

(iii) The current position of file pointer.

Table 13.2 displays the various values of location of file pointer.

TABLE 13.2 Locations of file pointer

Integer Value	*Constant*	*Location in the File*
0	SEEK_SET	Beginning of the file
1	SEEK_CUR	Current position of the file pointer
2	SEEK_END	End of the file

Example:

```
fseek(fp,10,0); or fseek(fp,10,SEEK_SET);
```

The file pointer is repositioned in the forward direction by 10 bytes.

13.6 SEARCHING ERRORS IN READING/WRITING FILES

While performing read or write operation, few times we do not get result successfully. The reason may be that the attempt of reading or writing operation may not be correct. The provision must be provided for searching the error while read/write operations are carried out.

The C language provides standard library function `ferror()`. This function is used for detecting any error that might occur during read/write operation of a file. It returns a '0' while the attempt is successful, otherwise non-zero in case of failure.

`ferror()`: The `ferror()` is used to find out error when file read/write operation is carried out.

`perror()`: It is a standard library function which prints the error messages specified by the compiler.

13.7 LOW-LEVEL DISK I/O

Text files can be copied from one file to the other or in many files, whereas binary files such as .EXE if attempted to open in text mode, unexpectedly process of getting characters would stop. This is because whenever ASCII value 26 is observed copying work stops due to EOF(). Another approach to copy such binary files is with low-level disk I/O.

In the low-level disk I/O operations, data cannot be written as character by character or with sequence of characters as it is carried in the high-level disk I/O operations. In the low-level disk I/O operations, buffers are used to carry the read and write operations.

Buffer plays an important role in the low-level disk I/O program. The programmer needs to declare the appropriate buffer size. The low-level disk I/O operations are more efficient and quick than the high-level disk I/O operations.

Opening a file: To open a file or files, open() function is used. This function is defined in io.h. The syntax of open() is given below.

***Syntax*:**

```
int open(const char *f_name, int access,
unsigned mode);
```

In the low-level operation, a number is assigned to the file and the number is used to refer the file. If open() returns -1, it means that the file could not be opened, otherwise the file is successfully opened.

Table 13.3 describes the file opening modes in the low-level disk I/O operations.

When O_CREAT flag is used, it also requires one of the arguments described in Table 13.4 to verify the read/write status of the file. These arguments are called as permission argument. The programmer need to #include the header file stat.h and types.h along with fcntl.h.

TABLE 13.3 File opening modes

Mode	*Meaning*
O_APPEND	Open a file in append mode
O_WRONLY	Opens a file for writing only
O_RDONLY	Opens a file for writing only
O_RDWR	Opens a file for read/write operations
O_BINARY	Opens a file in binary mode
O_CREAT	Creates a new file for writing
O_EXCL	When used with O_CREAT, if the file exists, it is not overwritten
O_TEXT	Creates a text file

TABLE 13.4 Permission argument

Mode	*Meaning*
S_IWRITE	Writing to the file allowed
S_IREAD	Reading from the file allowed

Writing a file: The write() function is used to write() data into the file. This function is defined in io.h. The syntax of write() function is as given below.

***Syntax*:**

```
int write(int handle, void *buf, unsigned nbyte);
```

Returns the number of bytes written or -1 if an error occurs.

Reading a file: The read() function reads a file. The syntax of read() function is as given below.

***Syntax*:**

```
int read(int handle, void *buf, unsigned len);
```

Upon successful end, it returns an integer specifying the number of bytes placed in the buffer; if the file was opened in text mode, read does not count carriage returns or Ctrl-Z characters in the number of bytes read. On error, it returns -1 and sets errno.

Closing a file: The close() function closes the file. This function is defined in io.h. The syntax of close() is as given below.

***Syntax*:**

```
int _close(int handle);
int close(int handle);
```

Upon successful finish, close() and _close() return 0; otherwise, they return -1 and set errno.

13.8 COMMAND LINE ARGUMENTS

An executable program that performs a specific task for operating system is called as command. The commands are issued from the prompt of operating system. Some arguments are to be associated with the commands, and hence these arguments are called as command line arguments. These associated arguments are passed to the program.

In C language, every program starts with a `main()` function and that it marks the beginning of the program. We have not provided any arguments so far in the `main()` function. Here, we can make arguments in the main like other functions. The `main()` function can receive two arguments and they are: (i) `argc` and (ii) `argv`. The information contained in the command line is passed on to the program through these arguments when the `main()` is called up by the system.

(i) Argument `argc`: An argument `argc` counts total number of arguments passed from command prompt. It returns a value which is equal to total number of arguments passed to the `main()`.

(ii) Argument `argv`: It is a pointer to an array of character strings which contains names of arguments. Each word is an argument.

***Example*:**

```
Copy file1 file2.
```

Here, `file1` and `file2` are arguments and copy is a command. The first argument is always an executable program followed by associated arguments. If you do not specify argument, the first program name itself is an argument but the program will not run properly and will flag an error.

EXERCISES

13.A Fill in the blanks

1. _________ function searches the disk for opening of the file.
   (a) `fopen()`
   (b) `fwind()`
   (c) `fread()`

2. This mode opens a new file on the disk for writing.
   (a) `r`
   (b) `w`
   (c) `a`

3. In low-level disk I/O operations ________ are used to carry the read/write operations.
   (a) array
   (b) buffer
   (c) structure

4. In random access file, the data is read ________.
   (a) randomly
   (b) sequentially
   (c) circularly

5. In `a+` mode, records are added ________.
   (a) at the beginning of the file
   (b) at the end of the file
   (c) nowhere

6. The `write()` function is used to write data into the file. This function is defined in the header file ________.
   (a) `io.h`
   (b) `sys.h`
   (c) `types`

7. Whenever a file is opened, the pointer points to the ________.
   (a) first character
   (b) last character
   (c) 10th character

8. The macro ________ is defined in the header file `stdio.h`.
   (a) null
   (b) NULL
   (c) NUL

9. When the file opened by `fopen()` is huge, then the file is loaded ________.
   (a) at once
   (b) part by part
   (c) half

10. While opening a file with "r" mode, the operation ________ can be performed.
    (a) write
    (b) read/write
    (c) deletion

11. In the ________ type of file, records can be read one after another.
    (a) random access file
    (b) sequential file
    (c) binary file

12. The file opening mode ________ can be used to perform read and write operation.
    (a) `r+`
    (b) `r`
    (c) `w`

13. The option `wb` opens a ____________ file.
    (a) text
    (b) binary
    (c) ASCII

14. All files opened by `fopen()` can be closed by _____ at a time.
    (a) `fclose()`
    (b) `fcloseall()`
    (c) `close()`

15. The SEEK_SET is equivalent to ________.
    (a) 0
    (b) 1
    (c) 2

16. The SEEK_CUR is equivalent to ________.
    (a) 0
    (b) 1
    (c) 2

17. The SEEK_END is equivalent to ________.
    (a) 0
    (b) 1
    (c) 2

18. File is a ___________.
    (a) set of records
    (b) group of characters
    (c) a part of memory

19. This mode opens a pre-existing file for reading.
    (a) `w`
    (b) `r`
    (c) `a`

20. This mode opens a pre-existing file for appending data.
    (a) `r`
    (b) `w`
    (c) `a`

13.B True or false

1. A file is a set of records.
2. The FILE pointer contains all information about a file.
3. Without the file pointer, file can be operated in C.
4. In sequential file, data can be read directly.
5. In a random file, the last record can be read first.
6. The `fopen()` is used to open a file.
7. The statement FILE *p declares file pointer.
8. The "r" mode means file is opened for writing only.
9. The "w" mode opens a new file on the disk.
10. The function `fputc()` writes data to the file.
11. The `fprintf()` is similar to `printf()`.
12. The function `feof()` finds the end of file.
13. The `getw()` is not associated with any file operation.
14. The SEEK_CUR indicates current position of the file pointer.
15. The `ferror()` reports error occurred during file read/write operation.
16. The function `rewind()` reverse the contents of file.
17. The "wb" creates a file in binary mode.
18. The O_APPEND is a low-level disk operation.
19. The `argc` and `argv` are not command line arguments.

13.C Match the following correct pairs given in Group A with Group B

I

Group A		Group B	
Serial No.	**File Functions**	**Serial No.**	**Used to**
1.	`fputs()`	A	Write character one by one to a file
2.	`fputc()`	B	Write string to the file
3.	`fwrite()`	C	Detect the end of file
4.	`feof()`	D	Write block of structured data to the file

II

Group A		Group B	
Serial No.	**File Functions**	**Serial No.**	**Used to**
1.	`rewind()`	A	Return the current pointer position
2.	`perror()`	B	Set the record pointer at the beginning of the file
3.	`ftell()`	C	Remove the specified file from the disk
4.	`unlink()`	D	Print compiler error messages along with user defined messages

III

Group A		Group B	
Serial No.	**Writing**	**Serial No.**	**Reading**
1.	`fputs()`	A	`fscanf()`
2.	`fputc()`	B	`fread()`
3.	`fwrite()`	C	`read()`
4.	`write()`	D	`fgets()`
5.	`fprintf()`	E	`fgetc()`

IV

Group A		Group B	
Serial No	**Alphabet**	**Serial No.**	**ASCII value**
1	B	A	75
2	K	B	65
3	Z	C	66
4	G	D	72
5	A	E	80
6	X	F	71
7	H	G	79
8	P	H	49
9	O	I	88
10	1	J	90

V

Group A		Group B	
Serial No.	**Keyword**	**Serial No.**	**Function**
1	`auto`	A	Long integer data type
2	`break`	B	Decision making statement
3	`void`	C	Makes variable constant
4	`long`	D	Auto storage class
5	`if`	E	Exit from loop
6	`const`	F	Creates while loop
7	`struct`	G	Function not returning value
8	`while`	H	Static storage class
9	`static`	I	Returns value from function
10	`return`	J	Creates user struct data type

VI

Group A		Group B	
Serial No.	**Functions**	**Serial No.**	**Use**
1.	`fputs()`	A	Binary files
2.	`fputc()`	B	Character string
3.	`fwrite()`	C	Low-level binary
4.	`write()`	D	Individual character
5.	`fprintf()`	E	Formatted ASCII

13.D Select the appropriate option from the multiple choices given below

1. The following file mode searches for the file, and if it is found contents are destroyed.
   (a) `w`
   (b) `w+`
   (c) `r`

2. What is the use of `putc()`?
   (a) writes characters one by one to a file
   (b) reads characters one by one from a file
   (c) both (a) and (b)
   (d) none of the above

3. One of the tasks of `fopen()` is
   (a) opening the file
   (b) closing the file
   (c) none of the above

4. A file opened in `wb` mode can
   (a) open a file in binary mode for writing
   (b) open a file in binary mode for reading
   (c) open a file in text mode for reading

5. Environment variables are available in
   (a) C editor
   (b) MS-DOS
   (c) both (a) and (b)
   (d) none of the above

6. The current position of the file pointer can be checked with a function
   (a) `unlink()`
   (b) `fseek()`
   (c) `remove()`
   (d) none of the above

7. Which file handling function is used to detect the errors
   (a) `feof()`
   (b) `ferror()`
   (c) `fputs()`
   (d) `fgetch()`

8. The EOF is equivalent to
   (a) –1
   (b) 0
   (c) 1
   (d) none of the above

9. The environment variables are used to display
   (a) system setting
   (b) compiler setting
   (c) editor setting
   (d) none of the above

10. The argument `argc`
    (a) counts total number of arguments
    (b) display total arguments
    (c) none of the above

11. The argument `argv` is a pointer to an array of
    (a) character string
    (b) integer array
    (c) `float` array
    (d) none of the above

12. The size of the buffer can be set using function
    (a) `set()`
    (b) `setbuf()`
    (c) `setsys()`

13. The file can be deleted from the disk using the function
    (a) `remove()`
    (b) `delete()`
    (c) `erase()`

14. The file can be renamed by using the function
    (a) `rename()`
    (b) `change()`
    (c) `alter()`

15. The file pointer can be set to the beginning of the file using
    (a) `reverse()`
    (b) `rewind()`
    (c) `rev()`

16. The current position of the file pointer can be known by
    (a) `ftell()`
    (b) `fprintf()`
    (c) `ftalf()`

17. The `fopen()` opens file with the help of
    (a) `file pointer`
    (b) `char pointer`
    (c) none of the above

18. The file pointer is of the type
    (a) FILE
    (b) file
    (c) POINTER

19. In sequential file, data is stored
    (a) non-sequentially
    (b) sequentially
    (c) randomly

20. The file object contains
    (a) current pointer position
    (b) end of file
    (c) pointer to any error
    (d) all of the above

13.E What will be the output/s of the following program/s?

1. Assume a file named `data.txt` in the read mode that contains `ab` information. Append some information in the file and see the contents after appending.

```
#include <stdio.h>
#include <conio.h>
#include <process.h>
void main()
{
FILE *f;
char c;
clrscr();
printf("Contents of file before
    appending:\n");
 f=fopen("data.txt","r");
   while(!feof(f))
        {
        c=fgetc(f);
        printf("%c",c);
        }

 f=fopen("data.txt","a");

 if(f==NULL)
 {
 printf("File can not appended");
 exit(0);
 }
 printf("\n Enter string to
    append:");

 while(c!='.')
 {
 c=getche();
 fputc(c,f);
 }
 fclose(f);

 printf("\n Contents of file After
    appending:\n");

 f=fopen("data.txt","r");
 while(!feof(f))
 {
 c=fgetc(f);
 printf("%c",c);
 }
 }
```

Explanation: Pre-existing file `data.txt` is read first that contains `ab`. The data appending process starts at the end of the file. The file pointer points to the last character of the file. Append some information say "`cd.`". As soon as .(dot) is entered, exit operation takes place in the program and one can see the output.

2. Read the contents of the file `data` with `w+` mode and input `ABCD.` through the keyboard and see the output with the same mode.

```
#include <stdio.h>
#include <conio.h>
#include <process.h>

void main()
{
FILE *f;
char c=' ';
clrscr();
f=fopen("data","w+");
if(f==NULL)
{
printf("Can not open file");
exit(1);
}

printf("Write data & to stop press
    '.':");
while(c!='.')
{
c=getche();
fputc(c,f);
}
 rewind(f);
```

```
printf("\n Contents read:");
while(!feof(f))
printf("%c",getc(f));
}
```

Explanation: Pre-existing file `data` is read with `w+` mode first that contains some information. With the same mode we can delete old information and enter new information.

3. Read the contents of the file in the `a+` mode and append it with some additional text and read with the same mode.

```
#include <stdio.h>
#include <conio.h>
#include <process.h>

void main()
{
FILE *f;
char c=' ';
clrscr();
f=fopen("data","a+");
if(f==NULL)
{
printf("Can not open file");
exit(1);
}

printf("Write data & to stop press
    '.':");
while(c!='.')
{
c=getche();
fputc(c,f);
}
 rewind(f);
printf("\n Contents read:");
while(!feof(f))
printf("%c",getc(f));
}
```

Explanation: Pre-existing file `data` is read with `a+` mode first that contains some information. With the same mode we can add new information and old and new information can be seen on the screen.

4. Open a file in `wb` mode and write "`Wonderful gift of life`" and display it with `rb` mode.

```
#include <stdio.h>
#include <conio.h>
#include <process.h>
void main()
{
FILE *f;
char c=' ';
clrscr();
f=fopen("data","wb");
if(f==NULL)
{
printf("Can not open file");
exit(1);
}

printf("Write data & to stop press
    '.':");
while(c!='.')
{
c=getche();
fputc(c,f);
}
 fclose(f);
f=fopen("data","rb");
printf("\n Contents read:");

while(!feof(f))

printf("%c",getc(f));
}
```

Explanation: A file `data` is opened in wb mode first and information "Wonderful gift of life" is invoked through the keyboard. With the `rb` mode, we can read the same information.

5. Write the contents of the file with `w` mode when contents of it are "Have a nice day." When * is encountered, process of writing in the file should be stopped.

```
#include <stdio.h>
#include <conio.h>
void main()
{
 FILE *fp;
 char c;
 clrscr();
 fp=fopen("lines.txt","w");
 if(fp==NULL)
 return;
 else
{
 while((c=getche())!='*');
 fputc(c,fp);
}
 fclose(fp);
}
```

6. If the contents of a file are "asdghhjjj", what would be the output of the following file?

```
#include <stdio.h>
#include <conio.h>
void main()
{
FILE *fp;
char ch;
fp=fopen("lines.txt","r");
fseek(fp,8,SEEK_SET);
ch=fgetc(fp);
clrscr();
while(!feof(fp))
{
printf("%c\t",ch);
printf("%d",ftell(fp));
ch=fgetc(fp);
}
fclose(fp);
}
```

13.F Find the bug/s in the following program/s

1.

```
#include <stdio.h>
#include <conio.h>
#include <process.h>
void main()
{
FILE *fp;
char c=' ';
clrscr();
fp=fopen("data.txt","w");
if(fp==NULL)
{
 printf("Cannot read file");
 exit(0);
 }
 printf("Write data & to stop press
   .: ");
 while(c!='.')
 {
 c=getche();
 fputc(c,fp);
 }
 printf("\n Contents Read:");
 fp=fopen("data.txt","r");
 while(!feof(fp))
 printf("%c",getc(fp));
}
```

2.

```
#include <stdio.h>
#include <conio.h>
#include <process.h>
void main()
{
FILE *fp;
char c=' ';
clrscr();
fp=fopen("data.txt","w");
if(fp==NULL)
{
 printf("Cannot read file");
 exit(0);
 }
 printf("Write data & to stop
   press.: ");
 while(c!='.')
 {
 c=getche();
 fputc(c,fp);
 }
 printf("\n Contents Read:");
 fp=fopen("data.txt","r");
 while(!feof(fp))
 printf("%c",getc(fp));
}
```

3.

```
#include <stdio.h>
#include <conio.h>
void main()
{
 FILE *fp;
char text[30];
clrscr();
fp=fopen("text.txt","w");
clrscr();
puts("\n Enter Text Here ");
gets(text);
fprintf("%s",text);
}
```

4.

```
#include <stdio.h>
#include <conio.h>
```

```
#include <process.h>
void main()
{
FILE *fp;
char c;
clrscr();
fp=fopen("text.txt","r");
if(fp==NULL)
{
 printf("\n cannot open file");
 }
 while((c=getc(fp)) !=EOF)
 printf("%c",c);
 fclose(fp);
 }
```

5.

```
#include <stdio.h>
#include <conio.h>

void main()
{
FILE *fr;
Char c,file[]="text.txt";
Fr=fopen(file,"w");
clrscr();
while(feof(fr))
{
c=fgetc(fr);
if(ferror(fr))
{
perror(file);
exit(0);
}
else
printf("%c",c);
}
fclose(fr);
}
```

6.

```
#include <stdio.h>
#include <conio.h>

void main()
{
char buff[10];
clrscr();
setbuf(stdout,buff);
printf("This Book is
   very good");
fflush(stdout);
}
```

7.

```
#include <stdio.h>
#include <conio.h>

void main(int argc, char argv[])
{
int x;
clrscr();
printf("\n Total Number of arguments
   are %d \n",argc);
for(x=0;x<argc;x++)
printf("%s",argv[x]);
}
```

13.G Attempt the following programming exercises

1. Write a program to generate a data file containing the student names, their ages, exams appeared, marks scored and grades (A to D). Use structure variables.
2. Write a program to print the current position of the file pointer in the file using `ftell()` function in association with `fseek()` function.
3. Write a program to display contents of a file on the screen. The program should ask for file name. Display the contents in lower case.
4. Write a program to find total words in a file.
5. Write a program to combine contents of two files in a third file. Find the total number of paragraphs in the new one.
6. Write a program to display numbers from 50 to 75. Redirect the output of the program to text file.
7. Write a program to encrypt the contents of one file to another with shifting each character by four positions on higher side.
8. Write a program to display the contents of two files containing text in one file and corresponding ASCII numbers in another file.

ANSWERS

13.A Fill in the blanks

1. (a) `fopen`
2. (b) `w`
3. (b) buffer
4. (a) randomly
5. (b) at the end of the file
6. (a) `io.h`
7. (a) first character
8. (b) NULL
9. (b) part by part
10. (b) read/write
11. (b) sequential file
12. (a) `r+`
13. (b) binary
14. (b) `fcloseall()`
15. (a) 0
16. (b) 1
17. (c) 2
18. (a) set of records
19. (b) `r`
20. (c) `a`

13.B True or false

1.T 2.T 3.F 4.F 5.T 6.T 7.T 8.F 9.T
10.T 11.F 12.T 13.F 14.T 15.T 16.F 17.T
18.T 19.F

13.C Match the following correct pairs given in Group A with Group B

I 1. B, 2. A, 3. D, 4. C
II 1. B, 2. D, 3. A, 4. C
III 1. D, 2. E, 3. B, 4. C, 5. A
IV 1. C, 2. A, 3. J, 4. F, 5. B, 6. I, 7. D, 8. E, 9. G, 10. H
V 1. D, 2. E, 3. G, 4. A, 5. B, 6. C, 7. J, 8. F, 9. H, 10. I
VI 1. B, 2. D, 3. A, 4. C, 5. E

13.D Select the appropriate option from the multiple choices given below

1. (b) `w+`
2. (a) Writes characters one by one to a file.
3. (a) Opening the file
4. (a) opens a file in binary mode for writing
5. (b) MS-DOS
6. (b) `fseek()`
7. (b) `ferror()`
8. (a) –1
9. (a) system setting
10. (a) counts total number of arguments
11. (a) character string
12. (b) `setbuf()`
13. (a) `remove()`
14. (a) `rename()`
15. (a) `rewind()`
16. (a) `ftell()`
17. (a) file pointer
18. (a) FILE
19. (b) sequential
20. (d) all of the above

13.E What will be the output/s of the following program/s?

1. Contents of file before appending: `ab`
   Enter string to append: cd.
   Contents of file After appending: `abcd`.
2. Write data & to stop press '.': ABCD.

   Contents read : ABCD.
3. Write data & to stop press '.' : This is append and read mode.

   Contents read : This is append and read mode.
4. Write data & to stop press '.' : Wonderful gift of life.

   Contents read : Wonderful gift of life.

5. Have a nice day
6. j 9

13.F Find the bug/s in the following program/s

1. After writing data file should be closed.
2. The file opening mode `"w"` is invalid.
3. The file pointer is missing in `fprintf()` and file must be closed.
4. In `if()` statement `exit(0)` is required.
5. `while(!eof(fr))` is correct condition.
6. The size of the buffer is to small.
7. No bug.

14

Graphics

CHAPTER OUTLINE

14.1 INTRODUCTION

The objective of this chapter is to look at information on graphics. Pictorial information is conveyed rather than oral information in our day to day life. The reason is humans can remember the pictorial information for a long period.

Pictorial presentation can be done with graphics. We can draw all figures of various shapes with computer graphics. Lines, circles, ellipse, rectangle, triangle, etc. of various shapes can be drawn with computer graphics. Besides, nowadays we deal with animation, multimedia, etc. which works predominantly using graphics. The intention for introducing this chapter is to interact with graphics using C language in an easy way. The basic concepts of graphics are explained with examples. In this chapter, standard library functions are described together with illustrations. We will see in brief about the computer graphics.

Video display unit is one of the most useful output components of the computer system. The video display system comprises of the following components.

(i) Video screen where text and picture can be displayed.

(ii) Video display adapter card, which is plugged into one of the expansion slots, provided on the motherboard.

14.2 INITILIZATION OF GRAPHICS

The header file `graphics.h` is to be included at the beginning of the program. This header file comprises the definitions and explanations of all the graphics functions. The functions described in this chapter are defined in `graphics.h` file, which should be included in every graphics program.

To switch over to graphics mode, a function `initgraph()` must be invoked. It selects the best resolution and puts the corresponding number in `gm`, where `gm` is the graphics mode.

14.3 FEW GRAPHICS FUNCTIONS

(i) `initgraph();`

This function initializes the graphics system. Prototype is defined in `"graphics.h"`. It is declared as given below:

```
void far initgraph(int far *gd, int far *gm, char far *pathtodriver);
```

where `gd` is graphics driver and `gm` is graphics mode.

In real application to detect graphics drives DETECT macro is used.

(ii) `closegraph();`

This function shuts down the graphics system. The declaration is as under. Prototype is defined in `"graphics.h"`.

```
void far closegraph(void);
```

(iii) `restorecrtmode();`

This function restores the screen mode to its pre-`initgraph` setting. Its prototype is defined in `"graphics.h"`.

```
void far restorecrtmode(void);
```

(iv) `graphresult();`

This function returns an error code for the last failed graphics operation. This function is defined as under.

```
int far graphresult(void);
```

Returns the error code for the last graphics execution that reported an error and resets the error level to `grOK`, where `grOK` is an enumerated error code.

(v) `getmaxx();` and `getmaxy();`

The `getmaxx()` returns maximum 'x' screen coordinate and `getmaxy()` returns maximum 'y' screen coordinate. Its prototype is defined in `"graphics.h"`. These functions can be declared as under.

```
int far getmaxx(void);
int far getmaxy(void);
```

(vi) `line();`

Draws a line between two specified points. This function is declared as under.

```
void far line(int x1, int y1, int x2, int y2);
```

Draws a line from `(x1, y1)` to `(x2, y2)` using the current color, line style and thickness.

(vii) `circle();`

This function draws a circle at `(x, y)` of the given radius. This function is declared as under.

```
void far circle(int x, int y, int radius);
```

(viii) `arc();`

This function draws an arc. This function is declared as under.

```
void far arc(int x, int y, int sa, int ea, int r);
```

where `(x, y)` is the centre point. The variables `sa` and `ea` are the start and end angles in degrees and variable `r` is the radius.

(ix) `ellipse();`

This function draws an elliptical arc. This function is declared as under.

```
void far ellipse(int x, int y, int sa, int ea, int xr, int yr);
```

where `(x, y)` is the centre point. The variables `sa` and `ea` are start and end angles in degrees, respectively. The variables `xr` and `yr` are horizontal and vertical radii.

(x) `bar();`

This function draws a bar using given coordinates. This function can be declared as under.

```
void far bar(int left, int top, int right, int bottom);
```

(xi) `setcolor();`

This function sets the current drawing color. This is declared as under.

```
void far setcolor(int color);
```

(xii) `outtextxy();`

Displays a string at the specified location (graphics mode). This function is declared as given under.

```
void far outtextxy(int x, int y, char far *textstring);
```

(xiii) `settextstyle();`

This function sets the current text attributes. This function is declared as under.

`void far settextstyle(int font, int direction, int fontsize);`

(xiv) `settextjustify();`

This function sets text justification for graphics mode. This function is declared as given below.

`void far settextjustify(int horiz, int vert);`

Affects text output with `outtext()` function, etc. Text is justified horizontally and vertically.

(xv) `getcolor();`

Returns the current drawing color. This function is declared as follows.

`void far getcolor(void);`

14.4 PROGRAMS USING LIBRARY FUNCTIONS

(i) `arc()`

This function is useful to draw a circular arc. It requires five arguments. The syntax would be

`arc(int x, int y, int sa, int ea , int r);`

Here, the first two arguments, i.e. `x` and `y` are the centre points. The arguments `sa` and `ea` are starting and ending angles and finally `r` is the radius. Following programming example can be referred for drawing an arc.

14.1 Write a program to demonstrate the use of `arc()` function.

```
#include <graphics.h>

void main()
{
  int gd =DETECT,gm,x,y;
  initgraph(&gd,&gm,"d:\turboc2\bgi");

arc(50,20,50,300,100);

getch();
closegraph();
restorecrtmode();
}
```

Explanation:

Consider the statement `initgraph(&gd,&gm,"d:\turboc2\bgi");` which initializes the graphic mode. The required adapter files are present in the specified directory. The `arc()` function draws arc by simply using parameter values. The function `closegraph()` shuts the graphics mode. The function `restorecrtmode();` restores the screen mode to its previous setting. The DETECT is enum data type of BGI graphics drivers.

(ii) `rectangle()`

The `rectangle()` function draws the rectangle. It has four arguments. The syntax of rectangle is as follows:

`rectangle(int left, int top, int right, int bottom);`

The following program illustrates this function.

14.2 Write a program to demonstrate the use of `rectangle()` function.

```
#include <graphics.h>
void main()
{
  int gd =DETECT,gm,x,y;
  initgraph(&gd,&gm,"d:\turboc2\bgi");
  setcolor(WHITE);
  rectangle(50,20,150,200);
  getch();
  closegraph();
  restorecrtmode();
}
```

Explanation:

This program draws the rectangle using given arguments. The `setcolor()` sets the color of drawings.

(iii) `circle()`

Draws circle of the given radius. It has three arguments.

`circle(int x, int y, int r);`

where `(x, y)` is the centre point and `r` is the radius.

14.3 Write a program to draw the circle of the given radius.

```
#include <graphics.h>
void main()
{
  int gd =DETECT,gm,x,y;
  initgraph(&gd,&gm,"d:\turboc2\bgi");
  setcolor(WHITE);
  circle(160,260,35);
  getch();
  closegraph();
  restorecrtmode();
}
```

Explanation:

This program draws circle using given arguments.

(iv) `line(int a, int b, int c, int d)`

This function draws line from `(a,b)` to `(c,d)`

14.4 Write a program to draw the line.

```
#include <graphics.h>
void main()
{
  int gd =DETECT,gm,x,y;
  initgraph(&gd,&gm,"d:\turboc2\bgi");
line(100,100,100,400);
getch();
closegraph();
restorecrtmode();
}
```

(v) `ellipse()`

The following function draws ellipse using given arguments.

14.5 Write a program to draw ellipse.

```
#include <graphics.h>
void main()
{
  int gd =DETECT,gm,x,y;
  initgraph(&gd,&gm,"d:\turboc2\bgi");
  ellipse(100,100,100,300,300,200);
  getch();
  closegraph();
  restorecrtmode();
}
```

14.6 Write a program to draw circle, line, and arc using graphics function.

```
#include <graphics.h>

void main()
{
    int gd=DETECT,gm,x,y,c=0;
    initgraph(&gd,&gm,"d:\turboc2\bgi");

    x=getmaxx();
    y=getmaxy();
    setcolor(WHITE);
    outtextxy(1,20,"Circle");
    circle(40,100,40);
    outtextxy(200,10,"Arc");
    arc(x/3,y/8,180,70,30);

    line(210,150,110,150);
    outtextxy(150,140,"Line");
```

```
    ellipse(215,150,0,70,150,150);
    outtextxy(290,10,"Ellipse");

getche();
 closegraph();
 restorecrtmode();
}
```

Explanation:

In the above program, a "`graphics.h`" header file is included. This header file contains all prototype and definition of all graphics functions.

Before starting any drawing action, we need to initialize graphics mode. The `initgraph()` function find outs the best graphics mode and sets the corresponding number in the variable `gm`. Using the value of `gm`, we can find out the details of monitor like its type, resolution, number of video pages and supporting colors.

The variable `gd` is used for graphics driver. Graphics drivers are subset of device drivers and used in only graphics mode. The graphics driver files have an extension `.bgi`. Depending on the type of the adapter, one of the supporting devices driver file is selected. In graphics mode, cursor disappears and the top left corner (0,0) of the console is considered as beginning.

The above program draws circle, arc, ellipse and line depending upon the given values. The user can put different values for different shapes.

Program on moving moon

The following program illustrates a moving moon.

14.7 Write a program to draw circle and move it on the screen.

```
#include <graphics.h>

void main()
{
   int gd =DETECT,gm,x,y;
   initgraph(&gd,&gm,"d:\turboc2\bgi");
clrscr();
for(x=30;x<400;x+=10)
{
fillellipse(x,50,30,30);
sleep(1);
clrscr();
}
closegraph();
restorecrtmode();
}
```

Explanation:

In this program, using `fillellipse()` function moon like shape is drawn. Using the loop, the drawn figure moved on the screen. The `sleep()` function halts the execution for a second.

(vi) `bar(int left, int top, int right, int bottom)`

The function `bar()` has four arguments. The `bar()` displays bar mostly shown in graphs.

14.8 Write a program to display bar.

```
#include <graphics.h>
void main()
{
  int gd =DETECT,gm,x,y;
  initgraph(&gd,&gm,"d:\turboc2\bgi");
   bar(10,20,50,190);
   getch();
   closegraph();
   restorecrtmode();
}
```

(vii) `sector()`

This function is used to draw a sector.

14.9 Write a program to draw a sector.

```
#include <graphics.h>
void main()
{
  int gd =DETECT,gm,x,y;
  initgraph(&gd,&gm,"d:\turboc2\bgi");
   sector(150,170,50,60,90,150);
   getch();
   closegraph();
   restorecrtmode();
}
```

(viii) `getdrivername()`

This function displays the name of graphics driver. For example, EGAVGA, EGA VGA, etc.

(ix) `getmaxcolor()`

Returns the maximum color available with the adapter.

(x) `getmaxmode()`

Returns number of display modes available.

(xi) `getmaxx()`

Returns number of maximum `x` coordinate on the screen.

(xii) `getmaxy()`

Returns number of maximum `y` coordinate on the screen.

(xiii) `getmodename(int)`

This function returns the name of the graphics mode. `int` specifies graphics mode number.

(xiv) `lineto(int x, int y)`

This function draws a line. It requires two integer arguments. It draws a line from current position to `(x,y)` where `x` and `y` are the coordinates to be specified by the user.

(xv) moveto(int x, int y)

This function moves the current position to (x, y), where x and y are the coordinates to be specified by the user.

Following program illustrates these concepts.

14.10 Write a program to shift the line coordinates to other positions with movto() and lineto() functions.

```
#include <graphics.h>
#include <stdlib.h>
void main()
{
     int gd =DETECT,gm,x,y;
     initgraph(&gd,&gm,"d:\turboc2\bgi");
     line(20,30,200,30);
     moveto(250,50);
     lineto(200,50);
     getch();
     closegraph();
     restorecrtmode();
}
```

Explanation:

In this program, line() function is used for drawing a line. Also the effect of moveto() and lineto() functions can be seen by executing this program. You will observe that the line coordinates get changed with these functions.

14.5 WORKING WITH TEXT

There are several functions for displaying text in different fonts, sizes and directions. Consider the following functions:

(i) outtextxy(int, int, string): This function is used to display the text in graphic mode.

(ii) settextstyle(int, int, int): This functions have three integer arguments. First argument indicates font, second direction and third size.

14.11 Write a program to display text in different font and size.

```
#include <graphics.h>
void main()
{
  int gd =DETECT,gm,x,y;
  initgraph(&gd,&gm,"d:\turboc2\bgi");
   settextstyle(1,0,30);
   outtextxy(0,120,"AMOL");
```

```
    getch();
    closegraph();
    restorecrtmode();
}
```

Explanation:

After the execution of the program, the string "AMOL" is displayed. This is performed by giving different values in the `settextstyle()` function. Another new function that can be used is `settextjustify()` which takes care of alignment of the text. This function is explained in the following program.

14.12 Write a program to display text in different size, font, vertically and horizontally using graphics functions.

```
#include <graphics.h>
#include <stdlib.h>

void main()
{
     int gd=DETECT,gm;
     initgraph(&gd,&gm, "d:\turboc2\bgi");

     settextstyle(1,0,10);
     settextjustify(0,2);
     outtextxy(10,2,"Hello");
     settextjustify(2,3);
     settextstyle(3,1,5);
     outtextxy(14,150,"Hello");

 getche();

 closegraph();
 restorecrtmode();
}
```

Explanation:

After the execution of the program the string "Hello" is displayed horizontally and vertical with different font and font size. This is performed by giving different values in the `settextstyle()` function. Another new function used is `settextjustify()` which takes care of alignment of text.

Stylish lines

14.13 Write a program to display stylish lines.

```
#include <graphics.h>
void main()
{
    int gd =DETECT,gm,x,y;
    initgraph(&gd,&gm,"d:\turboc2\bgi");
    clrscr();
    line(20,9,20,70);
```

```
    setlinestyle(1,1,1);
    line(40,9,40,60);
    setlinestyle(2,1,1);
    line(60,9,60,70);
    getch();
    closegraph();
    restorecrtmode();
}
```

***Explanation*:**

In this program, using `setlinestyle()` function, a line drawn can be displayed in different styles. It requires three integer arguments. The first represents style of line, second represents pattern and the third represents thickness.

14.14 Program to draw lines of different styles with increasing length and displaying text.

```
#include <graphics.h>
void main()
{
  int gd =DETECT,gm,x,y,i,k=20,j=200;
  initgraph(&gd,&gm,"d:\turboc2\bgi");
  settextstyle(1,0,30);
  settextjustify(100,50);
  setcolor(GREEN);
  outtextxy(20,40,"line");
   if(k<220)
   for(i=0;i<5;i++)
   {
   setlinestyle(i,10,2);
   line(k,30,j,30);
   k=k+20;
   j=j+20;
   sleep(1);
   }
   else
   getch();
   closegraph();
      restorecrtmode();
}
```

***Explanation*:**

This program is the same as what explained in the previous. In this program, additional functions for texts are used. The programmer can run the program and see its effects.

14.6 FILLING PATTERNS WITH DIFFERENT COLORS AND STYLES

Now we will use a function to fill the different patterns with different colors using different styles. In the following program, a `setfillstyle()` function is used for drawing a bar. This function needs to pass two parameters, the first being the pattern and the second being the color.

14.15 Write a program to use the `setfillstyle()` and show its effect on the VDU.

```
#include <graphics.h>
#include <stdlib.h>
void main()
{
    int gd =DETECT,gm,x,y;
    initgraph(&gd,&gm,"d:\turboc2\bgi");
    setcolor(GREEN);
    setfillstyle(SOLID_FILL,RED);
    bar(20,30,200,40);
    moveto(250,50);
    bar(200,50,250,60);
    getch();
    closegraph();
    restorecrtmode();
}
```

***Explanation*:**

This program uses `setfillstyle()` function for filling various colors with different styles. A bar is drawn with green color. The programmer can run the program and see its effects.

14.16 Write a program to draw the triband flag with using `setfillstyle()` and show its effect on the VDU.

```
#include <graphics.h>
#include <stdlib.h>
void main()
{
    int gd =DETECT,gm,x,y;
    initgraph(&gd,&gm,"d:\turboc2\bgi");
    setfillstyle(1,3);
    bar(20,30,200,40);
    rectangle(20,30,200,40);

    setfillstyle(1,4);
    bar(20,40,200,50);
    rectangle(20,40,200,50);

    setfillstyle(1,5);
    bar(20,50,200,60);
    rectangle(20,50,200,60);
    line(20,30,20,150);

    getch();
    closegraph();
    restorecrtmode();
}
```

***Explanation*:**

This program uses `setfillstyle()` function for filling various bars with different colors. Bars are drawn with different colors. The programmer can run the program and see the output.

14.17 Write a program to draw the rectangles duly filled with different patterns using `setfill-style()` and show its effect on the VDU.

```
#include <graphics.h>
#include <stdlib.h>
void main()
{
    int gd =DETECT,gm, x=20,y=20,i;
    initgraph(&gd,&gm,"d:\turboc2\bgi");
    for(i=0;i<10;i++)
    {
    setfillstyle(i,2);
    bar(x,y,x+50,y+50);
    rectangle(x,y,x+50,y+50);
    x=x+50;
     if(x>500)
     {
      y=y+50;
      x=20;
     }
     }
     getche();
    closegraph();
    restorecrtmode();
}
```

Explanation:

This program uses `setfillstyle()` function for filling the rectangles with different patterns. Rectangles are drawn with different colors. The programmer can run the program and see the output.

14.18 Write a program to draw boxes using bar() function. Fill the boxes with different designs.

```
#include <graphics.h>
#include <stdlib.h>

void main()
{
     int gd=DETECT,gm,a=40,b=40,ptr,k;
     char txt[10];
char *design[]={"EMPTY_FILL", "SOLID_FILL", "LINE_FILL","LTSLASH_FILL",
    "SLASH_FILL", "BKSLASH_FILL","LTBKSLASH_FILL", "HATCH_FILL", "XHATCH_
    FILL","INTERLEAVE_FILL", "WIDE_DOT_FILL","CLOSE_DOT_FILL", "USER_FILL"};
     initgraph(&gd,&gm, "d:\turboc2\bgi");

     setcolor(RED);
     settextstyle(0,0,2);
     outtextxy(100,1,"User-defined Styles");
     settextstyle(0,0,0);
     setcolor(WHITE);
     for(ptr=0;ptr<12;ptr++)'
```

```
        {
            setfillstyle(ptr,ptr);
            bar(a,b,a+70,b+70);
            rectangle(a,b,a+70,b+70);
            k=1+ptr;
            itoa(k,txt,10);
            outtextxy(a,b+100,txt);
            setcolor(ptr+1);
            outtextxy(a,b+110,design[ptr]);
            a=a+150;
            if(a>490)
            {
                b=b+150;
                a=40;
            }
        }
    getche();
    closegraph();
    restorecrtmode();
}
```

***Explanation*:**

In the above program, the `settextstyle()` function sets text attributes like font size, direction of text horizontal or vertical and size of the character. The message "User-defined styles" is displayed in larger size with red color. Again the text attributes are set to 0, so that further they will not affect the outputting text. The character pointer is initialized with pre-defined patterns (designs). The `setfillstyle()` function has two argument patterns and color to be filled. The `bar()` function draws the bar using attribute of `setfillstyle()`. The `rectangle()` function draws border to the various bars created by `bar()` function. The `itoa()` function converts an integer to string. The number 1 to 12 displayed below each bar are due to this function.

14.19 Write a program to draw the rectangle using `floodfill()` function and show its effect on the VDU.

```
#include <graphics.h>
#include <stdlib.h>
void main()
{
   int gd =DETECT,gm,x,y;
   initgraph(&gd,&gm,"d:\turboc2\bgi");
   setcolor(WHITE);
   outtextxy(30,20,"RECTANGLE");
   setcolor(GREEN);
   rectangle(20,40,200,60);
   setfillstyle(1,3);
   floodfill(21,41,GREEN);
   getch();
   closegraph();
   restorecrtmode();
}
```

***Explanation*:**

This program uses `setfillstyle()` and `floodfill()` functions for filling the rectangles with any pattern. It is not necessary to use `bar()` at first and then enclose it by rectangle as used in the previous program. Straightaway, one can use `floodfill()` function for filling a pattern with different colors. The programmer can run the program and see the output.

14.7 MOUSE PROGRAMMING

14.20 Write a program to display status of mouse button pressed and restrict the mouse between given coordinates on the screen. Use `int86()` function to call different ROM-BIOS services.

```
#include <process.h>
#include <dos.h>
#include <graphics.h>

union REGS i,o;

int initmouse(void);
void showarrow(void);
void mousearea(int, int, int,int);
void m_pointerat(int *, int *, int *);

void main()
{
     int gd=DETECT, gm,maxx,maxy,button,x,y;
     initgraph(&gd,&gm,"d:\turboc2\bgi");
     maxx=getmaxx();
     maxy=getmaxy();
     rectangle(0,56,maxx,maxy);
     setviewport(1,57,maxx-1,maxy-1,1);
     gotoxy(26,1);
     printf("\n Mouse Button pressed ");

     if(initmouse()==0)
     {
          closegraph();
          restorecrtmode();
          printf("\n Mouse driver not found");
          exit(1);
     }

     mousearea(0,100,maxx-50,maxy-10);
     showarrow();
     gotoxy(52,3);
     printf("\n Press any key to exit");

     while(!kbhit())
     {
          m_pointerat(&button,&x,&y);
          gotoxy(5,3);
          (button & 1)==1 ? printf("LEFT ") : printf("****");
          gotoxy(20,3);
```

```
            (button & 2)==2 ? printf("RIGHT ") : printf("*****");
            gotoxy(65,2);
            printf("Cursor Position");
            gotoxy(65,3);
            printf("X=%03d y= %03d",x,y);
        }
}
        initmouse()
        {
            i.x.ax=0;
            int86(0x33,&i,&o);
            return(o.x.ax);
        }
void showarrow()
        {
            i.x.ax=1;
            int86(0x33,&i,&o);
        }
void mousearea(int x1,int y1,int x2,int y2)
        {
            i.x.ax=7;
            i.x.cx=x1;
            i.x.dx=x2;
            int86(0x33,&i,&o);
            i.x.ax=8;
            i.x.cx=y1;
            i.x.dx=y2;
            int86(0x33,&i,&o);
        }
void m_pointerat( int *button, int *x,int *y)
        {
            i.x.ax=3;
            int86(0x33,&i,&o);
            *button=o.x.bx;
            *x=o.x.cx;
            *y=o.x.dx;
        }
```

***Explanation*:**
In the above program, the function `initgraph()` switches the mode from text to graphics. The DETECT is a macro which requests the `initgraph()` to set the graphics driver. The functions `getmaxx()` and `getmaxy()` obtain the maximum row and columns available on the screen. The function `setviewport()` defines the viewport area which bounds the drawing operation inside the area.

The `initmouse()` function checks whether the mouse drive is loaded or not. If mouse is not initialized, then the `closegraph()` function off-loads the graphics driver. The `restoremode()` function restores the mode.

The function `mousearea()` defines the area in which mouse pointer can be pointer. In this function, `int86()` is invoked by initializing CPU register with appropriate values.

The functions mousearea() and showarrow() call ROM-BIOS services under 33h with appropriate values. The while() loop checks the button pressed and displays messages accordingly. The function m_pointerat() displays the current cursor position. When the user presses a key, the program terminates.

14.21 Write a program to change the mouse cursor.

```
#include <graphics.h>
#include <dos.h>
#include <process.h>
union REGS i,o;
struct SREGS s;
int cursor[50]={0xaaaa,0xbbbb,0xdddd,0xbbbb,
                0xaaaa,0xffff,0xdddd,0xbbbb,
                0xaaaa,0xffff,0xdddd,0xbbbb,
                0xaaaa,0xffff,0xdddd,0xbbbb,
                0xaaaa,0xffff,0xdddd,0xbbbb,
                0xaaaa,0xffff,0xdddd,0xbbbb,
                0xaaaa,0xffff,0xdddd,0xbbbb,
                0xaaaa,0xffff,0xdddd,0xbbbb,
                0xaaaa,0xffff,0xdddd,0xbbbb,
                0xaaaa,0xffff,0xdddd,0xbbbb};

void main()
{

int mouse(void);
void cur_shape(int *);
void showpointer(void);
int gd=DETECT, gm;
initgraph(&gd,&gm, "d:\turboc2\bgi");

if( mouse()==0)
{
closegraph();
printf("\n Mouse Supporting files are not installed");
exit(1);
}

gotoxy(10,1);
printf("\n Press any key to exit..");
cur_shape(cursor);
showpointer();
getch();
}
mouse()
{
i.x.ax=0;

int86(0x33,&i,&o);
}

void showpointer()
{
```

```
    i.x.ax=1;
    int86(0x33,&i,&o);
  }

  void cur_shape(int *shape)
  {
  i.x.ax=9;
  i.x.bx=0;
  i.x.cx=0;
  i.x.dx=(unsigned) shape;
  segread(&s);
  s.es=s.ds;
  int86x(0x33,&i,&o,&s);
  }
```

Explanation:

In the above program, an integer array cursor is initialized with certain hexadecimal numbers. The structure SREGS is declared. The function `mouse()` and `showpointer()` are described in the previous program. In function `cur_shape()`, appropriate values are initialized in the CPU registers. The `segread()` function reads segment registers. The address of structure of segment registers `s` with interrupt `0x33` and addresses of variables of REGS `i` and `o` are passed to the function `int86x()`. The cursor shape changes to square like shape.

14.8 DRAWING NON-COMMON FIGURES

The following program illustrates the use of `drawpoly()` function. With this patterns of non-common shapes can be drawn.

14.22 Draw non-common shape pattern.

```
#include <graphics.h>
#include <stdlib.h>
void main()
{
    int maxx,maxy;
    int array[8];
    int gd =DETECT,gm,x,y;
    initgraph(&gd,&gm,"d:\turboc2\bgi");

    setcolor(WHITE);
    outtextxy(30,20,"NONCOMMON SHAPE");
    setcolor(GREEN);
   maxx=getmaxx();
   maxy=getmaxy();
   array[0]=20;
   array[1]=40;
   array[2]=60;
   array[3]=80;
   array[4]=maxx/3;
   array[5]=maxy/3;
   array[6]=array[0];
```

```
    array[7]=array[1];
    drawpoly(4,array);
    getch();
    closegraph();
    restorecrtmode();
}
```

Explanation:

This program uses drawpoly() function. The programmer can run the program and see the output. You will get non-regular shape figure on the screen.

14.9 SUMMARY

In this chapter, the reader is exposed to the basics of graphics programming in C. Initialization of graphics with library graphics functions and concepts are explained. A number of programming examples are provided. The reader is advised to go through other functions provided in HELP of C. Last few programs teach you how to do mouse programming.

EXERCISES

14.A Fill in the blanks

1. To switch over to graphics mode a function ______ must be invoked.

   (a) initgraph()
   (b) restorecrtmode()
   (c) graphresult()

2. The prototype for closegraph() is defined in ______.

   (a) graphics.h
   (b) stdio.h
   (c) conio.h

3. The bar() function draws a bar using ______ coordinates.

   (a) 2
   (b) 4
   (c) 6

4. ______ returns maximum y screen coordinate.

   (a) getmaxy()
   (b) getmaxx()
   (c) getmayy()

5. The function displays a string at the specified location

   (a) outtextxy()
   (b) settextstyle()
   (c) setcolor()

14.B True or false

1. The function getmaxx() returns maximum x screen coordinate.
2. One must specify the value of diameter for drawing circle using function circle().
3. Video screen is used only for displaying text.
4. The function setcolor() sets the current drawing color.
5. The outtextxy() function displays a string at the specified location.
6. The function closegraph() shuts the graphics mode.
7. The function settextjustify() sets text justification for graphics mode.
8. The header file graphics.h comprises the definitions and explanations of all the graphics functions.
9. The initgraph() function find outs the best graphics mode.
10. The function cirarc() is a library function.

14.C Match the following correct pairs given in Group A with Group B

I

Group A		Group B	
Serial No.	**Words**	**Serial No.**	**Meaning/Use**
1.	Resolution	A	Printout
2.	Display adapter	B	Pixel
3.	Video screen	C	SVGA
4.	Printer	D	Text and Graphis

II

Group A		Group B	
Serial No.	**Functions**	**Serial No.**	**Use**
1.	`initgraph();`	A	pre-initgraph setting mode
2.	`closegraph();`	B	initializes the graphics system
3.	`restorecrtmode()`	C	returns an error code
4.	`graphresult();`	D	shuts down the graphics system

III

Group A		Group B	
Serial No.	**Functions**	**Serial No.**	**No. of Arguments**
1.	`line()`	A	6
2.	`arc()`	B	4
3.	`circle()`	C	5
4.	`ellipse()`	D	3

IV

Group A		Group B	
Serial No.	**Functions**	**Serial No.**	**Use**
1.	`outtexty()`	A	Sets the color
2.	`color()`	B	Display string at specific location
3.	`settextstyle()`	C	Text justification for graphics mode
4.	`settextjustify()`	D	Sets the current text attributes

V

Group A		Group B	
Serial No.	**Functions**	**Serial No.**	**Arguments**
1.	`bar()`	A	Coordinate and radius
2.	`line()`	B	Coordinates left,top,right, bottom
3.	`arc()`	C	Center point. start and end angles in degrees and variable r is the radius.
4.	`circle()`	D	Start and end coordinates

14.D Select the appropriate option from the multiple choices given below

1. For drawing a bar number of arguments to be passed are
   (a) 3
   (b) 4
   (c) 5
   (d) 6

2. The initialization of graphics under C is done with the function
   (a) `loadgraph()`
   (b) `initgraph()`
   (c) `modegraph()`

3. Name the function to close the graphics mode in C
   (a) `closeall()`
   (b) `closegraph()`
   (c) `cls()`

4. Video display unit is ______ device of the computer system.
   (a) input
   (b) output
   (c) input/output

5. Name the function that returns maximum *x* screen coordinate
   (a) `getmaxx()`
   (b) `getmayy()`
   (c) `getmaxy()`

14.E Attempt the following programing exercises

1. Write a program to draw two overlapping circles.
2. Write a program to fill overlapping circles with different colors.
3. Write a program to draw 10 rectangles having similar size one after the other in one vertical line.
4. Draw alternately bars and rectangles one after the other.
5. Draw rectangles of different shapes and fill them with different colors.

14.F Answer the following questions

1. Write the initialization procedure of graphics under C.
2. What are the functions of video display adapter?
3. What are the display adapters available in the market?
4. List any 10 graphics library functions and explain their details.

ANSWERS

14.A Fill in the blanks

1. (a) `initgraph()`
2. (a) `graphics.h`
3. (b) 4
4. (a) `getmaxy()`
5. (a) `outtextxy`

14.B True or false

1. T 2. F 3. F 4. T 5. T 6. T 7. T 8. T 9. T 10. F

14.C Match the following correct pairs given in Group A with Group B

I

1. B, 2. C, 3. D, 4. A

II

1. B, 2. D, 3. A, 4. C

III

1.B, 2. C, 3. D, 4. A

IV

1. B, 2. A, 3. D, 4. C

V

1. B, 2. D, 3. C, 4. A

14.D Select the appropriate option from the multiple choice given below

1. (b) 4
2. (b) `initgraph()`
3. (b) `closegraph()`
4. (b) output
5. (a) `getmaxx()`

APPENDIX A

AMERICAN STANDARD CODE FOR INFORMATION INTERCHANGE

ASCII Value	*Symbol*	*Description*
000	(NUL)	Null char
001	☺ (SOH)	Start of Heading
002	☻ (STX)	Start of Text
003	♥ (ETX)	End of Text
004	♦ (EOT)	End of Transmission
005	♣ (ENQ)	Enquiry
006	♠ (ACK)	Acknowledgment
007	• (BEL)	Bell
008	◘ (BS)	Back Space
009	○ (HT)	Horizontal Tab
010	◙ (LF)	Line Feed
011	♂ (VT)	Vertical Tab
012	♀ (FF)	Form Feed
013	♪ (CR)	Carriage Return
014	♫ (SO)	Shift Out / X-On
015	☼ (SI)	Shift In / X-Off
016	► (DLE)	Data Line Escape
017	◄ (DC1)	Device Control 1 (often XON)
018	↕ (DC2)	Device Control 2
019	‼ (DC3)	Device Control 3 (often XOFF)
020	¶ (DC4)	Device Control 4
021	§ (NAK)	Negative Acknowledgement
022	▬ (SYN)	Synchronous Idle
023	↨ (ETB)	End of Transmit Block
024	↑ (CAN)	Cancel
025	↓ (EM)	End of Medium
026	→ (SUB)	Substitute
027	← (ESC)	Escape
028	∟ (FS)	File Separator
029	↔ (GS)	Group Separator

(continued)

ASCII Value	*Symbol*	*Description*
030	▲ (RS)	Record Separator
031	▼ (US)	Unit Separator
032	(BL)	Space (Blank)
033	!	Exclamation mark
034	"	Double quotes (or speech marks)
035	#	Number
036	$	Dollar
037	%	Percentage
038	&	Ampersand
039	’	Single quote
040	(	Open parenthesis (or open bracket)
041	)	Close parenthesis (or close bracket)
042	*	Asterisk
043	+	Plus
044	‘	Comma
045	-	Hyphen
046	.	Period, dot or full stop
047	/	Slash or divide
048	0	Zero
049	1	One
050	2	Two
051	3	Three
052	4	Four
053	5	Five
054	6	Six
055	7	Seven
056	8	Eight
057	9	Nine
058	:	Colon
059	;	Semicolon
060	<	Less than (or open angled bracket)
061	=	Equals
062	>	Greater than (or close angled bracket)
063	?	Question mark
064	@	At symbol
065	A	Uppercase A
066	B	Uppercase B

(*continued*)

ASCII Value	Symbol	Description
067	C	Uppercase C
068	D	Uppercase D
069	E	Uppercase E
070	F	Uppercase F
071	G	Uppercase G
072	H	Uppercase H
073	I	Uppercase I
074	J	Uppercase J
075	K	Uppercase K
076	L	Uppercase L
077	M	Uppercase M
078	N	Uppercase N
079	O	Uppercase O
080	P	Uppercase P
081	Q	Uppercase Q
082	R	Uppercase R
083	S	Uppercase S
084	T	Uppercase T
085	U	Uppercase U
086	V	Uppercase V
087	W	Uppercase W
088	X	Uppercase X
089	Y	Uppercase Y
090	Z	Uppercase Z
091	[	Opening bracket
092	\	Backslash
093	]	Closing bracket
094	^	Caret – circumflex
095	_	Underscore
096	‘	Grave accent
097	a	Lowercase a
098	b	Lowercase b
099	c	Lowercase c
100	d	Lowercase d
101	e	Lowercase e
102	f	Lowercase f
103	g	Lowercase g

(*continued*)

ASCII Value	*Symbol*	*Description*
104	h	Lowercase h
105	i	Lowercase i
106	j	Lowercase j
107	k	Lowercase k
108	l	Lowercase l
109	m	Lowercase m
110	n	Lowercase n
111	o	Lowercase o
112	p	Lowercase p
113	q	Lowercase q
114	r	Lowercase r
115	s	Lowercase s
116	t	Lowercase t
117	u	Lowercase u
118	v	Lowercase v
119	w	Lowercase w
120	x	Lowercase x
121	y	Lowercase y
122	z	Lowercase z
123	{	Opening brace
124	|	Vertical bar
125	}	Closing brace
126	~	Equivalency sign – tilde
127	(DEL)	Delete
128	Ç	Latin capital letter C with cedilla
129	ü	Latin small letter u with diaeresis
130	é	Latin small letter e with acute
131	â	Latin small letter a with circumflex
132	ä	Latin small letter a with dieresis
133	à	Latin small letter a with grave
134	å	Latin small letter a with ring above
135	ç	Latin small letter c with cedilla
136	ê	Latin small letter e with circumflex
137	ë	Latin small letter e with dieresis
138	è	Latin small letter e with grave
139	ï	Latin small letter i with dieresis
140	î	Latin small letter i with circumflex

(*continued*)

ASCII Value	*Symbol*	*Description*
141	ì	Latin small letter i with grave
142	Ä	Latin capital letter A with dieresis
143	Å	Latin capital letter A with ring above
144	É	Latin capital letter E with acute
145	æ	Latin small letter ae
146	Æ	Latin capital letter AE
147	ô	Latin small letter o with circumflex
148	ö	Latin small letter o with dieresis
149	ò	Latin small letter o with grave
150	û	Latin small letter u with circumflex
151	ù	Latin small letter u with grave
152	ÿ	Latin small letter y with dieresis
153	Ö	Latin capital letter O with dieresis
154	Ü	Latin capital letter U with dieresis
155	¢	Cent
156	£	Lira
157	¥	Yen
158	₧	Peseta
159	ƒ	Latin small letter f with hook
160	á	Latin small letter a with acute
161	í	Latin small letter i with acute
162	ó	Latin small letter o with acute
163	ú	Latin small letter u with acute
164	ñ	Latin small letter n with tilde
165	Ñ	Latin capital letter N with tilde
166	ª	Feminine ordinal indicator
167	º	Masculine ordinal indicator
168	¿	Inverted question mark
169	⌐	Reversed not
170	¬	Not
171	½	Vulgar fraction one half
172	¼	Vulgar fraction one quarter
173	¡	Inverted exclamation
174	«	Left-pointing double angle quotation
175	»	Right-pointing double angle quotation
176	░	Light shade

(*continued*)

ASCII Value	Symbol	Description
177	▒	Medium shade
178	▓	Dark shade
179	│	Box drawings light vertical
180	┤	Box drawings light vertical and left
181	╡	Box drawings vertical single and left double
182	╢	Box drawings vertical double and left single
183	╖	Box drawings down double and left single
184	╕	Box drawings down single and left double
185	╣	Box drawings double vertical and left
186	║	Box drawings double vertical
187	╗	Box drawings double down and left
188	╝	Box drawings double up and left
189	╜	Box drawings up double and left single
190	╛	Box drawings up single and left double
191	┐	Box drawings light down and left
192	└	Box drawings light up and right
193	┴	Box drawings light horizontal and up
194	┬	Box drawings light horizontal and down
195	├	Box drawings light vertical and right
196	─	Box drawings light horizontal
197	┼	Box drawings light vertical and horizontal
198	╞	Box drawings vertical single and right double
199	╟	Box drawings vertical double and right single
200	╚	Box drawings double up and right
201	╔	Box drawings double down and right
202	╩	Box drawings double up and horizontal
203	╦	Box drawings double down and horizontal
204	╠	Box drawings double vertical and right
205	═	Box drawings double horizontal
206	╬	Box drawings double vertical and horizontal
207	╧	Box drawings up single and horizontal double
208	╨	Box drawings up double and horizontal single
209	╤	Box drawings down single and horizontal double
210	╥	Box drawings down double and horizontal single
211	╙	Box drawings up double and right single
212	╘	Box drawings up single and right double

(continued)

ASCII Value	Symbol	Description
213	╒	Box drawings down single and right double
214	╓	Box drawings down double and right single
215	╫	Box drawings vertical double and horizontal single
216	╪	Box drawings vertical single and horizontal double
217	┘	Box drawings light up and left
218	┌	Box drawings light down and right
219	█	Full block
220	▄	Lower half block
221	▌	Left half block
222	▐	Right half block
223	▀	Upper half block
224	α	Greek small letter Alpha
225	β	Greek small letter Beta
226	Γ	Greek capital letter Gamma
227	π	Greek small letter Pi
228	Σ	Greek capital letter Sigma
229	σ	Greek small letter Sigma
230	µ	Greek small letter Mu
231	τ	Greek small letter Tau
232	Φ	Greek capital letter Phi
233	θ	Greek small letter Theta
234	Ω	Greek capital letter Omega (ohm)
235	δ	Greek small letter Delta
236	∞	Infinity
237	ø	Latin small letter o with stroke
238	Є	Cyrillic capital letter Ukrainian IE
239	∩	Intersection
240	≡	Identical to
241	±	Plus–minus
242	≥	Greater than or equal to
243	≤	Less than or equal to
244	⌠	Top half integral
245	⌡	Bottom half integral
246	÷	Division
247	≈	Almost equal to
248	°	White bullet

(*continued*)

ASCII Value	*Symbol*	*Description*
249	•	Bullet
250	·	Decimal point
251	√	Square root
252	η	Greek small letter Eta
253	^{2}	Superscript two
254	■	Black square
255		

APPENDIX B

PRIORITY OF OPERATORS AND THEIR CLUBBING

Operators	*Operation*	*Clubbing*	*Priority*
()	Function call	Left to right	1st
[]	Array expression or square bracket		
->	Structure operator		
.	Structure operator		
+	Unary plus	Right to left	2nd
−	Unary minus		
++	Increment		
−−	Decrement		
!	Not operator		
~	Ones complement		
*	Pointer operator		
&	Address operator		
sizeof	Size of an object		
type	Type cast		
*	Multiplication	Left to right	3rd
/	Division		
%	Modular division		
+	Addition	Left to right	4th
−	Subtraction		
<<	Left shift	Left to right	5th
>>	Right shift		
<	Less than	Left to right	6th
<=	Less than or equal to		
>	Greater than		
>=	Greater than or equal to		
==	Equality	Left to right	7th
!=	Inequality		
&	Bitwise AND	Left to right	8th

(*continued*)

<table>
<tr><th>Operators</th><th>Operation</th><th>Clubbing</th><th>Priority</th></tr>
<tr><td>^</td><td>Bitwise XOR</td><td>Left to right</td><td>9th</td></tr>
<tr><td>|</td><td>Bitwise OR</td><td>Left to right</td><td>10th</td></tr>
<tr><td>&&</td><td>Logical AND</td><td>Left to right</td><td>11th</td></tr>
<tr><td>||</td><td>Logical OR</td><td>Left to right</td><td>12th</td></tr>
<tr><td>?:</td><td>Conditional operator</td><td>Right to left</td><td>13th</td></tr>
<tr><td>=, *=, /=, %=,
- =, &=, +=, ^=,
|=, <<=, >>=</td><td>Assignment operators</td><td>Right to left</td><td>14th</td></tr>
<tr><td>,</td><td>Comma operator</td><td>Right to left</td><td>15th</td></tr>
</table>

APPENDIX C

HEADER FILES AND STANDARD LIBRARY FUNCTIONS

Every C compiler provides the standard library functions. The following table describes few C library functions that can be used by programmers' in their programs. Since standard library functions are huge in numbers, it is not possible to include all of them in this appendix. Programmer can refer to the help of the C compiler. Functions supported by compilers may vary from compiler to compiler.

Header files and functions supported by a compiler are as under.

1. stdio.h

Function Name & Syntax	*Description*	*Examples*
printf: int printf(const char *format ,argument, ...);	It applies each argument to corresponding format specifier in *format and sends formatted output to stdin. If successful, returns non-zero; otherwise EOF#.	• printf("%d",d) : prints value of d. (65) • printf("%c",65) : prints ASCII character of 65 i.e. 'A' • printf("s=%f,t=%d", s,t) : prints float value of s and int value of t. (s=4.5,t=2)
scanf: int scanf (const char *format,address, ...);	It scans a series of input fields one character at a time, format each field according to a corresponding format specifier in *format and stores the formatted input at an address passed as an argument. If successful, returns number of fields scanned; returns zero, if no fields are stored. Returns EOF# when it attempts to read end of file.	• scanf("%d",&s) : reads the value for s and stores in s. • scanf("%d%c",&i,&c) : reads value for i as int and value for c as char and stores in i and c. • scanf("%s",p) : reads string for p and stores in char array p.
gets: char *gets(char *s);	It collects a string of characters terminated by a new line from the standard input stream stdin and puts it into s by replacing newline by null character (\0). It allows whitespaces in string. If successful, returns string s otherwise null.	If we enter "C language" in screen for input; • scanf only takes "C" as string • gets takes "C Language" as string • gets(a) : entered string will be stored in char array a.
puts: int puts(const char *s);	It copies the null-terminated string s to the standard output stream stdout and appends a newline character. If successful, returns non-zero; otherwise EOF#.	puts(a) : The entire string with whitespaces stored in char array will get printed on screen.
fopen: FILE *fopen(const char *filename, const char *mode);	fopen opens a file and associate a stream with it and returns a pointer that identifies the stream in subsequent operations. Mode indicates in which mode a file will be accessed (r,w,a).	• FILE *fp=fopen("a.txt", "r") : opens file a.txt in read mode. • FILE *fc=fopen("s.C","w") : opens file s.C in write mode. • FILE *fd=fopen("p.doc","a") : opens file p.doc in append mode.

(continued)

Function Name & Syntax	*Description*	*Examples*

`fclose:`
`int fclose(FILE *stream);`
	`fclose` closes the named stream and returns 0 on success otherwise `EOF`[#]. All buffers associated with the stream are flushed before closing. System-allocated buffers are freed upon closing.	`fclose(fp);`
		`fclose(fc);`
		`fclose(fd);`

`fprintf:` `int fprintf(FILE *stream, const char *format , argument, ...);`	It applies each argument to corresponding format specifier in *format and sends formatted output to stream. If successful, returns non-zero; otherwise `EOF`[#].	`fprintf(fp,"s=%f,t=%d", s,t);` Writes "s=4.5,t=2" to a file indicated by `fp`.
`fscanf:` `int fscanf(FILE *stream, const char *format , address, ...);`	It scans a series of input fields one character at a time from a stream, format each field according to a corresponding format specifier in *format and stores the formatted input at an address passed as an argument. If successful, returns number of fields scanned; returns zero, if no fields are stored. Returns `EOF`[#] when it attempts to read end-of-file.	`fscanf(fp,"%s",&str);` Reads a string from a file indicated by fp and stores it in `char` array `str`.
`fgets:` `char *fgets(char *s, int n, FILE *stream);`	It reads characters from stream into the string s. It stops when it reads either n - 1 characters or a newline character, whichever comes first. `fgets` retains the newline character at the end of s and appends a null byte to s to mark the end of the string. `fgets` returns the string pointed to by s.	`fgets(str,10,fp);` Reads 9 characters or newline character, whichever comes first from a file pointed by fp and stores them into `char` pointer `str`.
`fputs:` `int fputs(const char *s, FILE *stream);`	`fputs` copies the null-terminated string s to the given output stream. It does not append a newline character, and the terminating null character is not copied. `fputs` returns the last character written.	`fputs(str,fp);` Writes the characters in string `str` to a fle pointed by `fp`.
`fgetc:` `int fgetc(FILE *stream);`	It returns the next character on the named input stream. It returns the character read, after converting it to an `int` on success; `EOF`[#] otherwise.	`fgetc(fp);` Reads next character from file indicated by `fp` .
`fputc:` `int fputc(int c, FILE *stream);`	It outputs character c to the named stream. It returns the character written on success; `EOF`[#] otherwise.	`fputc(65,fp);` Writes 'A' to a file indicated by `fp`.
`fflush:` `int fflush(FILE *stream);`	If the given stream has buffered output, `fflush` writes the output for stream to the associated file.	

[#]EOF: end-of-file

2. conio.h

Function Name & Syntax	Description	Example
clrscr: void clrscr(void);	It clears the current text window and places the cursor in the upper left-hand corner (at position 1,1).	clrscr();
getch: int getch(void);	It reads a single character directly from the keyboard, without echoing to the screen and returns the character read from keyboard.	getch();

3. alloc.h

Function Name & Syntax	Description	Example
malloc: void *malloc(size_t size);	It allocates a block of size bytes from the memory heap. It allows a program to allocate memory explicitly as it's needed, and in the exact amounts needed. On success, returns pointer to newly allocated block of memory; otherwise null.	char *str=(char *) malloc(10); Allocates space for 10 chracters pointed by str. Typecasting is needed here.
calloc: void *calloc(size_t nitems, size_t size);	calloc provides access to the C memory heap, which is available for dynamic allocation of variable-sized blocks of memory. calloc allocates a block (nitems * size) bytes and clears it to 0. On success, returns pointer to newly allocated block of memory; otherwise null.	int *str=(int *) malloc(10, sizeof(int)); Allocates space for 10 chracters as 10*sizeof(int)=10*2=20 bytes pointed by str. Typecasting is also needed here.
free: void free(void *block);	free deallocates a memory block allocated by a previous call to calloc, malloc, or realloc.	free(str); Frees the allocated block pointed by str.

Note: Above three functions are also available in stdlib.h file.

4. math.h

Function Name & Syntax	Description	Example
abs: int abs(int x);	It returns absolute value of its argument.	abs(-1); returns 1
ceil: double ceil(double x);	It finds the smallest integer not less than x.	ceil(2.6); returns 3.0
floor: double floor(double x);	It finds the largest integer not greater than x.	floor(2.6); returns 2.0
exp: double exp(double x);	It calculates the exponential function; e to the xth power.	exp(2); returns e^2=7.389056

(*continued*)

Function Name & Syntax	Description	Example

`log:`
`double log(double x);`
`double log10(double x);`
	log calculates the natural logarithm of x while log10 calculates the base 10 logarithm of x.	`log(5);`
		returns 1.609438
		log10(5);
		returns 0.698970

`pow:` `double pow(double x, double y);`	It calculates x**y i.e. x to the power y.	`pow(2,5);` `returns 32`

Trigonometric:
`double cos(double x);`
`double sin(double x);`
`double tan(double x);`
	`cos` computes the cosine of the input value. sin compute the sine of the input value. tan calculates the tangent of the input value. The value to be passed as argument must be in radians.	`cos(30*M_PI/180);`
		#returns 0.866025
		`sin(30*M_PI/180);`
		returns 0.500000
		`cos(30*M_PI/180);`
		returns 0.577350

`sqrt:` `double sqrt(double x);`	It calculates the positive square root of the input value.	`sqrt(6.25);` returns 2.500000

#`M_PI=π=3.141593`

5. stdlib.h

Function Name & Syntax	Description	Example
`atoi:` `int atoi(const char *s);`	It converts a string pointed to by s to int. If s is inconvertible, it returns zero.	`char *s="123"atoi(s);` returns an integer 123.
`exit:` `void exit(int status);`	It terminates the calling process. Before termination, it closes all files and writes buffered output. status=0 indicates normal exit and non-zero indicates error.This function is also available in `process.h` file.	`exit(0);` stops the execution of main function hence terminates the program.
`itoa:` `char *itoa(int value, char *string, int radix);`	It converts value to a null-terminated string and stores the result in string. radix specifies the base to be used in converting value (2to36).	`itoa(123,a,16);` The hexadecimal string format of 123 i.e. 7b will be stored in string a.
`random:` `int random(int num);`	It returns a random number between 0 and (num-1).	`random(999);` may return 10

INDEX

```
printf("Size of union :
    %d\n",sizeof(data.perf));
printf("Size of Structure : %d\n",
    sizeof(data));
}
```

Explanation: The union requires bytes that are equal to the number of bytes required for the largest size members. Here, `int` requires 2 bytes whereas `char` needs 1 byte. Hence, the first answer is 2 and the second answer is 19. Structure calculates total bytes required to store 15 characters and integer data 2 byte and for union `perf` 2 bytes.

Programs on calling BIOS and DOS services

23. Use of REGS.

```
#include <dos.h>
void main()
{
 union REGS in,out;
 in.h.ah=02;
 in.h.dl=89;
 clrscr();
 intdos(&in, &out);
}
```

Explanation: In the above program, the register variable 'ah' is initialized with service number 02 which controls standard output devices. The register variable 'dl' is initialized with ASCII code of character that is to be displayed on the screen. After execution of `intdos()` function, the given character is displayed on the screen.

24. Use of REGS.

```
#include <dos.h>
void main()
{
union REGS in,out;
int86(19, &in, &out);
clrscr();
printf("\n Total Memory = %d
    KB",out.x.ax);
}
```

Explanation: In the above program, `in` and `out` are objects of type `union` REGS. In this example, we need not require to send any values to the ROM-BIOS function. Thus, nothing is to be passed to any of the registers before invoking `int86()`. Here, the first argument 19 is the interrupt number followed by two arguments of `union` REGS. The result obtained here is the memory size displayed by calling `ax` register.

25. Use of REGS.

```
#include <dos.h>
/* displays specified character */
void main()
{
union REGS in,out;
in.h.ah=02;
in.h.dl=65;
intdos(&in, &out);
}
```

Explanation: In the above program, the register variable 'ah' is initialized with service number 02 which controls standard output devices. The register variable 'dl' is initialized with ASCII code of character that is to be displayed on the screen. After execution of `intdos()` function, the given character A is displayed on the screen.

12.F Find the bug/s in the following program/s

1.

```
void main()
{
struct book
 {
 int pages;
 float price;
 } *b1;
 b1.pages=500;
 b1.price=255;
 clrscr();
 printf("\n Pages : %d",b1.pages);
 printf("\n Price : %g",b1.price);
}
```

2.

```
void main()
{
 struct book
 {
   int pages;
   float price;
   } b1
 b1.pages=450;
 b1.price=450.55;
 clrscr();
}
```

3.

```
void main()
```

```
{
 struct book
{  int pages;
 float price;
} b2,*b3;
b3=&b2;
b3->pages=400;
b2.price=700.00;
clrscr();
printf("\n Pages : %d", b2->pages);
 printf("\n Price :%g", b3->price);
}
```

4.
```
void main()
{
struct book
 {
 int pages;
 float price;
 } b2;
 b2.pages=400;
 b2.price=700.00;
 clrscr();
show(b2);
}
show(struct book b1)
{ printf("\n Pages : %d",b1.pages);
 printf("\n Price : %f",b1.price);
}
```

5.
```
void main()
{
typedef hours int;
hours hrs;
hrs=120/60;
clrscr();
printf("\n 120 minutes=%d
   Hours",hrs);}
```

6.
```
void main()
{

struct vehicle
{
unsigned type : 3;
int fuel :32;
};

struct vehicle v;
 v.type=2;
 v.fuel=1;
 clrscr();
 printf("\n%d",v.type);
 printf("\n%d",v.fuel);
}
```

7.
```
void main()
{
enum month {Jan,Feb,March};
clrscr();
printf("\n January : %d",month.Jan);
}
```

8.
```
void main()
{
enum {Jan,Feb,March,April};
clrscr();
printf("\n January : %d",March);
}
```

9.
```
void main()
{
union REGS in ,out;
int86(18,&in,&out);
clrscr();
printf("\n Total Memory = %d
   KB",out.x.ax);
}
```

10.
```
void main()
{
struct emp
{
int k;
int a;
int s;
};
struct emp e={1,2,4};
e++;
clrscr();
printf("%d %d %d",e.k,e.a,e.s);
}
```

11.
```
struct month
{
char *month ;
};
void main()
{
struct month m={"August"};
```